The Score, the Orchestra, and the Conductor

The Score, the Orchestra,

and the Conductor

GUSTAV MEIER

OXFORD
UNIVERSITY PRESS
2009

OXFORD
UNIVERSITY PRESS

Oxford University Press, Inc., publishes works that further
Oxford University's objective of excellence
in research, scholarship, and education.

Oxford   New York
Auckland   Cape Town   Dar es Salaam   Hong Kong   Karachi
Kuala Lumpur   Madrid   Melbourne   Mexico City   Nairobi
New Delhi   Shanghai   Taipei   Toronto

With offices in
Argentina   Austria   Brazil   Chile   Czech Republic   France   Greece
Guatemala   Hungary   Italy   Japan   Poland   Portugal   Singapore
South Korea   Switzerland   Thailand   Turkey   Ukraine   Vietnam

Copyright © 2009 by Gustav Meier

Published by Oxford University Press, Inc.
198 Madison Avenue, New York, New York 10016

www.oup.com

Oxford is a registered trademark of Oxford University Press.

All rights reserved. No part of this publication may be reproduced,
stored in a retrieval system, or transmitted, in any form or by any means,
electronic, mechanical, photocopying, recording, or otherwise,
without the prior permission of Oxford University Press.

Library of Congress Cataloging-in-Publication Data
Meier, Gustav, 1929–
The score, the orchestra, and the conductor / Gustav Meier.
    p.   cm.
Includes bibliographical references and index.
ISBN 978-0-19-532635-2; 978-0-19-532636-9 (pbk.)
1. Conducting. 2. Orchestral music—Interpretation (Phrasing, dynamics, etc.)
I. Title.
MT85.M337 2009
781.45—dc22   2008027044

9 8 7 6 5 4 3 2 1

Printed in the United States of America
on acid-free paper

FOR EMY

With love and appreciation I dedicate this book
to Emy, my wife and best friend, who made
it possible for the book to become a reality.

CONTENTS

Introduction 3

CHAPTER 1 *The Beat* 5

    Introduction 5
- A. Basic Techniques 6
  1. The Baton 6
  2. Placement of the Beat 6
  3. The Size of the Beat 6
  4. A System for Notating Beats 7
- B. The Preparatory Beat 8

  Introduction 8
  1. Response to the Preparatory Beat 9
  2. Influence of Orchestration on the Preparatory Beat 10
  3. Preparatory Beat to Count 1 (without Setting Tempo) 15
  4. Preparatory Beat to Count 1 (Setting Tempo): The Rebound 17
  5. Beat Patterns 18
  6. Preparatory Beat to Counts Other Than 1 19
  7. Preparatory Beat to Upbeats 21
- C. Types of Beats 26
  1. Standard Beat 26
  2. Staccato Beat 27
  3. Legato Beat 29
  4. Nonrebound Beat 30
  5. Neutral Beat 31
  6. Circular Beat 32
- D. Other Preparatory Beats 33
  1. Multiple Preparatory Beats 33
  2. The Added Nondurational Preparatory Beat 35
  3. No Preparatory Beat for Solo Entrances 36
- E. Irregular Meters 37
  1. Description of the Patterns 37
  2. Preparatory Beat to Count 1 39

3. Preparatory Beat to Other Counts 43
4. Preparatory Beat to Upbeats 43
F. Subdivision 44
1. Full Subdivision 44
2. Modified Subdivision 45
G. Ritardando and Accelerando 46
1. Definition 46
2. Subdivision in Ritardandos 47
3. Compounding Beats in Accelerandos 47
H. Bars to Be Conducted in One 48
1. Individual Bars 48
2. Groups of Bars 50
I. Subito Tempo and Dynamic Changes 53
1. Subito Tempo Changes from Slow to Fast at the Same Dynamic Level 53
2. Subito Tempo Changes from Fast to Slow at the Same Dynamic Level 54
3. Combination Fast to Slow, Slow to Slower, and Slow to Fast 54
4. Subito Dynamic Changes from *ff* to *p* 55
5. Subito Dynamic Changes from *p* to *ff* 56
6. *sfz* and *fp* 58
7. Successive Preparatory Beats 58
8. Splitting a Single Preparatory Beat 59
J. Beat Options 61
1. Choosing the Beat Unit 61
2. Some Metrical Problems 61
   a. Hemiola and Rebarring 61
   b. Other Conflicting Patterns and Rebeaming 65
   c. Polyrhythmic Sections 66
3. Suppressing the Rebound 67
4. Dictating 68
5. Cutoffs and Exits 71
6. The *Luftpause* 72
7. Fermatas 74
8. Tied Notes 81
9. Syncopations 82
10. Tacet Bars and Grand Pauses 84
11. Sudden Silences and Their Continuation 86
12. Stopping the Beat 88
13. To Conduct or Not to Conduct 88
14. Composite Rhythmic Textures 89

CHAPTER 2 *Reading the Score* 97
  A. Notation 97
  B. Rhythm and Tempo 98
  C. Metronome Markings 100
  D. The Common Denominator 105
  E. Dynamics 128
  F. Phrasing and Articulation 129

CHAPTER 3 *Preparation of the Score for Conducting* 131
  A. Analysis 131
  B. Reading Through the Orchestral Part of Each Instrument 131
  C. Notation Issues 133
  D. Cuing 142
  E. Security 147
  F. Marking the Score for Irregular Meters 149

CHAPTER 4 *Seating Arrangements: Symbols for a Cuing System* 151
  A. General and Historical Information 151
  B. The String Section 152
  C. The Woodwind Section 153
  D. The Brass Section 154
  E. The Percussion Section, Harp, Piano, and Celesta 155
  F. Symbols and Positions 156
    1. The String Section 156
    2. The Woodwind Section 159
    3. The Brass Section 165
  G. Using Numbers Instead of Symbols to Indicate the Order of Entrances 169
    1. The String Section 170
    2. The Woodwind Section 192
    3. The Brass Section 206
  H. Combined Traffic Patterns 208

CHAPTER 5 *Sorting the Orchestration* 223

CHAPTER 6 *The Zigzag Way* 243
  A. Leading the Orchestra 243
  B. The Zigzag Way 257
    1. Beethoven, Symphony no. 2, First Movement—Adagio molto 258

2. Beethoven, Symphony no. 2, Second Movement—Larghetto 265
3. Beethoven, Symphony no. 2, Third Movement—Scherzo (Allegro) 268
4. Beethoven, Symphony no. 2, Fourth Movement—Allegro molto 268
5. Beethoven, *Egmont Overture* 269
6. Sibelius, Violin Concerto, First Movement—Allegro moderato 273
7. Debussy, *Prelude to the Afternoon of a Faun* 275
8. Bartók, *Concerto for Orchestra*, First Movement (Introduzione)—Andante non troppo and Allegro vivace 280
9. Copland, *Appalachian Spring* Suite 284
10. Tchaikovsky, *Romeo and Juliet* Fantasy-Overture 285

CHAPTER 7 *Special Techniques* 299

A. Accompanying 299
B. Operatic Conducting 308
   1. General Procedures 308
   2. Casting an Opera 311
   3. Voice Categorization 312
   4. Voice Charts 313
   5. Opera Chart 318
   6. Recitative Conducting 321
      a. Opera 321
      b. Sample Zigzag Way: Mozart, *The Magic Flute* 325
      c. Oratorio 327
      d. Orchestra 327
C. Choral Conducting 329
D. Band Conducting 334
E. Ballet Conducting 335
F. Backstage Conducting 336
G. Cross-Rhythms 336

CHAPTER 8 *Additional Concerns* 341

A. Ear Training 341
B. Memorization 341
C. Specialization 342
D. Cosmetics 342
E. General Attitude and Behavior 344

    F. Orchestra Musicians on Probation 345
    G. Programming 345
    H. Auditions 347
    I. At the Rehearsal 350
    J. Intonation 352
    K. Bowings 354
    L. About Breathing 354

APPENDICES

    A. *Instrumental Charts* 357

    B. *Notation of Instruments* 361

    C. *Harmonics* 447

    D. *Harmonics Charts* 453

    E. *Cross-Rhythm Charts* 463

Acknowledgments 477

Index of Musical Examples 481

General Index 485

The Score, the Orchestra, and the Conductor

INTRODUCTION

> *One man or woman stands in front of 100 fellow human beings—unlike them, without the capacity to make sound—and yet has the power to shape the great works of sonic art. The conductor's eyes dart about, seemingly all-seeing, ears all-hearing, a musical intelligence called upon to grasp a work's architecture and then convey it. He or she is curator of masterpieces, incubator of new works and public performer.—New York Times,* Daniel J. Wakin

Singers and instrumentalists are able to look at a musical work and transform it immediately into musical sound. Aural and physical feedback allows them to discover technical and musical problems early on and begin at once to work on solutions. In contrast, conductors spend the majority of their preparation time for a performance without access to their "instrument," the orchestra. Their musical and technical experimentation occurs in a vacuum. Conductors lack an opportunity to predict ensemble problems, experiment with tools of communication, or test their effectiveness in forming musical ideas prior to the first orchestra rehearsal.

The score provides all the information needed to form a musical interpretation of a composition; however, a conductor must be able to read and understand the score; know the various clefs; be familiar with transposing instruments; imagine sound, colors and textures; develop a deep and true musical concept; and decide how to communicate and lead most effectively through physical gestures.

Generally the orchestra plays the score together only a few days before an audience hears the performance. In addition, rehearsal time is limited, and frequently musicians have at best only a few opportunities to rehearse their parts together. Conductors must be aware that, from the first rehearsal, orchestra members expect a musical framework within which the composition will be performed and a consistent set of physical signals.

All of this requires intense preparation. Depending on the particular demands of each score and the conductor's training, different methods or even fundamentally different techniques may be used. This text is a practical approach to the conductor's preparation of a score for performance; it categorizes and illuminates the essential tools of the conductor's craft. I hope it will help conductors gain the knowledge and confidence needed to step on the podium.

Since beginning my teaching at Yale University, I have wanted to write a book about the conductor's craft. I have had the great privilege of long association with fine teachers, wonderful colleagues, and dedicated orchestra musicians, singers, and soloists. The many excellent conductors who have participated in my classes and seminars have taught me firsthand what leading an orchestra is all about. In this book I try to relate what I have learned: how to listen to music, read a score, connect to the composer's thought and emotion, and share the transcendent beauty of music with listeners.

Often I am asked what a person needs in order to become a fine conductor. I can offer a few suggestions: study an instrument and listen to music as early in life as possible, learn all you can about music and composers, study with a fine teacher, become educated in languages and the humanities, observe other conductors, harness energy for hard work, cultivate patience to work long hours alone without an instrument, and garner strength to deal with the inevitable rejections. The lifelong company of other musicians is a wonderful bonus.

The most frustrating part of my experience as a conducting teacher has been the need to limit the size of my classes and workshops. I dislike having to choose only a few participants from a number of sincere and talented conductors. Many have been disappointed, and some wonderful conductors may not have been given the opportunities they deserved. For this I am truly sorry.

Being a conducting teacher is always interesting and exciting; the students and the music are constantly stimulating. I look forward to every class and seminar, and I am very proud of my students. Fate doesn't always bring what each person deserves, but their lives are enhanced by association with this great art. My best wishes and affection go out to all of you whom I've had the privilege to teach.

CHAPTER ONE

The Beat

INTRODUCTION

A performance, whether a violin sonata, piano quintet, or any other ensemble, succeeds only if the players have worked out a system of communication among themselves. Rehearsals help to resolve ensemble challenges, but without designated signals, the musicians cannot effectively monitor the musical flow of a composition. The players need flexibility during performances to make spontaneous changes. Proper signaling allows this and prevents disruption in the music or actual breakdowns.

In ensemble playing, a leader from within the group uses physical signals to guide the others. The signals are transmitted with the head, eyes, arms, hands, breath, an instrument, or a combination of them. All signals are gestures that anticipate forthcoming musical happenings. Some indicate when to start or end a work, while others show when to retain, change, monitor, or set up a tempo. Signals give cues or cutoffs and show when to hold or end a fermata. The leader in traditional chamber groups is usually the player of the highest-pitched instrument: the first violin in a string quartet, the flutist in a woodwind quintet, or the first trumpeter in a brass quintet. In a mixed ensemble, the player whose part has priority from a compositional point of view takes over the leadership.

When the task of signaling and cuing becomes complex, or when too many musicians must be led from within an ensemble, a separate person—the conductor—is designated to direct the group and make musical and technical decisions. The conductor becomes a spokesperson for the composer and a facilitator for the musicians.

Conducting gestures are equivalent to the signaling motions used by leaders in chamber ensembles; the "fingering" of the conductor and the signals of the leader in chamber music serve the same purpose. Obviously a leader cannot simultaneously play an instrument and simulate the conductor's beat patterns, but the leader can shape gestures using a mental image of the patterns. In fact, many leaders do use a compressed beat pattern, with the beats resembling vertical downbeat motions.

Most subtleties of phrasing and refinement in articulation can be transmitted through appropriate body language. How to express them is an individual matter. The strength of the communication comes from the conductor's awareness, understanding, and total commitment to the composition.

A. BASIC TECHNIQUES

1. The Baton

Though not essential, most conductors use a baton to increase the visibility of the beat information. When a baton is used (in either hand), it serves as an extension of the arm and points toward the center of the ensemble.

2. Placement of the Beat

The physical placement of the beat—the spot where information is passed on to the orchestra—is very important for effective communication. To locate the proper placement of the beat, let both arms hang down naturally, lift the hands and the forearms to a horizontal position, and then move the hands toward each other. This position, with the hands positioned directly in front of the conductor's body at the base of the sternum, is the ideal location for delivery of the beat.

From here the hands and arms are able to move horizontally, vertically, and diagonally, either alone or together. They can move up or down with a wrist motion and pivot at the same time. For powerful attacks, the hands are positioned with the thumb on top.

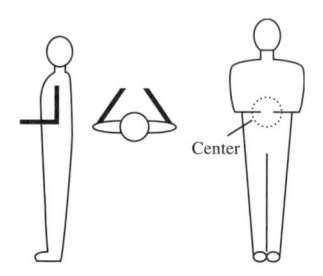

As the hands move away from the center of the body, the strength and effectiveness of the beat decrease. Conducting information is not confined to this area, but rhythmic control is most effective when hand movements issue from this central location.

3. The Size of the Beat

All information physically expressed by a conductor should reflect the prevailing dynamic level as it occurs in the composition. Generally speaking, large movements represent *f* playing and small ones *p* playing. However, the physical size of the conductor's beat is less important than the character and expressivity of the gesture. In a passage marked *ff*, small gestures projected with great inner strength have the same dynamic power as larger ones. Conversely, a *pp* passage may be conducted with rather large motions if both body language and facial expression support the *pp*.

Although many well-known and successful conductors routinely use large beats to communicate with their orchestras, the effectiveness of these motions is limited in the long run. Musicians tire of rhythmic information delivered in this manner and have difficulty understanding where and when the beat begins and ends. Economy of movement promotes the musicians' self-reliance and encourages them to listen to one another. Moreover, constant use of large beats prevents the conductor from shaping phrases and indicating the architecture of the composition.

4. A System for Notating Beats

The beginning of a preparatory beat, indicated by "ST" (start), moves upward until it reaches the apex. At that point, the beat notation is interrupted and moves horizontally to the right.

The beat notation resumes at the next count in the music. The point at which the beat notation continues is marked "C." The downward movement ends, and at this point a new beat begins.

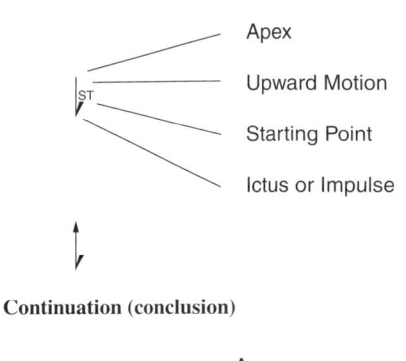

Preparatory Beat

- Apex
- Upward Motion
- Starting Point
- Ictus or Impulse

Continuation (conclusion)

- Apex
- Downward Motion

The following symbols are used to indicate the different types of beats:

Basic Symbols

Downbeat Pattern continuing to the left	\	Start	ST ↑	| ST
Downbeat Pattern continuing to the right	/	Continue	C ↑	| C
Crossover	V	Stop	SP ↑	| SP
		Hold	⌒ ↑	| ⌒

Alterations to Basic Symbols

Regular to Legato Beat	V	∪
Regular to Strong Ictus	V	V V
Measured to Unmeasured Beat	V	V (dashed)
Regular to Neutral Beat	V	v
Regular to Short Duration	V	v
Specified Duration	♩. | ST	♩ | ST

B. THE PREPARATORY BEAT

Introduction

The first piece of information—the initial signal—needed to start an ensemble is called the *preparatory beat*. It may establish the upcoming tempo, or it may initiate an orchestral entrance without setting a tempo.

The preparatory beat begins with the hand or hands in a stationary position directly in front of the body. After an extremely small but intense downward push called the *ictus*, the hand, as though having received an imaginary electrical shock, moves upward in a pull-away motion. As this motion reaches the apex of the trajectory, it gradually exhausts itself as if pulled down by the force of gravity, and falls downward to its original point of departure. The ensemble enters at the end of the downward motion, at which point the beat simply stops. The beat's trajectory—a boomerang motion—helps the musicians predict the exact time of their entrances. When executed properly, the complete trajectory, beginning with the initial ictus and ending with the return to the same point, contains all the information needed to initiate a unified entrance of the ensemble. Although any other spot can be equally effective if the ictus is properly delivered, the beat is clearest when the downward motion concludes in the vicinity in which the ictus originated. The strength of the ictus and the resulting speed of the upward motion predict the precise arrival of the forthcoming entrance. Once the ictus is given, its upward motion must be allowed to continue without any physical interference. It simply runs its course. The downward path of the beat is the final confirmation of the communication to the orchestra.

Breathing is synchronized with the physical movement of the preparatory beat: inhalation as the ictus begins and exhalation as the beat concludes. The ictus itself initiates tension, with relaxation setting in at the completion of the preparatory beat.

The physical size of the beat, which may vary from conductor to conductor, should have no bearing on the rhythmic information. The formation of the ictus, the surge of the upward motion, and the synchronized breathing convey the information needed for a precise entrance.

1. Response to the Preparatory Beat

Each orchestral musician will respond to the preparatory beat according to his or her individual technical proficiency and experience. Reaction time to the signals received varies considerably from one instrument or section to another; consequently, the instrument or combination of instruments making the entrance significantly influences the shape of the preparatory beat.

Lower-pitched instruments respond to signals more slowly than higher-pitched ones. In the string section, the heavier and thicker strings of the lower-pitched instruments require more physical effort to vibrate than the higher strings. As the conductor moves from the violins to the double basses, responses to signals become slower. Similarly, in the brass section, the lower-pitched instruments must set in motion a larger column of air than the higher-pitched ones.

The situation is different in the woodwinds, where variations in response to the conductor's preparatory beat are based not on the instrument's volume of sound, but rather on the means of tone production. The attacks of the double-reed instruments are generally more distinct than those of the single reeds. For example, the clarinets, owing to the particular way players produce a tone, have a tendency toward late entrances. The range of response to the conductor's signals, from the fastest to the slowest, is oboe, piccolo, flute, English horn, bassoon, contrabassoon, clarinet, and bass clarinet.

Another factor affecting the musicians' response to the conductor's beat information is the physical distance separating the players from the conductor. A delayed response becomes more likely the farther a musician is seated from the podium.

2. Influence of Orchestration on the Preparatory Beat

The most significant influence on the preparatory beat is the orchestration: what instruments enter, whether they enter alone or with others, and under what technical, dynamic, and musical circumstances they make their entrance.

Producing consistently reliable attacks in the extreme registers (high or low) is difficult for wind instruments. Additional challenges occur throughout the entire range when extreme dynamics or specific articulations (accents, sforzatos, tenutos, and forte-pianos) or special effects such as flutter-tonguing or muted notes in the brasses are required.

String players, on the other hand, do not have problems with tone production in the lower registers or difficulties with extreme dynamics; however, high positions on any string may cause some hesitation. In addition, a delay may occur while a string player searches for the proper division point (node) on the open or shortened string for a harmonic, because certain harmonics "speak" more readily than others. Pizzicato production is distinct and final; therefore, pizzicato entrances often are not together. A clear and pointed preparatory beat is needed for a precise and unified pizzicato entrance.

In summary, there is a risk of a late response when a musician or section faces technical challenges such as notes placed in an extreme register, excessive dynamic requests, demanding articulations, difficult harmonics, double stops, pizzicatos, requests for mutes or stopped pitches (in the horn section), or any combination of the above.

The following examples illustrate how the preparatory beat can be shaped to meet the complexity and subtlety of the orchestration. The overture to Wagner's *Rienzi* demonstrates how the orchestration in three entrances with the same pitch, duration, and dynamic level nevertheless requires three different preparatory beats. The first entrance is orchestrated for solo trumpet. Because the trumpet enters alone in a comfortable range, little assistance is needed. Securing a precise attack from the two trumpets in the next entrance, however, requires a stronger and more assertive preparatory beat. The third entrance needs a less aggressive preparatory beat than the second because the combination of four trumpets more easily absorbs a slight imprecision.

Wagner, Overture to Rienzi, *bars 69–73*

As in the previous example, the two trumpets in Dvořák's Symphony no. 8 require a distinct ictus to guarantee a unified attack.

Dvořák, Symphony no. 8, fourth movement, bars 1–4

Frequently a number of musicians enter simultaneously, each requiring a different kind of preparatory beat. Those most in need of the conductor's assistance are given priority.

The entrance of the strings in the second movement of Bizet's Symphony no. 1 would normally call for a preparatory beat without ictus to produce a true *pp*. But the simultaneous entrance of the three horns calls for an alternative approach. Each horn plays a different partial of the chord, so a strong preparatory beat is needed to secure a precise attack, especially given the dynamic level required of *pp*. Hence, the preparatory beat required for the benefit of the three horns takes precedence over the preparatory beat more suited to the string entrance. A left-hand signal will prevent the strings from entering at a louder level than desired.

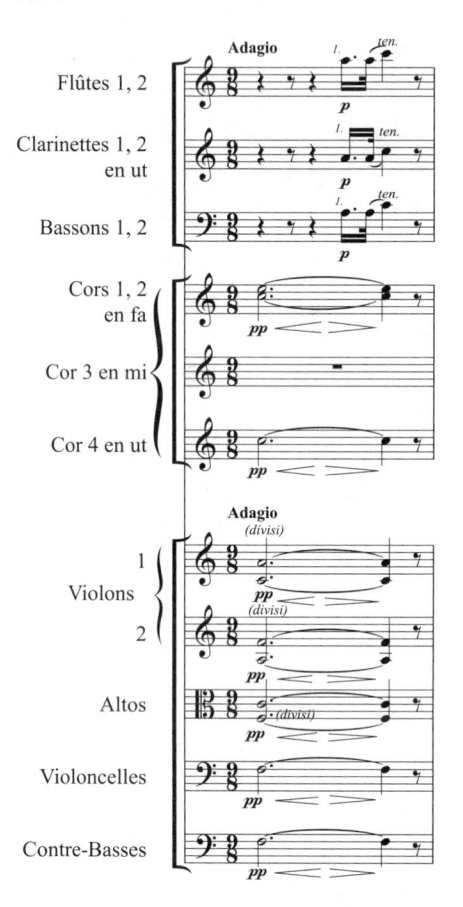

Bizet, Symphony no. 1, second movement, bar 1

Haydn, Symphony no. 101, first movement, bar 1

In Haydn's Symphony no. 101, the woodwind sextet determines the strength of the preparatory beat.

In the passage from the Overture to Weber's *Der Freischütz,* special consideration must be given to the oboes and second bassoon, who have a *pp* entrance in their low range. Many conductors have the oboes and bassoons enter at a *pp* level approximately in the middle of the bar after the strings and clarinets have reached a *mf*.

Weber, Overture to *Der Freischütz*, bars 1–2

In the second and fourth movements of Brahms's Symphony no. 1, the conductor should focus on the strings and let the bassoonist and contrabassoonist identify the appropriate moment to enter.

Brahms, Symphony no. 1, second movement, bars 1–2

Brahms, Symphony no. 1, fourth movement, bar 1

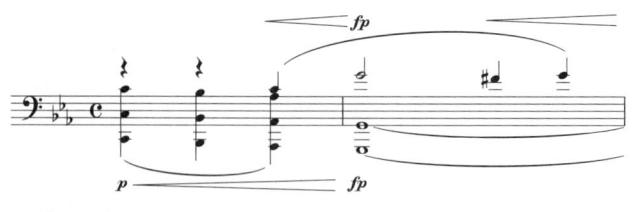

Contrabassoon
Viola
Cello
Bass

The pizzicatos in the following examples are the priority and need a strong preparatory beat, although both the violas and cellos in Dukas's *Sorcerer's Apprentice* and the muted upper strings in Tchaikovsky's Symphony no. 1 would be better served with a smoother preparatory beat and a less strongly emphasized ictus.

Dukas, *The Sorcerer's Apprentice,* bar 1

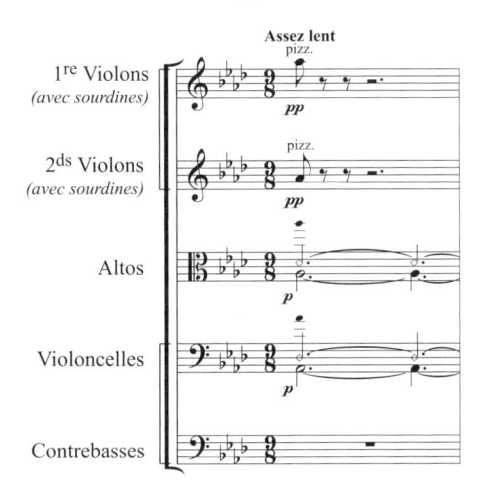

Tchaikovsky, Symphony no. 1, second movement, bar 1

3. Preparatory Beat to Count 1 (without Setting Tempo)

In the following examples the preparatory beat does not need to contain rhythmic information for an anticipated tempo. It reflects the music, and its duration may vary; the strength of the ictus matches the orchestration and dynamic level.

Each of the following examples requires a strong preparatory beat.

Beethoven, *Egmont Overture,* bar 1

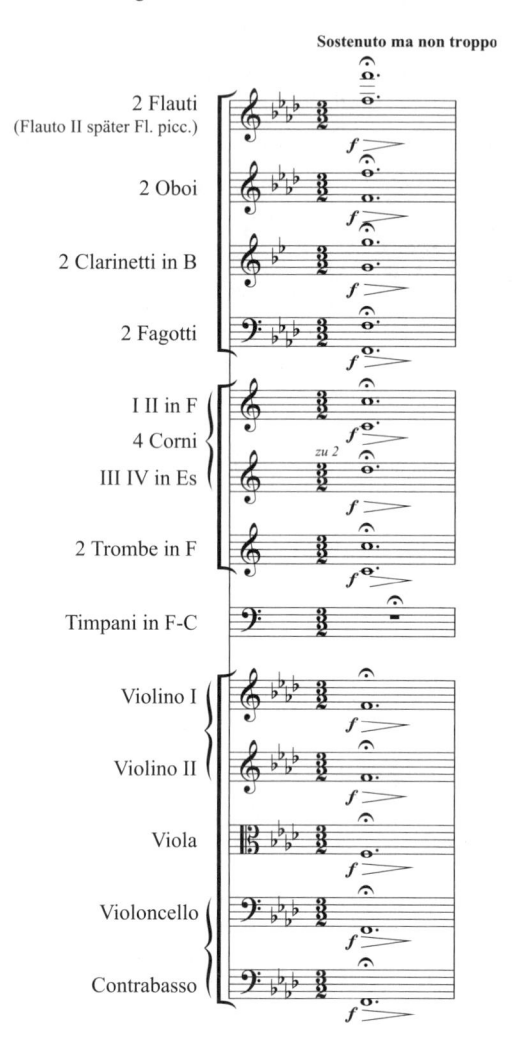

Haydn, Symphony no. 93, first movement, bars 1–2

By contrast, the opening of the third movement of Hindemith's *Symphonie Mathis der Maler* is orchestrated for strings only and starts as softly as possible; therefore, the preparatory beat must not contain an ictus. The preparatory beat is intentionally vague. The hands move upward cautiously and then return downward slowly, encouraging every musician to start playing, but not at any specific moment. The individual players will enter at slightly different times, resulting in an extremely *pp* opening. The orchestra may not enter unless the conductor remembers to breathe and exhale and mentally project the moment when the sound is expected to emerge.

Hindemith, *Symphonie Mathis der Maler,* third movement, bar 1*

4. Preparatory Beat to Count 1 (Setting Tempo): The Rebound

If the conductor wishes to set a tempo, the preparatory beat must contain the duration of the desired pulse. At its completion, the end of the downward motion, the ensemble begins to play, and a new ictus is initiated. This causes an upward motion identical to the original preparatory beat. The renewed preparatory beat, the *rebound,* prepares the following count. The process is repeated with each successive pulse.

The preparatory beat should reveal whether the inner rhythmic division of the upcoming beat is in 2 (♩ ♩) or 3 (♩ ♩ ♩) . When the first count contains two halves (inner 2), the upward motion stops briefly and almost unnoticeably at the apex, then moves quickly downward to the position from which the next beat originates. When the beat contains three parts (inner 3), or any uneven number of parts, the beat sails smoothly around the apex, giving the entire beat the impression of an uninterrupted boomerang motion. In slow tempos, ♩ = 70 or less, preparatory beats containing an uneven number of inner beats lead to precise entrances because the travel path is not interrupted.

The rebound of beat 1 is crucial for setting the desired tempo. Although the preparatory beat to count 1 should be sufficient to establish a tempo, the pulse has to be confirmed by moving convincingly toward count 2.

---

*© 1934 B. Schott Söhne, Mainz. © Renewed. All Rights Reserved. Used by permission of European American Music Distributors LLC, sole U.S. and Canadian agent for Schott Music.

5. Beat Patterns

The beat pattern is generally shown with the baton hand. Special gestures for indicating dynamics, articulations, cutoffs, cues, and other information are usually assigned to the non-baton hand. Within the beat pattern itself, the motions of the two hands occasionally mirror one another, moving together vertically but in opposite directions horizontally. The conductor must know when it is possible to deviate from, or even abandon, a beat pattern without jeopardizing effective control of the ensemble.

Beats connect to form patterns based on the number of counts in each bar. A few basic patterns have evolved and are universally accepted today. These are represented in the following examples. Using approximately the same amount of space for each beat and beginning each ictus on more or less the same horizontal plane is important.

Beat Patterns

Conducted Beats	Standard	Legato

2 — beats 1, 2

3* — beats 1, 2, 3

4 — beats 1, 2, 3, 4

6 — beats 1, 2, 3, 4, 5, 6

6 — beats 1, 2, 3, 4, 5, 6   (2 + 4)

5**   1 + 4   4 + 1   2 + 3   3 + 2   1 + 3 + 1
      2 + 2 + 1 1 + 2 + 2 2 + 1 + 2

7**   4 + 3   3 + 4   2 + 2 + 3 3 + 2 + 2 2 + 3 + 2
      1 + 3 + 3 3 + 1 + 3 3 + 3 + 1

* The first downbeat may be slightly moving to the left in order to place the second beat more into the center.

** The first beat of each bar should be physically recognizable in order to distinguish it from any other beat within the bar. This is accomplished by giving it a slightly larger size, minimizing any other vertical downbeat.

Different Meters

Conducted Beats per Measure	Meter Combinations
1	1 2 3 4 5 6 7 / 64 32 16 8 4 2 1
2	2 4 6 8 10 12 / 64 32 16 8 4 2 1
3	3 9 15 18 / 64 32 16 8 4 2 1
4	4 8 12 16 / 64 32 16 8 4 2 1
5	5 10 15 / 64 32 16 8 4 2 1
6	6 12 / 64 32 16 8 4 2 1
7	7 14 / 64 32 16 8 4 2 1

Meters are formed by choosing one number from the numerator and one from the denominator.

5 10 15 / 64 32 16 **8** 4 2 1   **3** 6 9 12 / 64 32 16 8 **4** 2 1

6. Preparatory Beat to Counts Other Than 1

All preparatory beats discussed thus far serve to bring in the ensemble on the first count of a bar. The preparatory beat to any other count within a bar is basically the same, but it must originate within the space of the given beat pattern, one count prior to the point at which the orchestra enters.

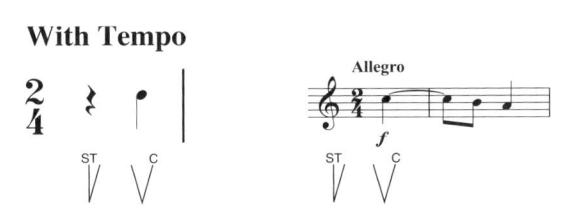

With Tempo

Mozart, *The Abduction from the Seraglio,* act 1, no. 5, bar 1

Hindemith, *Kammermusik no. 4,* fourth movement, bars 1–2*

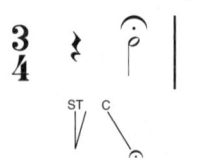

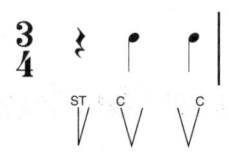

Schumann, Symphony no. 4, first movement, bar 1

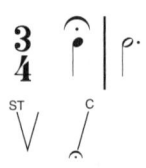

Shostakovich, Symphony no. 5, third movement, bar 1

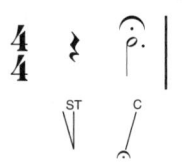

---

*© 1925. © Renewed. All Rights Reserved. Used by permission of European American Music Distributors LLC, sole U.S. and Canadian agent for Schott Music.

Without Tempo

Mozart,
Eine kleine Nachtmusik,
second movement,
bar 1

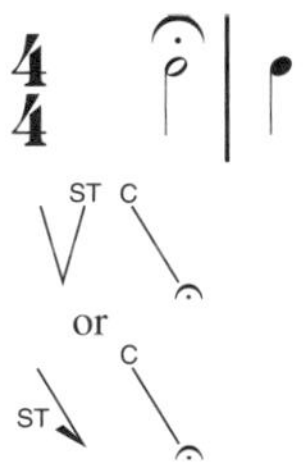

With Tempo

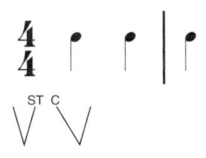

*Assuming that the upbeats are conducted with 2 quarter-note beats

Without Tempo

Brahms,
Symphony no. 2,
second movement,
bar 1

With Tempo

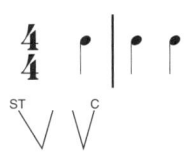

7. Preparatory Beat to Upbeats

The preparatory beats described so far have been for notes or chords that begin on one of the main counts of a bar. A rhythmic fragment that directly precedes a main count and is shorter in duration than one complete count is an *upbeat*.[1]

The duration of the upbeat affects the preparatory beat itself. If the upbeat's duration is half of the basic pulse or less, the normal preparatory beat for bringing in the orchestra on the main count is sufficient. A slightly stronger impulse or ictus at the

---

1. When bars are conducted in one, any number of notes, even an entire bar or more, may constitute an upbeat.

beginning of the preparatory beat adds clarity. Breathing must always accompany and reinforce the preparatory beat.

Pick-ups Given With One Preparatory Beat
(Half of the basic pulse or shorter)

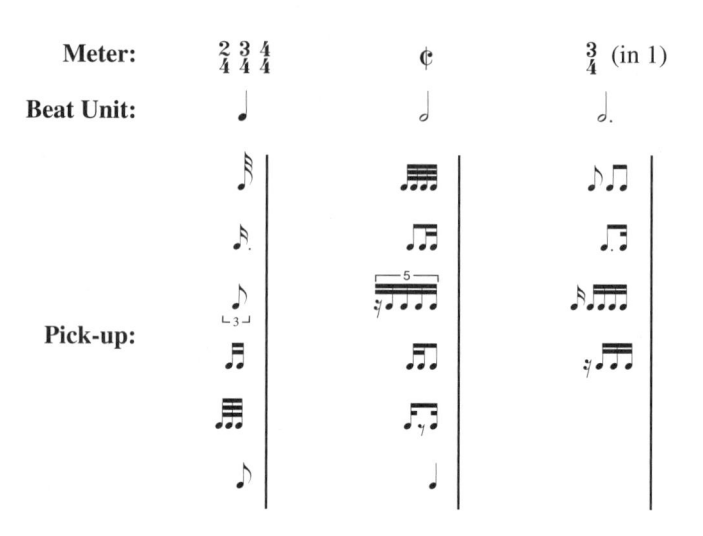

Meter:	2/4 3/4 4/4	¢	3/4 (in 1)
Beat Unit:	♩	♩	♩.
Pick-up:	(various note values)	(various note values)	(various note values)

Beethoven, Symphony no. 2, fourth movement, bar 1

Schumann, Symphony no. 3, fifth movement, bar 1

Smetana, Overture to *The Bartered Bride*, bar 1

Allegro animato e grazioso (musical excerpt with ST and C markings)	Schumann, Symphony no. 1, fourth movement, bar 1
 **Allegro con fuoco** (musical excerpt with ST and C markings)	Mendelssohn, Symphony no. 1, fourth movement, bar 1
 **Moderato assai, molto ritmico e pesante** (musical excerpt with ST and C markings)	Falla, *The Three-Cornered Hat*, Suite no. 2, second movement, bar 15
(musical excerpt in 2/4 with ST and C markings)	Stravinsky, *L'histoire du soldat*, The Soldier's March, bar 1
 **Nicht schnell** (musical excerpt with ST and C markings)	Schumann, Symphony no. 3, third movement, bar 1
 **Con moto moderato** (musical excerpt in 3/4 with ST and C markings)	Mendelssohn, Symphony no. 4, third movement, bars 1–2
 **Allegro non troppo e molto maestoso** (musical excerpt in 3/4 with ST and C markings)	Tchaikovsky, Piano Concerto no. 1, first movement, bars 1–2

Rossini, Overture to *L'Italiana in Algeri,* bars 32–33

If the upbeat's duration is longer than half of the basic pulse, an additional preparatory beat is required. This beat occupies the space within the pattern just prior to the final upbeat. The first preparatory beat does not contain an ictus; it must be smooth and nonaggressive, otherwise some member of the orchestra may begin to play prematurely. The first preparatory beat conveys the exact speed of the upcoming pulse and leads to the second one with a sense of anticipation (as though a crescendo connected the two), moving intensely to the point at which the final preparatory beat begins. When there are two preparatory beats, the inhalation occurs with the first one. Some conductors prefer to give the first preparatory beat with the left hand.

Pick-ups Given With Two Preparatory Beats
(Longer than half of the basic pulse)

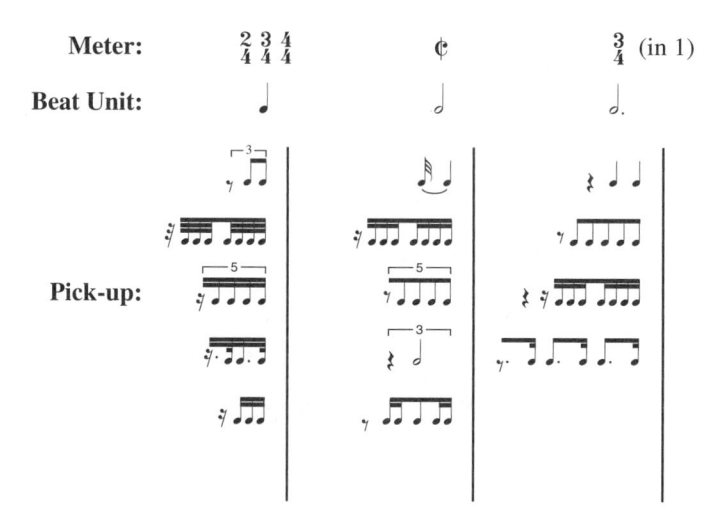

Rimsky-Korsakov, *Scheherazade,* third movement, bar 1

Dvořák, Symphony no. 7, third movement, bar 1

Beethoven, Symphony no. 5, first movement, bars 1–2

Beethoven, Symphony no. 1, fourth movement, bar 7

Weber, Overture to *Der Freischütz*, bar 282

Wagner, Overture to *The Flying Dutchman*, bars 321–322

Schumann, Symphony no. 2, second movement, bar 1

R. Strauss, *Don Juan*, bar 1

Schumann, Symphony no. 4, fourth movement, bar 211

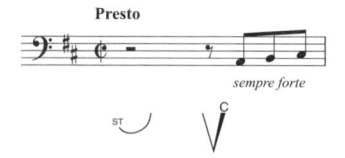

Mozart, *Eine kleine Nachtmusik*, fourth movement, bar 1

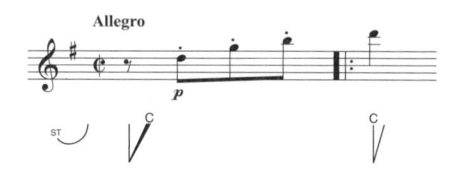

Stravinsky, *Pulcinella* Suite, Tarantella, bars 1–2

Tchaikovsky, Serenade, second movement, bars 1–2

When bars are conducted in one, the first preparatory beat always begins at the level of the sternum.

C. TYPES OF BEATS

The shape of the beat depends on the orchestration, compositional context, dynamics, articulation, and mood. In the following examples, the music always starts on the first count of a full bar.

1. Standard Beat

The standard, most common beat, best described as neither legato nor staccato, begins with an ictus of moderate strength. The upward motion determines the speed of the upcoming pulse. At the apex the beat moves downward, and at its conclusion the orchestra enters. At that moment the beat (rebound) renews itself, and the entire process is repeated. The rebound may move in any chosen direction depending on the beat pattern.

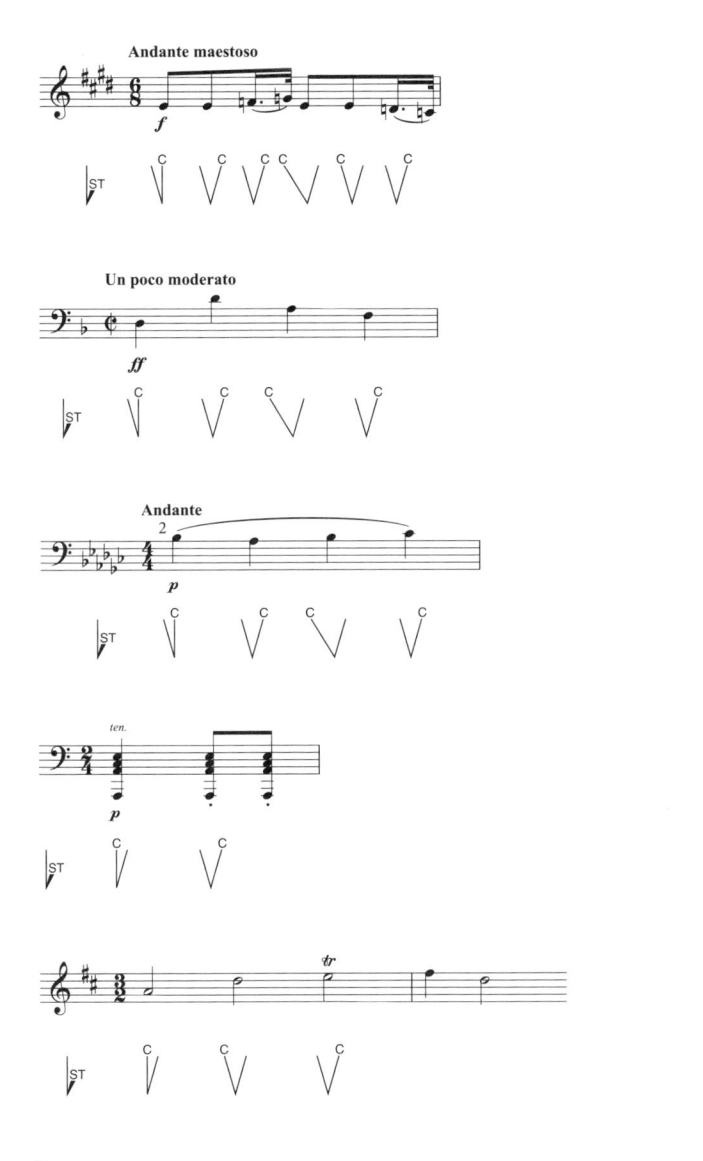

Brahms, Symphony no. 4, second movement, bar 1

Gluck, Overture to *Alceste,* bar 1

Stravinsky, *Firebird* Suite (1919 version), Berceuse, bar 1*

Beethoven, Symphony no. 7, second movement, bar 3

Handel, *Water Music,* Suite no. 2, Alla Hornpipe, bars 1–2

2. Staccato Beat

The *staccato beat* requires a change in the character of the ictus and the speed of the rebound. The ictus is more pronounced and is followed by an increase in the

---

2. Viola and harp.

*With kind permission of European American Music Distributors LLC, sole U.S. and Canadian agent for Schott Music.

speed of the upward motion. Because the beat reaches the apex earlier than usual, the beat stops at the apex for a split second before continuing with the downward motion. The follow-through downward motion to the original point of departure is executed quickly, as is the rebound. This process is repeated for each successive beat. In slow tempos the conductor may elect to prepare each consecutive staccato beat with a fast, renewed preparatory beat given after the rebound has stopped.

Deliberately stopping the rebound at its apex lessens the predictability of the succeeding beat and reduces the conductor's rhythmic control of the ensemble. However, if the basic pulse is steady, this particular type of beat works well. If there is a change of tempo, the rebound returns to its original function of clearly predicting the anticipated tempo of the next pulse.

Schumann, Symphony no. 4, fourth movement, bar 17

Rossini, Overture to *La scala di Seta*, bar 1

Mussorgsky, *Pictures at an Exhibition* (arr. Ravel), no. 5, rehearsal no. 48, Ballet of the Chicks in Their Shells

Stravinsky, *Firebird* Suite (1919 version), Danse infernale du roi Kastcheï, bar 1*

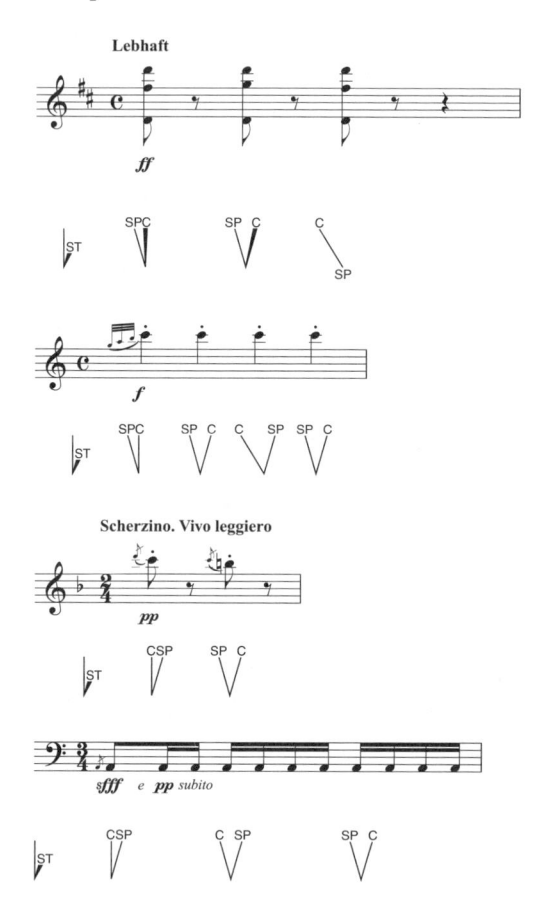

The staccato beat is not suitable for string staccato music in fast tempos. Its inflexibility distracts the players. A circular beat works better (see below), because it allows the players to focus on listening.

---

*With kind permission of European American Music Distributors LLC, sole U.S. and Canadian agent for Schott Music.

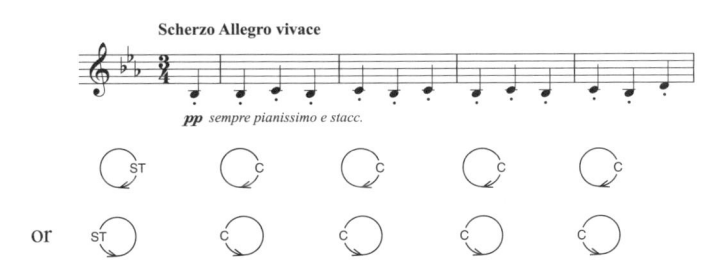

Beethoven, Symphony no. 3, third movement, bars 1–4

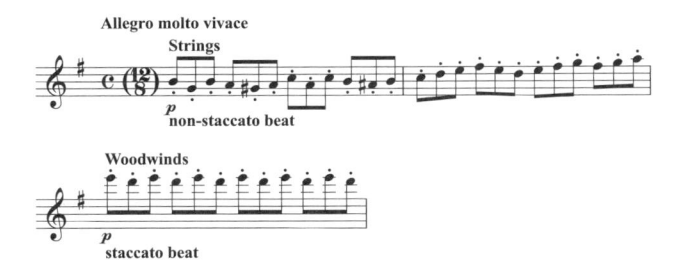

Tchaikovsky, Symphony no. 6, third movement, bars 1–3

3. Legato Beat

The ictus is deactivated for the *legato beat*. The upward motion is smooth, and the return motion touches the arrival point of each succeeding beat as discreetly as possible. This beat pattern has no corners—just smooth sailing, with downbeat and rebound connecting gently. Like the staccato beat, the legato beat provides less rhythmic control than the standard beat. The decision on when to return to a more informative and assertive ictus will depend entirely on the compositional texture and the need to focus on keeping the ensemble together.

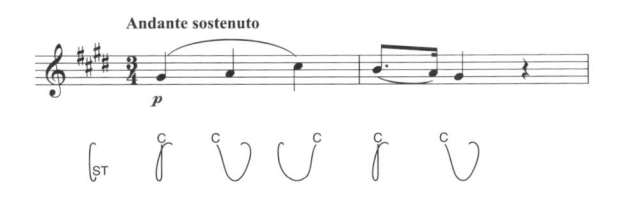

Brahms, Symphony no. 1, second movement, bars 1–2

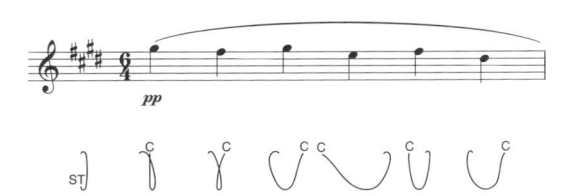

Debussy, *Nocturnes,* first movement, bar 1

Brahms, Symphony no. 2, first movement, bars 1–2

Beethoven, Symphony no. 2, second movement, bars 1–2

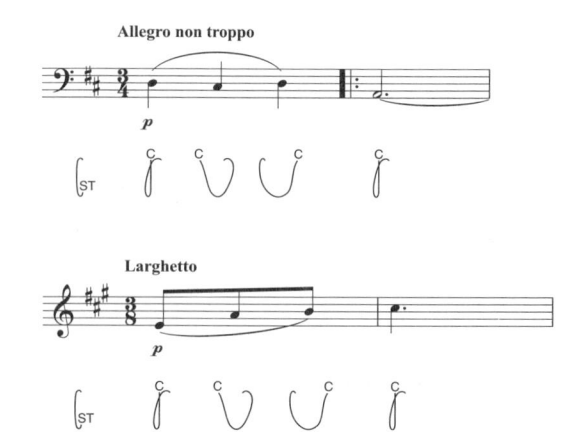

4. Nonrebound Beat

In the *nonrebound beat,* the beat, deprived of its rebound, stops at the end of the downward motion. The conductor waits until the arrival of the next pulse and then moves quickly to the next beat. This beat has limited flexibility and control. The traditional pattern need not be strictly followed, provided that the first beat in each bar reflects a downbeat motion. If the rebound stops for more than a split second, the musicians cannot accurately predict the arrival of the next beat; therefore, this beat should only be used when the tempo is relatively fast (M.M. = 100+) and the rhythm is steady. All nonrebound beats must be small, and the use of the wrist is recommended.

Tchaikovsky, Symphony no. 6, third movement, bar 212

Tchaikovsky, Symphony no. 4, third movement, bars 170–171

Salieri, Sinfonia, third movement, bar 1

5. Neutral Beat

Although smaller in size, the *neutral beat* moves in the normal beat patterns of the regular meters. It has no ictus, and the conductor moves through the beat pattern as smoothly as possible. The neutral beat is best suited for passages containing sustained notes, measured silences, and the grand pause. The ictus returns when affirmative leading is required.

Beethoven, *Coriolan Overture*, bars 1–4

Tchaikovsky, Symphony no. 6, first movement, bars 18–20

Tchaikovsky, Symphony no. 4, first movement, bars 26–27

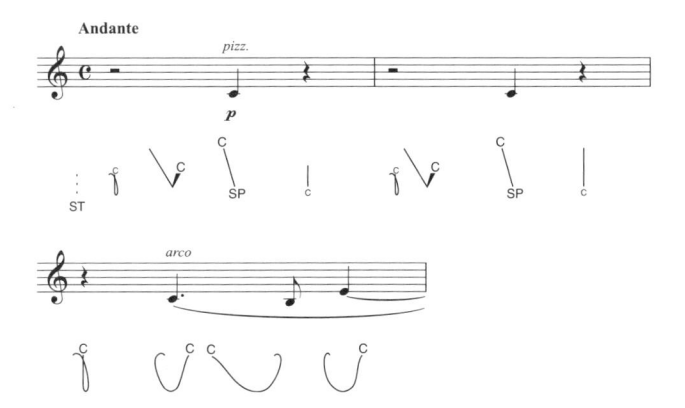

Liszt, *Les Préludes*, bars 1–3

6. Circular Beat

The *circular beat* moves to the following beat without an ictus. This beat surges ahead through each pulse and gives an impression of music in perpetual motion. Most effective in fast tempos where time does not allow for execution of a full-fledged ictus, the circular beat is also useful for accelerandos and string staccato sections. If it is not possible to show a semblance of a pattern, the downbeat for count 1 in each bar should be enlarged.

Tchaikovsky, Symphony no. 6, third movement, bar 1

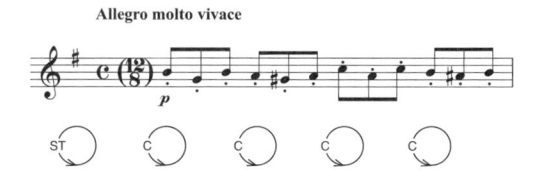

Beethoven, Symphony no. 7, fourth movement, bars 302–303

Beethoven, Symphony no. 3, third movement, bars 1–4

Bartók, *Concerto for Orchestra*, first movement, bars 64–66

Beethoven, Symphony no. 9, second movement, bars 9–12

Beethoven, Symphony no. 5, fourth movement, bars 353–356

D. OTHER PREPARATORY BEATS

1. Multiple Preparatory Beats

Many conductors add a secondary preparatory beat to any upbeat, even if its duration is half or less than half of the basic pulse. The secondary preparatory beat precedes the regular one and uses the space of the previous count in the pattern. The added preparatory beat gives additional security to the musicians and gives wind players more time to prepare for an entrance. Giving two full preparatory beats, however, may result in some premature entrances if the first preparatory beat contains an ictus.

Mendelssohn, Symphony no. 4, third movement, bar 1

Tchaikovsky, Piano Concerto no. 1, first movement, bars 1–2

Falla, *The Three-Cornered Hat*, Suite no. 2, second movement, bar 15

Leaders of jazz ensembles often set the tempo for their fellow musicians by conducting, tapping, or snapping *multiple preparatory beats.* The orchestra conductor may find times when as many as three individual preparatory beats are helpful in establishing a secure tempo. Multiple preparatory beats do provide more specific information about the upcoming inner rhythm, particularly in works written in $\frac{3}{4}$ or $\frac{3}{8}$ that are to be conducted in one, or in works in $\frac{6}{8}$, $\frac{9}{8}$, or $\frac{12}{8}$ that are conducted in two, three, or four, respectively. Fast multiple preparatory beats are small and lead without delay into the first entrance. The final preparatory beat must be slightly larger in size so that the musicians know exactly when to enter. Under no circumstance should this last preparatory beat show the slightest change of tempo, since that would defeat the purpose of the multiple preparatory beats.

Berlioz, Overture to *Beatrice and Benedict*, bar 1

Beethoven, Symphony no. 8, first movement, bar 1

Ravel, *Daphnis and Chloé*, Suite no. 2, bar 1

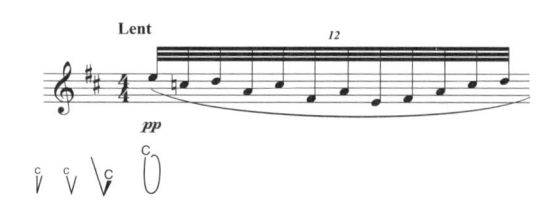

Beethoven, Symphony no. 3, first movement, bars 1–2

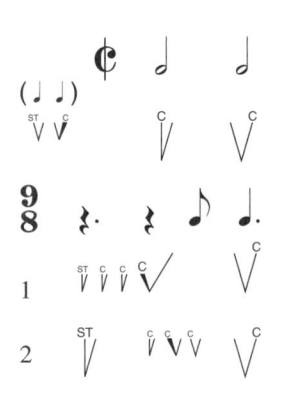

In alla breve (₵) or $\frac{4}{4}$ bars conducted in two, the conductor may decide to give two quarter-note preparatory beats instead of one or two half-note beats. These multiple upbeats provide increased rhythmic security.

If the music does not begin on a main count, a mixture of inner- or full-beat units may be employed. As a rule, the unit that contains the upbeat is conducted with the inner-beat unit, preceded by a full-sized beat. The reverse can be equally effective depending on the musical circumstances.

In some situations, the conductor may maintain the inner-beat unit until the count that follows the upbeat.

2. The Added Nondurational Preparatory Beat

As pointed out previously, one preparatory beat is sufficient for any upbeat no longer than half of a single pulse in the bar, yet many conductors prefer to give two preparatory beats. Another solution is to add a *nondurational preparatory upbeat* preceding the final preparatory beat. This additional move does not contain any rhythmic information. Its duration can vary but should contain, at a minimum, the length of two beats of the ongoing tempo. There should be no break between the preparatory beats; rather, the nondurational beat should lead gently into the ictus of the final preparatory beat and convey a feeling of anticipation. The inhalation should be delayed until the ictus of the final preparatory beat is about to begin. Any breathing during the nondurational upbeat may confuse it with the final preparatory beat and lead some musicians to make a faulty entrance.

As the conductor prepares to start conducting, the arms separate in opposite directions rather than moving toward each other.

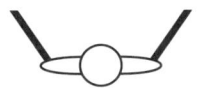

The conductor then begins a slow, nondurational move toward the center. A sense of anticipation prevails until the actual preparatory beat emerges unexpectedly and brings in the orchestra.

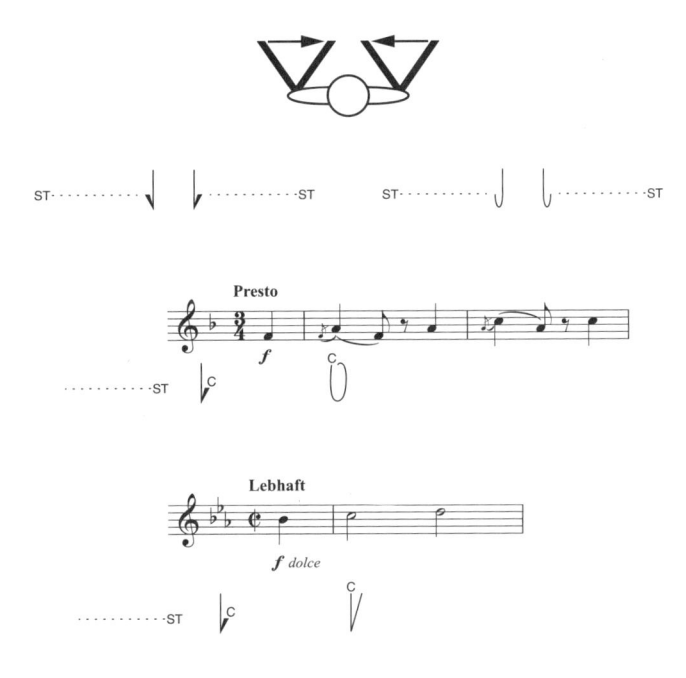

Beethoven, Symphony no. 7, third movement, bars 1–2

Schumann, Symphony no. 3, fifth movement, bar 1

Brahms, Symphony no. 4, first movement, bar 1

3. No Preparatory Beat for Solo Entrances

When a single player enters in a moderate tempo with an upbeat that has the duration of a full count, a preparatory beat is unnecessary. The preparatory beat for the orchestra is given at the moment the soloist begins to play, one count before the entrance of the orchestra.

Rossini, Overture to *La scala di Seta*, bars 4–6

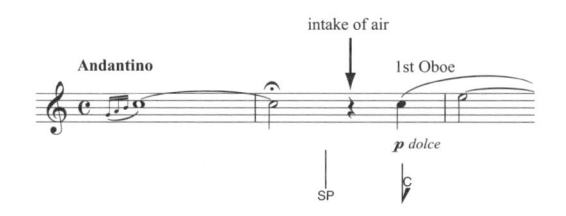

The next examples assume that the musicians and the conductor make a break between the fermata and the beginning of the solo line.

Brahms, Symphony no. 3, third movement, bars 97–99

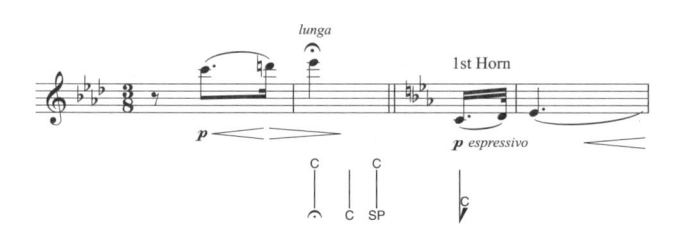

Beethoven, Symphony no. 3, fourth movement, bars 348–349

Beethoven, Symphony no. 7, first movement, bars 300–301

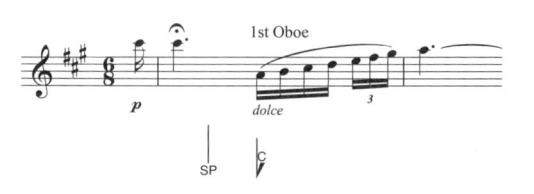

If the solo upbeat is longer than a major count, the preparatory beat starts one count before the orchestra enters.

Tchaikovsky, Symphony no. 4, second movement, bars 1–2

Beethoven, Symphony no. 8, third movement, bar 44

E. IRREGULAR METERS

1. Description of the Patterns

The standard beat patterns are used for irregular meters, except that the duration of one or more individual counts is expanded or reduced by a fraction of its basic pulse. (The term "irregular meter" does not apply when the time signature's denominator is the conducted beat unit, as, for example, when a $\frac{5}{8}$ bar is conducted in eighth notes.) The rebounds of the irregular beats must be altered to accommodate the changed duration, by changing either the speed of the rebound or the length of the rebound's travel path.

THE SCORE, THE ORCHESTRA, AND THE CONDUCTOR

Basic Meter $\frac{3}{4}$ ♩ ♩ ♩ $\frac{2}{4}$ ♩ ♩

                                    Beat   Beat
                         Expansion   Reduction

Irregular Meter $\frac{7}{8}$ ♩ ♩. ♩ $\frac{7}{16}$ ♩ ♪.

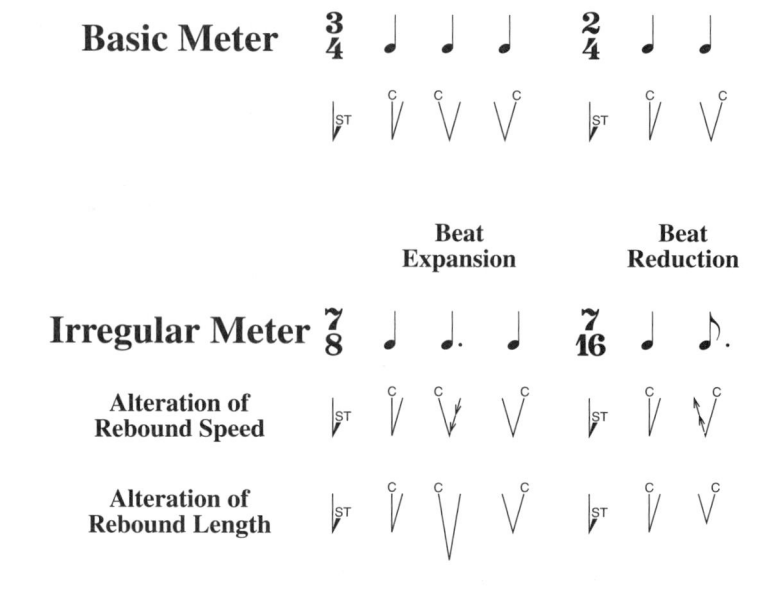

Alteration of Rebound Speed

Alteration of Rebound Length

The following is a list of the most common irregular meters.

Irregular Meters

Half of the basic ♩ is added (♪) to one or more basic beats in a measure:

Breakdown	$\frac{2}{4}$ + 1♪	$\frac{3}{4}$ + 1♪	$\frac{3}{4}$ + 2♪	$\frac{4}{4}$ + 1♪	$\frac{4}{4}$ + 2♪	$\frac{4}{4}$ + 3♪
No. of Beats	2	3	3	4	4	4
Meter	$\frac{5}{8}$	$\frac{7}{8}$	$\frac{8}{8}$	$\frac{9}{8}$	$\frac{10}{8}$	$\frac{11}{8}$
Subdivisions	2+3	2+2+3	2+3+3	3+2+2+2	3+3+2+2	3+3+3+2
	3+2	2+3+2	3+2+3	2+3+2+2	3+2+3+2	3+3+2+3
		3+2+2	3+3+2	2+2+3+2	2+2+3+3	3+2+3+3
				2+2+2+3	2+3+2+3	2+3+3+3
					2+3+3+2	etc.
					3+2+2+3	

Less than half of the basic ♩ is subtracted (♪) from one or more basic beats in a measure:

Breakdown	$\frac{2}{4}$ - 1 ♪	$\frac{3}{4}$ - 1 ♪	$\frac{4}{4}$ - 1 ♪	$\frac{4}{4}$ - 2 ♪	$\frac{4}{4}$ - 3 ♪
No. of Beats	2	3	4	4	4
Meter	$\frac{7}{16}$	$\frac{11}{16}$	$\frac{15}{16}$	$\frac{14}{16}$	$\frac{13}{16}$
Subdivisions	4 + 3	4 + 4 + 3	4 + 4 + 4 + 3	4 + 3 + 4 + 3	4 + 3 + 3 + 3
	3 + 4	4 + 3 + 4	4 + 4 + 3 + 4	etc.	etc.
		3 + 4 + 4	4 + 3 + 4 + 4		
			3 + 4 + 4 + 4		

2. Preparatory Beat to Count 1

As a rule, the preparatory beat to count 1 of an irregular bar is of the same duration as the first rhythmic unit of the bar. In $\frac{5}{8}$, for example, the preparatory beat may be a quarter note or a dotted quarter note, depending on the rhythmic grouping of the bar.

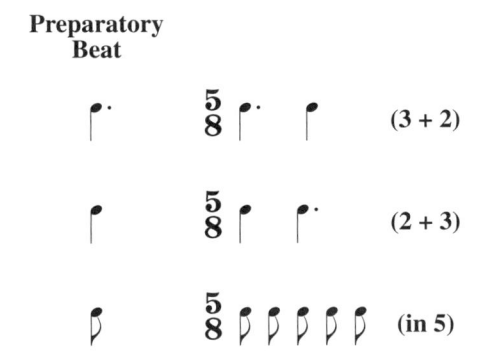

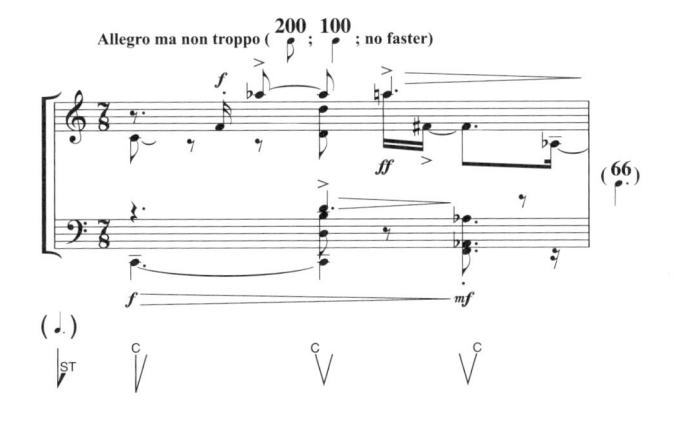

Kirchner, Concerto for Violin, Cello, Ten Winds, and Percussion, first movement, bar 1

Foss, *Time Cycle*, second movement, bar 61

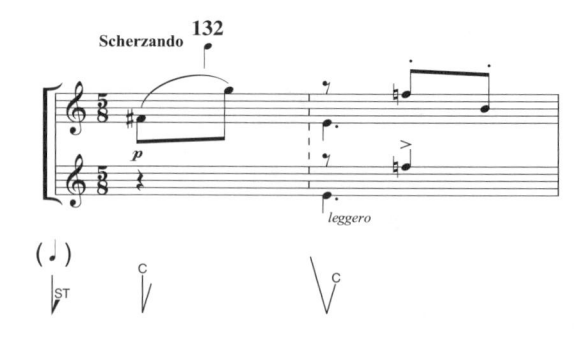

Floyd, *Of Mice and Men*, act 3, rehearsal no. 1

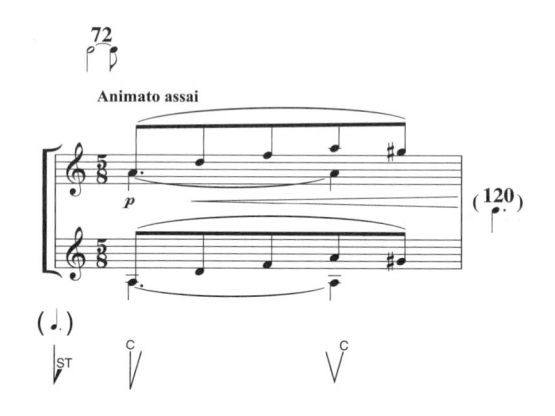

Floyd, *Of Mice and Men*, act 3, rehearsal no. 42

Tchaikovsky, Symphony no. 6, second movement, bar 1

When no rhythmic grouping is evident, the duration of the preparatory beat can be based on the tempo of the passage: a shorter unit if the tempo is slow; a longer one if it is fast.

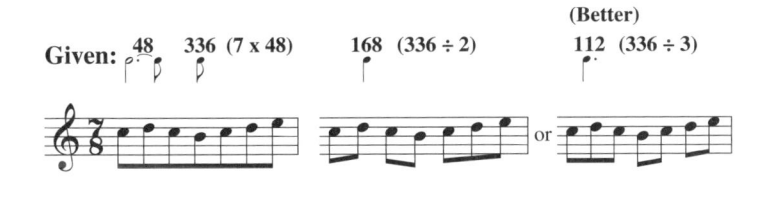

If more than one inner grouping appears simultaneously in different instrumental parts, the duration of the preparatory beat is based on the grouping that includes a majority of the players. An exception occurs when the main thematic material is played by a minority.

Floyd, *Of Mice and Men,* act 2, rehearsal no. 90

Other considerations may influence the rhythmic duration of the preparatory beat. In the following example, a quarter-note preparatory beat is the best choice because the 112 reflects the forthcoming march tempo.

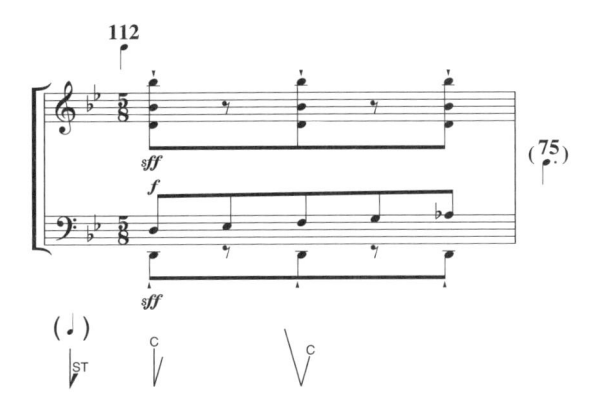

Stravinsky, *L'histoire du soldat,* Royal March, bar 1

If the meter is consistently divided into the same rhythmic pattern throughout a passage, the conductor may prefer to give multiple preparatory beats, reflecting the beat pattern of an entire bar.

Kay, *Suite for Strings*, third movement, bars 1–3

Tchaikovsky, Symphony no. 6, second movement, bar 1

In these two examples, the preparatory beat matches the duration of the first rhythmic unit to be conducted.

Moore, *The Ballad of Baby Doe*, act 1, Scene 6, bar 1

Bernstein, *Divertimento for Orchestra*, second movement, Waltz, bars 1–2

3. Preparatory Beat to Other Counts

In irregular meters, preparatory beats to counts other than the first one in the bar are identical to those in regular meters. The preparatory beat uses the appropriate space of the particular beat pattern.

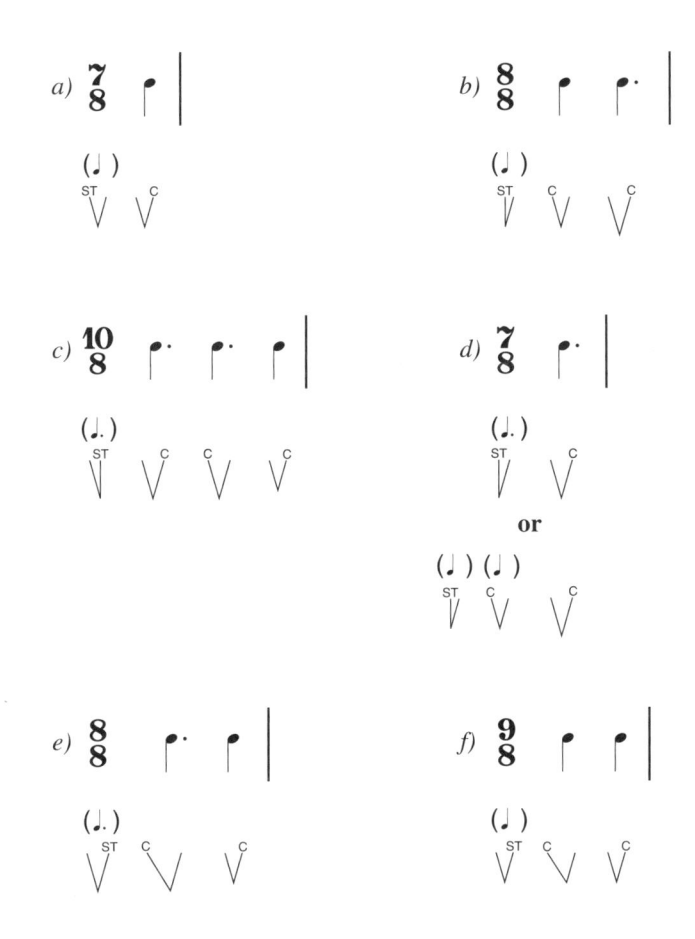

a) 7/8 — (♩) ST, C

b) 8/8 — (♩) ST, C, C

c) 10/8 — (♩.) ST, C, C, C

d) 7/8 — (♩.) ST, C

or

(♩)(♩) ST, C, C

e) 8/8 — (♩.) ST, C, C

f) 9/8 — (♩) ST, C, C

4. Preparatory Beat to Upbeats

Preparatory beats to a fraction of any count of an irregular meter are treated in the same manner as upbeats for regular meters. Although not necessary, additional preparatory beats may be added within the ongoing pattern prior to the musicians' entry.

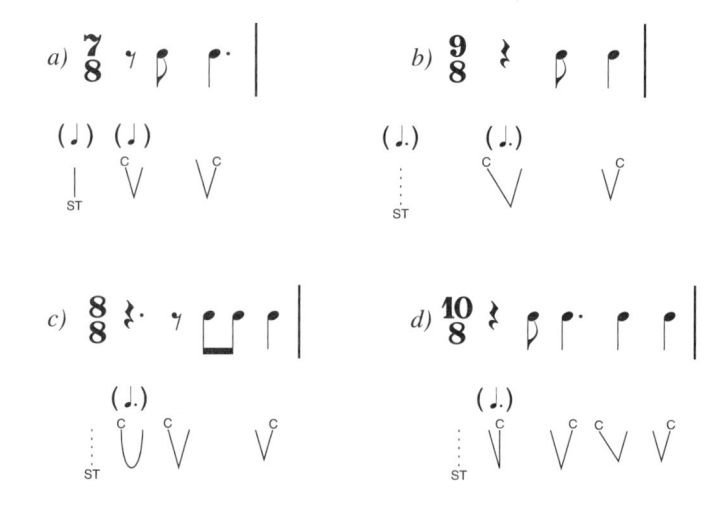

Irregular bars containing four or more basic counts (3 + 2 + 2 + 3, 3 + 3 + 2 + 2 + 3, etc.) can be conducted with a variety of beat patterns as long as the first beat in the bar is a downward motion and the beat preceding it moves upward.

F. SUBDIVISION

1. Full Subdivision

Composers often imply that a beat should be subdivided by choosing a metronomic unit given to a fraction of the main count (e.g., ♪ = 60 in $\frac{3}{4}$, $\frac{4}{4}$, or $\frac{5}{4}$, etc.), by introducing a time signature that implies a beat unit different from the basic count of the bar in question (e.g., $\frac{8}{8}$ in $\frac{4}{4}$, or $\frac{4}{8}$ in $\frac{2}{4}$), or by following a notated request by the composer. Musical considerations, such as the need to project inner rhythmic pulses, ultimately determine when to subdivide. The complexity of the composition may require subdivision for the benefit of clarity and communication. In most cases, subdivision should not disturb the overall beat pattern of the time signature. Each count is subdivided using the same pattern.

Beethoven, Symphony no. 4, second movement, bar 1

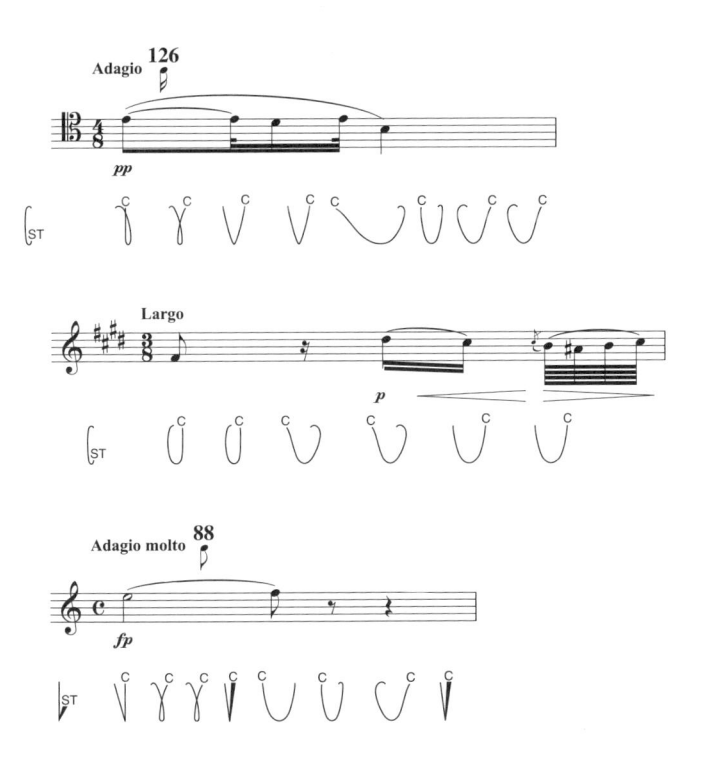

Dvořák, Symphony no. 9 (*From the New World*), first movement, bar 1

Beethoven, Piano Concerto no. 3, second movement, bar 32

Beethoven, Symphony no. 1, first movement, bar 1

When a simple duple meter (i.e., 2/4 or ¢) is subdivided, the conductor must decide whether to use a subdivided two-beat pattern or a regular four-beat pattern. The traditional four-beat pattern lends itself better to legato passages; however, in this pattern the second beat may become too dominant and disturb the musical flow of the passage.

2. Modified Subdivision

Rather than giving a full beat for each ♪, the main beat is divided into two equal motions.

Brahms, Symphony no. 1, second movement, bar 1

Downward and upward motions of constant speed throughout, reflecting the inner ♪.

In a 3/4 bar conducted in three, the conductor may wish to show a 𝅗𝅥+♩ or a ♩+𝅗𝅥.

J. Strauss, *On the Beautiful Blue Danube*, no. 1, bars 2–3

This subdivided motion happens at the exact moment that the third quarter note is played and should reflect its articulation, be it tenuto or staccato. The motion can be executed in any direction.

Beethoven, Symphony no. 6, second movement, bar 1

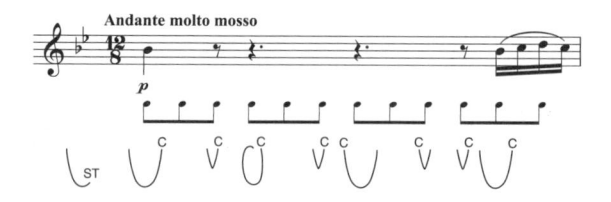

When the basic pulse is slow, more inner rhythmic divisions can be shown. At faster tempos, however, this becomes impractical. When squeezed too closely together, signals lose their effectiveness.

G. RITARDANDO AND ACCELERANDO

1. Definition

In a steady tempo, the rebound contains the duration of the regular pulse. Altering the duration of the rebound communicates a gradual change of tempo. In a ritardando, expansion of the rebound signals a delay in the arrival of the next count. This expansion is accomplished not merely by physically slowing down the speed, but also by creating a visual resistance to the upward motion of the rebound.

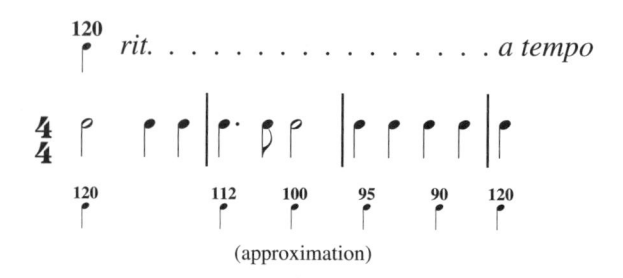

(approximation)

A ritardando has a predictable momentum of its own; overregulating the slowdown process is not necessary. The ritardando should be distributed throughout the designated passage in an organic fashion by slowing the pulse gradually and proportionately. The timing of the second and third beats sets up the progression of the tempo of the ritardando. No two beats are equal in duration in a ritardando. If the process of slowing down begins properly and the musicians trust it, heavy-handed control is not necessary.

The description of an organic ritardando applies also to the accelerando. Here a compression of the rebound signals an early arrival of the next beat. Each successive rebound quickens its pace and gradually reduces its duration; it surges forward, eager to get to the next beat, and compels the musicians to play faster and faster.

2. Subdivision in Ritardandos

When a musical passage slows down, at what point does subdivision begin? The right moment is determined by (1) the musical content; (2) the amount of information that must be communicated, given the complexity of the music; and (3) the declining effectiveness of the conductor's beat as the basic pulse changes. (See the Beat Options section later in this chapter.) The modified subdivision can serve as a transition into full subdivision.

3. Compounding Beats in Accelerandos

The factors determining when to compound beats during an accelerando are the same as those governing the decision on when to begin subdividing in a ritardando. (See the preceding section.)

Meter	Original Beat Unit	Compounding Method	Compounded Beat Unit
4/4	♩	2 ♩ =	♩
3/4	♩	3 ♩ =	♩.
6/8	♪	3 ♪ =	♩.
6/8	♩.	2 ♩. =	♩.

etc.

In general, ritardandos and accelerandos are approximate tempo alterations that defy consistent duplication. During each one, a variety of technical and musical circumstances comes into play. Successful execution depends on listening, adjusting, and refraining from overconducting or making overly strenuous efforts to control the musical flow.

H. BARS TO BE CONDUCTED IN ONE

1. Individual Bars

If not explicitly requested by the composer, the decision on whether or not to conduct a full bar in one is based on the time signature ($\frac{1}{1}$, $\frac{1}{2}$, $\frac{1}{\rho}$, etc.) or a metronome marking that refers to a full bar. The preparatory beat to a bar conducted in one always starts from the bottom (at the level of the sternum). All beats are equal—there is no pattern—and contain the duration of the entire bar. In bars that are divided into two equal rhythmic units, a small signal at the apex may mark the middle of the bar.

Verdi, Overture to *Nabucco*, bars 108–111

Schubert, Symphony no. 9, third movement, bars 1–2

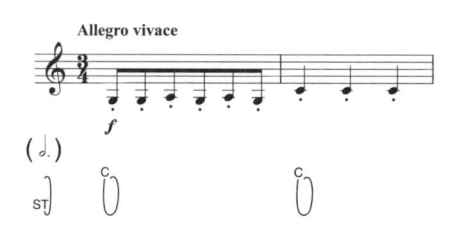

Rimsky-Korsakov, *Scheherazade*, fourth movement, bar 30

When there is an upbeat, its preparatory beat is subject to the guidelines discussed earlier. If the upbeat's duration is shorter than half of the entire bar, a single preparatory beat will suffice.

The Beat 49

Schubert, Symphony no. 9, fourth movement, bar 1

J. Strauss, *Tales from the Vienna Woods,* no. 3, bar 1

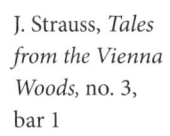

J. Strauss, *Tales from the Vienna Woods,* no. 4, bar 1

Dvořák, Symphony no. 8, third movement, bars 1–2

If the upbeat's duration is longer than half of the bar, a second preparatory beat without ictus is added.

Beethoven, Symphony no. 5, first movement, bars 1–2

Brahms, Serenade, Op. 11, second movement, bar 1

Tchaikovsky, Serenade, second movement, bar 1

Puccini, *La Bohème*, act 1, Introduction, bars 1–2

2. Groups of Bars

The melodic and harmonic structure, phrasing, articulation, bowing, dynamics, and orchestration determine when bars should be grouped into larger units. The terms *ritmo di tre battute* and *ritmo di quattro battute* appear in the second movement of Beethoven's Symphony no. 9. They indicate that several bars are grouped (phrased) into units of three or four. The question arises of whether these groups of bars should be conducted in beat patterns that correspond to the number of bars in each group. Remaining in one throughout is preferable because the musicians may become confused by beat patterns that do not match the time signatures in their printed parts. A barely perceptible beat pattern can be implemented by squeezing the beats closely together. This gives security to the conductor without distracting the musicians.

The Beat   51

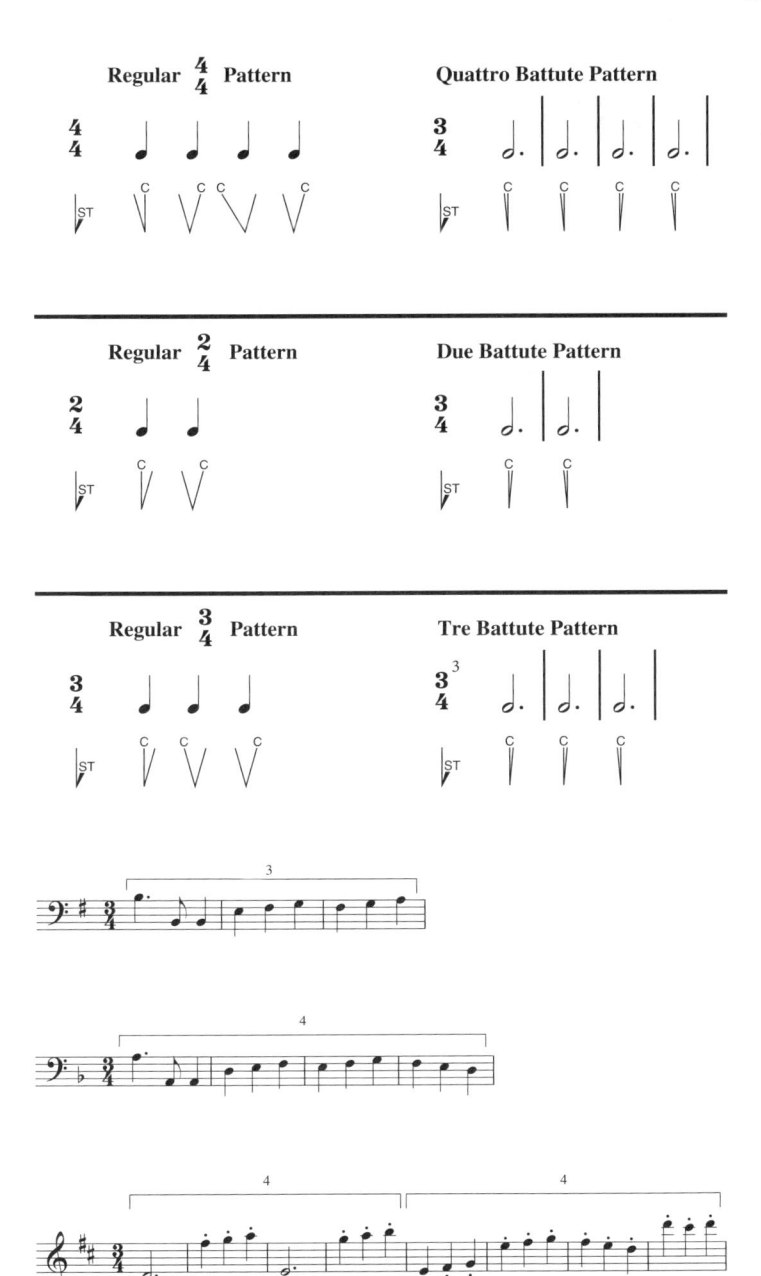

Regular 4/4 Pattern   **Quattro Battute Pattern**

Regular 2/4 Pattern   **Due Battute Pattern**

Regular 3/4 Pattern   **Tre Battute Pattern**[3]

Beethoven, Symphony no. 9, second movement, bars 177–179

Beethoven, Symphony no. 9, second movement, bars 234–237

Beethoven, Symphony no. 2, third movement, bars 1–8

---

3. Any other time signature applies, as long as each bar is conducted in one ($\frac{2}{4}$ - $\frac{5}{4}$ - $\frac{6}{8}$ - $\frac{7}{16}$ - $\frac{9}{8}$, etc.).

52 THE SCORE, THE ORCHESTRA, AND THE CONDUCTOR

Dukas, *The Sorcerer's Apprentice*, bars 42–59

J. Strauss, *Tales from the Vienna Woods*, Introduction, bars 1–15

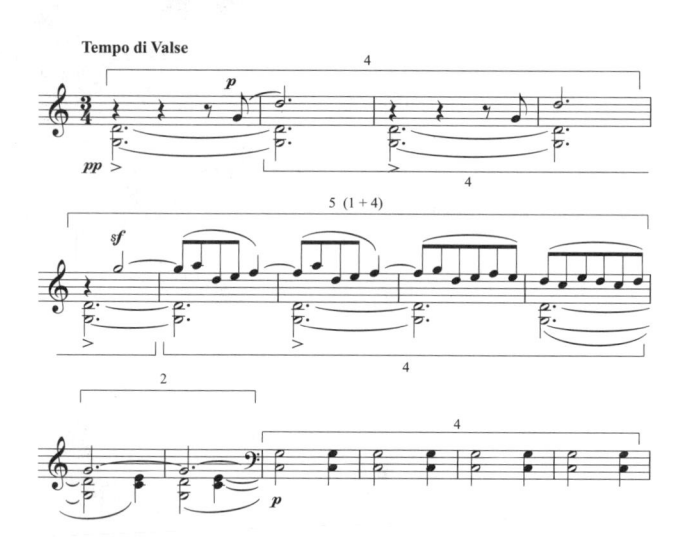

Bartók, *Concerto for Orchestra*, first movement, bars 76–89

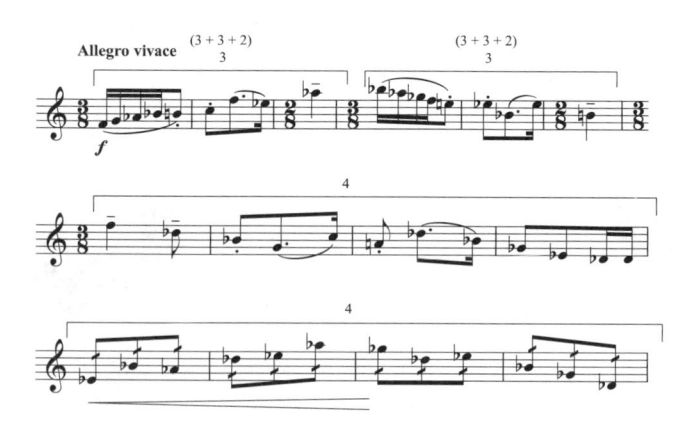

Bartók, *Concerto for Orchestra,* first movement, bars 488–508

I. SUBITO TEMPO AND DYNAMIC CHANGES

1. Subito Tempo Changes from Slow to Fast at the Same Dynamic Level

When moving from a slow section to a fast section, conductors in the past gave a preparatory beat establishing the speed of the new tempo just as the slow section was about to end. This disrupted the final moment of the old tempo and weakened the surprise of the tempo change.

Today, the orchestral musicians' level of playing is excellent, so a conductor can maintain the prevailing tempo until the moment of the tempo change. The new section begins with a rebound that contains the pulse of the new tempo, and, if the rebound shows the new pulse properly, the musicians will execute the change without difficulty.

Mozart, Overture to *The Abduction from the Seraglio,* bars 152–153

Beethoven, *Leonore Overture* no. 3, bars 513–514

Mozart, Overture to *The Magic Flute,* bars 15–16

Tchaikovsky, Symphony no. 4, first movement, bars 380–381

2. Subito Tempo Changes from Fast to Slow at the Same Dynamic Level

No advance preparation is possible when moving suddenly from a fast tempo to a slow tempo. The speed of the rebound of the first slower pulse establishes the new tempo. The rebound slows down, as though the upward motion of the beat were suddenly encountering resistance from above.

Brahms, Piano Concerto no. 2, second movement, bars 186–189

Brahms, *Academic Festival Overture*, bars 377–379

Bartók, *Concerto for Orchestra*, fourth movement, bars 41–42

3. Combination Fast to Slow, Slow to Slower, and Slow to Fast

Beethoven, Symphony no. 9, fourth movement, bars 202–205

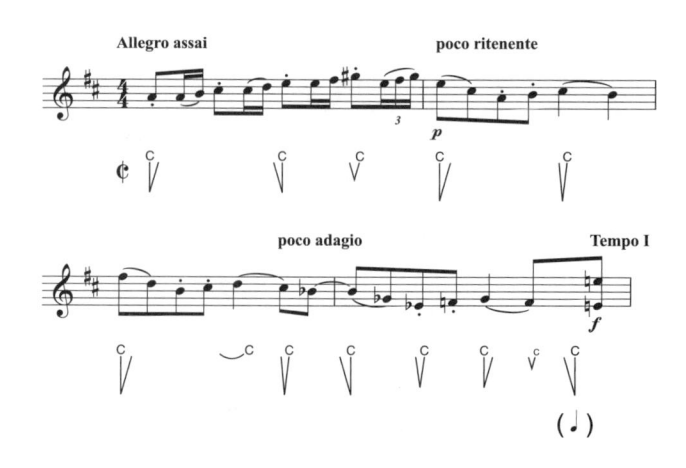

When a composer uses a prolonged note, chord, or pause to link two sections of different tempos, a fermata can be superimposed and followed by a preparatory beat for the new section at its conclusion. Another approach is to continue the flow of the present tempo with small and neutral beats that observe the pattern. While maintaining the mood and energy of the musical line until the tempo shifts, an element of surprise is added.

Dvořák, Symphony no. 9 (*From the New World*), second movement, bars 45–46

Weber, Overture to *Der Freischütz*, bars 35–37

Many musicians find common denominators between different tempos. If a common denominator can be identified or created by adjusting either tempo, the transition is seamless. (See the discussion of common denominators in chapter 2.)

Tchaikovsky, Symphony no. 5, fourth movement, bars 55–58
Tchaikovsky, Symphony no. 5, fourth movement, bars 545–546
Beethoven, Symphony no. 7, first movement, bars 62–63
Beethoven, Symphony no. 7, third movement, bars 149–153

4. Subito Dynamic Changes from *ff* to *p*

A sudden *p* following a *ff* passage can be achieved by reducing the beat to the smallest possible size, short of stopping it altogether, at the exact moment of the dynamic change. However, if a complex rhythmic change occurs with the start of the *p*, a beat must be found that transmits all of the necessary rhythmic information.

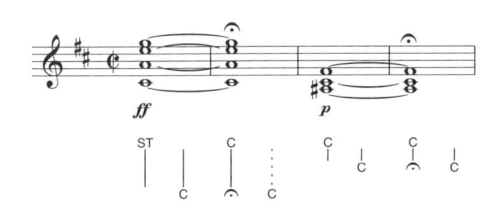

Beethoven, Symphony no. 2, fourth movement, bars 334–337

Marking the two bars prior to the fermata bars is unnecessary.

In *ff* passages the beat maintains its strength until the exact point of the dynamic change; under no circumstance should the conductor anticipate the forthcoming *p*. To maintain the *f* or *ff* level until the arrival of the subito *p* or *pp*, the conductor mentally divides the last beat unit before the dynamic change into smaller rhythmic units, then projects the *f* or *ff* level for each subdivided note until the moment of the dynamic change.

Beethoven, Symphony no. 2, first movement, bars 243–245

Beethoven, Symphony no. 7, second movement, bars 148–150

Beethoven, Symphony no. 2, third movement, bars 107–110

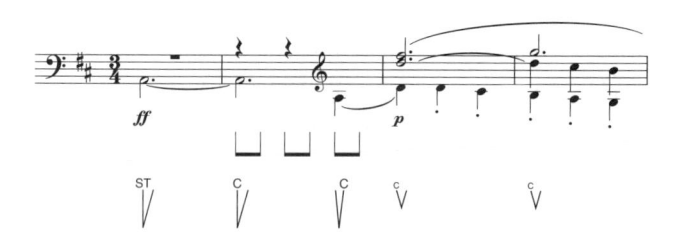

Beethoven, Symphony no. 2, first movement, bars 118–120

5. Subito Dynamic Changes from *p* to *ff*

A strong preparatory beat generally precedes a sudden *ff* entrance following a *p* passage. A challenge arises when the tempo is extremely slow and a lengthy preparatory beat for the *ff* is necessary, since there is a contradiction between the physical motion of a *ff* preparatory beat and the prevailing *p* beneath it. To avoid early interference with the conclusion of the *p* section, a faster beat unit can be created for the *ff*'s preparatory beat by subdividing the last pulse of the slow tempo.

Bartók, *Concerto for Orchestra,* first movement, bars 48–52

Haydn, Symphony no. 99, second movement, bars 93–95

Haydn, Symphony no. 94, second movement, bars 13–16

Berlioz, *Symphonie fantastique,* fourth movement, bars 128–130

Tchaikovsky, Symphony no. 5, first movement, bars 27–28

Beethoven, Symphony no. 9, first movement, bars 28–29

Tchaikovsky, Symphony no. 5, second movement, bars 157–158

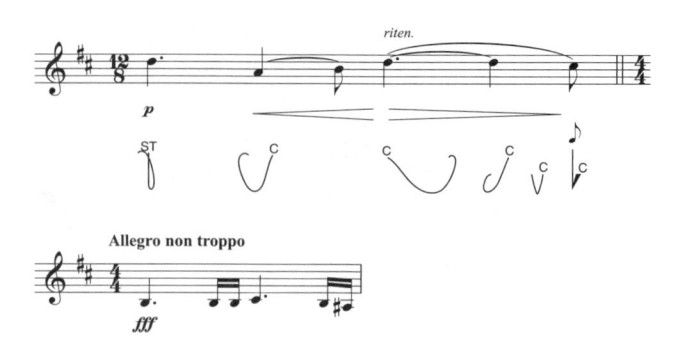

Mozart, Symphony no. 41, first movement, bars 1–6

6. *sfz* and *fp*

The preparatory beat for both the *fp* and the *sfz* (*sfz* and *sf* are considered to be the same) contains a strong ictus. At the conclusion of the preparatory beat and immediately after the *fp* or *sfz* attack, the rebound pulls back toward the conductor's body, either restoring the previous dynamic level or setting up a new one. Successive beats continue in the prevailing beat pattern within the framework of the given dynamics. These beats can easily disintegrate into stabbing motions directed into the orchestra that are both ineffective and offensive to the musicians.

7. Successive Preparatory Beats

A succession of *sfz*s or *fp*s is difficult to conduct. The rebound of the first *sfz* must rejuvenate itself immediately and produce the same vital energy and power for the next one; otherwise, the second *sfz* is not adequately anticipated or prepared, resulting in a weak attack.

Beethoven, Symphony no. 7, fourth movement, bars 459–460

Beethoven, Symphony no. 4, fourth movement, bars 66–67

Powerful successive entrances require the same approach.

Tchaikovsky, Symphony no. 4, first movement, bars 5–9

Tchaikovsky, Symphony no. 6, first movement, bars 189–192

8. Splitting a Single Preparatory Beat

Splitting a single preparatory beat into two allows for different signals to two different musicians or groups. In the following examples, a strong ictus serves the pizzicato and the wind entrance, while a smooth downbeat motion for the sustained first violins concludes the beat.

Beethoven, *Coriolan Overture*, bars 295–296

The first half of the preparatory beat serves as the cutoff for the *ff* and the second half (downbeat motion) shows the *p*.

Beethoven, Symphony no. 5, first movement, bars 3–7

Beethoven, Symphony no. 2, first movement, bar 1

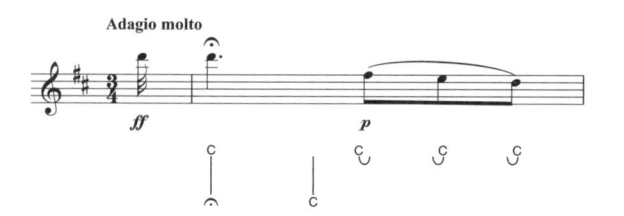

J. BEAT OPTIONS

1. Choosing the Beat Unit

Choosing the proper beat unit for any given bar is generally based on information explicitly provided in the score: a time signature, a metronome marking, or a notated instruction by the composer.[4]

A different beat unit from the one given by the composer may be more effective because of (1) the intricacy of the rhythmic texture; (2) the complexity of the orchestration; (3) excessively large orchestral forces; (4) the unusual physical layout of the musicians, such as excessive distances between players and conductor; (5) limitations in the effectiveness of the conductor's beat as it slows down or speeds up; and (6) rhythmic or technical limitations of certain instrumentalists, sections, or the entire ensemble.

Problems may emerge as the beat approaches either end of the tempo spectrum. In slow tempos more time elapses between successive beats. The musicians are on their own longer, and control of the ensemble becomes increasingly difficult. Subdividing the beat establishes control. In fast tempos, less time elapses between successive beats, and the musicians may have difficulty understanding and absorbing the information being communicated. Compounding two or more beat units into one larger and slower beat solves this problem.

In deciding when to change to a different beat unit, each conductor will formulate his or her own guidelines based on personal skill and experience. Some conductors may need to introduce a subdivision when the pulse falls below ♩ = 60, while others may still be comfortable at ♩ = 50. Some may easily be able to conduct up to ♩ = 180 before changing to ♩ = 90 or ♩. = 60, while others may need to compound the accelerating beats much earlier. Ideally, the beat unit that is chosen will feel inherently right to the conductor, and the pulse will be musically correct and the most effective one for controlling the ensemble.

2. Some Metrical Problems

a. Hemiola and Rebarring

The common definition of a hemiola is a musical alteration when two equal rhythmic units, each containing three equal inner beats, are regrouped into three units, each

---

4. Composers, particularly those who are conductors themselves (e.g., Mahler, Strauss, Stravinsky, Copland, Bernstein, Adams, Knussen, and Harbison), often indicate which beat unit to use. If at all possible, the conductor should abide by these requests.

containing two equal inner beats, or vice versa: for example, two $\frac{3}{4}$ bars become three $\frac{2}{4}$ bars, a $\frac{6}{8}$ bar becomes a $\frac{3}{4}$ bar, or a $\frac{3}{4}$ bar becomes a $\frac{6}{8}$ bar that is beaten in two.

When the hemiola applies to all participating musicians, most conductors alter the beat pattern to match the grouping of the hemiola or the inflections of the text.

Handel, *Messiah*, no. 3, bars 35–38

Brahms, Symphony no. 2, first movement, bars 282–285

Brahms, Symphony no. 2, first movement, bars 40–43

Mozart, Symphony no. 38, second movement, bar 132

Mozart, *The Magic Flute*, no. 17, bars 38–39

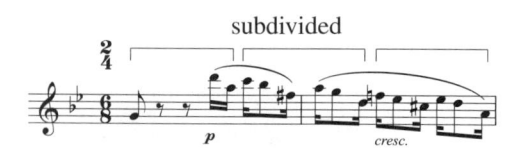

Tchaikovsky, Symphony no. 5, first movement, bars 96–100

Tchaikovsky, Symphony no. 4, first movement, bars 211–212

When only part of the orchestra participates in the hemiola, the conductor may choose to retain the original beat pattern, rather than rebarring the music for the benefit of the hemiola.

R. Strauss, Also sprach Zarathustra, 2 bars after rehearsal no. 24

Note: See four bars after rehearsal number 24, where the trumpet line no longer conflicts rhythmically; here rebarring is easier.

Berlioz, Symphonie fantastique, fifth movement, bars 394–403

If the phrasing clearly contradicts the time signature, the conductor may want to rebar the music mentally and allow the beat pattern of the prevailing time signature to continue.

Mussorgsky, *Night on Bald Mountain*, bars 299–303

Brahms, Symphony no. 2, first movement, bars 78–81

Beethoven, Symphony no. 2, second movement, bars 68–72

Brahms, Symphony no. 2, first movement, bars 118–121

Tchaikovsky, Symphony no. 6, fourth movement, bars 75–78

Debussy, Prelude to the Afternoon of a Faun, bar 27

Rebarring their parts is time-consuming for the musicians and may be confusing to those who are not participating in the hemiola. An alternative is to minimize the gestures of the beat pattern and show the notated time signature as discreetly as possible. The musicians will be able to follow without being distracted by contradictory beat patterns.

b. Other Conflicting Patterns and Rebeaming

The music of the twentieth century often requires simultaneous conducting of several instrumental groups with conflicting metric patterns.

In a $\frac{5}{8}$ bar, for instance, one section of the orchestra may be beamed in 2 + 3 and the other in 3 + 2.

In 3	In 4	In 5	In 6
2 + 1	2 + 2	3 + 2	2 + 2 + 2 (3 x 2)
1 + 2	3 + 1	2 + 3	3 + 3 (2 x 3)
	1 + 3	1 + 2 + 2	etc.
		2 + 1 + 2	
		2 + 2 + 1	

Beaming together groups of notes that contradict the main rhythmic structure and synchronizing them with the ongoing main pulse or the majority of players facilitates ensemble playing.

Stravinsky, *L'histoire du soldat,* The Devil's Dance, bar 20

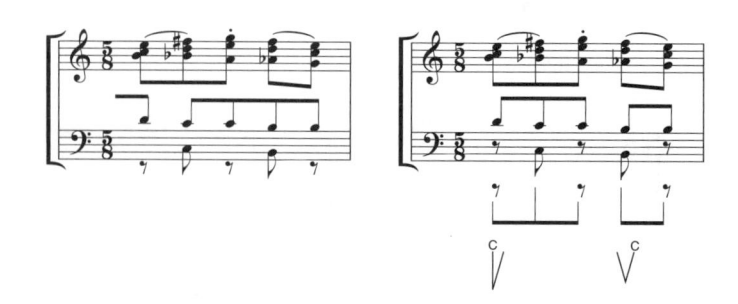

Bartók, *Concerto for Orchestra,* fourth movement, bars 75–78

c. Polyrhythmic Sections

Orchestra musicians conform to the time signature of the bar; however, at times, the players are divided into two groups, each with a different time signature for the same bar and each requiring separate beat information from the conductor. Theoretically each hand could lead a different group, but conducting two simultaneous beat patterns is confusing to the musicians. They prefer doing without beat information until major points where the rhythmic pulses of both groups coincide.

In the following example, the downbeat simply stops. Without any particular durational value, the next upbeat is given toward the end of the bar.

Carter, Double Concerto for Harpsichord and Piano, bar 619

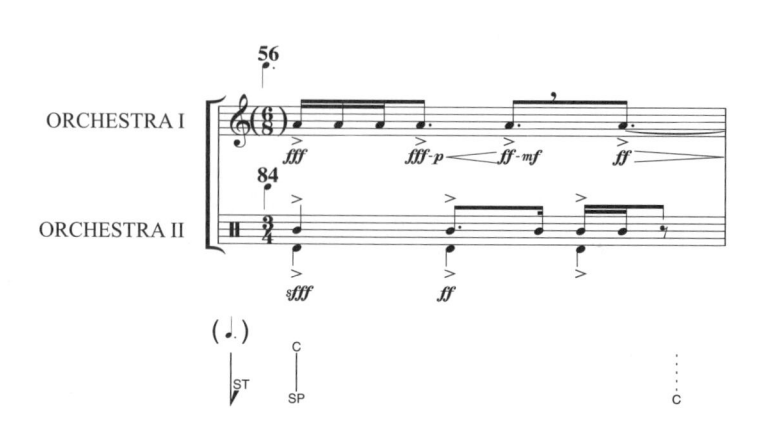

In this example, some conductors recommend shifting to 3 ($\frac{3}{4}$ $\overset{132}{\downarrow}$) for the first three bars at rehearsal number 25.

Stravinsky,
Petrouchka
(1947 version),
1 bar before
rehearsal no. 25

3. Suppressing the Rebound

In general the rebound functions as a preparatory beat for the next count; however, if no rhythmic activity is forthcoming, a rebound is unnecessary.

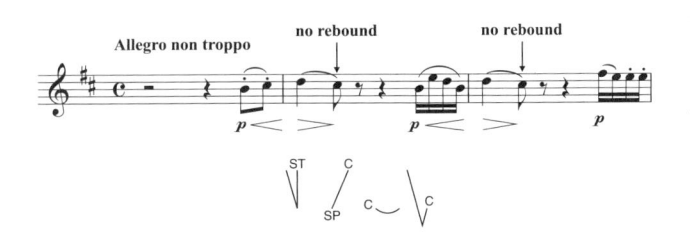

Tchaikovsky,
Symphony no. 6,
first movement,
bars 19–21

The rebound may be delayed to create a short stop in the musical flow (*Luftpause*). The interruption is usually of extremely short duration, but it can be expanded easily.

Brahms, Symphony no. 3, third movement, bars 13–14

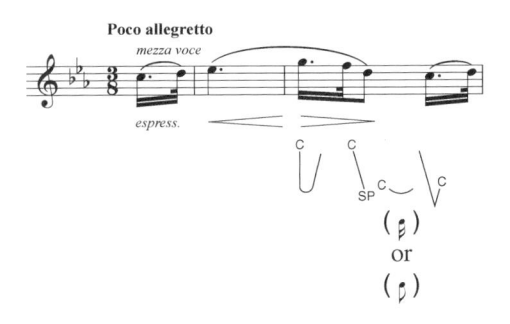

Beethoven, Symphony no. 2, second movement, bar 16

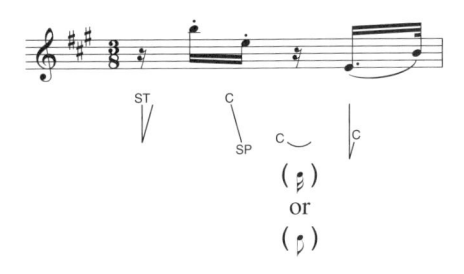

When rhythmic motion resumes after a tied-over note (♩♪♪) or a pause (𝄽 ♪ ♪), the rebound can be eliminated by stopping the beat immediately—freezing it. This procedure works only when the conductor moves into the inactive beat with a sense of forward direction similar to a crescendo motion.

Tchaikovsky, Symphony no. 6, fourth movement, bars 71–72

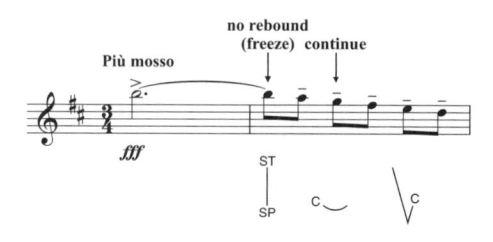

Tchaikovsky, Symphony no. 5, fourth movement, bars 58–59

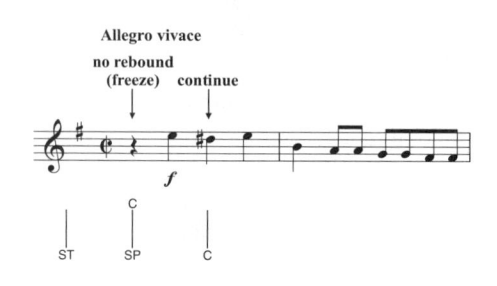

Falla, *The Three-Cornered Hat*, Suite no. 2, second movement, bars 15–17

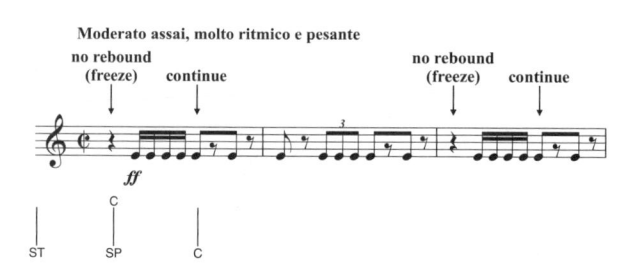

4. Dictating

If part of a phrase consists of sustained notes or chords, or if a measured silence of considerable length occurs, the conductor does not need to mark each and every metric pulse. Single gestures representing the total duration of each musical sound or silence are more suitable. The term *dictating* is often used to describe this approach.

In rehearsals, choral conductors make regular use of dictating in order to expedite learning; often, they give signals only when the rhythm, pitch, harmony, or text changes. Each sustained note, chord, word, syllable, or silence is held for its duration without any beat motion while the pulse continues in the conductor's mind. The beat is reactivated when a preparatory beat for a rhythmic change is needed.[5] From a musical point of view, dictating is better than giving monotonous and unnecessary beats. On the other hand, when a choral conductor leads orchestra musicians, they often object strenuously to dictating because of its "poor traffic information." They are accustomed to recognizable beat patterns. Giving regular beat patterns with small, discreet, neutral beats during sustained notes and rests is a satisfactory compromise. This is especially beneficial for those musicians in the ensemble who are counting bars during lengthy tacet sections and depend on the beat pattern to maintain their places.

In a slow passage, the preparatory beat to a sustained note or chord can be fast or slow (unmeasured). Naturally, the conductor must clearly feel the underlying regularity of the pulse and observe the exactness of the composer's rhythmic outline.

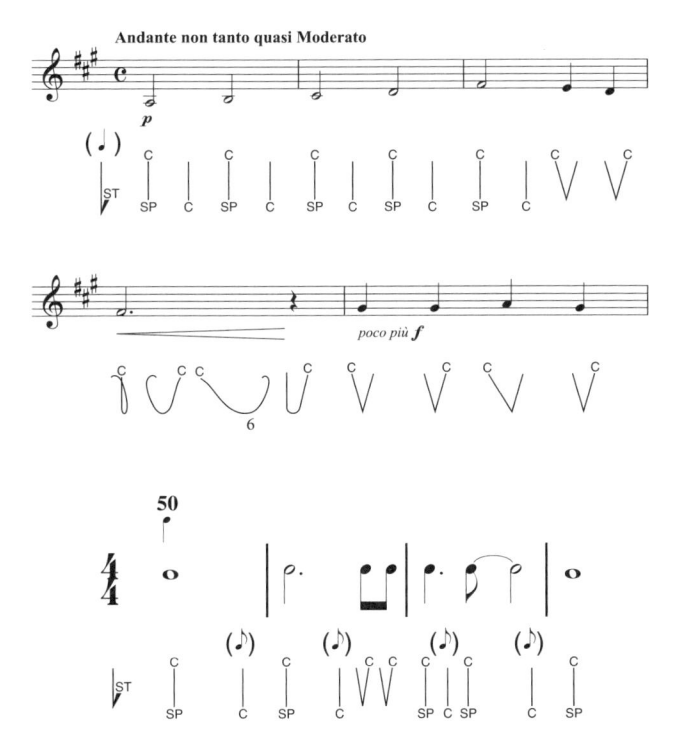

Tchaikovsky, *Romeo and Juliet* Fantasy-Overture, bars 1–5

---

5. Obviously, successive fast notes cannot be conducted individually but must be compounded into larger units.

6. In ♩ beats, each increases in size, in order to show the crescendo.

Mozart, Requiem, Dies Irae, bars 1–5

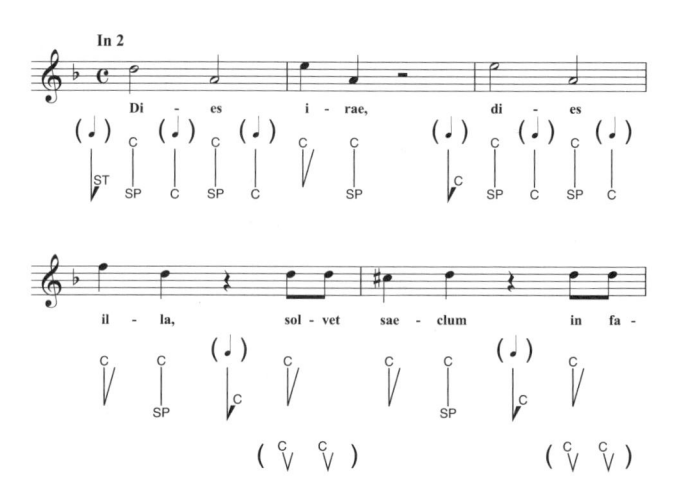

The shortness of a single staccato note can be indicated by adding a fast rebound and downbeat motion, each as small as possible. This can be done if there is enough time after the stopped staccato beat to execute the preparatory beat needed for the next entrance.

Deciding when to dictate depends upon several factors, ranging from the experience of the conductor to the level of the orchestra and the availability of rehearsal time. A clear beat pattern reassures musicians that they are in the right place. In the long run, however, increasing familiarity with the score in rehearsals provides them with greater security than does relying on a beat pattern and counting bars. Through listening, the musicians come to understand their roles within the compositional structure, gain musical independence, and acquire the freedom to respond to the artistic and musical subtleties the conductor is trying to transmit.

Dictating is an effective tool for reinforcing rhythmic progressions, especially at the end of works. In the following examples, the rhythmic outline is better realized by dictating than by beating ♩s throughout each bar.

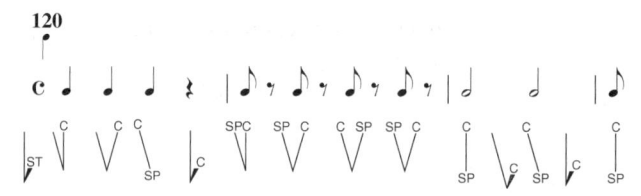

On count 3 the beat stops with no rebound. Cutting off the third ♩ is not necessary. The ictus of the beat on count 4 will substitute for a cutoff.

Each rebound stops.

The stopping of beats 1 and 3 must show the sustaining of the ♩'s.

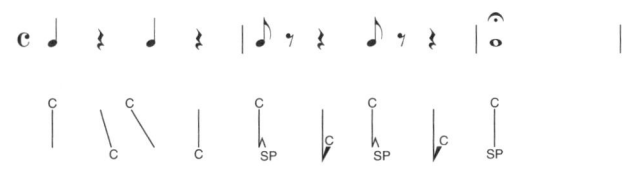

No rebounds.   Short rebound or small cutoff
                            depending on the tempo.

5. Cutoffs and Exits

Cutoffs, like entrances, require a full preparatory motion. The preparatory beat causes the participating musicians to enter together, while the cutoff assures their coordinated exit. Both signals require the same strength and physical effort; hence, a sustained *ff* chord orchestrated for a large ensemble requires a strong preparatory beat and an equally strong cutoff.

Orchestration, dynamic level, and musical and emotional concept guide the shaping of the cutoff. If no further rhythmic activity occurs after a sustained note or chord at the end of a movement or work, for instance, the cutoff may have an independent duration. A sustained string *pp* chord requires only a small cutoff. String players adjust their bowing to exit at the tip; each arrives at the moment of silence at a slightly different time, creating a fade-out. Generally, the players vibrate until the end of the bow is reached and often afterward as well. If wind instruments are included in the chord, the cutoff is adjusted. Flutes and clarinets are able to participate in a fade-out if their pitches lie in a comfortable range. Although they do not apply to rolls on bass drum, cymbals, and timpani or to sustained notes on mallet, keyboard, and bell-like instruments, clearly articulated cutoffs are necessary. The cutoff should reflect the composer's intent to end a note or chord at a specific dynamic level.

Exits do not always occur at the end of the basic count; often the notes spill over into the next count (or). The short overlap is signaled either by adding a slight pressure on the final beat and rebounding quickly, or by pulling back the beat motion. Depending upon the tempo, a subdivision can cut off the sound. Often musicians need encouragement to sustain the final notes or chords to the full duration requested by the composer.

Cutoffs offer a variety of musical possibilities. A pitch or a chord may ring into the silence or the music may stop suddenly. A fast and nervous cutoff has a far different musical impact from one that is broad and expressive.

The orchestra must never be cut off with an aggressive or negative gesture as though the musicians had dared to extend the duration of the final note or chord.

6. The *Luftpause*

A *Luftpause* (ʼ) is a short interruption in a musical line or passage during which the musicians make a quick break and then resume playing. It may apply to one or several instruments or include the entire ensemble.

If only some musicians participate, a *Luftpause* is achieved by shortening the length of the note or chord directly preceding it. When a series of rapid notes occurs prior to the *Luftpause*, a slight accelerando in the passage may be unavoidable or even desirable. A *Luftpause* that does not include the entire ensemble never interrupts the ongoing basic pulse.

If the composer indicates a *Luftpause* for the entire ensemble, the continuation of the musical passage immediately thereafter must be delayed momentarily. The best way to achieve this delay is to stop the beat just prior to the *Luftpause*. If the tempo is slow, the last beat before the *Luftpause* is subdivided. The stop should be extremely brief, because the preparatory beat for the continuation in itself causes a rest. The *Luftpause* may be too long if the preparatory beat sets up a slow tempo.

Depending upon the rhythmic complexity and the orchestration of the musical material that follows, the preparatory beat after the *Luftpause* may be unmeasured, measured, or a subdivision of the basic pulse. It should resemble a push-away motion. The preparatory beat may continue from the exact point within the beat pattern where the beat stopped, or it may backtrack and repeat an entire beat. Deciding which procedure to use depends entirely on the compositional context surrounding the *Luftpause*.

R. Strauss, *Don Juan*, bars 473–474

Bartók, *Concerto for Orchestra*, fifth movement, bars 570–573

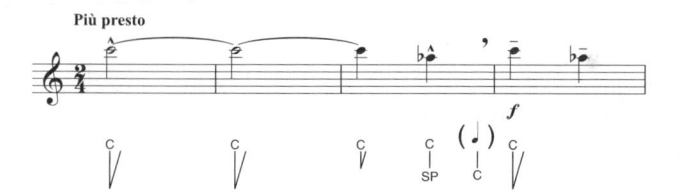

R. Strauss, *Don Juan*, bars 300–302

A brief *Luftpause* can be added to separate two phrases. If the tempo is steady, the beat is stopped without rebound for a split second at the conclusion of the phrase.

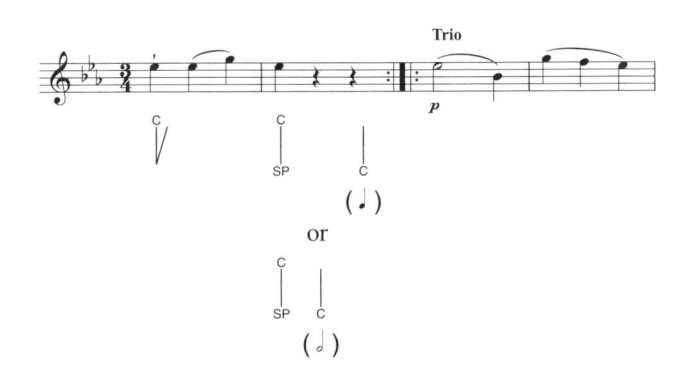

Mozart, Symphony no. 39, third movement, bars 43–46

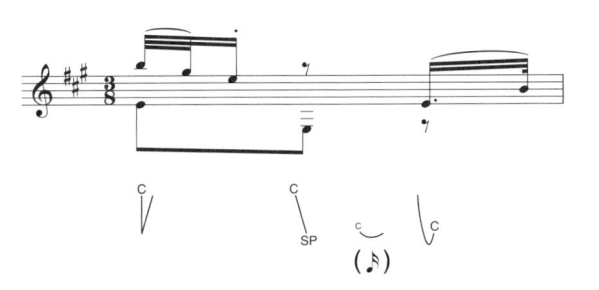

Beethoven, Symphony no. 2, second movement, bar 173

Mozart, Symphony no. 41, third movement, bars 57–61

Beethoven, Symphony no. 5, third movement, bars 139–141

---

7. Resembles a push-away motion. A pull-back motion can also be very effective.

Beethoven, Symphony no. 3, third movement, bars 165–167

Beethoven, Symphony no. 2, second movement, bar 16

Beethoven, Symphony no. 4, third movement, bars 89–91

Brahms, Symphony no. 3, third movement, bars 1–2

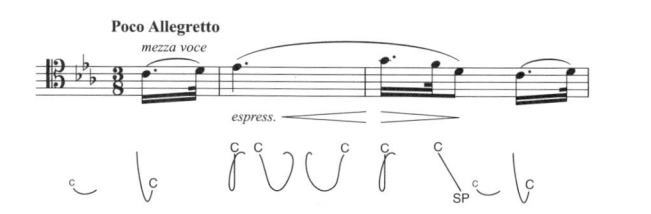

7. Fermatas

A *fermata* extends a pitch, chord, or silence beyond its notated duration. From a technical point of view, the moment of the fermata's arrival is straightforward. The beat stops without a rebound; there is a discontinuation of any rhythmic motion. Musically speaking, a prolonged pitch, chord, or silence is not static. The conductor actively participates in the holding of the fermata and reflects the flow of time by remaining focused. If the score indicates a change in dynamics within the fermata, the conductor expresses it physically with one or both hands.

After a fermata, a composer may insert a *caesura* (//) or a *breath mark* (ʼ) to indicate a clear break between the fermata and the music that follows. The left hand cuts the fermata off without any specific tempo information because the rest itself is of undetermined duration.

The beat stops at the conclusion of the cutoff. After the desired duration of the break, an appropriate preparatory beat is given to continue. In physical terms, the cutoff and the upcoming preparatory beat use the same space within the prevailing pattern. The left-hand cutoff concludes at a place from which the preparatory beat that follows can comfortably be initiated. At that point the right hand immediately starts the preparatory beat for the next entrance.

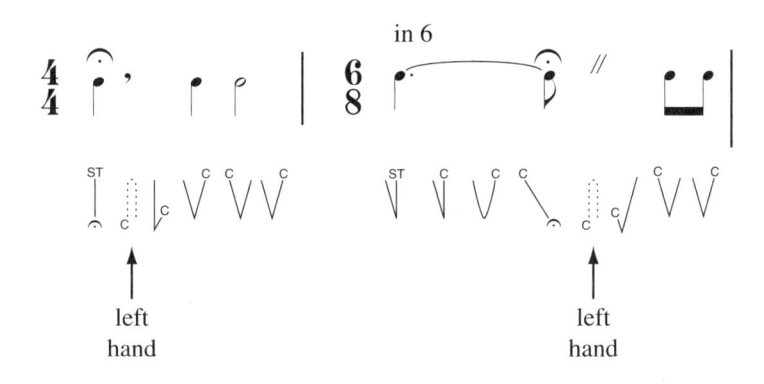

A push-away motion eliminates the need to use the left hand.

If a fermata over a pitch is followed by a fermata over a rest, the cutoff for the first concludes in the space where the second one begins. If the duration of the rest with the fermata equals a full count, the preparatory beat for the next entrance uses the space in the beat pattern that belongs to the second fermata. An upbeat with a duration of less than half of the basic count requires the same approach.

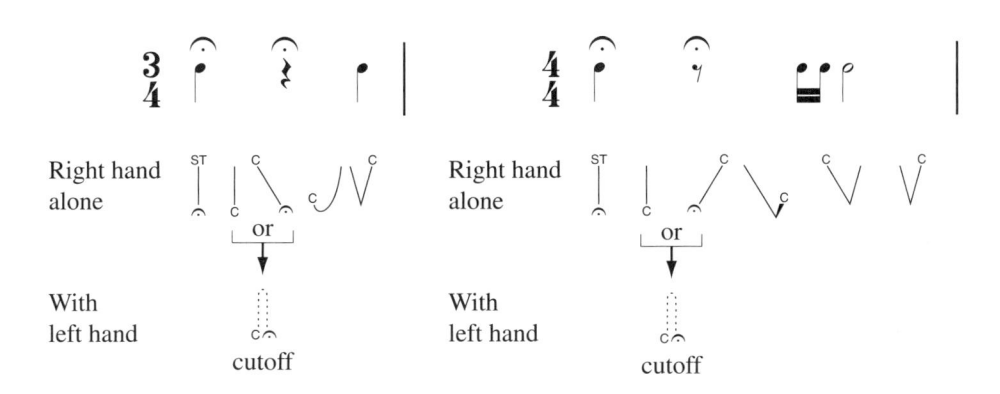

If the upbeat's duration is longer than half of the basic count, an additional preparatory beat is required.

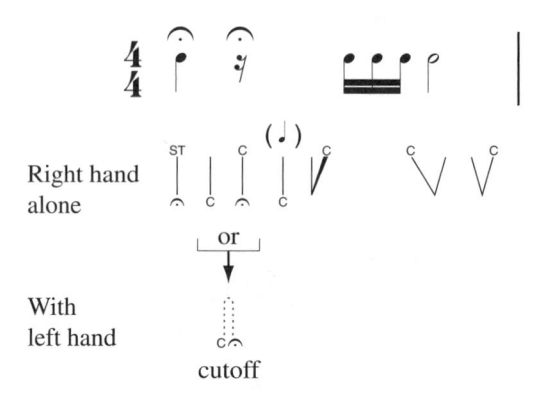

When a fermata is followed by a measured rest, the conclusion of the fermata's cutoff becomes part of the continuing beat pattern.

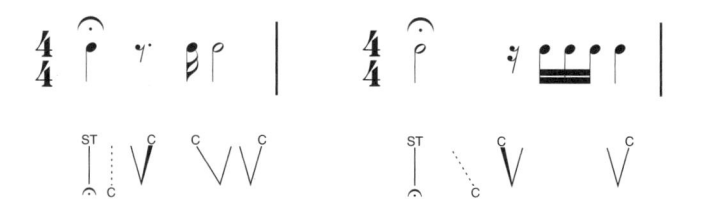

If more than one beat occurs before the orchestra reenters, all the tacet counts must be marked in a neutral fashion without ictus until the final preparatory beat is given that brings in the orchestra.

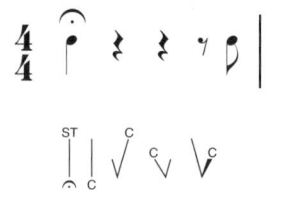

Matters become more problematic when no break is indicated between a fermata and the music that follows. Although the composer clearly wants to continue without a break, conductors often choose either to add a *Luftpause* or to separate the two with a break of considerable length.

A pause can be extended to accommodate bowing or breathing for singers and wind players. A break may also be justified when the dynamics shift from a *f* fermata to a *p* to prevent the post-fermata material from being obscured (Beethoven 2,I,1 and 5,I,1–5).

If there is no break after the fermata and the fermata is about to end, a preparatory beat is initiated for the music that follows. This preparatory beat should never contain a strong ictus; otherwise it might be mistaken for a cutoff.

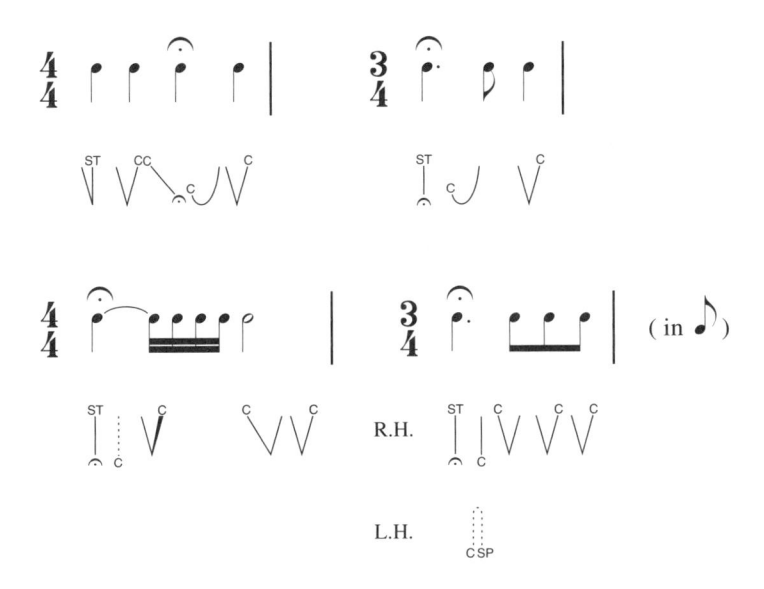

If the conductor decides to add a *Luftpause* after the fermata, the preparatory beat for the following note or chord must contain a strong ictus. The downward pressure of the ictus is increased as though the sound were being pushed away. This creates a moment of silence before continuing.

If a fermata is placed over a note, chord, or rest lasting more than one count, the conductor continues to beat through the held notes or silence within the bar's pattern until the final count is reached.[8] The beat remains neutral and is not necessarily in tempo.

---

8. If the entire orchestra participates in the fermata, the conductor can stop the beat at the beginning of the fermata and give no further information.

78 THE SCORE, THE ORCHESTRA, AND THE CONDUCTOR

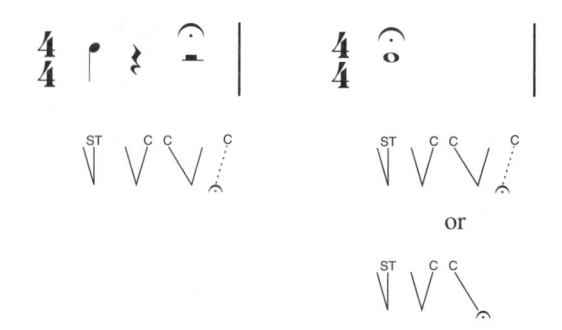

A collection of fermata excerpts follows:

Schumann, Symphony no. 1, first movement, bars 1–2

No ictus; no break

Beethoven, Symphony no. 7, first movement, bars 87–88

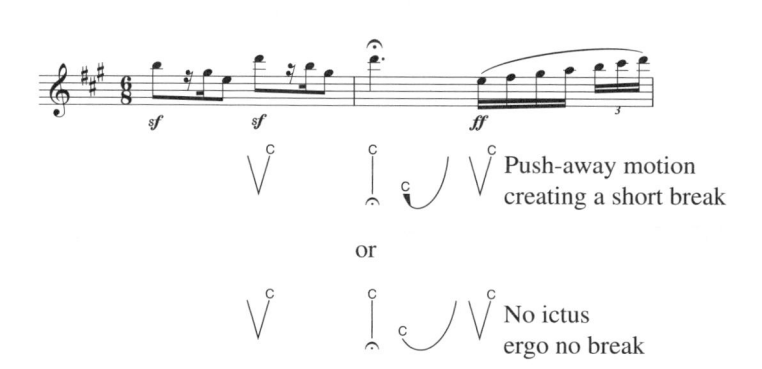

Push-away motion creating a short break

or

No ictus ergo no break

Tchaikovsky, Symphony no. 6, first movement, bars 160–161

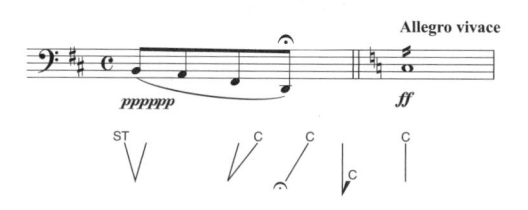

Mendelssohn, *A Midsummer Night's Dream*, Nocturne, bar 26

The Beat   79

Schumann, Symphony no. 3, part 2, bars 38–39

Mozart, Overture to *The Abduction from the Seraglio*, bar 151

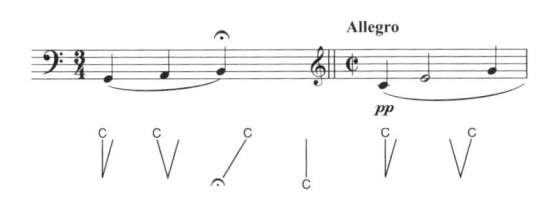

Beethoven, *Leonore Overture* no. 3, bars 36–37

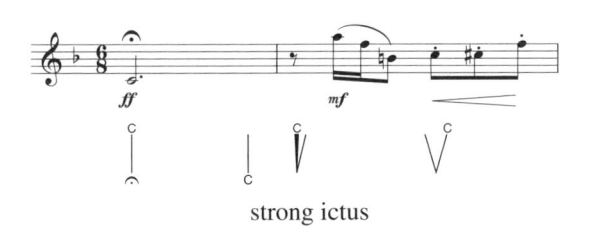

no ictus, no break

R. Strauss, *Till Eulenspiegels lustige Streiche*, bars 45–46

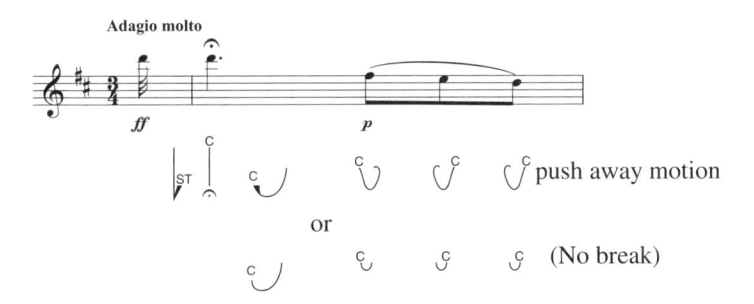

strong ictus

Beethoven, Symphony no. 2, first movement, bar 1

push away motion

or

(No break)

Beethoven, Symphony no. 1, fourth movement, bars 1–2

push away motion

80 THE SCORE, THE ORCHESTRA, AND THE CONDUCTOR

Schumann, Symphony no. 1, third movement, bars 199–200

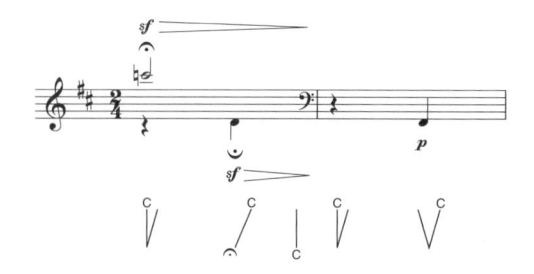

Mahler, Symphony no. 2, first movement, bar 4*

Weber, Overture to *Der Freischütz*, bars 281–282

Puccini, *La Bohème,* act 1, 9 bars before rehearsal no. 15

Rimsky-Korsakov, *Scheherazade,* third movement, bar 160

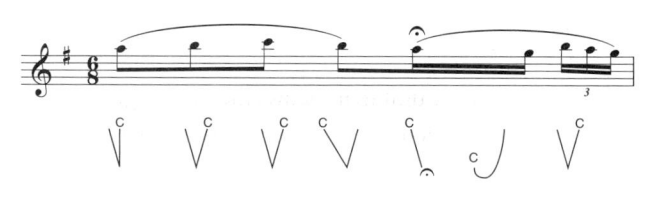

Beethoven, Symphony no. 3, fourth movement, bars 95–96

*© 1972 Universal Edition, Vienna. © Renewed. All Rights Reserved. Used by permission of European American Music Distributors LLC, U.S. and Canadian agent for Universal Edition Vienna, London.

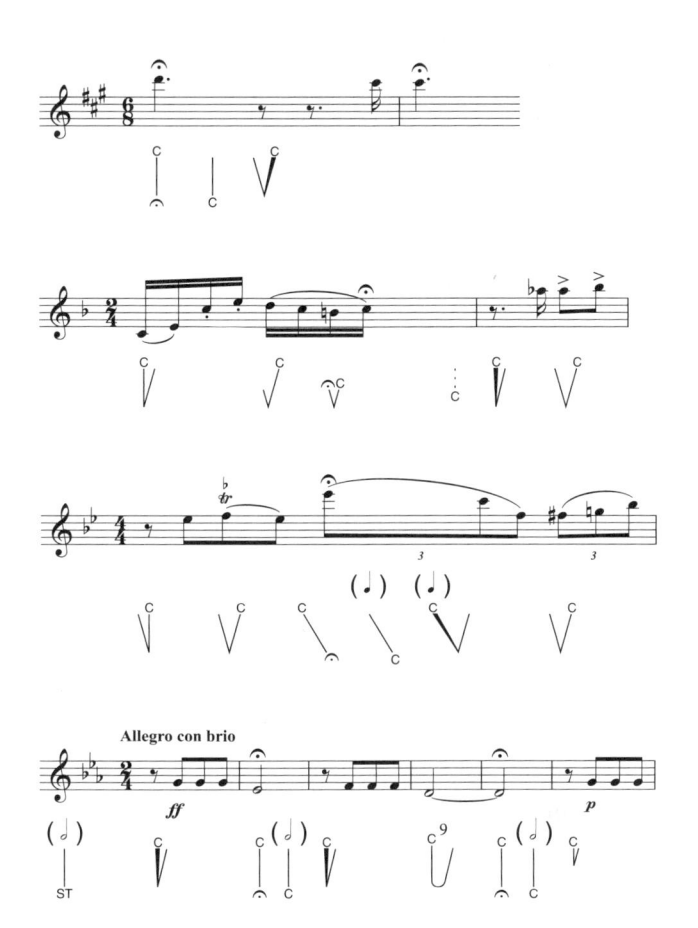

Beethoven, Symphony no. 7, first movement, bars 299–300

Schumann, Symphony no. 4, first movement, bars 143–144

Gershwin, *Rhapsody in Blue*, bar 10

Beethoven, Symphony no. 5, first movement, bars 1–6

8. Tied Notes

Notes or chords tied over into the next count often cause an unwanted delay before the music continues. If the basic tempo is moderate to fast, a strong ictus on the rhythmically inactive count will suffice to maintain the tempo. If the tempo is slower, it is better to dictate the rhythmic unit that follows the tie. Imagining a crescendo while leading into the count with the tied-over note or chord is helpful to the conductor.

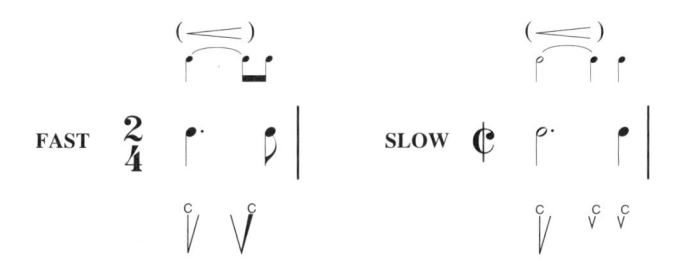

---

9. It is not necessary to mark this bar. Go to the ⌢ bar immediately.

9. Syncopations

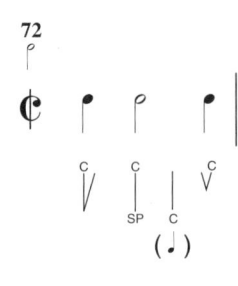

Syncopations lose force unless their relationship to the basic pulse is recognizable. During syncopations, control of the orchestra is maintained by signals that emphasize the main pulse. The musicians play against the pulse more easily when the main pulse is audible, visible, and steady. For a single syncopation in a slow tempo, the conductor subdivides the basic pulse and dictates the syncopation.

In a fast tempo, the beat that includes the syncopation must not rebound; instead, the motion should stop. The reentry following the stop must occur at exactly the right moment.

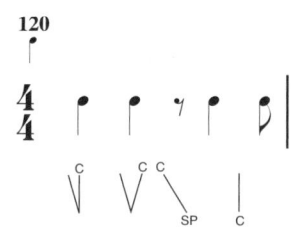

For a series of syncopations, the conductor concentrates strictly on the main pulse and leaves the syncopations alone. When no one plays on the beat, the conductor must still focus on the main pulse and resist the temptation to conduct or show the syncopations. Leading an imaginary on-the-beat group of musicians is suggested.

Weber, Overture to *Der Freischütz*, bars 53–54

In a faster tempo, the conductor moves from beat to beat in the fashion described in the section on the nonrebound beat.

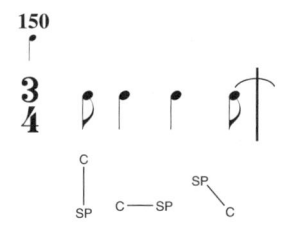

If some of the musicians play on the main counts, the conductor addresses them with full rebound beats.

Tchaikovsky, Symphony no. 5, third movement, bars 57–64

* There is no rebound on the second count.
Beat motion continues on the arrival of count 3.

When the tempo of the conducted beat is very fast, the musicians can comprehend the syncopations more easily if beats are compounded into a larger and slower unit. Again, the conductor must associate with the players who are articulating the main pulse.

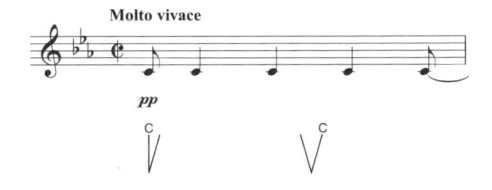

Weber, Overture to *Der Freischütz*, bar 37

The *offbeat,* an isolated note or chord played after a main pulse, is related to the syncopation. Unless the main pulse is projected strongly, the offbeat will be performed poorly. As with syncopations, the conductor stays in contact with the "on-the-beat" musicians, although their musical material may be of secondary importance. If no one plays on the beat, the conductor must give strong preparatory signals for each count.

R. Strauss, *Death and Transfiguration*, bar 1

10. Tacet Bars and Grand Pauses

Empty tacet bars for the entire orchestra are conducted within the normal beat pattern but with reduced size. By keeping beat information to a minimum, the musicians, as well as the listeners, experience both the silence and the surprise of the reentry. The preparatory beat for the reentry must take place at precisely the right moment. When little or no time is available for rehearsals, giving regular, full-size beats is safer. They are more effective than small ones for fast-moving passages where the musical content after the measured silence is rhythmically challenging (e.g., upbeats or after-the-beat entrances). Each section involving tacet bars should be examined from a practical point of view first and from a musical point of view second.

Mozart, Symphony no. 39, fourth movement, bars 106–108

Beethoven, Symphony no. 5, first movement, bars 121–125

Debussy, *Prelude to the Afternoon of a Faun*, bars 5–7

Beethoven, Symphony no. 7, fourth movement, bars 1–3

Dukas, *The Sorcerer's Apprentice,* bars 42–55

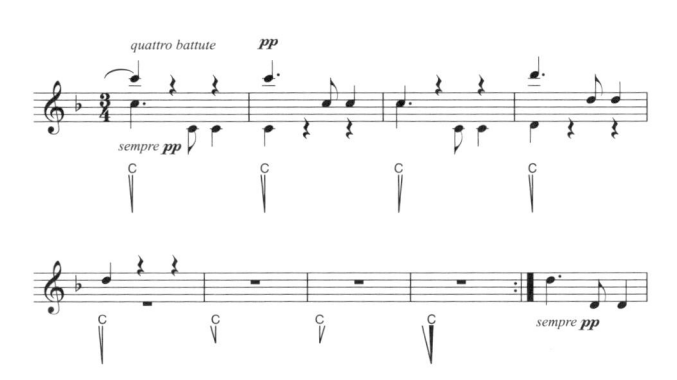

Beethoven, Symphony no. 9, second movement, bars 143–151

Today, bars of silence labeled G.P. (grand pause) or tacet are sometimes given different durations than those requested by the composer. Instead, the G.P. is treated as an unmeasured block of time.

Beethoven, Symphony no. 7, fourth movement, bars 1–5

Mozart, Symphony no. 40, first movement, bars 41–44

Mozart, Symphony no. 39, fourth movement, bars 105–109

Debussy, *Prelude to the Afternoon of a Faun,* bars 5–7

Beethoven, *Coriolan Overture,* bars 1–6

Haydn, Symphony no. 104, fourth movement, bars 164–168

Taking extra time is clearly not possible when the empty bars are part of a *quattro* or *tre battute* section.

11. Sudden Silences and Their Continuation

When the flow of the music is suddenly interrupted by a rest, the conductor stops the beat for a split second before the silence occurs. The stop reflects the silence. The last note or chord before the silence must be conducted by a subdivided beat if necessary.

Brahms, Symphony no. 4, fourth movement, bar 56

Brahms, Symphony no. 2, fourth movement, bars 407–409

Copland, *Appalachian Spring* Suite, 2 bars before rehearsal no. 33

Beethoven, Symphony no. 2, second movement II, bars 15–16

Brahms, Symphony no. 3, first movement, bars 193–194

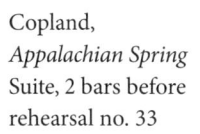

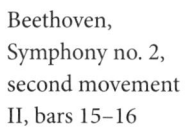

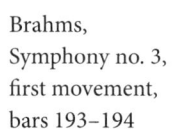

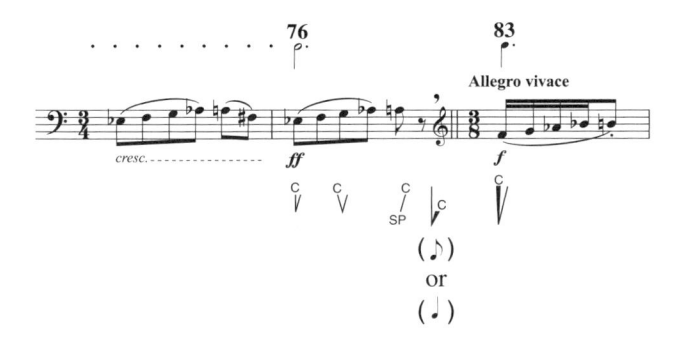

Bartók, *Concerto for Orchestra*, first movement, bars 74–76

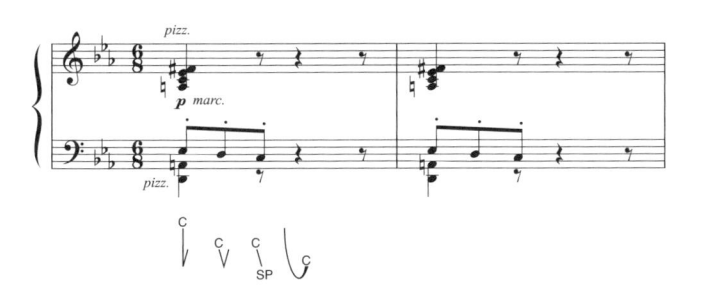

Brahms, Symphony no. 1, first movement, bars 430–431

If a cutoff is required, the conductor stops at its conclusion. No rebound is given because it would disturb the beginning of the silence. As the silence is about to end, a preparatory beat reestablishes the continuation of the musical material.

Weber, Overture to *Der Freischütz*, bars 284–287

12. Stopping the Beat

Conductors often fall into the habit of stopping the beat at the apex for longer than a brief moment. Usually accompanied by a held breath, the beat continues with a fast downward motion after this sudden, extended stop. When the travel motion of the rebound is blocked in this way, the musical line is disturbed, and synchronized attacks are impossible. The conductor should be on the lookout for interruptions in the travel path of the beat, abandon them, and return to a preparatory beat or rebound that moves ahead to its conclusion without hesitation.

13. To Conduct or Not to Conduct

Occasionally passages are played by only one orchestra player. Giving the musician a small and unmeasured preparatory beat is usually not done, but it is helpful because it informs the other musicians where they are in their parts. Although the beat pattern should be recognizable to the musicians, the motions following the preparatory beat are very small and neutral. The goal is for the soloist to feel that the conductor is in a supportive, accompanying role.

Weber, *Oberon Overture*, bar 1

Berlioz, *Symphonie fantastique*, third movement, bars 1–4

Debussy, *Prelude to the Afternoon of a Faun*, bars 1–4

14. Composite Rhythmic Textures

Following the rule that each musical shift—melodic, harmonic, or rhythmic—should be acknowledged, the conductor may want to create a mental composite of all rhythmic moves. These compound examples provide an overview of how rhythmic lines interlock. The Webern work and other fast examples serve as theoretical examples; practical application may not be possible.

Beethoven, Symphony no. 2, second movement, bars 142–143

Beethoven, Symphony no. 2, fourth movement, bars 98–99

Beethoven, Symphony no. 9, third movement, bars 1–3

Tchaikovsky, Symphony no. 5, second movement, bar 43

Debussy, *Prelude to the Afternoon of a Faun,* bars 76–78

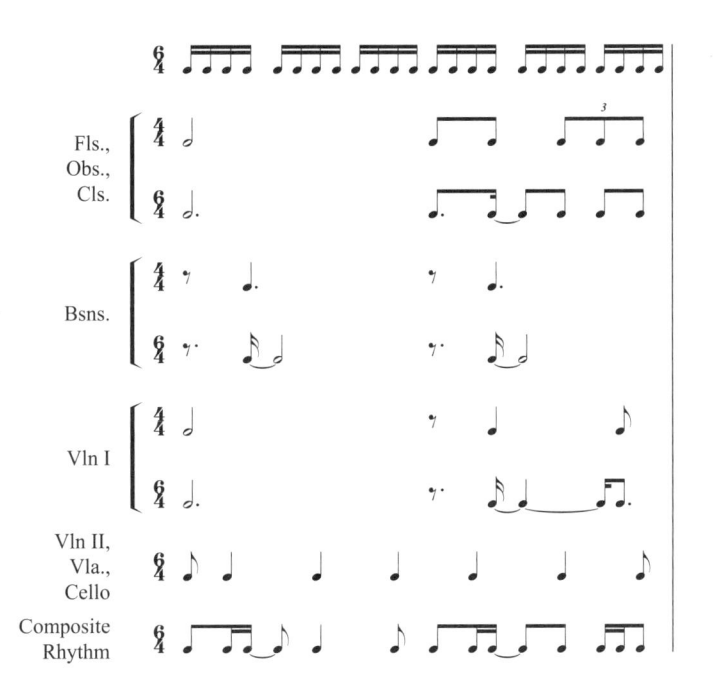

Sibelius, Symphony no. 1, second movement, bar 114

Webern, Symphony, op. 21, second movement, bars 65–68 *

*© 1992 by Universal Edition. © Renewed. All Rights Reserved. Used by permission of European American Music Distributors LLC, U.S. and Canadian agent for Schott Music.

Webern, Symphony, op. 21, second movement, bars 69–73*

*© 1992 by Universal Edition. © Renewed. All Rights Reserved. Used by permission of European American Music Distributors LLC, U.S. and Canadian agent for Schott Music.

Debussy, *Prelude to the Afternoon of a Faun,* bar 34

Mozart, Symphony no. 39, first movement, bars 1–2

Dvořák, Symphony no. 9 (*From the New World*), first movement, bars 9–12

CHAPTER TWO

Reading the Score

A. NOTATION

A conductor must have a thorough understanding of the notation of all orchestral instruments. The majority of the standard orchestral instruments are notated at *concert pitch* (in C).

    Flute   Trombone   Organ
    Oboe   Tuba   Vibraphone
    Clarinet in C   Timpani   Marimba
    Bassoon   Harp   Violin
    Horn in C alto   Harpsichord   Viola
    Trumpet in C   Piano   Cello[1]

Any time the fundamental key of an instrument is not at concert pitch, a transposition must take place. The following instruments require transposition:

Piccolo (sounds an octave higher)
Alto flute (in G)
Oboe d'amore (in A)
English horn (in F)
Heckelphone (sounds an octave lower)
Clarinet (in E♭, D, B♭, and A)
Basset horn (in F)
Bass clarinet (in B♭ and A)
Saxophone (in B♭ and E♭)
Contrabassoon (sounds an octave lower)
Horn (in B and B♭ alto; in A, A♭, G, F♯, F, E, E♭, D, and D♭; and in C, B, B♭, A, and A♭ basso)

Baritone (in B♭)
Wagner tuba (in F, E♭, and B♭)
Trumpet (in F♯, F, E, E♭, D, D♭, B, B♭, A, A♭, and G)
Bass trumpet (in C sounds an octave lower, B♭, and E♭)
Xylophone (sounds an octave higher)
Celesta (sounds an octave higher)
Orchestra Bells (sound two octaves higher)
Bass (sounds an octave lower)

---

1. For irregular octave transpositions, see Appendix A.

Clefs Used in Today's Orchestra

(**X** = Clef normally used; **R** = Clef rarely used)

Instrument/Clef	Treble	Alto	Tenor	Bass	Tr/Bs
Piccolo	X				
Flute	X				
Oboe	X				
English Horn	X	R*			
Clarinet	X				
Bass Clarinet	X			X	
Basset Horn	X			X	
Saxophone	X			X	
Bassoon	R		X	X	
Contrabassoon				X	
Horn	X	R*		X	
Wagner Tuba	X			X	
Trumpet	X			R	
Bass Trumpet	X			R	
Trombone, alto		X	R	X	
Trombone, tenor		R	X	X	
Trombone, bass			R	X	
Tuba				X	
Timpani	X			X	
Orchestra Bells	X				
Xylophone	X				
Vibraphone					
Marimba					X
Harp					X
Piano					X
Celesta					X
Organ					X
Harpsichord	X				X
Violin	X				
Viola	X	X			
Cello	R		X	X	
Bass			X	X	

*See Prokofiev 5, Barber scores, and others.

B. RHYTHM AND TEMPO

Tempo markings are self-explanatory. Movements or sections are generally headed by clear tempo indications, such as Allegro, Andante, or Lento. Bowings, phrasings, articulations, and dynamics are also indicative of tempo. The metronome markings of composers from earlier periods approximate the speed of a given pulse. Contemporary composers generally notate exact metronomic tempos, and musicians are expected to honor them. At times the technical abilities of the performers dictate a tempo and override the notated tempo markings.

Although sometimes well camouflaged, a common denominator may connect adjoining sections and reveal their rhythmic relationship. A conductor should be able to execute any rhythmic pattern accurately; however, polyrhythmic passages consisting of multiple layers of different, unrelated rhythms executed simultaneously create challenges.

Ritardando and accelerando are rhythmic tools. The *ritardando* is understood to mean a gradual slowdown of the tempo. It may lead into a new tempo or stop as it reaches a fermata or rest. The *accelerando* moves the tempo forward. Some composers have begun to pinpoint their intentions by utilizing increasing or decreasing metronome markings at short intervals, thereby setting the degree of a ritardando or accelerando more precisely. Generally, however, the conductor must search for an approximation that best serves the composer's intent.

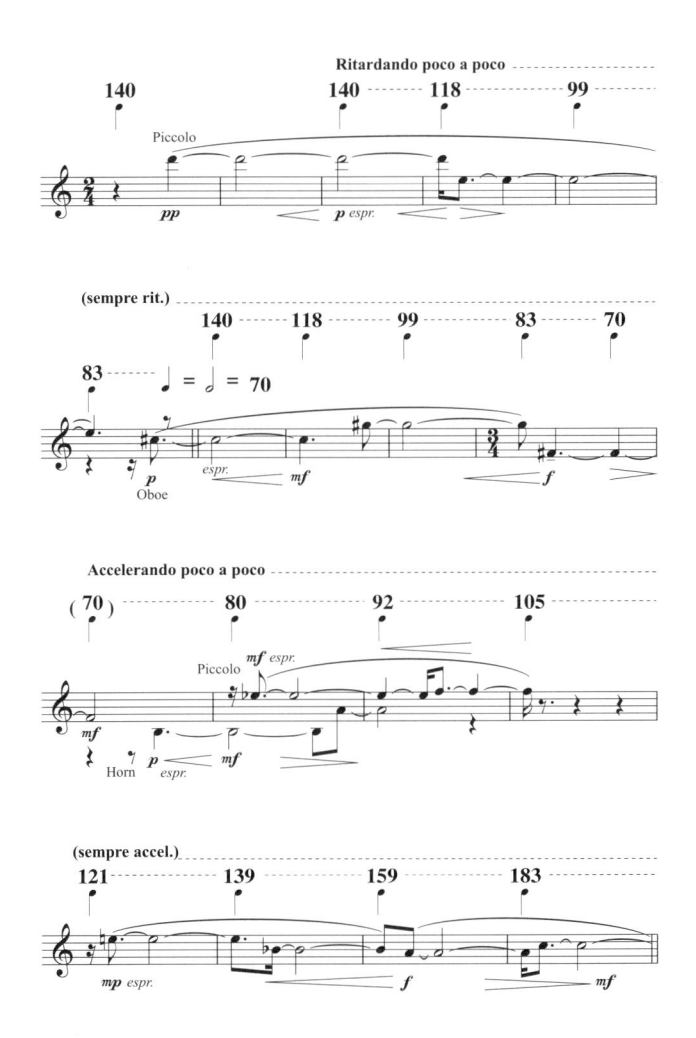

Carter, Double Concerto for Harpsichord and Piano, bars 319–336

The *rubato*, unique among the rhythmic variables, is a subtle rhythmic alteration of a passage or part of a passage of steady tempo created by minute slow-downs, speed-ups, delays, expanded silences, or whatever rhythmic flexibilities seem appropriate.

Composers may indicate a rubato, or performers may create a rubato where none is indicated. The rubato is used to highlight a phrase, part of a phrase, or a significant harmonic progression.

Depending on the musical circumstances, an arbitrary (unwritten) ritardando or accelerando may be stretched over several bars to set up a new tempo or return to a previous one. However, unwritten and prolonged ritardandos or accelerandos may lead to a rhythmic progression unintended by the composer and rob the listener of a musical surprise. The following examples illustrate this:

Tchaikovsky, Symphony no. 4, fourth movement, bars 195–199

Brahms, Symphony no. 1, fourth movement, bars 403–408

C. METRONOME MARKINGS

A note of any duration and metronomic speed can be divided into any number of shorter notes of equal length. The metronome marking of the shorter note can be determined by multiplying the metronome marking of the original note by the number of divisions it underwent. If the metronome marking is ♩ = 60, for example, and the conductor wants to know the metronome marking of the corresponding ♪, the metronome marking of the ♩ must be multiplied by four, the ♪ being four times faster. The metronome marking of the new ♪ is, therefore, 60 × 4 = 240.

$$♩ = 60 = 4♪ \qquad ♪ = 4 \times 60 = 240$$

The same answer can be obtained by dividing the metronome marking of the original note by the proportion of the requested unit.

$$\quarternote = 60 = \frac{1}{1} \qquad \eighthnote = \frac{1}{4} \qquad \eighthnote = 60 \div \frac{1}{4} = 240$$

The following diagram lists a number of different subdivisions of $\quarternote = 60$ and shows the resulting metronome marking for each of the new subdivisions.

Number of Subdivisions		Metronome Marking of New Subdivision
2	$2 \times 60 = 120 \qquad 60 \div \frac{1}{2}$	$\eighthnote = 120$
3	$3 \times 60 = 180 \qquad 60 \div \frac{1}{3}$	$\eighthnote_{\lfloor 3 \rfloor} = 180$
4	$4 \times 60 = 240 \qquad 60 \div \frac{1}{4}$	$\eighthnote = 240$
5	$5 \times 60 = 300 \qquad 60 \div \frac{1}{5}$	$\eighthnote_{\lfloor 5 \rfloor} = 300$
6	$6 \times 60 = 360 \qquad 60 \div \frac{1}{6}$	$\eighthnote_{\lfloor 6 \rfloor} = 360$
7	$7 \times 60 = 420 \qquad 60 \div \frac{1}{7}$	$\eighthnote_{\lfloor 7 \rfloor} = 420$
8	$8 \times 60 = 480 \qquad 60 \div \frac{1}{8}$	$\eighthnote = 480$

To combine two or more rhythmically identical notes into a larger, slower unit and find its corresponding metronome marking, the original metronome marking has to be divided by the number of notes needed to form the larger unit. If a metronome marking is $\eighthnote = 150$, for example, and the conductor wants to determine the metronome marking of the corresponding $\dottedquarter$, the metronome marking of the $\eighthnote$ (150) must be divided by three, the $\dottedquarter$ being three times slower. The metronome marking of the $\dottedquarter$ is therefore $150 \div 3 = 50$.

$$\eighthnote = 150 \qquad 3\,\eighthnote = \dottedquarter \qquad \dottedquarter = 150 \div 3 = 50$$

The same answer can be obtained by multiplying the metronome marking of the original note by the proportion of the requested note.

$$\eighthnote. = \frac{1}{1} \qquad \eighthnote = 150 = \frac{1}{3} \qquad \eighthnote. = 150 \times \frac{1}{3} = 50$$

The following diagram illustrates different examples of $\eighthnote = 180$ and shows the resulting metronome marking for each new compound unit.

Number of Sixteenths			Metronome Marking of New Unit
2	$180 \div 2 = 90$	$180 \times \frac{1}{2}$	$\eighthnote = 90$
3	$180 \div 3 = 60$	$180 \times \frac{1}{3}$	$\eighthnote. = 60$
4	$180 \div 4 = 45$	$180 \times \frac{1}{4}$	$\quarternote = 45$
5	$180 \div 5 = 36$	$180 \times \frac{1}{5}$	$\quarternote\eighthnote = 36$
6	$180 \div 6 = 30$	$180 \times \frac{1}{6}$	$\quarternote. = 30$

The first step in assigning a metronome marking to only a portion of a given note value is to find a rhythmic unit that divides evenly into both the original and the new note value. This common rhythmic unit is called the *common denominator*.

For example, to determine the metronomic pulse of a $\quarternote$, given the basic pulse of $\quarternote.\!\!\!{}^{50}$, the first step is to figure out the rhythmic unit that is the common denominator between the two, which in this case is the $\eighthnote$.

The next step is to figure out how many $\eighthnote$s are contained in the original $\quarternote.$ unit. Because the metronome marking is

$$\quarternote. = 50$$

and given that there are three $\eighthnote$s in a $\quarternote.$, the metronome marking for the $\eighthnote$ is three times faster.

$$3 \times 50 = 150 \, \eighthnote$$

The metronome marking of the ♩ can be derived from the ♪. Because the ♩ contains two ♪s, the metronome marking of the ♪ is divided by two, resulting in a ♩ pulse of

$$150 \div 2 = 75 \, \quarternote$$

If the metronome marking is ♩·· = 60 and the conductor wants to find the metronome marking of the ♩, a common denominator between the two rhythmic units has to be identified, which in this case is the ♬. Because there are a total of seven ♬s in the original ♩·· unit, the metronome marking for the ♬ is

$$7 \times 60 = 420 \, \sixteenthnote$$

Because the ♩ comprises four ♬s, its metronome marking is

$$420 \div 4 = 105 \, \quarternote$$

The metronome marking of this rhythmic unit is 𝅝 ♩ ♪ = 32.
There are thirteen ♪s in the combined unit, making the speed of the individual ♪

$$13 \times 32 = 416 \, \eighthnote$$

The metronome markings for several different note values are:

whole-note (i.e., eight ♪s) $416 \div 8 = 52 \, \wholenote$

half-note (i.e., four ♪s) $416 \div 4 = 104 \, \halfnote$

quarter-note (i.e., two ♪s) $416 \div 2 = 208 \, \quarternote$

dotted quarter-note (i.e., three ♪s) $416 \div 3 = 138 \, \quarternote.$

Question: If a ♪ (triplet) equals 180, what is the metronome marking of the ♩.?

(a) Using the previous method, this problem can be solved by finding a common denominator between the ♪ (180, triplet) and the ♩.. This is the

♪ (sextuplet)

The ♪ (180, triplet) contains two ♪ (sextuplet)s, so the metronome marking of the ♪ (sextuplet) is

2 × 180 = 360 or 360 ♪ (sextuplet)

Because the ♩. contains nine ♪ (sextuplet)s, its metronome marking will be

360 ÷ 9 = 40 or 40 ♩.

(b) The original metronome marking of the ♪ (180, triplet) can be changed by compounding three ♪ (triplet)s into a ♩, with a corresponding ♩ (60) (180 ÷ 3) metronome marking, which relates better to the ♩.. By comparing the ♩ and the ♩., we find that the common denominator is the ♪.

Because there are two ♪s in a ♩, the metronome marking of the ♪ is

2 × 60 = 120 or 120 ♪

Because there are three ♪s in the ♩., the metronome marking of the ♩. is

120 ÷ 3 = 40 or 40 ♩.

When an entire bar is divided into equal portions that have no direct rhythmic relationship to the basic pulse, the metronome marking of the inner unit can be found by first identifying the metronome marking of the entire bar, then multiplying the number of divisions by the metronome marking of the entire bar.

$\frac{3}{4}$ ♩ = 90   ♩. = 30   ♪ = 210 (septuplet)

[Musical example: Vivace ♩=138, with time signature changes 3/4, 2/4, 3/4; tuplet groupings of 7, 5, 5, 8 below the staff; with corresponding values 322, 345, 368 marked with tuplet brackets of 7, 5, 8]

Stravinsky, *Petrouchka* (1947 version), 2 bars after rehearsal no. 4 [bars 29–32]

$\frac{3}{4}$ ♩. = | 138 ÷ 3 = 46 (♩.) | ♪ (7-tuplet) = 7 × 46 = 322 (♪, 7-tuplet)

$\frac{2}{4}$ ♩ = | 138 ÷ 2 = 69 (♩) | ♪ (5-tuplet) = 5 × 69 = 345 (♪, 5-tuplet)

$\frac{3}{4}$ ♩. = | 138 ÷ 3 = 46 (♩.) | ♪ (8-tuplet) = 8 × 46 = 368 (♪, 8-tuplet)

D. THE COMMON DENOMINATOR

The common denominator connects two different tempos by means of a common rhythmic unit and is therefore one of the conductor's most useful tools in ascertaining a composer's intent. Some composers indicate clearly that a note value in a new tempo is to be equal in duration to a note from the previous one. However, other composers notate tempo changes differently, less clearly, or not at all. A conductor willing to do a little detective work may find hidden, unmarked common denominators.

The sign = directly above the bar line separating two tempos is the clearest notation of a common denominator. The notes on either side of the equal sign represent rhythmic units of identical duration.

Allegro ♩ = ♪ Andante
$\frac{4}{4}$ ‖ $\frac{3}{4}$

Other ways of indicating common denominators are shown in the next examples:

Allegro ♩=120 ♩=120 Andante (♩=60)
$\frac{4}{4}$ ‖ ¢
(♩ = ♩)

Allegro ♩=120 ♪=120 Andante (♩=60)
$\frac{4}{4}$ ‖ $\frac{4}{4}$
(♩ = ♪)

Brahms, *Tragic Overture*, bars 206–209

Sibelius, Symphony no. 2, first movement, bars 239–240

R. Strauss, *Till Eulenspiegels lustige Streiche*, bars 5–6

des² 4/8

R. Strauss, *Till Eulenspiegels lustige Streiche*, bars 177–178

des vorigen Zeitmasses³

Falla, *The Three-Cornered Hat*, Suite no. 2, third movement, 1 bar before rehearsal no. 24

Shostakovich, Symphony no. 12, first movement, bars 464–468

2. *of the*
3. *of the previous tempo*

An equation notated before or after the tempo change raises questions about which of the two notes relates to which of the two sections.

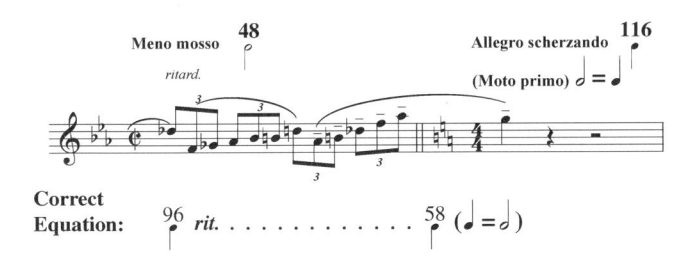

Rachmaninoff, Piano Concerto no. 2, third movement, 1 bar before rehearsal no. 38

Often composers do not indicate common denominators between tempos; the common denominators become apparent only after a conductor compares the metronome markings of each tempo.

Tchaikovsky, Symphony no. 5, fourth movement, bars 545–546

The easiest way to find a common denominator that is not directly indicated by a composer is to compare the metronome markings of the old and new tempos. Breaking down these markings into units of successively faster and slower duration will often reveal a common denominator.

108   THE SCORE, THE ORCHESTRA, AND THE CONDUCTOR

Is there a common denominator?

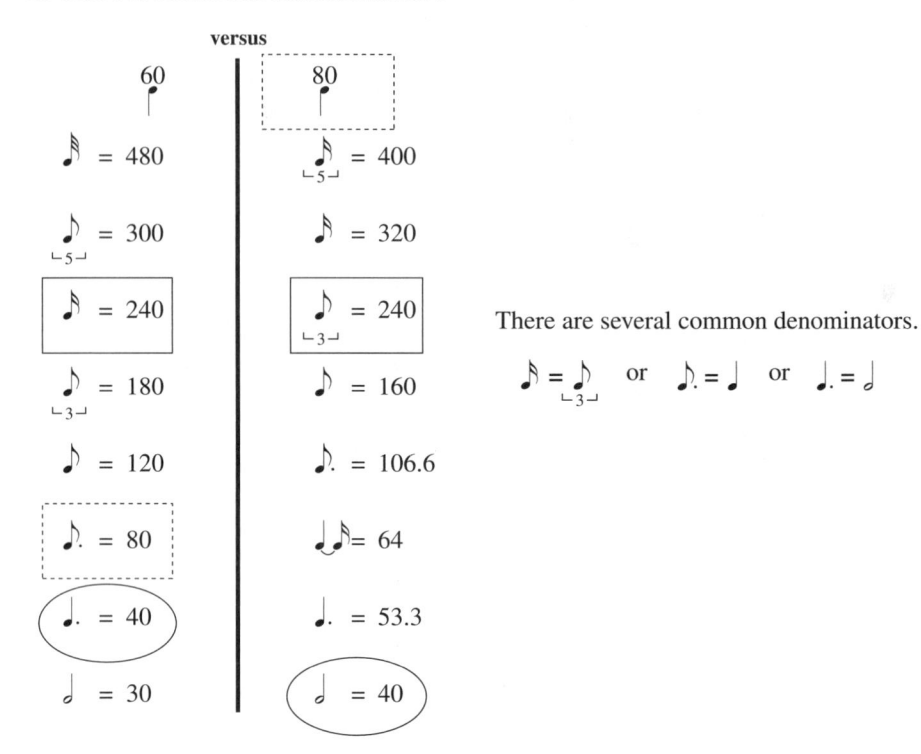

versus

60 ♩	80 ♩
𝅘𝅥𝅰 = 480	𝅘𝅥𝅯 (5) = 400
𝅘𝅥𝅯 (5) = 300	𝅘𝅥𝅯 = 320
𝅘𝅥𝅰 = 240	𝅘𝅥𝅯 (3) = 240
𝅘𝅥𝅯 (3) = 180	𝅘𝅥𝅯 = 160
𝅘𝅥𝅯 = 120	𝅘𝅥𝅯. = 106.6
𝅘𝅥𝅯. = 80	♩𝅘𝅥𝅯 = 64
♩. = 40	♩. = 53.3
♩ = 30	♩ = 40

There are several common denominators.

𝅘𝅥𝅯 = 𝅘𝅥𝅯 (3)   or   𝅘𝅥𝅯. = ♩   or   ♩. = 𝅗𝅥

Tchaikovsky,
Symphony no. 5,
fourth
movement,
bars 55–58

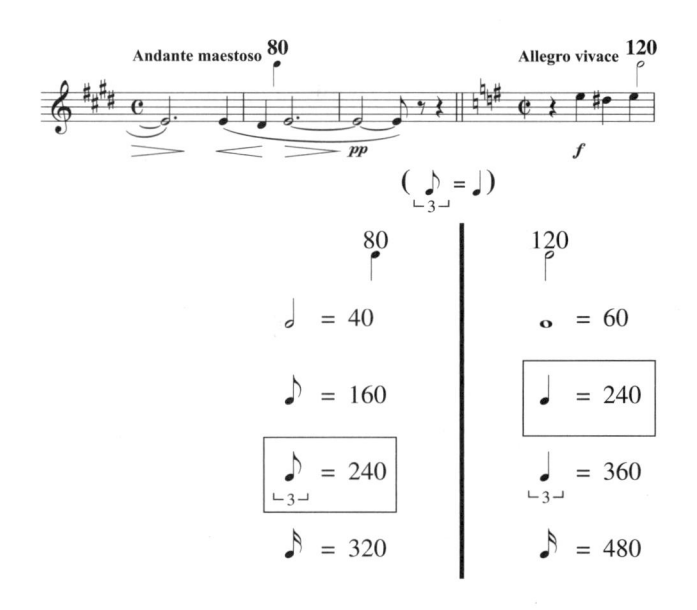

Andante maestoso 80 ♩   Allegro vivace 120 ♩

(𝅘𝅥𝅯 (3) = ♩)

80 ♩	120 ♩
♩ = 40	𝅝 = 60
𝅘𝅥𝅯 = 160	♩ = 240
𝅘𝅥𝅯 (3) = 240	♩ (3) = 360
𝅘𝅥𝅰 = 320	𝅘𝅥𝅯 = 480

In some instances the notation of transitions is ambivalent, while in others the two sides of the equation do not correspond.

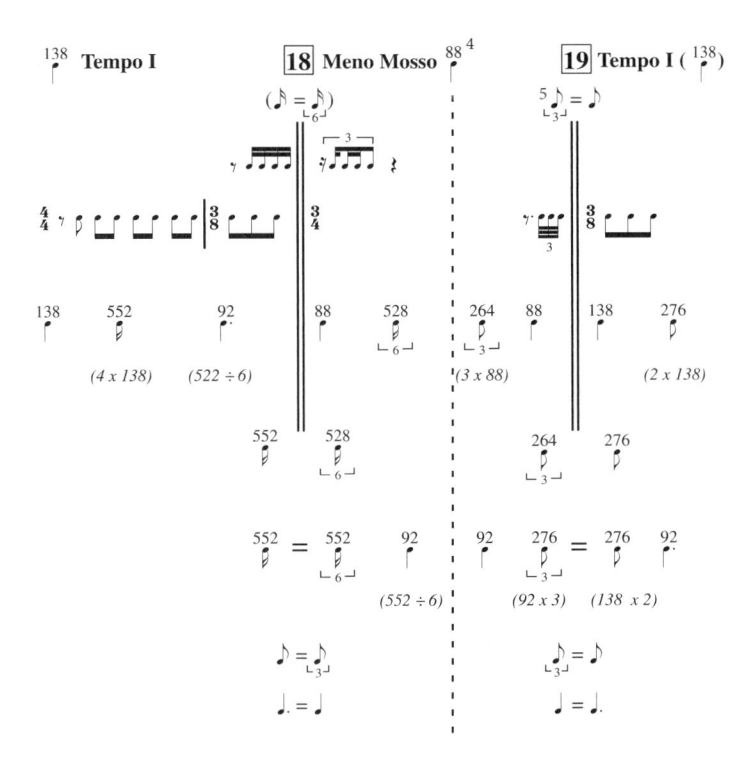

Stravinsky, *Petrouchka* (1947 version), 2 bars before rehearsal no. 18

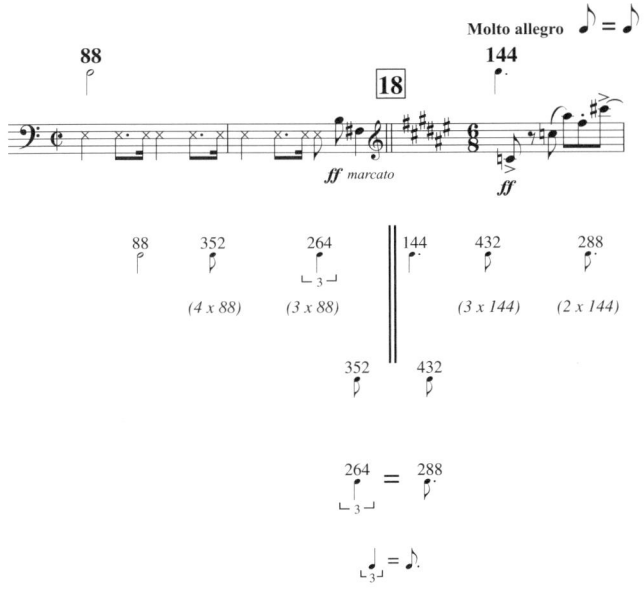

Bernstein, *Symphonic Dances from "West Side Story"* (revised edition), bars 728–730

---

4. Metronome marking should be $\genfrac{}{}{0pt}{}{92}{\flat.}$
5. The ⌐3⌐ is missing from the Boosey & Hawkes score.

Bernstein, *Divertimento for Orchestra*, second movement, Waltz, bar 1

A conductor may accelerate or slow down a pulse and reach a tempo at the double bar that results in a common denominator.

Debussy, *La mer*, first movement, bars 22–23

Debussy, *La mer*, first movement, bars 30–31

Tchaikovsky, Symphony no. 5, fourth movement, bars 503–504

The tempo of the Moderato assai e molto maestoso is close to the tempo of the Andante maestoso at the beginning of the fourth movement, marked ♩ = 80. If a common denominator with the Presto is intended, the Moderato assai e molto maestoso should be played at ♩ = 72, which leads to a common denominator, ♪ = ♩. If a different tempo for the opening theme is desired (faster or slower than ♩ = 80), a common denominator can

---
6. Metronome markings should be ♩. = 63, ♩ = 94.5 (♪ = 189).

be achieved by making a ritardando or accelerando in the bar before the Presto and reaching 𝄐 just before the tempo change to the Presto.

In the following Debussy example, two different metric units are connected simultaneously.

Debussy, *Prelude to the Afternoon of a Faun*, bars 105–106

or

Debussy, *Prelude to the Afternoon of a Faun*, bars 105–107

In the example below, the tempo of the introduction, Un poco sostenuto, and the following Allegro can be connected by a common denominator (♪ = ♩.). If the conductor does not see a connection, the last ♩. can be neutralized and a new tempo established for the Allegro by giving an appropriate upbeat.

Brahms, Symphony no. 1, first movement, bars 35–40

Matters become more complicated when ritardandos or accelerandos connect two sections and the score does not indicate whether the common denominator should be the original *a tempo* pulse or the pulse reached at the end of the ritardando or accelerando.

R. Strauss, *Death and Transfiguration*, bars 63–67

The question here is whether the ♪ in the original Largo tempo is to be the common denominator with the ♩ of the new Allegro, or whether the final ♪ pulse of the ritardando is the common denominator. If the basic Largo tempo is ♩ (♪ = 112, 2 × 56), then the Allegro is ♩; therefore, the ritardando ♪ cannot be a common denominator with the upcoming ♩ because the Allegro would turn out to be too slow.

It is assumed that the heartbeat motif in bar 1 and bar 63 are in the same Largo tempo. Consequently the poco rit. has to be implemented in bar 62 in order to reach the Largo tempo in bar 63 after the Un poco agitato. No ritard should occur afterward, so that a common denominator will exist with the Allegro molto agitato.

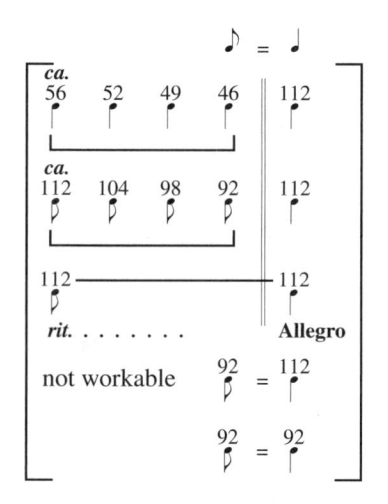

---

7. *of the previous tempo*

Before metronome markings and notated tempo relationships were in use, common denominators often could be identified by identical compositional material appearing in both of the connecting sections.

Mozart, Symphony no. 39, first movement, bar 2

Mozart, Symphony no. 39, first movement, bars 71–72

ergo

Mozart, Symphony no. 39, first movement, bars 23–29

Mozart, Overture to *Così fan tutte*, bars 10–11

Mozart, Overture to *Così fan tutte*, bars 231–234

Mozart, Overture to *Don Giovanni*, bars 30–32

Brahms, Symphony no. 1, fourth movement, bars 28–30

Brahms, Symphony no. 1, fourth movement, bars 47–51

Brahms, Symphony no. 1, fourth movement, bars 407–416

Tchaikovsky, Symphony no. 4, first movement, bars 411–412

Tchaikovsky, Symphony no. 4, first movement, bar 1

Tchaikovsky, Symphony no. 4, first movement, bar 193

(reappearance of the Leitmotiv in the Moderato con anima)

Tchaikovsky, Symphony no. 4, first movement, bars 27–28

Ergo!

Assuming that the ♩ tempo of the Leitmotiv is the same throughout the work, Tchaikovsky may have intended to relate all basic tempos of the four movements of the entire symphony to that pulse.

Tchaikovsky, Symphony no. 4, second movement, bars 1–2

Tchaikovsky, Symphony no. 4, third movement, bars 1–2

Tchaikovsky, Symphony no. 4, fourth movement, bars 1–2

Tchaikovsky, Symphony no. 4, fourth movement, bars 198–199

Conductors can connect sections by utilizing common denominators even though they are not indicated in the score. These *artificial common denominators* are established between two different tempos by using inner rhythmic units unrelated to the compositional content. Artificial common denominators are useful tools in facilitating transitions as long as they enhance the accuracy of the compositional intent.

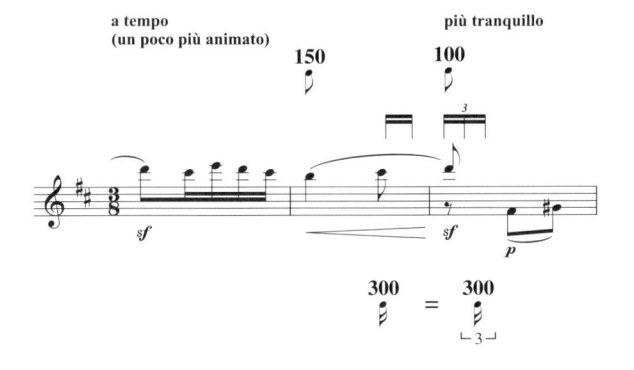

Rimsky-Korsakov, *Scheherazade*, second movement, 13 after Letter C

Berlioz, *Roman Carnival Overture*, bars 1–2

Berlioz, *Roman Carnival Overture*, bars 18–21

Beethoven, Symphony no. 9, fourth movement, bars 626–627

Tchaikovsky, Symphony no. 5, second movement, bars 65–66

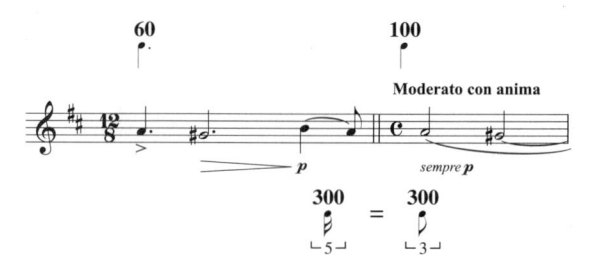

---

8. Assuming the Adagio starts a half note earlier (count 3 of bar 626).

Reading the Score 117

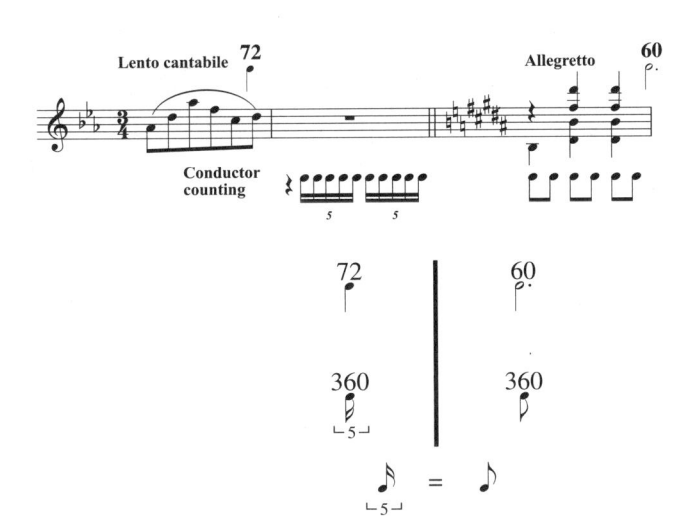

Stravinsky, *Petrouchka* (1947 version), 2 bars before rehearsal no. 143

CLOSE CALLS

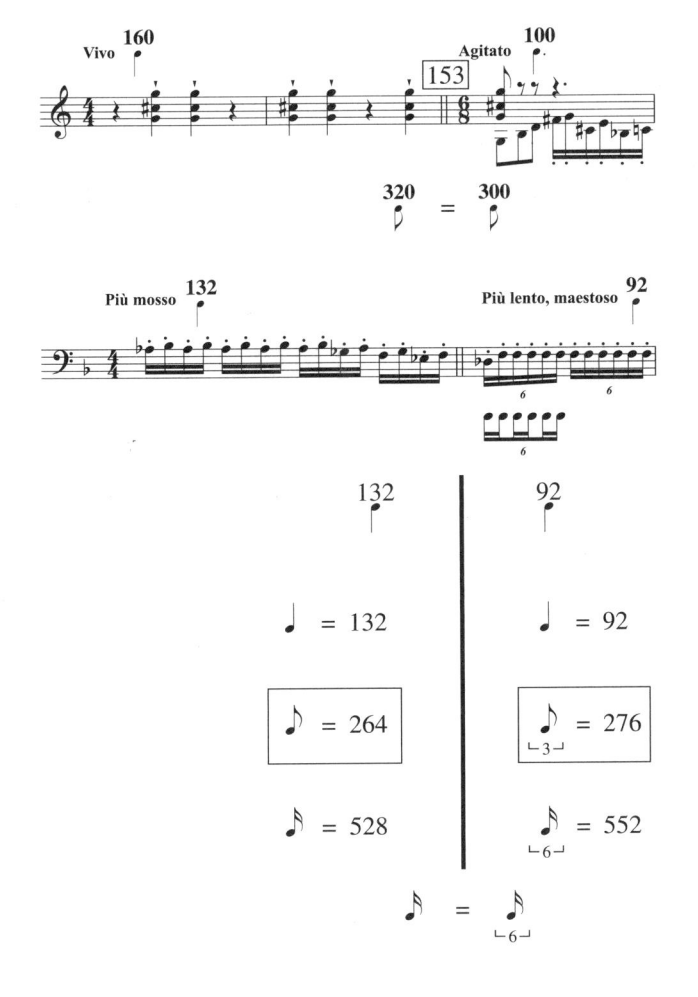

Stravinsky, *Petrouchka* (1947 version), 2 bars before rehearsal no. 153

Verdi, *Falstaff*, act 1, no. 1, 9 bars after rehearsal no. 8

118 THE SCORE, THE ORCHESTRA, AND THE CONDUCTOR

Brahms, Piano Concerto no. 2, fourth movement, bars 375–377

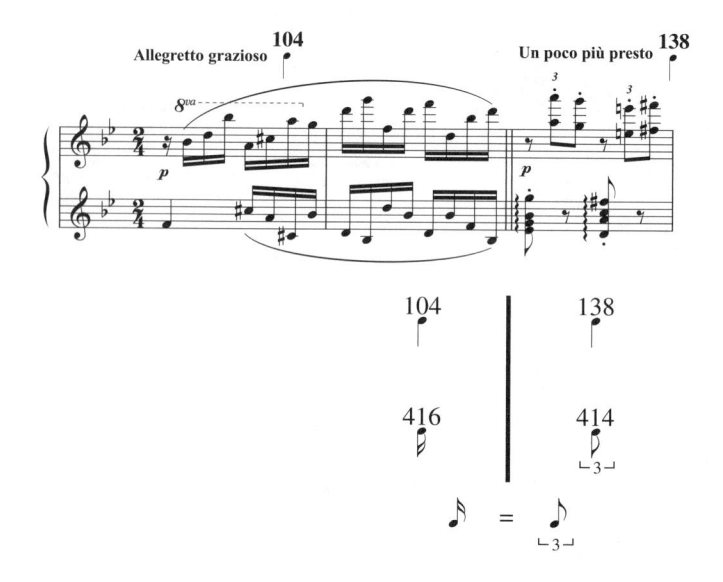

Stravinsky, *Petrouchka* (1947 version), 2 bars before rehearsal no. 123

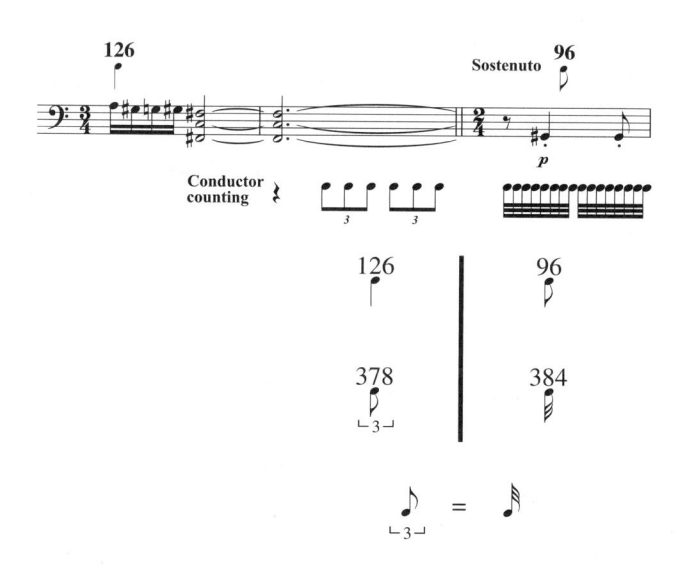

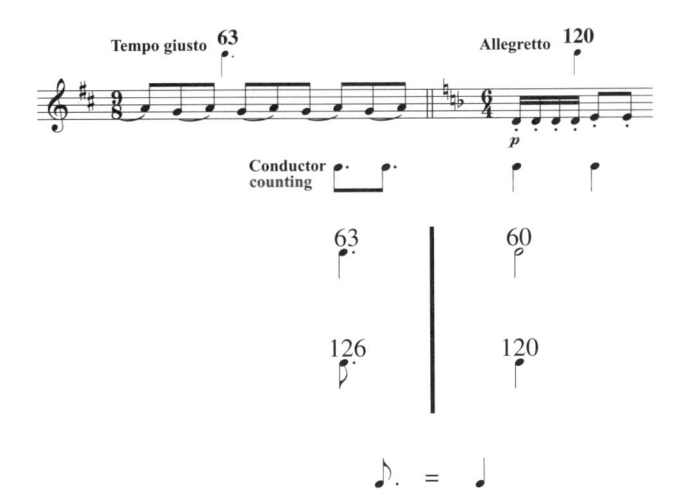

Stravinsky, *Petrouchka* (1947 version), 1 bar before rehearsal no. 170

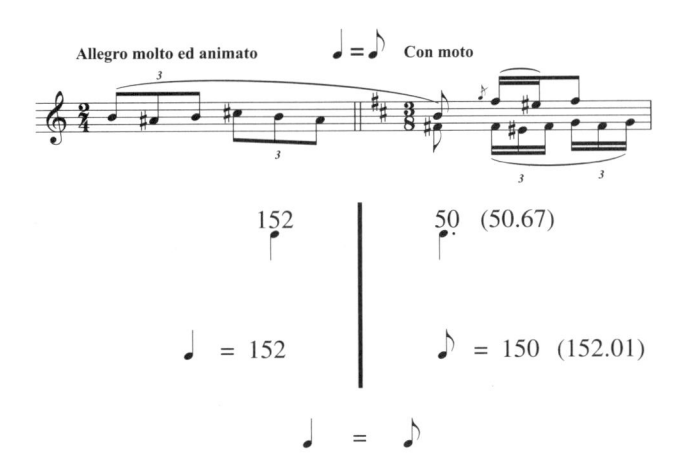

Rimsky-Korsakov, *Scheherazade*, second movement, 1 bar before letter N

Copland, *Appalachian Spring* Suite, 1 bar before rehearsal no. 50

The common denominator is $\overset{368}{\flat}$ (4 × 92) = $\overset{360}{\underset{\llcorner 3 \lrcorner}{\flat}}$ (3 × 120). Often the 3 ♫ upbeat is done in the slower tempo, matching the $\frac{3}{8}$ bar 3 bars later. Leonard Bernstein makes a rallentando throughout the first $\frac{5}{4}$ bar, going from $\overset{184}{\flat}$ to $\overset{120}{\flat}$ in the second $\frac{5}{4}$ bar. (See his score in the archives of the New York Philharmonic.) My suggestion is to divide the $\frac{5}{4}$ into two bars, a $\frac{6}{8}$ ($\overset{122}{\flat}$, $\overset{368}{\flat}$ ÷ 3) bar and a $\frac{2}{4}$ ($\overset{120}{\flat}$ bar).

120 THE SCORE, THE ORCHESTRA, AND THE CONDUCTOR

In the first Carter example that follows, the tempo relationships between bars 295 and 296 and bars 299 and 300 are self-explanatory. However, the relationship between bars 297 and 298 requires further investigation so that the two tempos are connected smoothly and accurately. The conductor can accomplish this by counting the 5 ♪s of the last ♩. ♩ unit of bar 297 ($\frac{15}{16}$) and then counting ♪ on the first half of the $\frac{6}{8}$ bar (bar 298). (The ♪s are played by one of the soloists in bar 298.)

Carter, Double Concerto for Harpsichord and Piano, bars 295–300

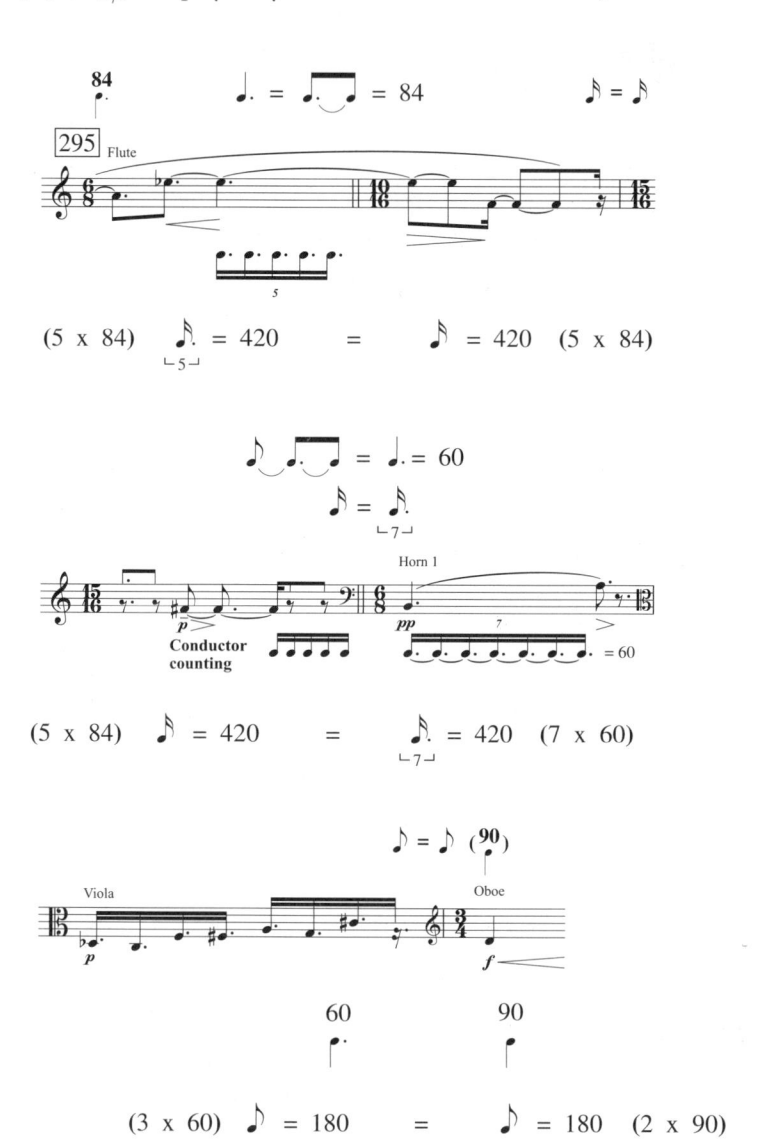

Carter, Double Concerto for Harpsichord and Piano, bars 558–559

Beethoven, Symphony no. 7, first movement, bars 62–63

It is not necessary to conduct the second half of bar 62 in 3 ⌞3⌟s. After the first ⌞3⌟, the beat simply stops. At the appropriate moment, the third ⌞3⌟ is given, serving as an upbeat for the upcoming $\frac{6}{8}$ tempo.

Beethoven, Symphony no. 7, third movement, bars 145–149

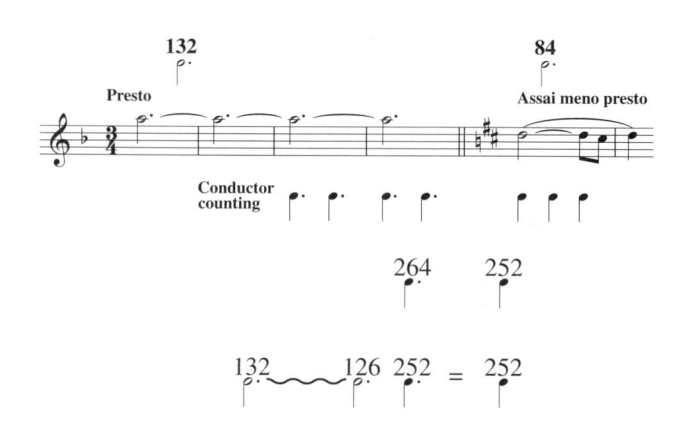

---

9. The ♪ upbeat changes to a ⌞3⌟ ♩, which equals the regular ♪ of the upcoming $\frac{6}{8}$ Vivace.

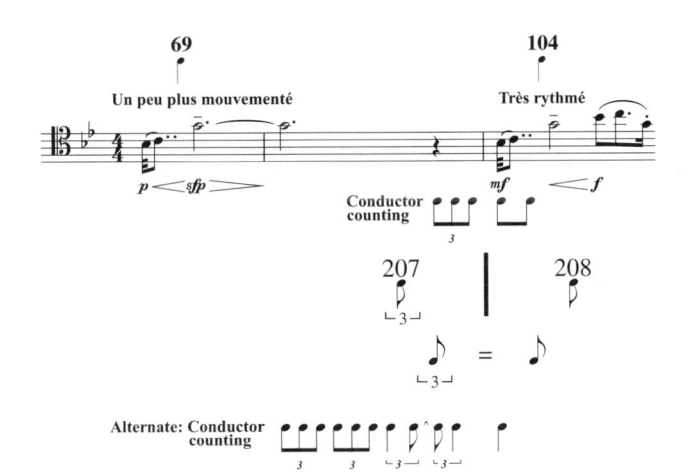

Debussy, *La mer*, first movement, 2 bars before rehearsal no. 9

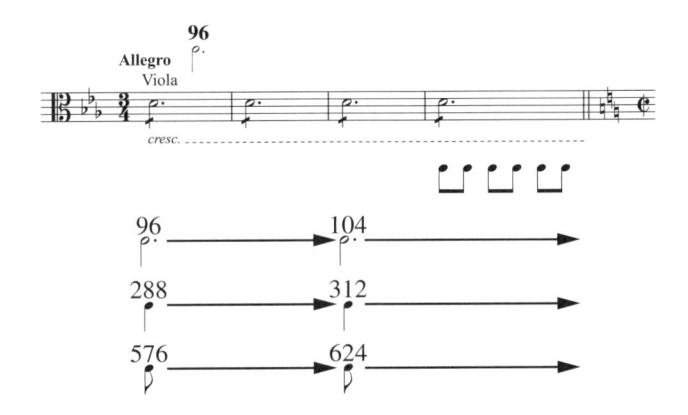

Beethoven, Symphony no. 5, third movement, bar 370–fourth movement, bar 2

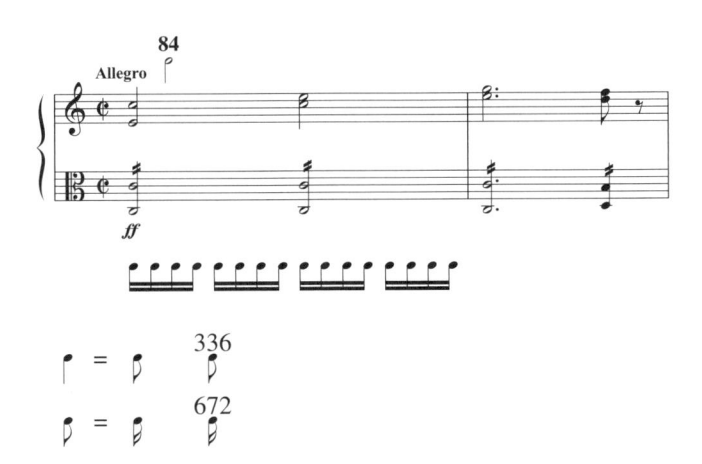

Beethoven, Symphony no. 5, second movement, bars 204–205

Beethoven, Symphony no. 5, second movement, bars 217–218

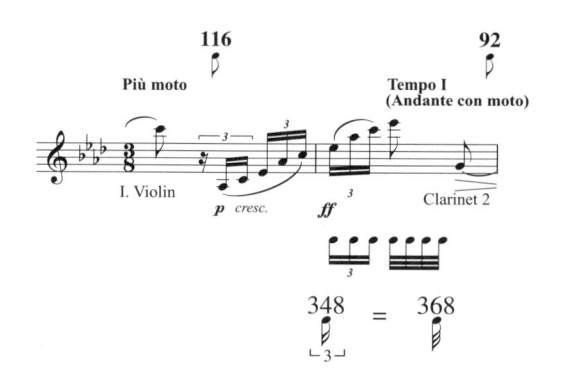

FAR FETCHED!

In the following examples, ritardandos and accelerandos are utilized to create artificial common denominators.

Beethoven, Symphony no. 2, first movement, bars 33–34

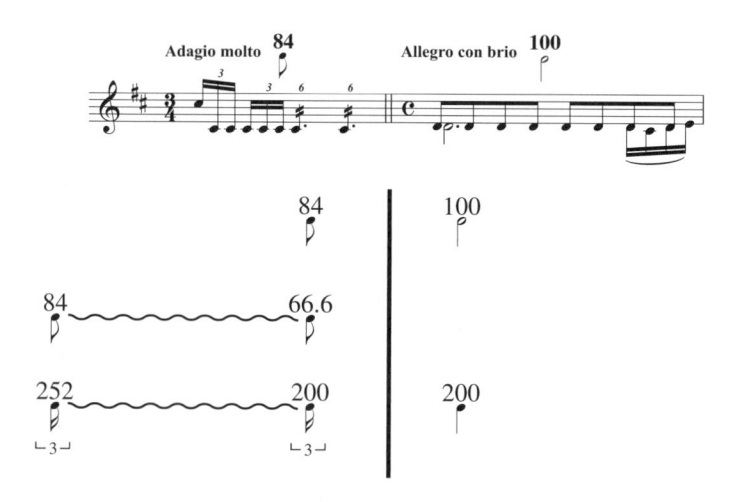

In the following two examples, it is assumed that the four- or five-note upbeats preceding the Allegro sections should be equal in duration to the four ♪ upbeats in the Allegro sections.

Beethoven, Symphony no. 4, first movement, bars 38–39

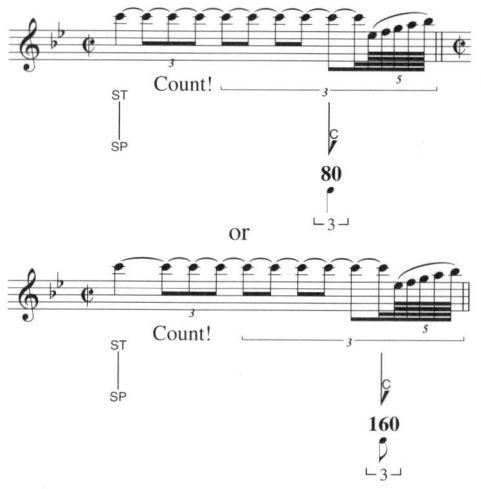

Beethoven, Symphony no. 4, first movement, bars 38–39

Beethoven, Symphony no. 1, first movement, bars 12–13

During one of Leonard Bernstein's many visits to the conducting seminars at Tanglewood, he stated passionately that all subito tempo changes in the classical period should be connected by a common denominator. He wanted seamless connections.

Berlioz, *Symphonie fantastique*, fifth movement, bars 19–22

Berlioz, *Symphonie fantastique*, fifth movement, bars 28–30

Berlioz, *Symphonie fantastique,* fifth movement, bars 38–41

Using artificial common denominators is very helpful when the conductor begins to study the score. Eventually the transitions will feel natural and musically correct. Recognizing and utilizing common denominators may not seem to be a priority; however, those conductors who include careful study of common denominators as an integral part of score preparation will find the time well spent.

E. DYNAMICS

The proper interpretation of dynamics is very difficult because the symbols used by composers are meant only as guidelines. A precise notation of the dynamic range (from the softest *pp* to the loudest *ff*) is virtually impossible.[10] Each instrument of the orchestra, and consequently each section or combination of instruments, has its own particular acoustical idiosyncrasies, and instruments of the same category differ depending on the manufacturer. Sound levels fluctuate from one performer to another, therefore a precisely measured and defined dynamic range does not exist.

Notations of dynamic markings may also pose interpretive problems. If different dynamic levels are simultaneously notated in different instrumental groups, is the composer requesting differences in the dynamic levels among the instruments or trying to balance the overall sound of the ensemble by using sophisticated dynamic markings?

Because of their physical location within the orchestra, the sounds of individual instruments and sections will vary in their ability to project. The acoustics of each individual auditorium will affect the dynamic balance as well.

The conductor's physical position is not the best spot from which to judge dynamic balances. Feedback from an assistant conductor during rehearsals can be helpful, although acoustics often change when the hall is filled or partially filled at the concert. Sometimes dynamics may differ enormously in various parts of the same hall, but often little can be done to correct these puzzling imbalances. For example, for no ex-

---

10. At present, precise dynamic notation is only possible in electronic music.

plainable reason, one instrument or section may dominate in certain parts of the auditorium while others are inaudible. To conclude, the acoustics in the hall, along with the individual strengths of each performer and each section of the orchestra, must be taken into consideration; continuous feedback and experimentation are required. Achieving an "ideal" acoustical balance is sometimes impossible.

F. PHRASING AND ARTICULATION

Accurate interpretation of a composer's notation of phrasing is difficult when the composer's notation does not give precise and comprehensive instructions to the performer. Even such basic symbols as the staccato (.) or tenuto (_) can be interpreted many different ways depending upon the compositional context. The wedge (|) and various accents (>, <, ∧, and ∨) complicate matters further. Simultaneous combinations of symbols add to the confusion. The markings are guidelines; interpretive decisions should be made only after first considering

1. the particular instrument's characteristics and historical use;
2. the speed, range, dynamic level, overall shape, and character of the musical passage in question; and
3. the general musical condition prevailing in the rest of the ensemble.

The only precise articulation marking is the *slur,* which serves to connect notes without a break. For wind players, this means playing the series of notes underneath a single slur without tonguing; for string players, it means playing without a change of the bow. The interpretation of the slur is less clear for keyboard and mallet players.

Although combinations of dynamic markings like the forte-piano (*fp*) and the sforzato (*sfz*) belong to the previous section on dynamics, they are more closely related to articulation. The difference between the *fp* and the *sfz* is difficult to determine, and technical conditions and musical context will influence their interpretation. Although it is certain that the *fp* specifies two distinct dynamic levels, interpretation of the *sfz* depends entirely on the dynamic surroundings of the passage involved.

Study of other works by the same composer, including chamber music and pieces for single instruments, often provides clues that help to define a particular articulation as it applies to a specific instrument within a particular work. Also, it should not be forgotten that each performer in the ensemble is an expert on his or her instrument. The conductor can learn a great deal about details of articulations, dynamics, and style from knowledgeable and experienced orchestra musicians.

CHAPTER THREE

Preparation of the Score for Conducting

A. ANALYSIS

Analysis is at the heart of the conductor's learning process. Form and structure, melodic and harmonic progressions and articulations, rhythmic relationships, distribution and use of dynamics, and musical priorities influence the final concept and interpretation of a composition. Approaching each work with analytical scrutiny leads to a deep appreciation of the composer's vision and offers the possibility of an illuminating re-creation in performance.

Studying the other works of a composer, such as non-orchestral pieces, can provide new insights. Extramusical information about the composer and the times in which a work was written will also enhance the learning process. When totally immersed in the score and history of a work, the conductor grows into a legitimate spokesperson for the composer.

A conductor's study of harmony, form, analysis, and counterpoint is lifelong. Recommended authors on these subjects include Reinhold Brinkmann, Edward T. Cone, Nicholas Cook, David Epstein, Allen Forte, Leonard B. Meyer, Ernst Oster, Walter Piston, Charles Rosen, William Rothstein, Felix Salzer, Carl Schachter, Heinrich Schenker, and Roger Sessions, among others.

B. READING THROUGH THE ORCHESTRAL
   PART OF EACH INSTRUMENT

By reading through each instrument's line in the score from the first bar to the last, the conductor sees what is required of each musician in a particular work. One player may have a great deal to do in one movement and very little in another. When a musician has a large number of tacet bars, the conductor marks the total number of bars of rest for that instrument in the score.

Beethoven, Symphony no. 3, first movement, bars 506–507

Beethoven, Symphony no. 2, first movement, bars 246–247

Tchaikovsky, *Romeo and Juliet* Fantasy-Overture, bar 150

By reading through each part in the score, the conductor may discover ambiguities about articulations and dynamics. A string part may not clearly indicate when to play pizzicato and when to return to arco, or when to use mutes and when to remove them. Some scores indicate pizzicato only when it first comes into use, although it continues for several more pages. The same ambiguity may apply to other effects, such as *col legno* and *sul ponticello*. It is helpful to notate this information in the score at the beginning of each player's staff line and to list the individual keys and positions (1st, 2nd, 3rd, or 4th) of the winds.

Some scores identify only the instruments playing in the first bars; the others are named in the score as they enter. Noting the full instrumentation of each movement at the beginning of the score and at the beginning of each movement provides a quick overview of the entire work.

A musician who is *doubling*—shifting between two instruments, such as flute and piccolo, oboe and English horn, clarinet and bass clarinet, or bassoon and contrabassoon—may be uncertain as to which instrument to play in a particular passage. Fortunately, in new editions, instruments and keys are generally identified at the beginning of each new staff line.

Brahms Symphony no. 1

I.	2	2	2	3*	/	4	2	-	-	Ti	/ Str
II.	2	2	2	3*	/	2	2	-	-	Ti	/ Str
III.	2	2	2	2	/	4	2	-	-	-	/ Str
IV.	2	2	2	3*	/	4	2	3	-	Ti	/ Str

*denotes the use of an auxiliary instrument such as Piccolo, English horn, E♭ Clarinet, Bass Clarinet and Contrabassoon by at least one player.

Preparation of the Score for Conducting 133

Berlioz Symphonie fantastique

I.	2	2	2	2	/	4	4	-	-	1 Ti	-	-	/ Str
II.	2*	1	2	-	/	4	-	-	-	-	2 Hps	/ Str
III.	2	2*	2	4	/	4	-	-	-	4 Ti	-	-	/ Str
IV.	2	2	2	4	/	4	4	3	2	3 Ti	3 Perc	-	/ Str
V.	2*	2	2*	4	/	4	4	3	2	2 Ti	4 Perc	-	/ Str

*denotes the use of an auxiliary instrument such as Piccolo,
English horn, E♭ Clarinet, Bass Clarinet and Contrabassoon
by at least one player.

Haydn Symphony no. 100

I.	2	2	-	2	/	2	2	-	-	Ti	-	/ Str
II.	2	1	2	2	/	2	2	-	-	Ti	3 Perc	/ Str
III.	2	2	-	2	/	2	2	-	-	Ti	-	/ Str
IV.	2	2	-	2	/	2	2	-	-	Ti	3 Perc*	/ Str

*(Only the last 70 bars!)

Mozart Contradances K. 609

                                                        Strings
1 - - - / - - - - - 1 Perc / x x - x x

A conductor should study the individual orchestra parts. Bowings are often revealing. Also, players may have written informative remarks in their parts such as "don't drag," "don't rush," "watch intonation," "listen to or ignore a particular instrument(s) or section(s)," "be aware of balance," "change dynamics," "count," "exaggerate articulations," "watch or ignore conductor," or "don't wait for cue." If rental material is used, the score may also contain helpful suggestions penciled in by previous conductors.

C. NOTATION ISSUES

Sometimes a conductor will find problems in notation that cannot be resolved easily. Aside from simple misprints, inconsistencies in dynamics and articulation are often found between parts. When faced with these dilemmas, the conductor asks:

1. Was the composer or publisher simply careless in matters of notation?
2. Did the composer assume that the performer would understand what was intended and modify and adjust dynamics and articulations accordingly?

3. Did the composer *intend* to be inconsistent in his or her notation of articulations and dynamics?
4. Should slight differences in dynamics and articulation between the exposition and the recapitulation be adjusted or left alone?

Beethoven, Symphony no. 9, fourth movement, bars 527–529

versus

Beethoven, Symphony no. 9, fourth movement, bars 533–535

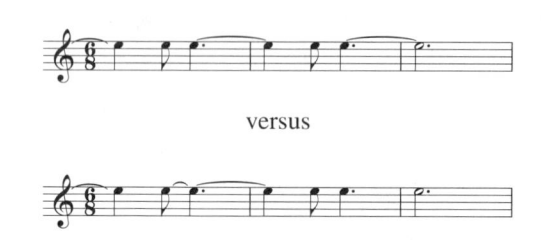

Composers are often ambiguous about shifts from *f* to subito *p*, especially in music of the classical period. The markings are usually clear for the players carrying the main thematic material, but not for the others. Careful study of the notated dynamics may reveal that a subito *pp* passage in the main voice is covered by other instruments marked *f*.

In the second bar of the following Mozart excerpt, some decisions are required. Should a diminuendo or *fp* be added to the *f* string chord that extends into the *p* material in the woodwinds? Should the upcoming *p* in the woodwinds be delayed in order to achieve the proper balance, or did Mozart want the dynamics to overlap? Mozart may have taken for granted that the downbow motion for the E♭ string chord would produce a natural diminuendo, thereby allowing the woodwinds to be heard when they enter *p*.

Preparation of the Score for Conducting   135

Mozart, Symphony no. 39, first movement, bars 1–2

In bar 2 of the Haydn symphony, the harmony is sustained until the appoggiatura resolves; in other words, the principal bassoon and second horn should elongate their quarter notes. It is equally important for the viola and bass sections to shorten their half notes in order to create a pause before the solo line continues.

Haydn, Symphony no. 88, second movement, bars 1–2

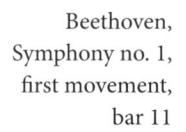

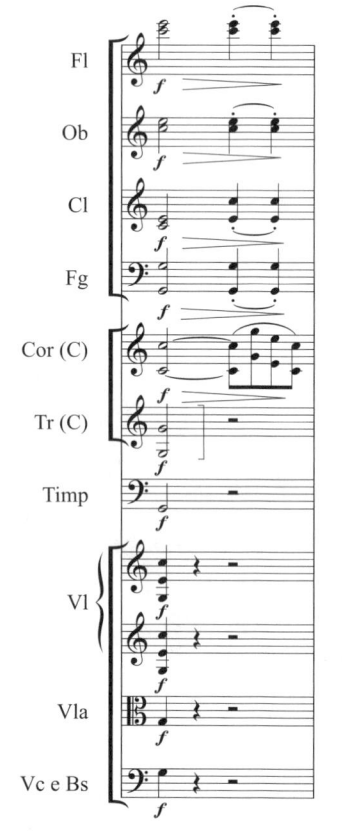

Beethoven, Symphony no. 1, first movement, bar 11

In a complex orchestration that includes multiple entrances of various instruments, the dynamic markings are often unclear. Crescendos are not always synchronized by the composer in the parts, confusing the overall dynamic picture. Generally, a crescendo progresses from one dynamic level to another. Every crescendo has a specific starting point—the dynamic level already in effect. If, after its conclusion, the new dynamic marking is identical to the one at the beginning of the crescendo, the composer obviously wants a return to the original dynamic level, requiring a subito dynamic change at the end of the crescendo. If a crescendo ends without a new dynamic marking at its conclusion, the composer must intend to continue at the higher dynamic level.

In the Beethoven example, the conductor may add a diminuendo for the trumpets (f to mf) or have the woodwinds begin their diminuendo at the start of the third count.

Should the horns add a crescendo?

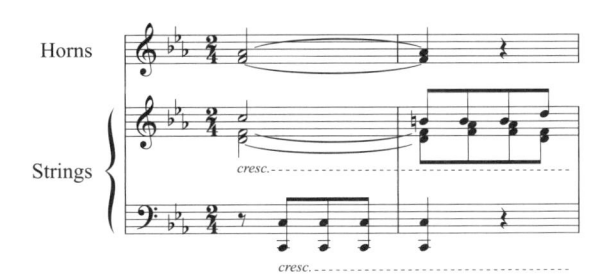

Beethoven, Symphony no. 5, first movement, bars 34–35

Beethoven, Symphony no. 2, fourth movement, bars 56–60

Players sometimes correct discrepancies between the exposition and the recapitulation. The conductor must be aware of these changes and advise the musicians about whether or not they should be observed.

Beethoven, Symphony no. 2, fourth movement, bars 61–65

Preparation of the Score for Conducting 139

Beethoven, Symphony no. 2, fourth movement, bars 240–244

* Missing *sf*

Beethoven, Symphony no. 2, fourth movement, bars 245–249

* Missing *sf*
** Added tie or slur

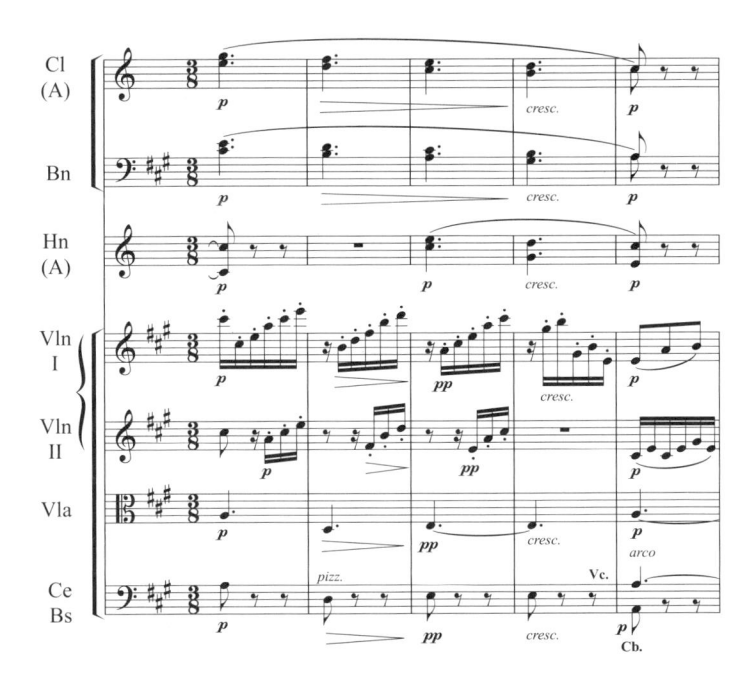

Beethoven, Symphony no. 2, second movement, bars 154–158

In this example, all instruments except the horns make a diminuendo from *p* to *pp*, followed by a crescendo back to *p*. The horns, however, crescendo from *p* to *mf* (approx.), followed by a subito *p*. Either Beethoven forgot to put a diminuendo in bar 156, or the subito *p* in the horns is intended to clear the way for the return of the theme.

Articulations, bowings, and phrasings pose the same type of interpretive dilemmas. For example, different instruments with conflicting articulations for the same melodic line may reflect the composer's conscious decision to utilize a mixture of different articulations. Checking against the original manuscript may resolve some of the confusion.

A *tremolo* is produced by repeating a pitch with fast up-and-down strokes of the bow or with rolls by timpanists or other percussion instruments. Tremolos are either *measured* or *unmeasured*. "Measured" means the tremolo has a certain number of strokes per beat. Generally, each stroke is given a notated rhythmic duration, such as a sixteenth, thirty-second, or sixty-fourth note. A half note, for example, can accommodate 16 thirty-second notes. However, depending on the metronome marking for the half note, the musicians may or may not be able to execute the tremolo as notated. As a consequence, the bow motions or rolls are played as rapidly as possible, without any specific rhythmic organization, resulting in an unmeasured tremolo. When a tremolo is part of a *colla parte* accompaniment or a rubato section (such as Tchaikovsky's Symphony no. 6, first movement, bars 277–300), it must be unmeasured to allow flexibility in the melodic line. In slow tempos, such as Largo and Adagio, a notated tremolo consisting of ♪ or ♪ may be playable as printed.

In the absence of indications in the score, conductors must decide how to assign doublings in the wind and brass sections. Composers occasionally neglect to notate whether a passage is for the first or second player, a2 (*a due*), all players, or first and second player together.

Orchestra musicians may ask, "Did the composer intend to use a piccolo or a flute here? Are two crashed cymbals or one suspended cymbal intended? When does the pizzicato end and the arco begin? At what point are the mutes removed? How far does the *sul ponticello* extend?" The conductor must be aware of these questions before the first rehearsal, but he or she may wait until the rehearsal for the musicians to supply answers for some of them.

At times brass parts have been "improved" by players' or previous conductors' adding pitches that were not available on natural horns and trumpets, for the benefit of voice leading or completion of chords. Timpani parts may also have been altered.

Beethoven, Symphony no. 8, fourth movement, bars 332–337

D. CUING

Cuing refers to bringing in one instrument, an entire section, or a combination of instruments with a preparatory gesture or signal, such as a nod, eye contact, or a hand motion. The main reasons for cuing are

1. to share an entrance with one or more musicians for purely musical reasons;
2. to give reassurance and support to a musician or group of musicians who are about to enter; and
3. to facilitate entrances of musicians even though very little time has elapsed since their last exit.

In addition to confirming an entrance, cues can provide additional information. They may restrain an overly eager player from exaggerating a solo passage, act as a reminder of a particular articulation or dynamic marking, encourage a discreet reentry, or underline the musical priority of a new entrance. When cues disrupt the musical line, they should be minimized.

Giving a cue does not end the conductor's responsibility; all cues must be integrated smoothly into the ensemble's musical fabric. Obviously, when a cue involves many players who are positioned in different places throughout the orchestra, it is not possible for the conductor to address each person individually. The solution is to cue with a broad and general gesture without singling out any particular musician or section.

Sometimes a cue cannot be completed because an immediate subsequent signal is required. The conductor may have to pivot to a second musician or group of musicians before the first cue is complete. Actually, the first group does not require further attention after the ictus has been given. The conductor continues with a fast but calm turn and gives mental and physical attention to the second individual or group to be cued. In the following example, the remainder of the beat, leaving the apex, serves as a cue for the violins.

Beethoven, Symphony no. 6, first movement, bars 1–2

* Pivot

Successive pivots:

Pivot to the first violins when the cellos have reached the F in bar 199, then pivot for the pizzicato in the lower strings.

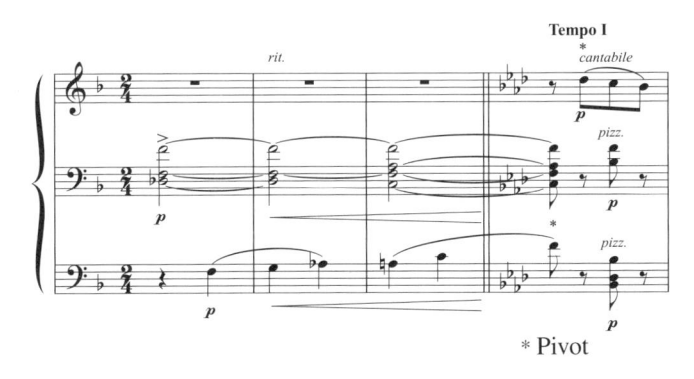

Tchaikovsky, Symphony no. 4, second movement, bars 196–199

* Pivot

After cuing in the first violins, pivot immediately to cue the remaining strings, who enter on the downbeat.

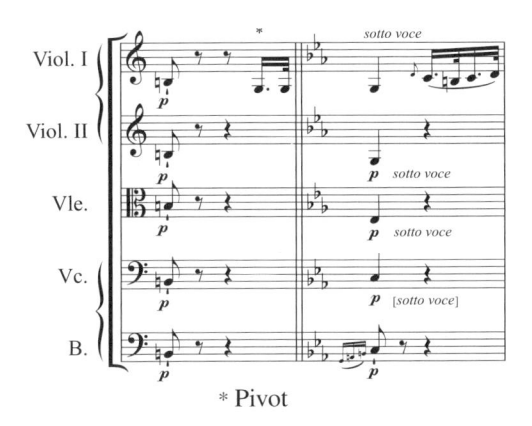

Beethoven, Symphony no. 3, second movement, bars 104–105

* Pivot

After starting to cue the timpani, pivot to the first flute, then to the trumpets.

Beethoven, Symphony no. 3, second movement, bars 90–91

*Pivot

Preparation of the Score for Conducting 145

After bringing in the woodwinds, pivot to the second violins, then to the cellos. On the cellos' last note, pivot to the second violins, then to the first.

Beethoven, Symphony no. 3, fourth movement, bars 43–47

* Pivot

After giving the downbeat, pivot to the cellos, then to the woodwinds.

Beethoven, Symphony no. 3, second movement, bar 220

* Pivot

146   THE SCORE, THE ORCHESTRA, AND THE CONDUCTOR

After the downbeat in bar 232, pivot to cue the woodwinds before returning to the first violins to help them get off the tied-over triplet low C. On the third count, pivot back to the woodwinds.

In bar 233, pivot from the woodwinds' B to the timpani and then to the first violins.

Beethoven, Symphony no. 3, second movement, bars 232–234

* Pivot

In bar 235 after the woodwind B, pivot to the first violins and then to the timpani. In bar 236, pivot on the downbeat to the first flute to ensure a prompt entry.

Beethoven, Symphony no. 3, second movement, bars 235–237

* Pivot

E. SECURITY

Composers often write repeated chord progressions or melodic sequences. In most instances, analysis reveals the composer's overarching structural framework. It is helpful to group these passages together into units according to their melodic and harmonic sequences and patterns.

Beethoven, *Leonore Overture* no. 3, bars 514–529

Exercise: Conduct in two and sing the first pitch of each six-, seven-, and eight-note scale.

Tchaikovsky, *1812 Overture*, bars 335–359

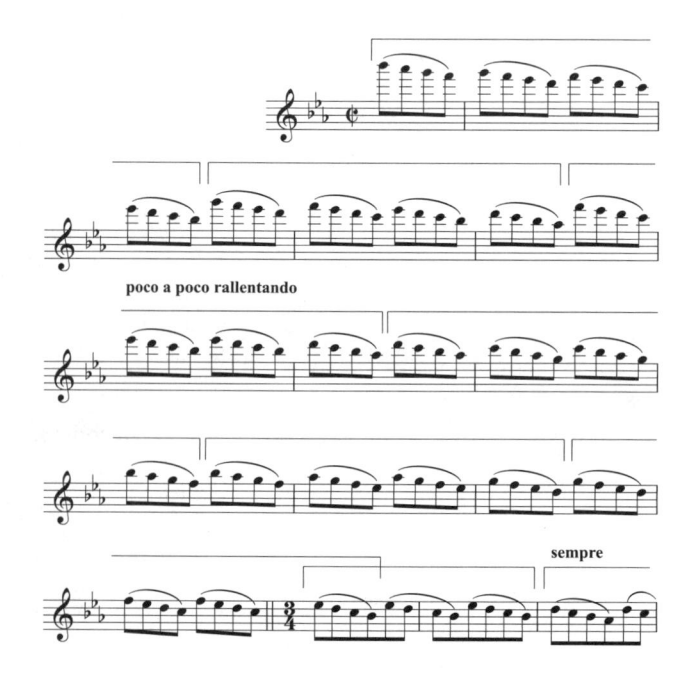

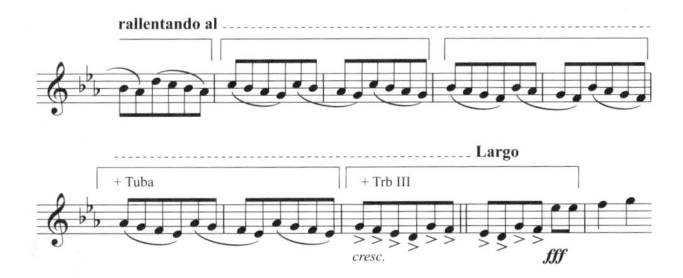

Some passages seem to lack structural organization; the music moves without any obvious harmonic or melodic patterns or sequences. In these passages, the conductor has the choice of doing one or more of the following:

1. Arbitrarily impose artificial phrases that will provide a sense of orientation
2. Count the number of bars
3. Use multiple beat patterns (see *tre* and *quattro battute*)
4. Use the orchestration, dynamic patterns, articulations, or bowings of the passage as a type of mnemonic device, if applicable

F. MARKING THE SCORE
   FOR IRREGULAR METERS

When the time signature changes constantly, marking the score with a variety of individualized symbols highlights pitch duration, patterns, and phrases. The symbols serve as visual confirmation of the time signature changes and provide security and stability. The following system reflects both the time signatures and the duration of the beats.

Stravinsky, *The Rite of Spring*, 2 bars before rehearsal no. 147

CHAPTER FOUR

Seating Arrangements: Symbols for a Cuing System

A. GENERAL AND HISTORICAL INFORMATION

The seating arrangement for the various string sections and wind instruments is by no means standardized. A rule for seating in all situations is impossible because each composition has its specific orchestration and each stage and auditorium has its own unique acoustical and logistical properties. However, by drawing on a combination of general principles, historical tradition, and an ability to improvise, a conductor can devise solutions that meet the particular challenges any given program presents.

The present-day arrangement of the various wind and string sections is the result of the orchestra's evolution from a small ensemble seated around a harpsichord into a large symphony orchestra. The size of the string section depends on the conductor's preference, the availability of string players, the financial strength of the orchestra, and the available space on stage. Although the exact number of wind and percussion personnel is noted in each score,[1] conductors may choose to double some instruments because of acoustics or players' lack of endurance. Some orchestras can afford to solve endurance problems by utilizing different sets of players for different works on the same program. Although the entire woodwind section is often doubled in tutti passages, only the principal horn of the brass family is doubled.

Locating and cuing a player or a group of players within the orchestra take careful study and practice. The conductor must know who is playing and where the sound comes from within the large and complex layout of the orchestra. During a performance, the conductor shifts attention quickly, continuously, and irregularly from one group to another, and the evolving choreography can be extremely complex. These "traffic patterns" must be practiced until they are as secure and ingrained as a solidly established fingering is for an instrumentalist. Notating this information in the score helps the conductor remain consistent in the distribution of attention, cues, and cutoffs. Orchestra musicians rarely depend on cues after a conductor has established regular contact; however, they tend to be apprehensive if the cuing is not consistently maintained.

---

1. It is often necessary to consult with the percussionists themselves to determine exactly how many players a composition will require.

152   THE SCORE, THE ORCHESTRA, AND THE CONDUCTOR

Often a conductor would like to concentrate on a solo passage and simultaneously cue entrances of other players. If attention to the soloist is more important, the location and musical contribution of the other players must be kept in mind.

This chapter sets forth a system for marking a score that indicates the positions of the musicians within the orchestra and the order and timing of their individual entrances. The system can also be applied to opera and choral works.

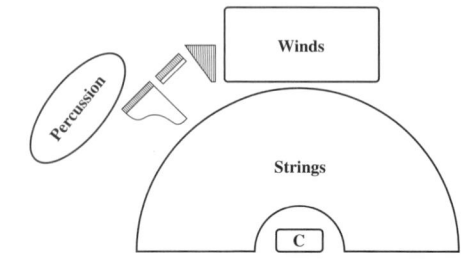

The first step is to survey the most common seating arrangements. The strings are consistently placed at the front of the stage, with the winds and brasses behind them. The percussion section is located either behind the winds or in one of the two back corners of the stage. The piano, celesta, and harp are usually placed behind the strings or on either side of the woodwind section.

B. THE STRING SECTION

The strings may range from a relatively small section of 6.4.3.2.1 in a baroque work (i.e., six first violins, four second violins, three violas, two cellos, and one bass) to a section of 8.6.5.4.2 in an early Mozart or Haydn symphony, to a section of 16.16.12.10.8 in a work by Strauss or Mahler. The lower string sections have fewer players because these instruments produce a large sound. Using fewer second violins in classical and romantic works can be justified because their function is often less important than that of the first violins; however, many conductors prefer to use an equal number of first and second violins. The viola section is smaller than the violin sections; enlarging the section is advisable when the composer writes two separate viola parts. If the score calls for more than ten cellos, the number of bass players can be increased.

Should one or two double basses be used in small string sections such as 8.6.5.4.2? A single player on any stand in any section should be avoided because players are unaccustomed to playing without a partner, and having two players on a stand facilitates page turning.

Various seating arrangements are currently in use for the strings. The following layouts represent the most common ones; the first two are generally given priority.

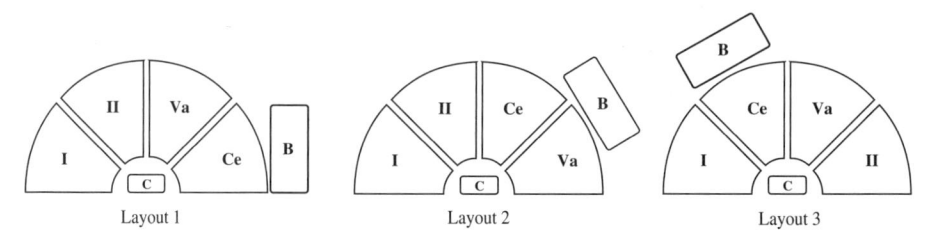

Layout 1   Layout 2   Layout 3

I = 1st Violin, **II** = 2nd Violin, **Va** = Viola, **Ce** = Cello, **B** = Bass

C. THE WOODWIND SECTION

The traditional seating arrangement for the woodwinds places the principal players next to one another; the flutes and oboes sit in the first row, with the clarinets and bassoons behind. The second players are seated next to their respective principals.

2. Cl | 1. Cl 1. Bn | 2. Bn
2. Fl | 1. Fl 1. Ob | 2. Ob

If string layout no. 3 is used, the clarinets and bassoons are usually reversed in the back row so that the bassoons (the bass voice of the woodwinds) are closer to the cellos and basses.

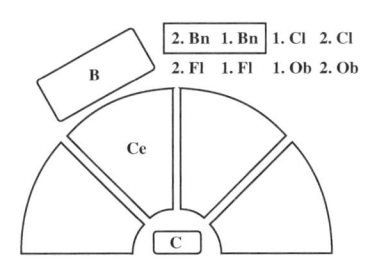

```
         2. Bn 1. Bn | 1. Cl 2. Cl
   B     2. Fl  1. Fl  1. Ob 2. Ob
          Ce
           C
```

In the woodwinds, additional players are seated next to the second player whether they are third instruments of the same kind or auxiliary instruments such as the piccolo, English horn, bass clarinet, or contrabassoon (which may be seated close to the bass section, depending on its role in the composition).

Bcl/3. Cl   2. Cl | 1. Cl 1. Bn | 2. Bn   3. Bn/Cbn
Picc/3. Fl 2. Fl | 1. Fl 1. Ob | 2. Ob   3. Ob/Ehn

More instruments may be added, extending the two lines as far out as necessary.

BCl   Eb Cl   3. Cl   2. Cl | 1. Cl 1. Bn | 2. Bn   3. Bn   1. Cbn   2. Cbn
2. Picc 1. Picc 3. Fl 2. Fl | 1. Fl 1. Ob | 2. Ob   3. Ob   1. Ehn   2. Ehn

Occasionally, conductors create a third row by seating the bass clarinets and contrabassoons together.

                2. BCl 1. BCl 1. Cbn 2. Cbn
           3. Cl 2. Cl | 1. Cl 1. Bn | 2. Bn 3. Bn
2. Picc 1. Picc 3. Fl 2. Fl | 1. Fl 1. Ob | 2. Ob 3. Ob 1. Ehn 2. Ehn

Nonstandard instruments, such as saxophones, are placed near a related instrument: soprano saxophone with oboes or flutes, alto saxophone with clarinets, and tenor or baritone saxophone with bassoons. Depending on its compositional function, a full saxophone section can be placed anywhere within the wind section.

D. THE BRASS SECTION

The seating arrangement of the brasses varies according to the size and shape of the stage and the acoustics of the hall. Generally, the principal trumpet and trombone are seated together, with the other players extending outward on both sides. Often the trombones are placed near the double basses, especially if a tuba is part of the orchestration.

            Tb   Tp   Tp   Tb
          3 2 1   1 2 3   3 2 1   1 2 3

The tuba is seated next to the third trombone.

              Tb   Tp   Tp   Tb
         Tu 3 2 1   1 2 3   3 2 1   1 2 3 Tu

The horn section, seated in the center or to the conductor's right, directs its sound into the orchestra.[2] For the purpose of leading, the principal horn is seated the farthest to the right of the conductor and plays into the section. When seated in a single row, the principal horn is followed on his or her right by the second, third, and fourth players.

In some orchestras the horns are seated in a square, with the first and second horn in front of the third and fourth horn. Some principal horn players prefer this seating because it brings the third and fourth horns closer to them.

                    4 3 2 1

                       4 3
                       2 1

---

[2]. If the horns are seated too far to the left, the sound will bounce back from the side wall.

These layouts for the entire brass section are the most common:

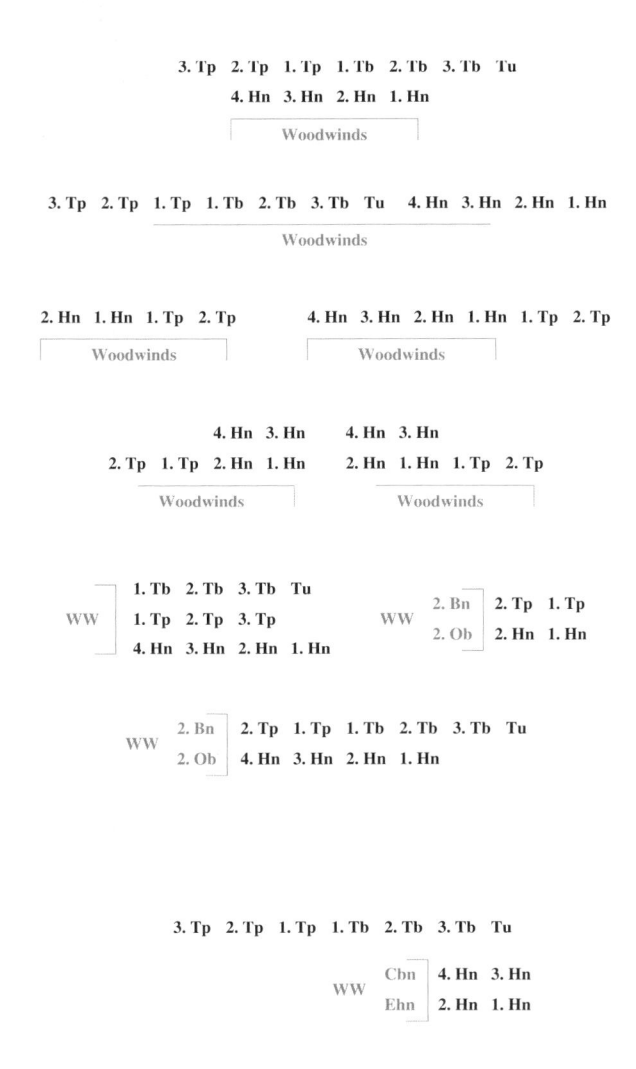

3. Tp 2. Tp 1. Tp 1. Tb 2. Tb 3. Tb Tu
4. Hn 3. Hn 2. Hn 1. Hn
Woodwinds

3. Tp 2. Tp 1. Tp 1. Tb 2. Tb 3. Tb Tu   4. Hn 3. Hn 2. Hn 1. Hn
Woodwinds

2. Hn 1. Hn 1. Tp 2. Tp   4. Hn 3. Hn 2. Hn 1. Hn 1. Tp 2. Tp
Woodwinds   Woodwinds

                4. Hn 3. Hn   4. Hn 3. Hn
2. Tp 1. Tp 2. Hn 1. Hn   2. Hn 1. Hn 1. Tp 2. Tp
Woodwinds   Woodwinds

         1. Tb 2. Tb 3. Tb Tu   2. Bn   2. Tp 1. Tp
WW   1. Tp 2. Tp 3. Tp   WW
         4. Hn 3. Hn 2. Hn 1. Hn   2. Ob   2. Hn 1. Hn

         2. Bn   2. Tp 1. Tp 1. Tb 2. Tb 3. Tb Tu
WW
         2. Ob   4. Hn 3. Hn 2. Hn 1. Hn

3. Tp 2. Tp 1. Tp 1. Tb 2. Tb 3. Tb Tu
              Cbn | 4. Hn 3. Hn
WW
              Ehn | 2. Hn 1. Hn

E. THE PERCUSSION SECTION, HARP, PIANO, AND CELESTA

The dimensions of the stage and the acoustics of the auditorium determine the placement of the percussion section, harp, piano, and celesta. Generally, the percussion section is placed near the back wall, either in the center or off to one side. The organization of the seating depends on the number of players, their particular specialization (mallets, drums, cymbals, triangle, or timpani), and the need for individual musicians to play more than one instrument. In the classical repertory, the timpani should be near the trumpets and horns because they often function as a single unit.

156   THE SCORE, THE ORCHESTRA, AND THE CONDUCTOR

The most common locations for the percussion section, harp, piano, and celesta are:

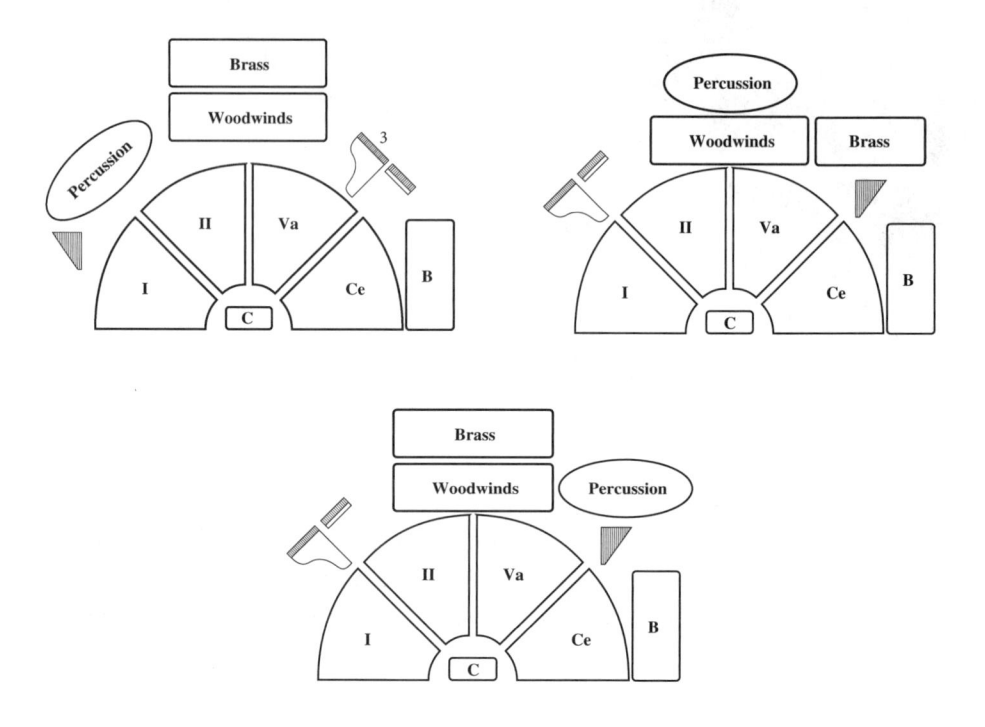

F. SYMBOLS AND POSITIONS

Graphic illustrations of the instruments and their physical locations are very helpful for cuing. The following system is suggested:

1. The String Section

---

3. The piano and celesta should be placed close together because often the same musician plays both keyboard instruments alternately.

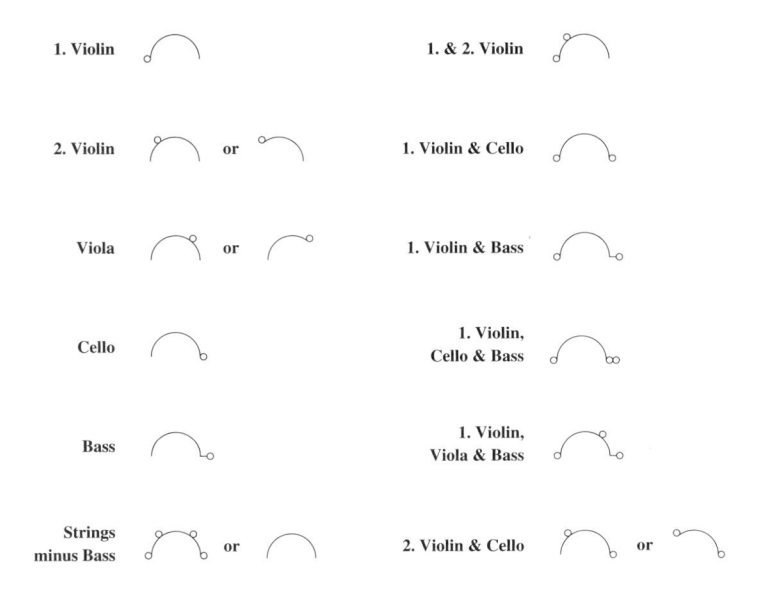

Seating Arrangements   157

1. Violin	⌒	1. & 2. Violin	⌒
2. Violin	⌒ or ⌒	1. Violin & Cello	⌒
Viola	⌒ or ⌒	1. Violin & Bass	⌒
Cello	⌒	1. Violin, Cello & Bass	⌒
Bass	⌒	1. Violin, Viola & Bass	⌒
Strings minus Bass	⌒ or ⌒	2. Violin & Cello	⌒ or ⌒

As the following examples illustrate, the symbols not only indicate very clearly which sections are playing, but also show their placement within the orchestra. All these symbols can be written into the score and then erased when the locations are memorized.

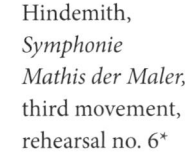

⌒ (1. Violin & Cello)

Hindemith, *Symphonie Mathis der Maler,* third movement, rehearsal no. 6*

⌒ (Violins & Viola)

Hindemith, *Symphonie Mathis der Maler,* second movement, bars 1–2*

---

*© 1934 B. Schott Söhne, Mainz. © Renewed. All Rights Reserved. Used by permission of European American Music Distributors LLC, sole U.S. and Canadian agent for Schott Music.

158 THE SCORE, THE ORCHESTRA, AND THE CONDUCTOR

Hindemith, *Symphonie Mathis der Maler*, third movement, bar 1

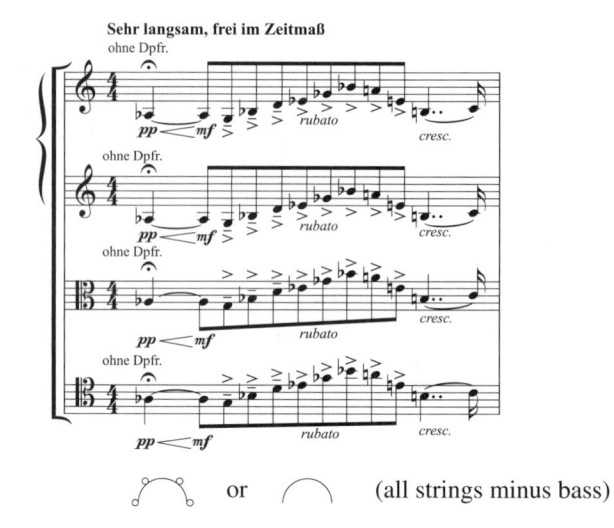

(all strings minus bass)

Franck, Symphony in D minor, first movement, bars 65–66

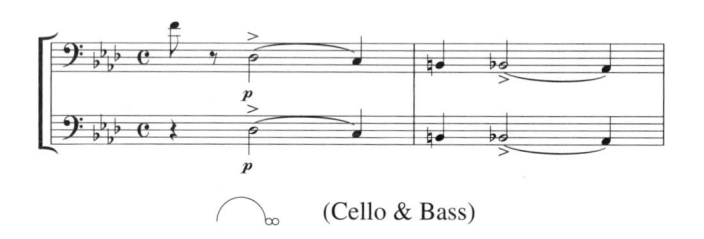

(Cello & Bass)

Franck, Symphony in D minor, first movement, bars 1–2

(Viola, Cello & Bass)

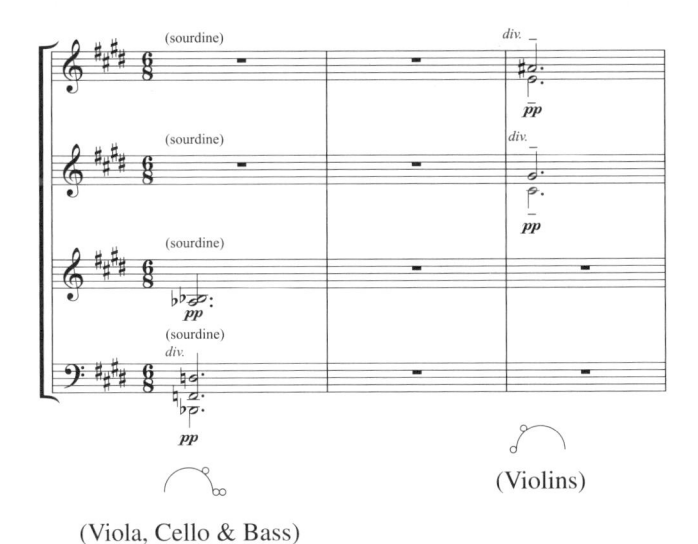

Debussy, *Prelude to the Afternoon of a Faun,* bars 5–7

2. The Woodwind Section

The woodwind section is the most complex to graph because it encompasses four different instrumental groups, each containing one or more players with individual parts. The positions of the four principal woodwind players are represented by a square with small circles at the corners. For double woodwinds, an additional circle is added for each second instrument. This results in the following designs:

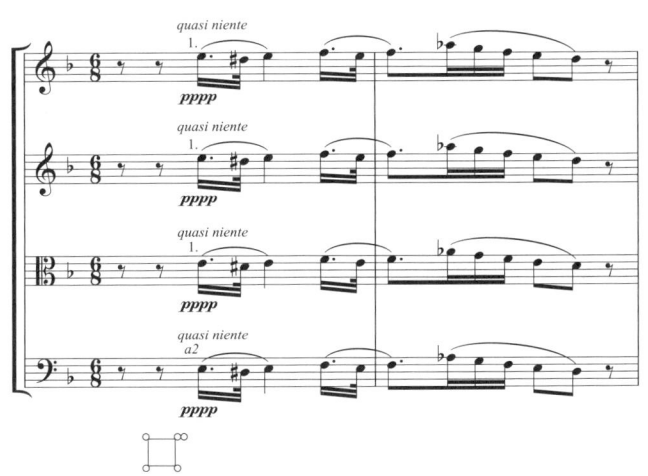

Berlioz, *Symphonie fantastique,* third movement, bars 137–138

Brahms, Symphony no. 2, first movement, bars 266–268

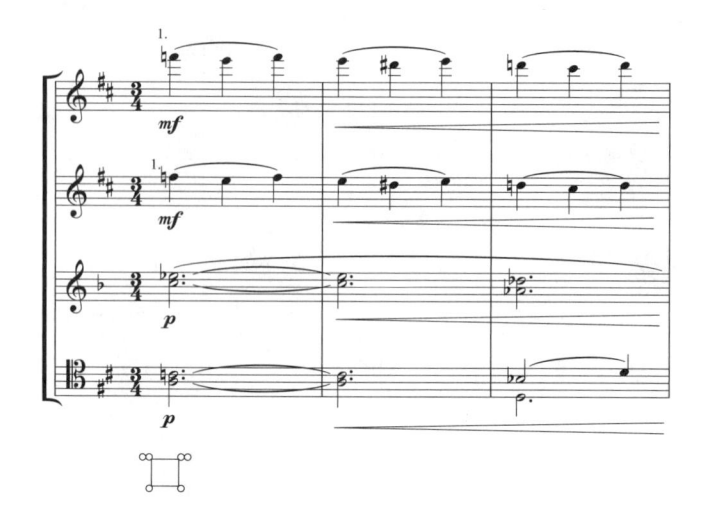

Beethoven, Symphony no. 3, second movement, bars 153–154

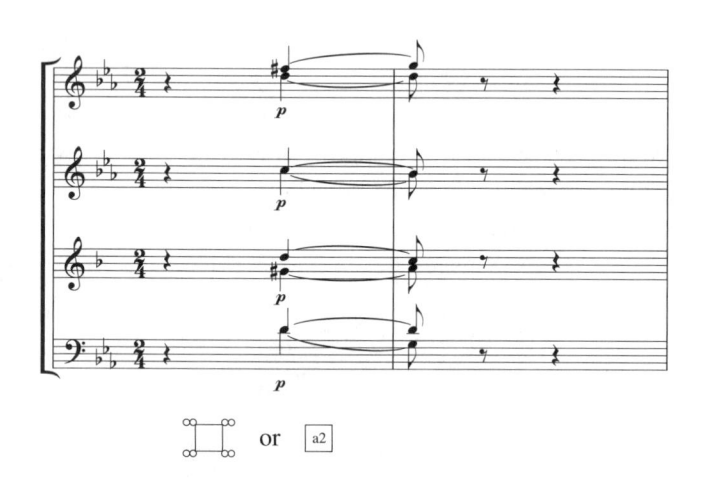

Beethoven, Symphony no. 7, third movement, bars 441–443

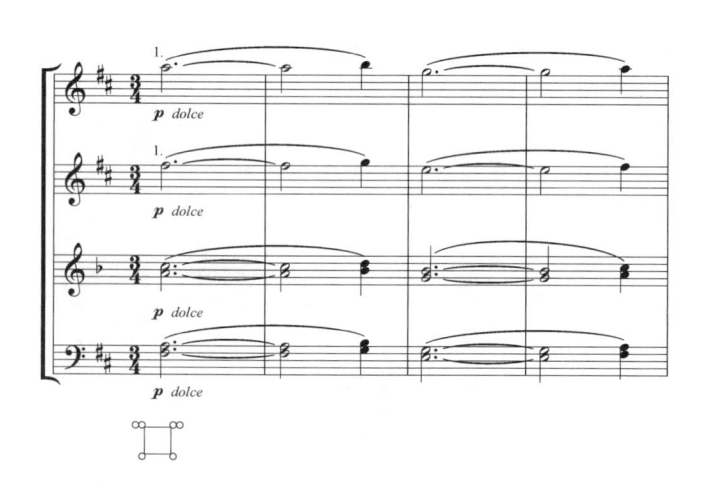

The following symbols briefly but effectively identify the positions of the various woodwinds.

Instruments from one family:

        2 Cls   2 Bns   2 Cls   2 Bns

                 or

        2 Fls   2 Obs   2 Fls   2 Obs

Instruments from two families:

2 Cls		2 Fls			1. Cl
2 Bns		2 Cls			1. Ob
1. Fl		1. Ob			1. Fl
1. Ob		1. Bn			1. Bn

Instruments from three families:

1. Fl			2 Cls
1. Cl			2 Bns
1. Bn			2 Obs
1. Cl			2 Fls
2 Fls			2 Obs
1. Ob			2 Bns

Mozart, Overture to *The Magic Flute*, bars 109–110

Brahms, Symphony no. 4, first movement, bars 317–318

Brahms, Symphony no. 2, first movement, bars 226–227

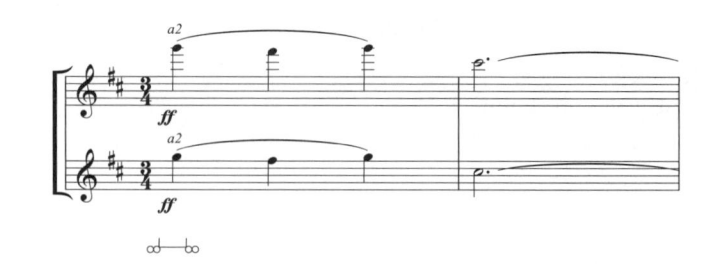

Brahms, Symphony no. 1, second movement, bars 11–13

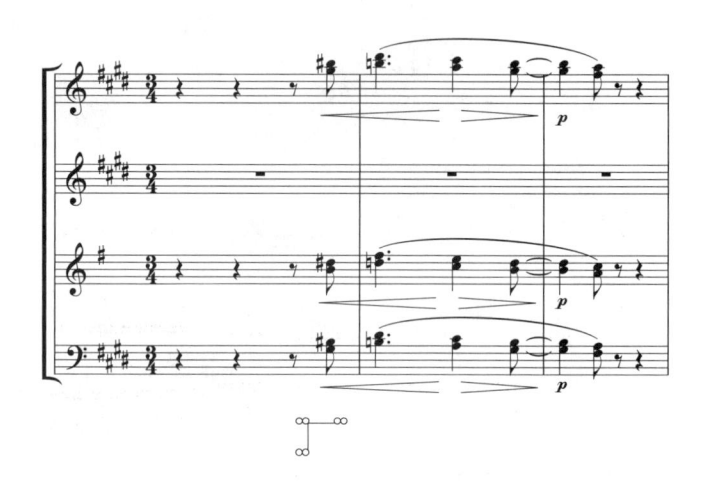

Beethoven, Symphony no. 3, third movement, bars 40–43

Tchaikovsky, Symphony no. 6, fourth movement, bars 2–3

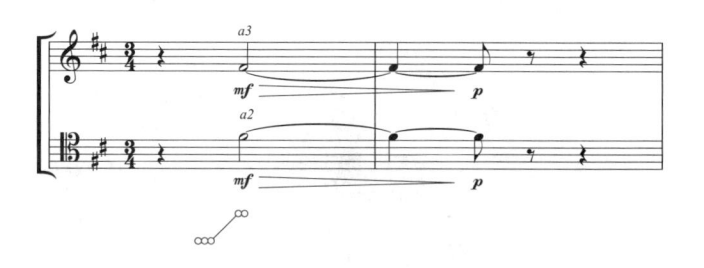

Brahms, Symphony no. 2, third movement, bars 107–108

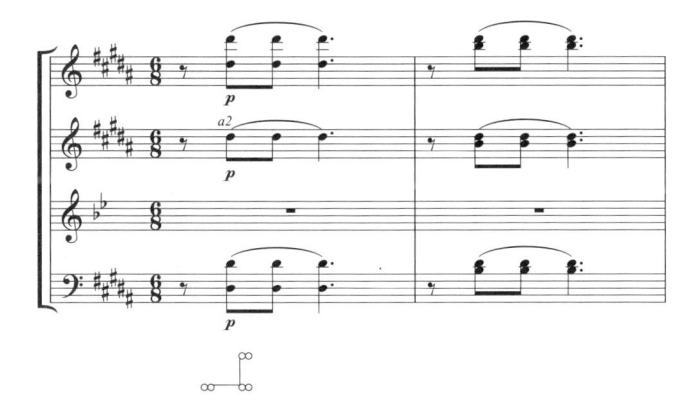

Brahms, Symphony no. 1, third movement, bars 71–72

Beethoven, Symphony no. 5, second movement, bars 135–137

Beethoven, Symphony no. 2, second movement, bars 43–44

An additional circle is added to represent a third instrument within each family (excluding auxiliary instruments). A dash indicates an inactive (tacet) player.

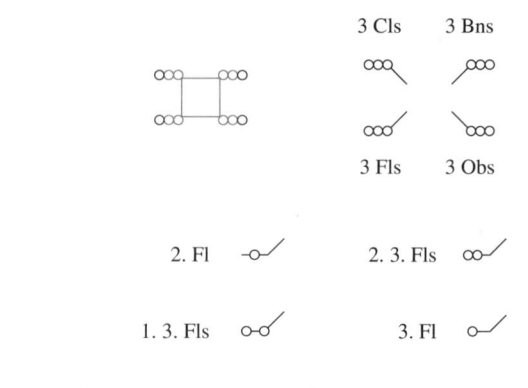

3 Cls   3 Bns

3 Fls   3 Obs

2. Fl   2. 3. Fls

1. 3. Fls   3. Fl

Bartók, *Concerto for Orchestra*, first movement, bars 474–475

Dvořák, Symphony no. 9 (*From the New World*), first movement, bars 374–377

For auxiliary instruments such as piccolo, English horn, E♭ clarinet, bass clarinet, and contrabassoon, the following notation is effective:

Picc   Ehn   BCl   Cbn   E♭

To show the exact position of these five instruments, the preceding notation is altered; only the first letter of the instrument is used.

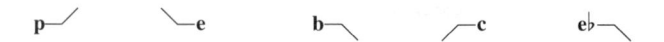

p   e   b   c   e♭

This system allows one to see at a glance precisely which instruments are playing.

2 Fls, Picc   E♭ Cl   2 A Cls, 2 B♭ Cls

2. Ob, Ehn   1. Cl, BCl   2 Bns, Cbn

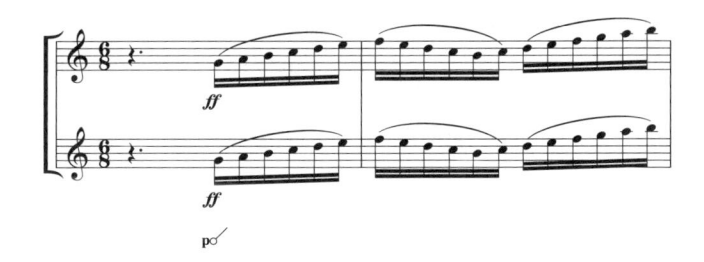

Berlioz, *Symphonie fantastique,* fifth movement, bars 422–423

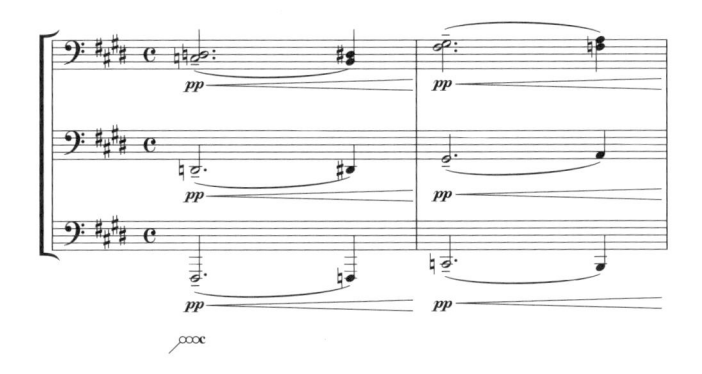

Debussy, *La mer,* third movement, bars 22–23

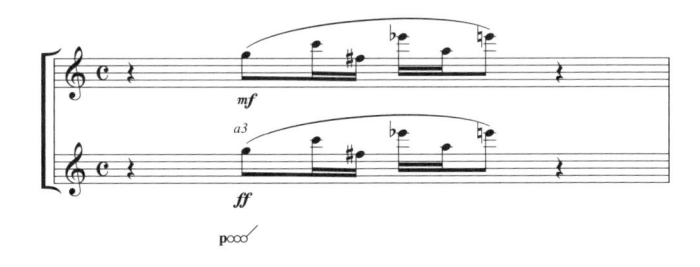

Perle, *Three Movements for Orchestra,* second movement, bar 39

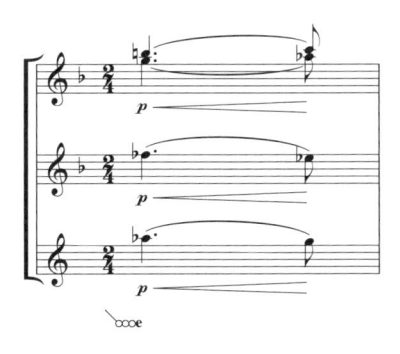

R. Strauss, *Till Eulenspiegels lustige Streiche,* bar 206

3. The Brass Section

The conductor must always know where each section of the brass family is located within the orchestra and also where every individual player within each section is seated.

Given the harmonic restrictions of the brass instruments of the classical period, the first and second players usually play as a single unit in the same key; therefore, locating and cuing them is relatively simple. Mozart expanded the number of available pitches by using horns in different keys within a pair (Symphony no. 40).

In the *Eroica* Beethoven added a third horn in F to the pair in E♭, and in the Symphony no. 9 he used two pairs, each playing in a different key. This practice did not become standard until the romantic period. The two pairs generally used different crooks that served different harmonic needs. The pairs played together only when their pitches fit the harmonic requirements. With the invention of the valve, brass writing and cuing became more challenging.

Although indicating exact positions in the score is unnecessary when only two horns are involved, symbols are helpful when three or more are scored. In the illustration below a system of horizontal circles describes the exact location of individual players. The dash represents an inactive (tacet) instrument.

3 Hns   ∞∞∞

1. Hn   —o   1.2. Hn   -∞∞
2. Hn   -o-   2.3. Hn   ∞∞-
3. Hn   o—   1.3. Hn   o-o

Beethoven, Symphony no. 3, first movement, bars 22–25

Beethoven, Symphony no. 3, first movement, bars 408–411

Beethoven, Symphony no. 3, first movement, bars 384–385

Beethoven, Symphony no. 3, first movement, bars 13–15

Beethoven, Symphony no. 3, first movement, bars 394–395

Seating Arrangements

To indicate four horns, an additional circle is added.

4 Hns	○○○○	1.2. Hn	—∞	1.4. Hn	○—○		
1. Hn	—○	2.3. Hn	-∞-	1.2.3. Hn	-∞○		
2. Hn	-○-	3.4. Hn	∞—	2.3.4. Hn	∞○-		
3. Hn	-○-	1.3. Hn	-○-○	1.2.4. Hn	○-∞		
4. Hn	○—	2.4. Hn	○-○-	1.3.4. Hn	∞-○		

4 Hns □   1. Hn ↘   3.4. Hn ⊓   1.4. Hn ↘

1.2.3. Hn ⊔   2. Hn ↗   1.3. Hn ⊥   2.3. Hn ↗

Stravinsky, *Firebird* Suite (1919 version), Danse infernale du roi Kastcheï, rehearsal no. 18*

or

Stravinsky, *Firebird* Suite (1919 version), Danse infernale du roi Kastcheï, rehearsal no. 13*

Franck, Symphony in D minor, first movement, bars 13–15

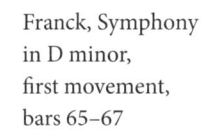

Franck, Symphony in D minor, first movement, bars 65–67

---

*With kind permission of European American Music Distributors LLC, sole U.S. and Canadian agent for Schott Music.

Franck, Symphony in D minor, first movement, bars 385–387

Stravinsky, *Firebird* Suite (1919 version), Ronde des princesses, 2 bars before rehearsal no. 2*

Tp	Tb
∞∂	∂∞Tu
	or
	∂∞T

∂ = principal

Brahms, Symphony no. 2, fourth movement, bars 234–240

Stravinsky, *Petrouchka* (1947 version), 3 bars before rehearsal no. 7

Stravinsky, *Firebird* Suite (1919 version), Danse infernale du roi Kastcheï, rehearsal no. 9*

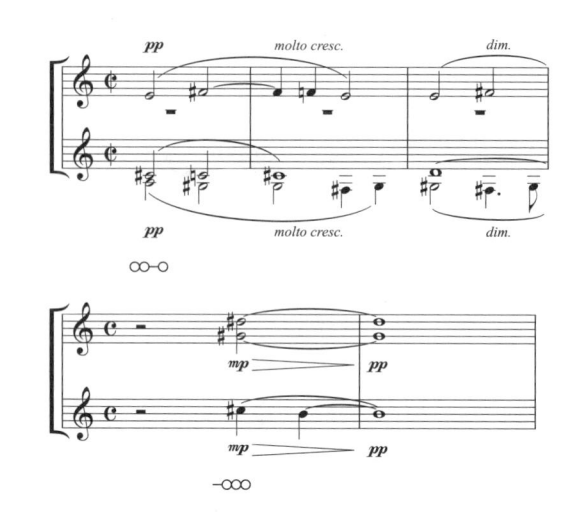

When the trumpets, trombones, and tuba play as an entire group, seating positions are not needed; however, symbols are helpful in polyphonic writing.

*With kind permission of European American Music Distributors LLC, sole U.S. and Canadian agent for Schott Music.

In compositions requiring more than four horns, three trumpets, or three trombones (such as works by Mahler, Strauss, Stravinsky, and Schoenberg, among others), different combinations are notated by indicating each instrument's part with an additional circle.

Stravinsky, *The Rite of Spring*, 4 bars after rehearsal no. 53

Mahler, Symphony no. 5, fifth movement, 5 bars before rehearsal no. 32

Stravinsky, *The Rite of Spring*, rehearsal no. 31

G. USING NUMBERS INSTEAD OF SYMBOLS TO INDICATE THE ORDER OF ENTRANCES

The order of individual entrances is indicated by using numbers instead of circles. This notation shows the placement of specific players or sections and also demonstrates the physical patterns created when the conductor shifts attention from instrument to instrument and from section to section. These complex movements can be absorbed and remembered easily by thinking graphically and notating the moves.

1. The String Section

A. Single moves between any two adjacent sections:[4]

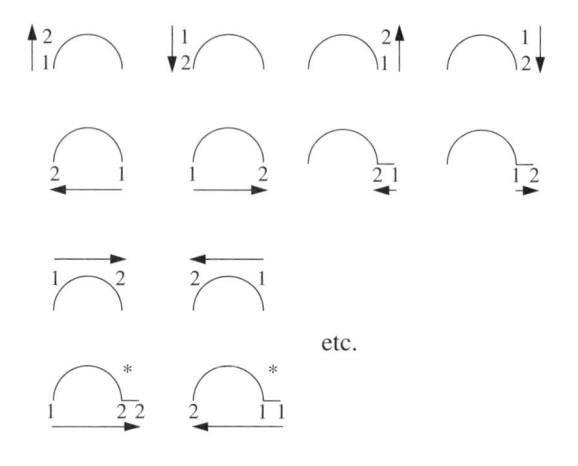

* Cellos and Basses are considered as one unit in a majority of the repertory, because their parts are often identical.

Franck, Symphony in D minor, fourth movement, bars 161–162

Franck, Symphony in D minor, first movement, bars 307–310

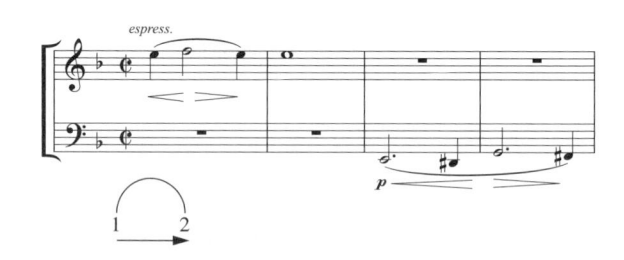

---

4. Examples in this section utilize layout no. 1. Should a different layout be desired, the traffic patterns would have to be altered accordingly. In layout no. 1, there is no other section between the first violins and the cellos and basses; therefore, movements between them are considered to be adjacent.

Beethoven, Symphony no. 3, third movement, bars 70–74

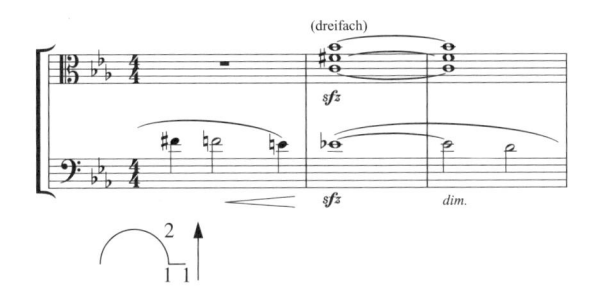

R. Strauss, *Ein Heldenleben*, 3 bars before rehearsal no. 16

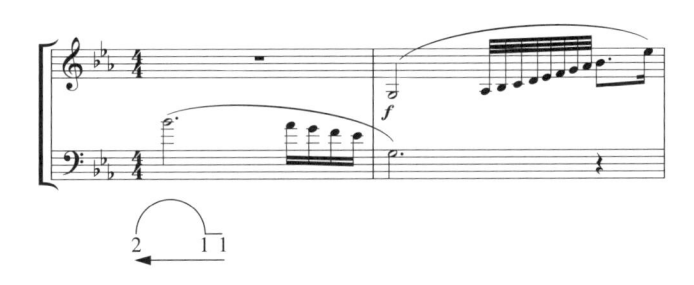

R. Strauss, *Ein Heldenleben*, 2 bars before rehearsal no. 2

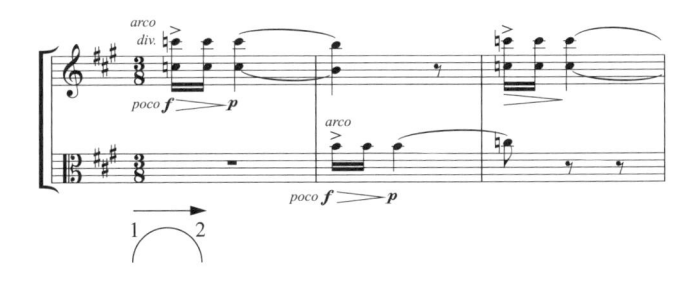

Berlioz, *Symphonie fantastique*, second movement, bars 215–217

Beethoven, Symphony no. 4, first movement, bars 312–314

Mahler,
Symphony no. 5,
fifth movement,
1 bar before
Rehearsal no. 1

B. Multiple moves are combinations of the above.
Two moves:

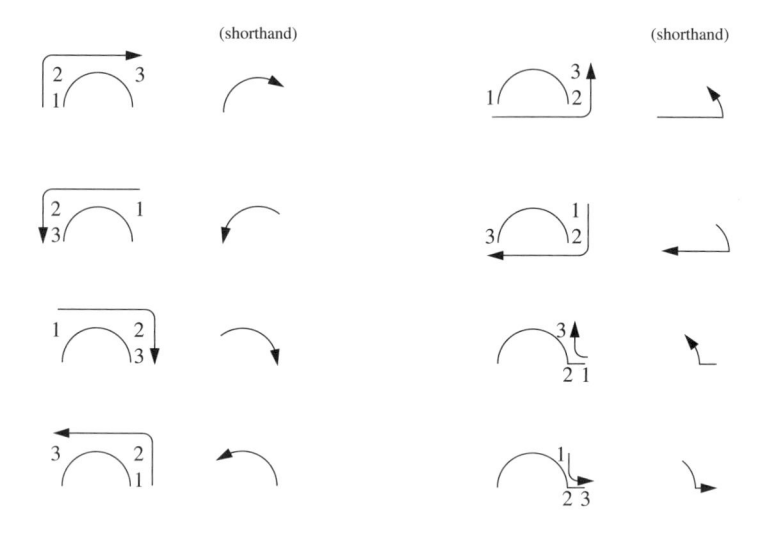

Brahms,
Symphony no. 2,
third movement,
bars 188–189

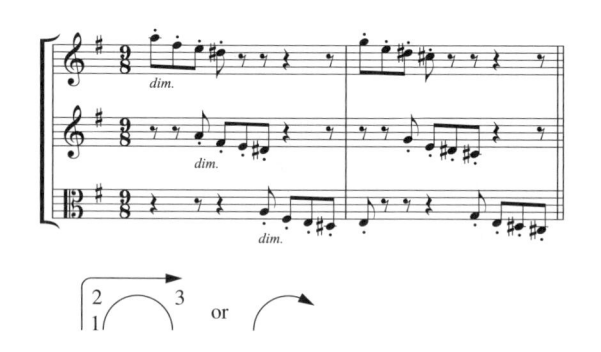

Seating Arrangements 173

Beethoven, Symphony no. 6, third movement, bars 75–78

Three moves:

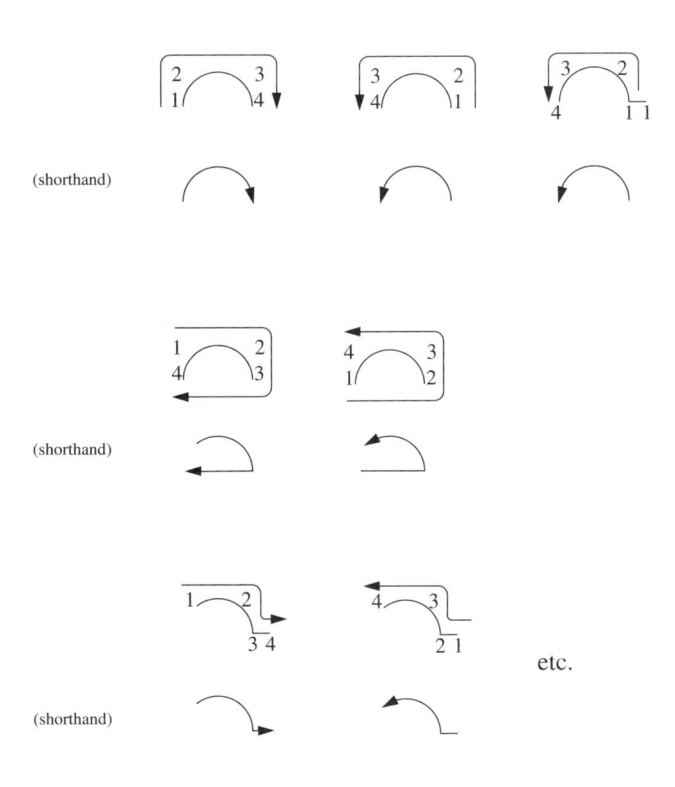

(shorthand)

(shorthand)

etc.

(shorthand)

Dvořák, Symphony no. 9 (*From the New World*), fourth movement, bars 316–320

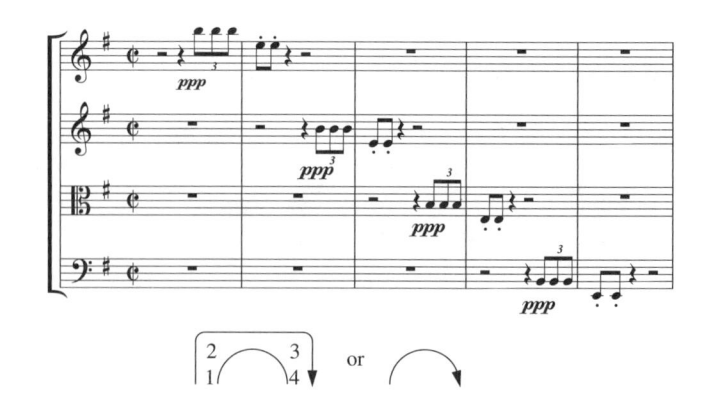

Beethoven, Symphony no. 7, third movement, bars 397–400

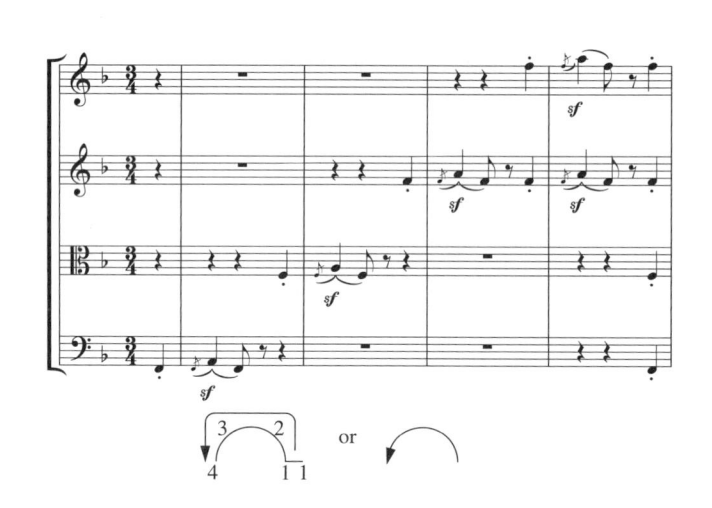

Prokofiev, *Classical Symphony*, fourth movement, bars 99–102

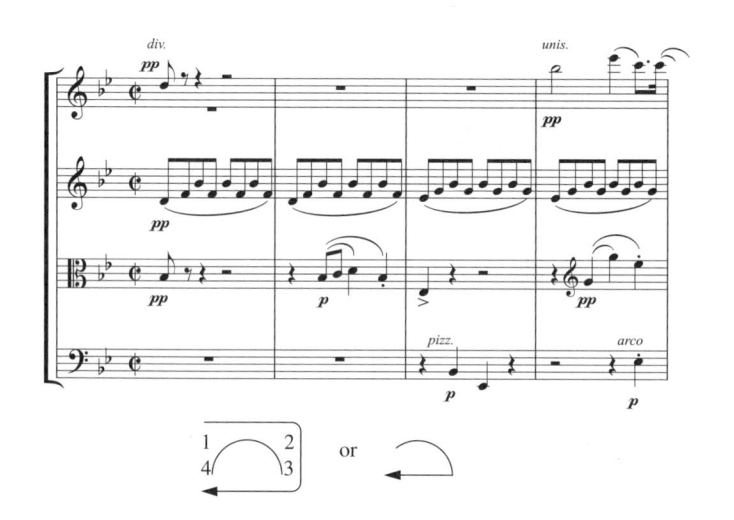

Reger, *Four Tone Poems after Arnold Böcklin,* second movement, bars 139–142

Four moves:

(shorthand)

Bartók, *Concerto for Orchestra,* first movement, bars 116–120

176   THE SCORE, THE ORCHESTRA, AND THE CONDUCTOR

C. Moves between nonadjacent sections creating a diagonal motion:

etc.

Wagner, *A Faust-Overture*, bars 8–10

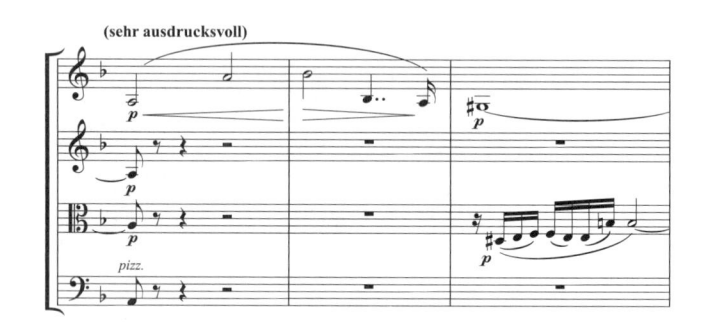

Wagner, *A Faust-Overture*, bars 274–276

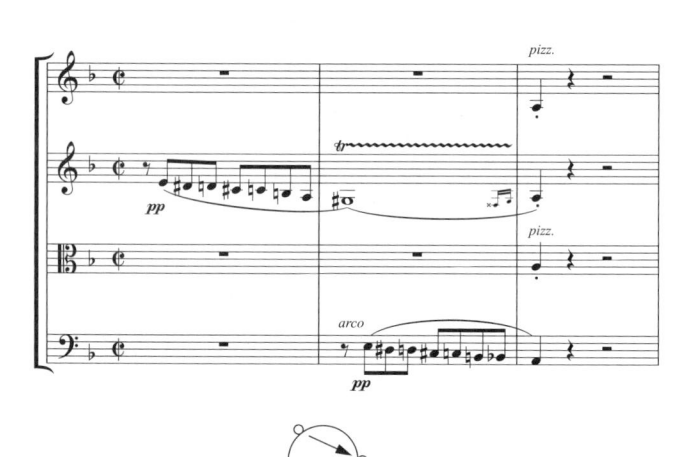

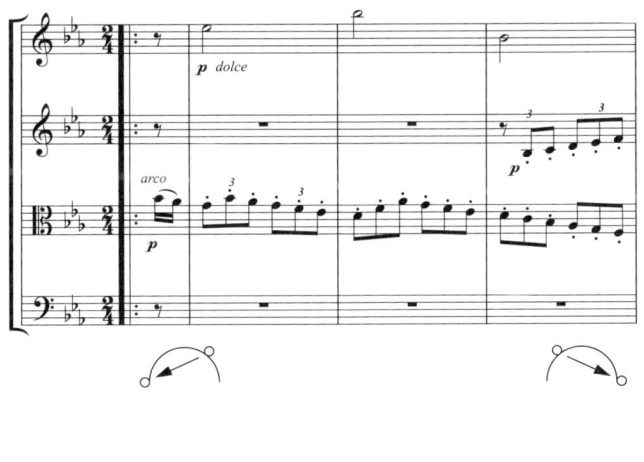

Beethoven, Symphony no. 3, fourth movement, bars 60–64

D. When diagonal moves are used in combination with adjacent moves (see sections A and B above), the following patterns result:

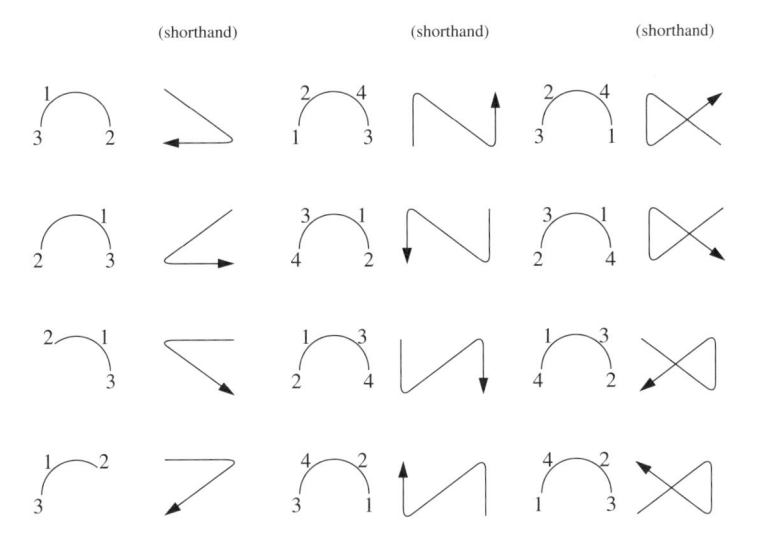

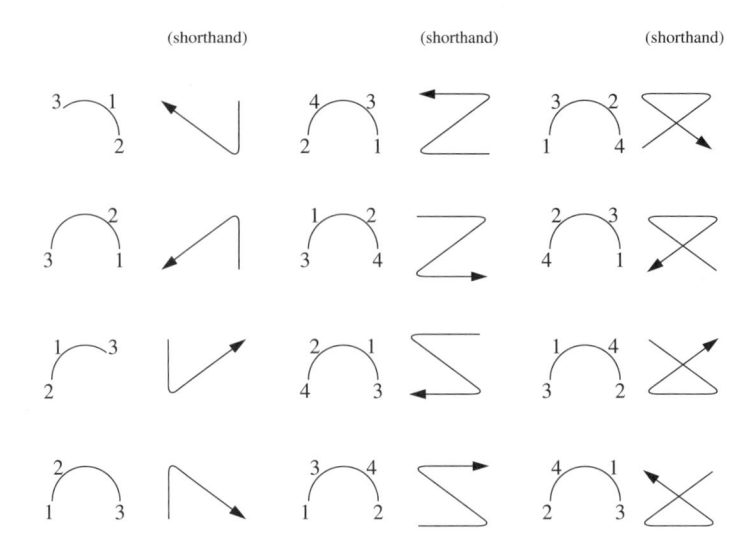

178　THE SCORE, THE ORCHESTRA, AND THE CONDUCTOR

Two moves:

Beethoven,
Symphony no. 3,
fourth movement,
bars 44–47

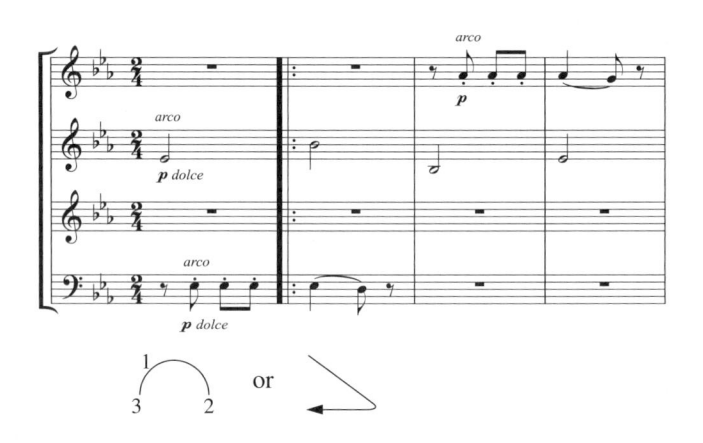

Beethoven,
Symphony no. 3,
fourth movement,
bars 52–54

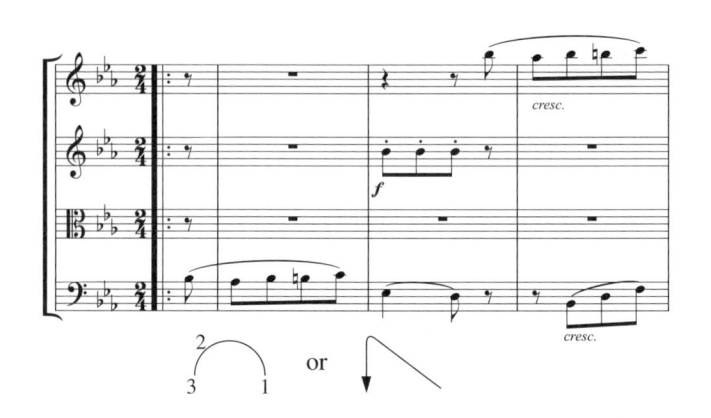

Beethoven, Symphony no. 3, first movement, bars 577–581

Beethoven, Symphony no. 3, second movement, bars 209–214

180 THE SCORE, THE ORCHESTRA, AND THE CONDUCTOR

Three moves:

Beethoven, Symphony no. 6, first movement, bars 64–68

Brahms, Symphony no. 2, first movement, bars 254–257

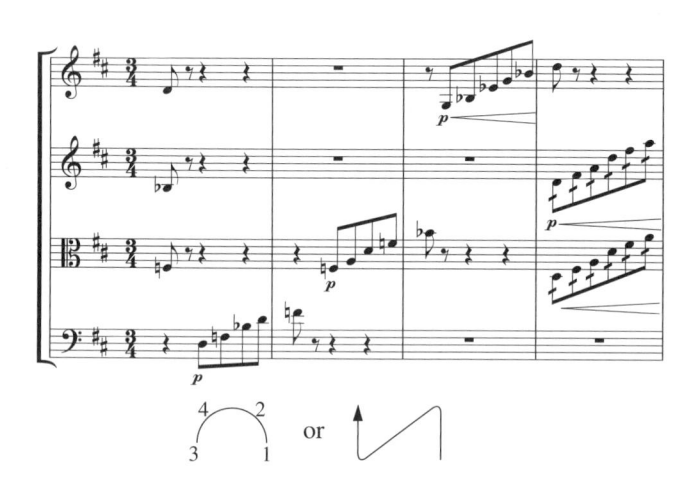

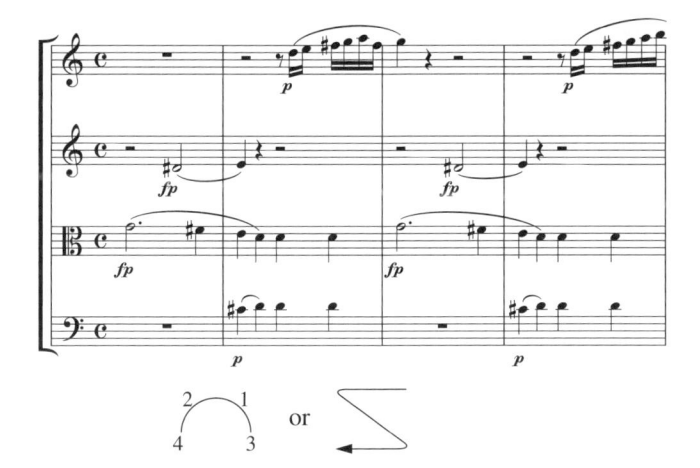

Beethoven, Symphony no. 5, fourth movement, bars 64–67

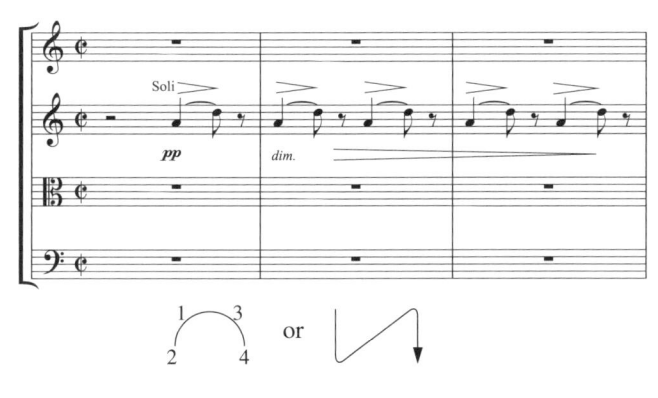

Berlioz, *Symphonie fantastique*, first movement, bars 234–238

Beethoven, Symphony no. 3, fourth movement, bars 60–64

Berlioz, *Symphonie fantastique*, third movement, bars 150–154

E. The string section can be divided horizontally, vertically, or diagonally.

Vertical: ⌢ (upper/lower)

Horizontal: ⌒ (inner/outer)

Diagonal:

R. Strauss, *Death and Transfiguration*, bars 11–14

R. Strauss,
Death and Transfiguration,
bars 72–74

Beethoven,
Symphony no. 3,
first movement,
bars 132–135

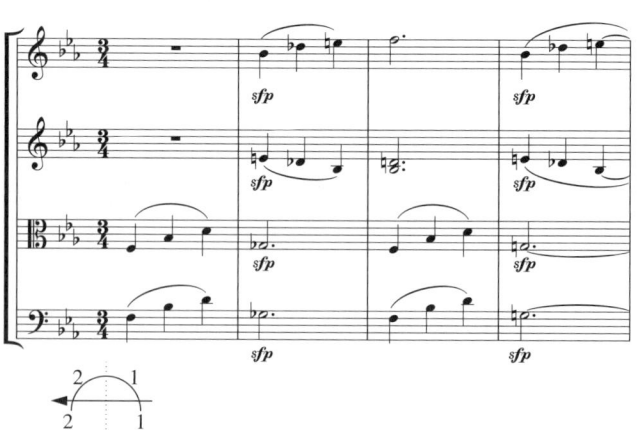

R. Strauss, *Till Eulenspiegels lustige Streiche*, 2 bars after rehearsal no. 5

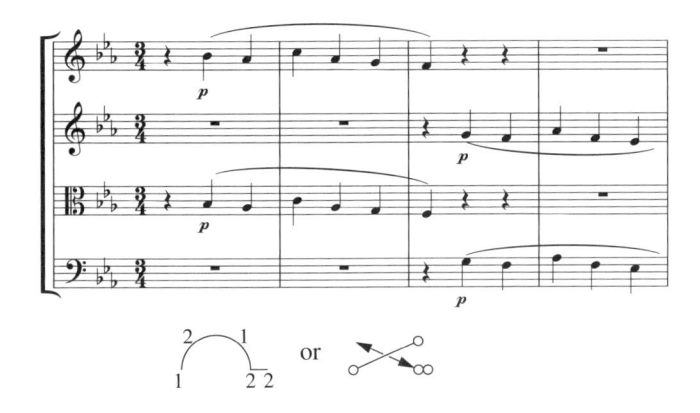

Beethoven, Symphony no. 3, third movement, bars 216–219

Beethoven, Symphony no. 5, second movement, bars 157–159

186   THE SCORE, THE ORCHESTRA, AND THE CONDUCTOR

F. The next few examples demonstrate the complexity of cuing and illustrate how symbols can assist in remembering the instrumentation.

R. Strauss,
Death and Transfiguration,
1 before letter D

Franck, Symphony in D minor, first movement, bars 199–202

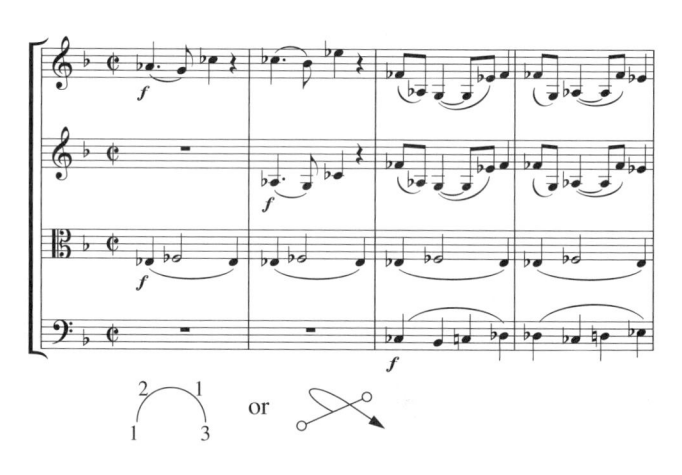

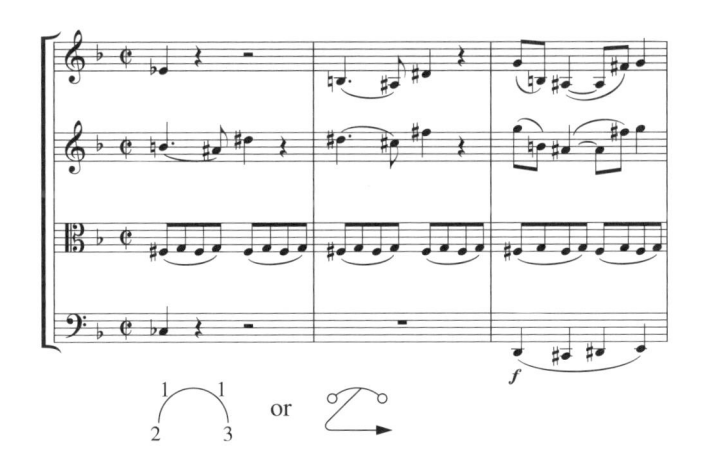

Franck, Symphony in D minor, first movement, bars 206–208

Dvořák, Symphony no. 9 (*From the New World*), third movement, bars 5–9

* Sometimes it may be necessary to divide the cuing into two segments for the sake of clarity.

188 THE SCORE, THE ORCHESTRA, AND THE CONDUCTOR

Beethoven, Symphony no. 7, first movement, bars 181–185

Beethoven, Symphony no. 6, fifth movement, bars 181–186

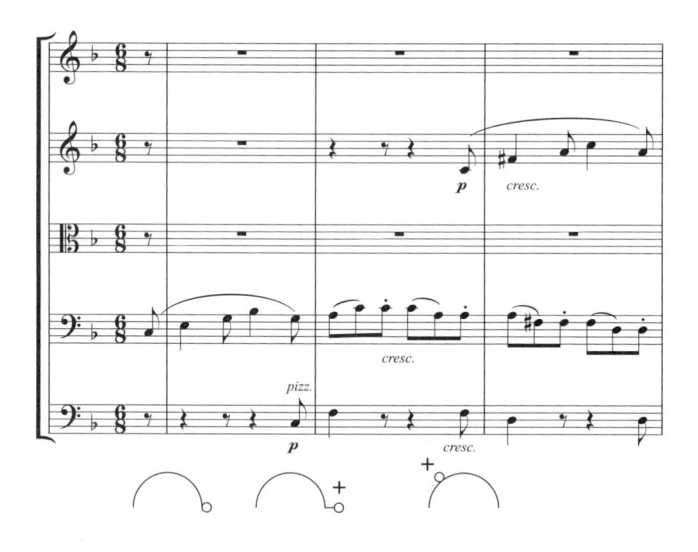

Composers may specify divisions of the string sections; otherwise, the conductor divides them. Because different divisions will affect the string sound, various combinations should be tried before a choice is made.

Two systems of divisi are prevalent: division by individual players (inside/outside) and division by stand. "Dividing the section by individual players" means that those players sitting on the outside of the stand play one part while those on the inside play the other. "Division by stand" means that, counting outward from the conductor, all uneven-numbered stands play one part and all even-numbered stands play another. When dividing a section into outside/inside, the players lose the benefit of playing the same part as their stand partners. Also, the musical line of the inside player's part will be interrupted whenever he or she has to turn the page.

Divisi into three or more parts is done either by individuals or by stand.

String Divisi Chart, Part 1

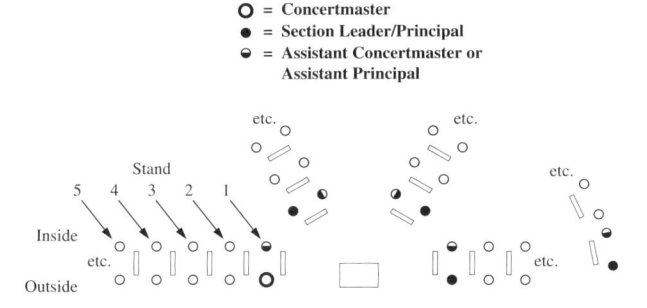

○ = Concertmaster
● = Section Leader/Principal
◐ = Assistant Concertmaster or Assistant Principal

190 THE SCORE, THE ORCHESTRA, AND THE CONDUCTOR

Divisi in 2

By Individual

By Stand

Divisi in 3

By Individual

By Stand

* Leader of the second, third or fourth divisi part

String Divisi Chart, Part 2

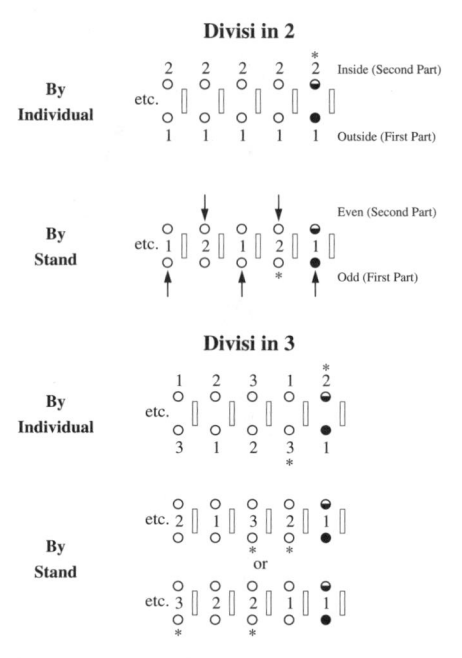

Divisi in 4

By Individual

By Stand

All Violins Divisi in 3 (A B C)

* Leader of the second, third or fourth divisi part

When the individual string sections are divided in different ways, their multiple entrances can lead to complex cuing patterns.

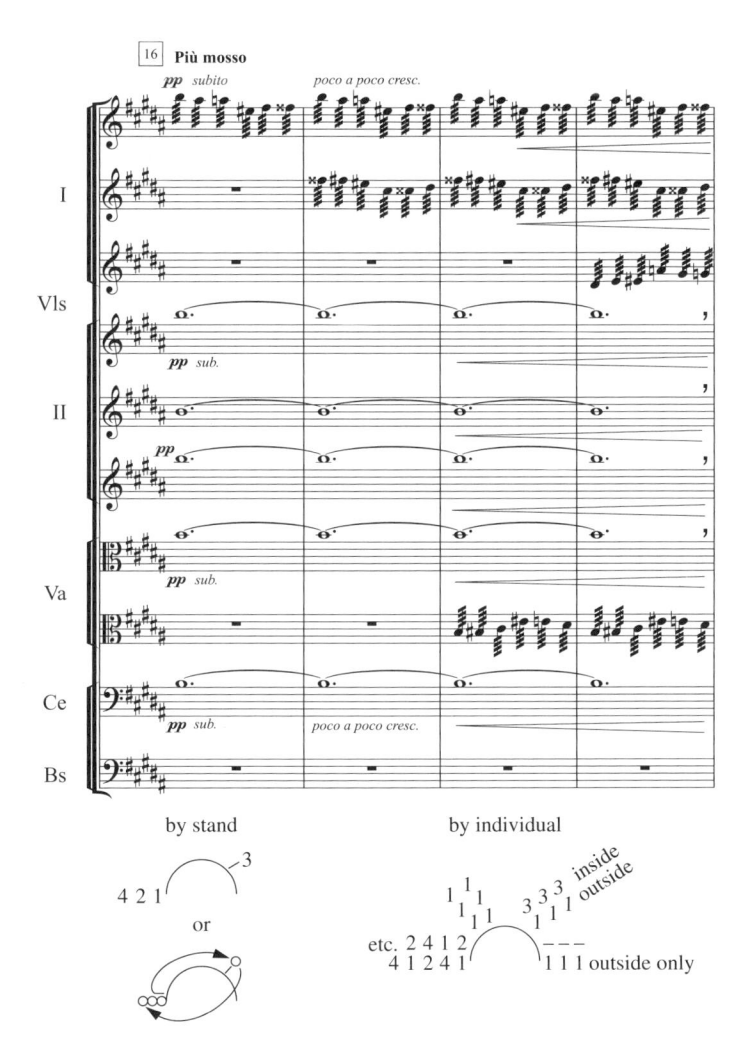

Stravinsky, *Firebird* Suite (1919 version), finale, rehearsal no. 16 to rehearsal no. 17*

---

*With kind permission of European American Music Distributors LLC, sole U.S. and Canadian agent for Schott Music.

R. Strauss, *Ein Heldenleben*, 2 bars before rehearsal no. 68

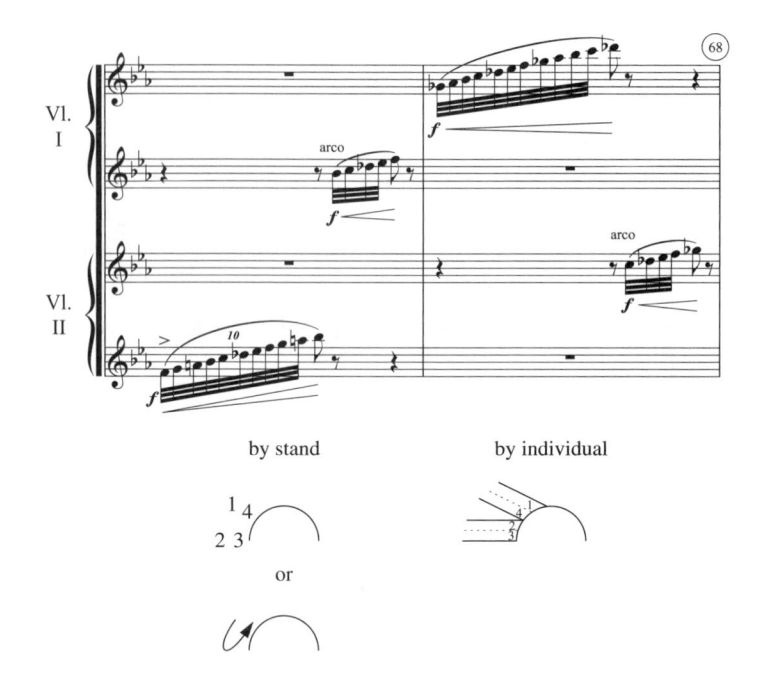

2. The Woodwind Section

Within the woodwind block, shifting attention from one instrument to another can be complicated. Numerical marking facilitates cuing and memorization. The directions of the markings are identical to those used for the strings: horizontal, vertical, and diagonal. Retaining these complex cuing patterns is facilitated by using symbols and numbers to indicate instrumentation and order of entrances.

Moving between two principal players horizontally, vertically, and diagonally:

Beethoven, Symphony no. 3, second movement, bars 69–71

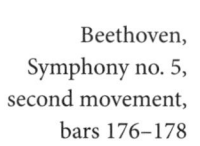

Beethoven, Symphony no. 5, second movement, bars 176–178

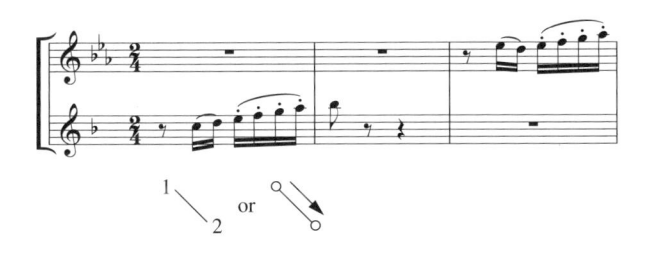

Beethoven, Symphony no. 3, fourth movement, bars 358–360

Beethoven, Symphony no. 3, fourth movement, bars 119–122

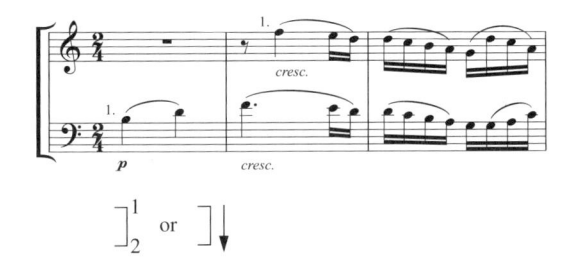

Beethoven, Symphony no. 3, second movement, bars 73–75

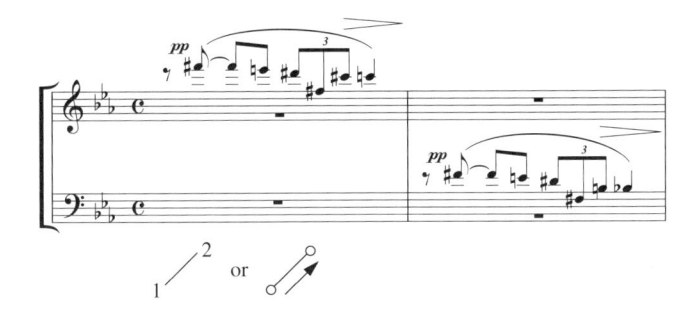

R. Strauss, *Death and Transfiguration*, bars 46–47

Moving between two different families of instruments:

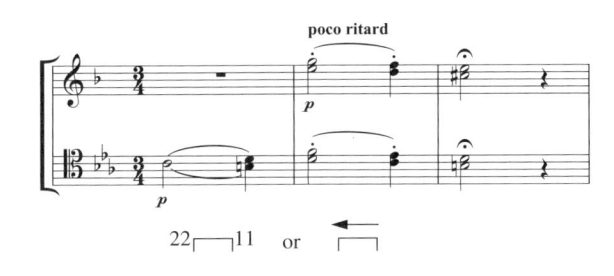

Beethoven, Symphony no. 5, third movement, bars 6–8

Dividing the entire woodwind block into equal halves may be helpful:

A. Horizontal division separates the front row of woodwinds from the back row; a division of upper versus lower woodwinds according to the score:

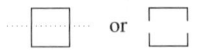

Mozart, Symphony no. 35, first movement, bars 13–16

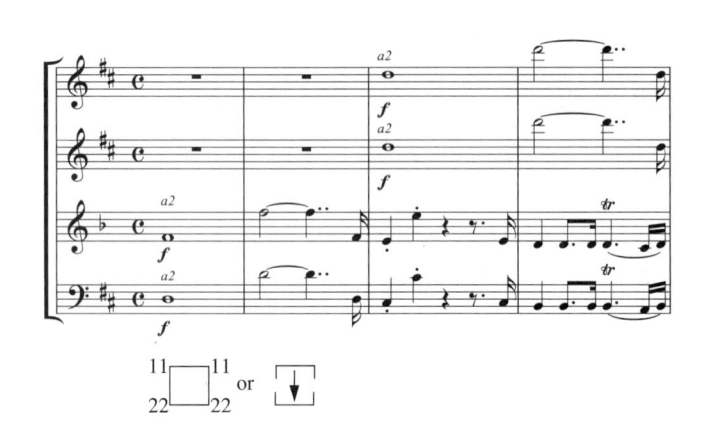

Brahms, Symphony no. 1, first movement, bars 152–155

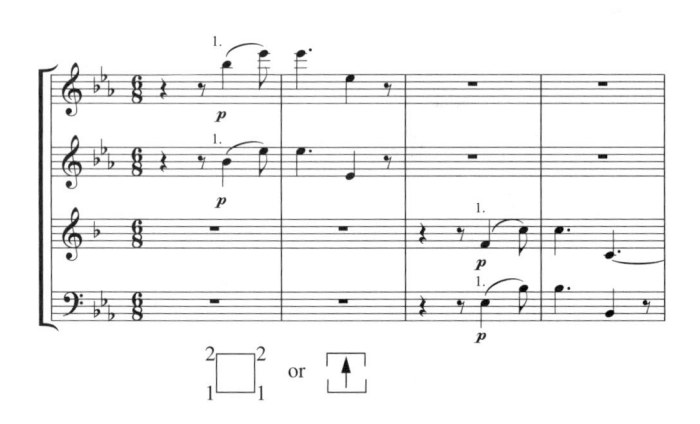

B. Vertical division groups the flute and clarinet on the left and the oboe and bassoon on the right side; this is a division between single reeds and double reeds:

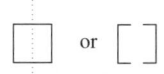

Seating Arrangements   195

Beethoven, Symphony no. 2, first movement, bars 2–5

C. The diagonal pairing divides the woodwind block into the outer woodwinds (flute and bassoon) and the inner ones (oboe and clarinet):

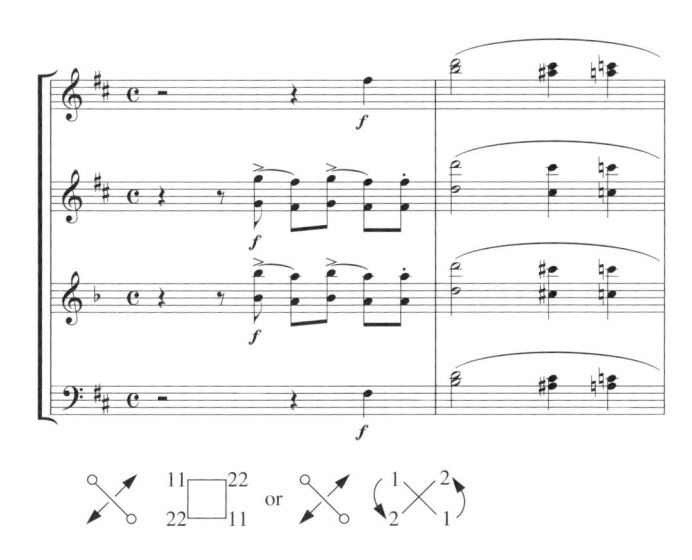

Mendelssohn, *Fingal's Cave Overture,* bars 243–244

196   THE SCORE, THE ORCHESTRA, AND THE CONDUCTOR

Brahms,
Symphony no. 4,
first movement,
bars 137–139

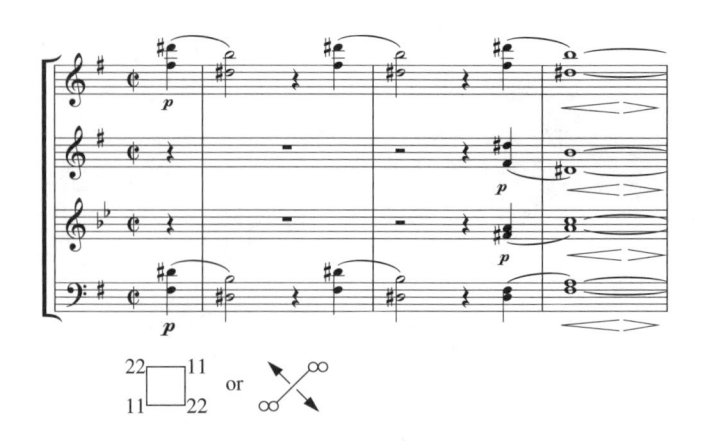

The following examples show combinations of moves between different instruments:

One move:

Beethoven,
Symphony no. 3,
third movement,
bars 22–29

Brahms,
Symphony no. 1,
third movement,
bars 45–49

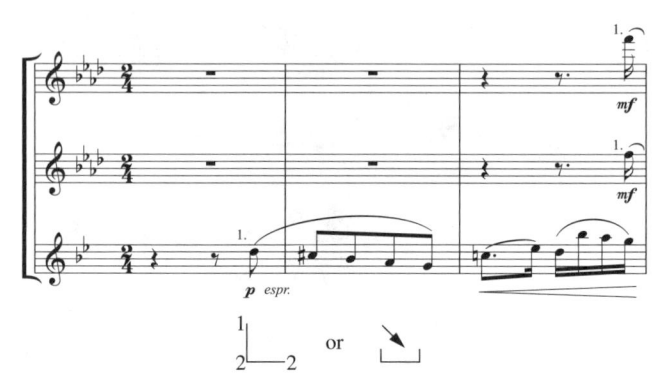

Seating Arrangements 197

Brahms,
Symphony no. 4,
fourth movement,
bars 213–218

Two moves:

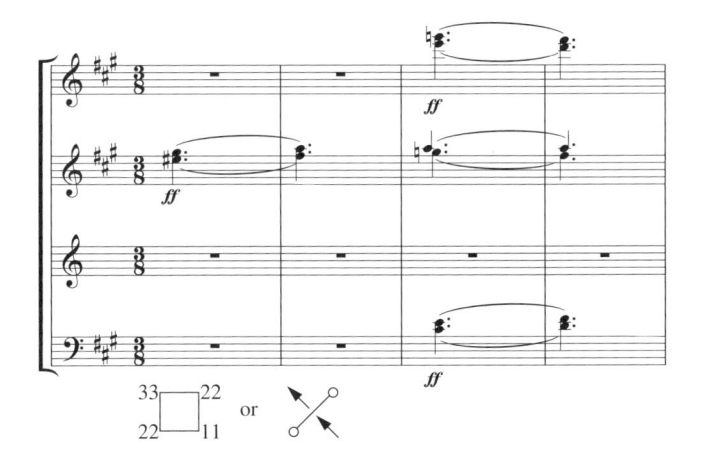

Beethoven,
Symphony no. 2,
second movement,
bars 148–154

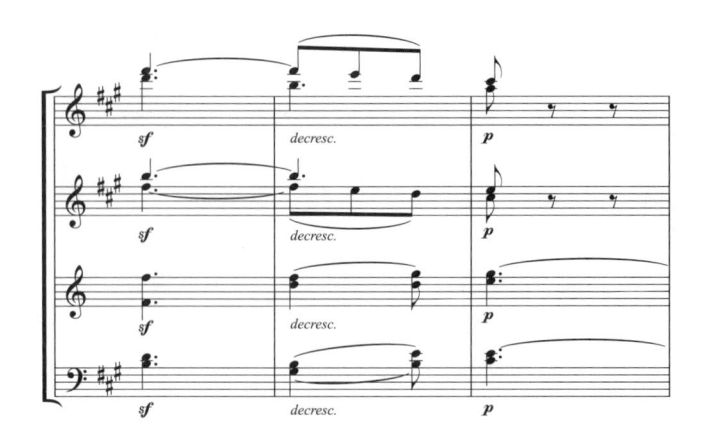

Brahms,
Symphony no. 4,
second movement,
bars 113–114

Beethoven,
Symphony no. 2,
fourth movement,
bars 52–55

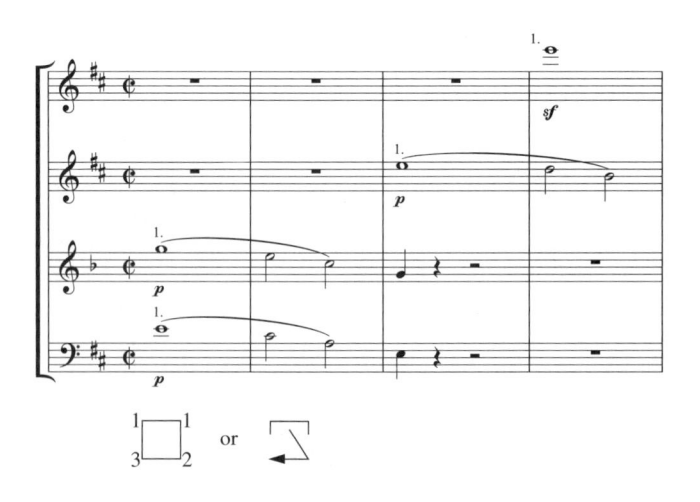

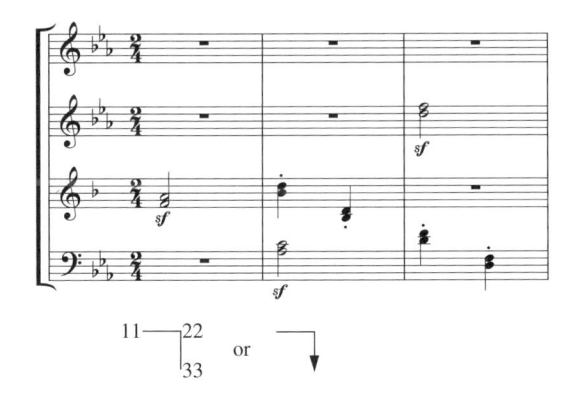

Beethoven, Symphony no. 3, fourth movement, bars 329–331

Brahms, Symphony no. 4, second movement, bars 15–16

Brahms, Symphony no. 4, fourth movement, bars 107–110

Beethoven, Symphony no. 6, fifth movement, bars 212–215

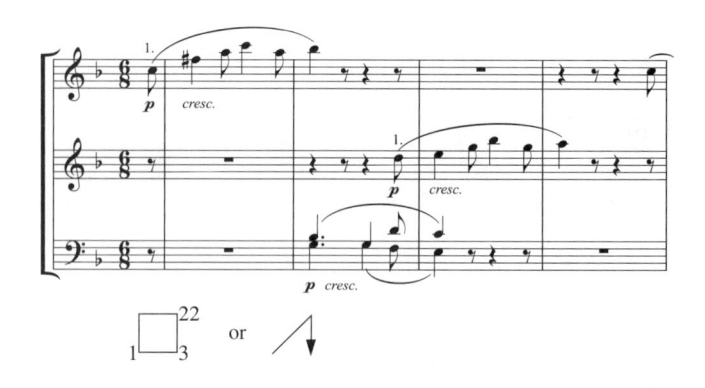

Three moves:

Beethoven, Symphony no. 5, fourth movement, bars 321–325

Seating Arrangements 201

Beethoven, Symphony no. 3, first movement, bars 244–247

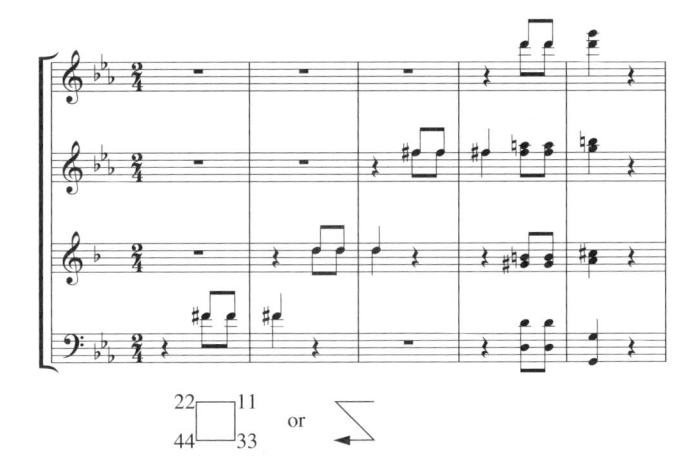

Beethoven, Symphony no. 5, first movement, bars 183–187

Beethoven, Symphony no. 3, first movement, bars 492–495

Bizet, *Carmen*,
act 2, no. 12,
bars 84–87

Beethoven,
Symphony no. 5,
second movement,
bars 127–132

These two examples demonstrate once again the benefits of graphics in score study. The first example makes use of the mirror image between the two entrances for a handy mnemonic; the second illustrates how a set of entrances becomes a simple shift to the left in the back row.

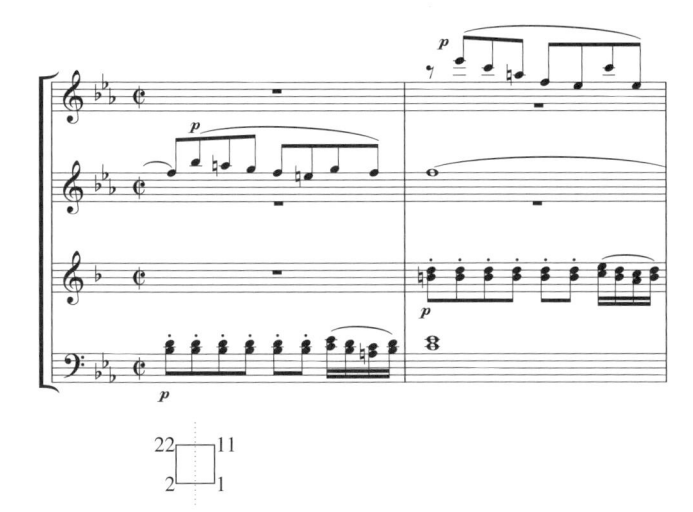

Mozart, Overture to *The Magic Flute*, bars 74–75

Beethoven, *Egmont Overture*, bars 279–286

204   THE SCORE, THE ORCHESTRA, AND THE CONDUCTOR

In these two bars from Stravinsky's *Firebird* Suite, the instrumentation is easy to remember. The two solo instruments (second flute and first horn) are compositionally separated from the two accompanying woodwind pairs, which consist of the right half of the woodwinds followed by the back row of the woodwinds.

Stravinsky, *Firebird* Suite (1919 version), Ronde des princesses, rehearsal no. 5*

Mastering the cuing of each entrance in the following passage from Beethoven's *Eroica* Symphony requires considerable practice. Within the short span of four bars, all eight woodwind instruments have important entrances. Although there is little time between each entrance (especially in the fourth bar, when a new entrance occurs on each eighth note), the conductor can manage to locate the position of each player, establish eye contact, and successfully cue each entrance.

Entrance 2 to 3 right to left in the back row:

Entrance 4 to 5 right to left in the front row:

---

*With kind permission of European American Music Distributors LLC, sole U.S. and Canadian agent for Schott Music.

Beethoven, Symphony no. 3, second movement, bars 47–50

In this passage from the same movement, there are four separate entrances, each involving a pair.

Beethoven, Symphony no. 3, second movement, bars 193–195

Many instrumental combinations can be remembered almost immediately because of the shape of their cuing patterns. In the following two examples, the theme and the two later entrances are a mirror of the participating musicians.

Beethoven, Symphony no. 3, second movement, bars 173–178

3. The Brass Section

As brass instruments developed and composers began to write for each instrument or section independently, their cuing patterns became as complex as those of the woodwinds.

Beethoven, Symphony no. 3, second movement, bars 184–187

Beethoven, Symphony no. 3, third movement, bars 174–176

Mahler, Symphony no. 2, fifth movement, rehearsal no. 30*

Brahms, Symphony no. 2, fourth movement, bars 397–402

*© 1972 Universal Edition, Vienna. © Renewed. All Rights Reserved. Used by permission of European American Music Distributors LLC, U.S. and Canadian agent for Universal Edition Vienna, London.

H. COMBINED TRAFFIC PATTERNS

Corresponding graphs for entrances that alternate between strings and winds help to retain the intricate polyphony and complex orchestration. If returning to an instrument for an additional cue is necessary, the appropriate entrance number is marked in parentheses next to the initial number.

Beethoven, *Egmont Overture*, bars 5–8

The first oboe initiates the four-note motive. The first clarinet follows playing the first three notes of the four-note motive. The first bassoon enters and also plays the first three notes of the original motive. The entrance of the second bassoon completes the dominant seventh chord.

Seating Arrangements 209

The first violins initiate the four-note motive, followed by the second violins, which play the first three notes of the four-note motive. The cellos and basses are added before the entrance of the violas and bassoons. The violas and the first bassoon elongate the first two notes of the four-note motive. With the arrival of count 6, the first bassoon, first violins, and violas complete the dominant seventh chord.

Beethoven, *Egmont Overture*, bars 9–11

210   THE SCORE, THE ORCHESTRA, AND THE CONDUCTOR

Beginning with bar 12, five successive entrances follow each other after each main count: first, the first clarinet; second, the first bassoon; third, the first oboe, second clarinet, and second bassoon enter simultaneously; fourth, first flute; and fifth, the first oboe.

Beethoven,
Egmont Overture,
bars 12–14

Memorizing the following four passages from Beethoven's *Eroica* Symphony is demanding. Each includes rhythmically identical three-note motives orchestrated for woodwinds and first violins. The order of the woodwinds is different each time.

In the first two examples from Beethoven's *Eroica* Symphony, cues 1 and 3 start and end at the same place. Cue 2 moves diagonally, the first time to the clarinet in the left corner and the second time to the bassoon directly behind the oboe in the back row.

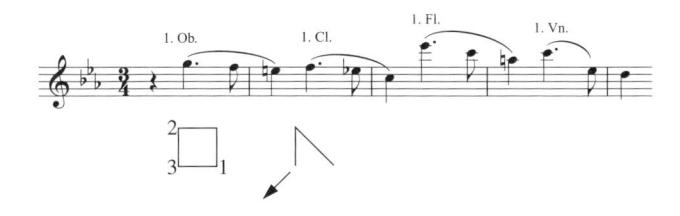

Beethoven, Symphony no. 3, first movement, bars 45–49

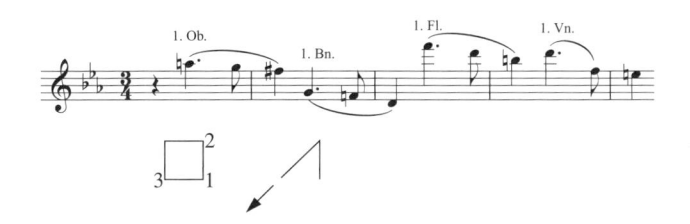

Beethoven, Symphony no. 3, first movement, bars 166–170

In the third and fourth examples from this symphony, the pattern is identical, except that the patterns begin in the back row the first time but change to the front row the second time. A diagonal move follows.

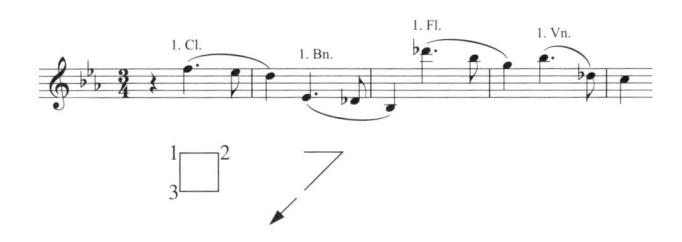

Beethoven, Symphony no. 3, first movement, bars 220–224

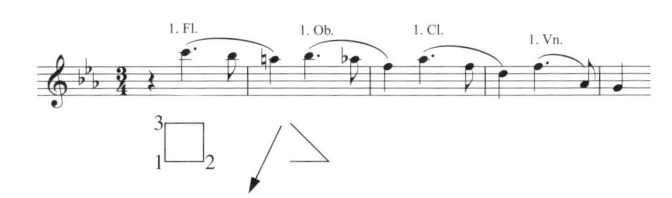

Beethoven, Symphony no. 3, first movement, bars 448–452

In this example, the conductor will want to reinforce the *sfz*s that occur on the first three eighth notes in the bar. This succession of *sfz*s begins with the double basses before moving to the cellos and horns. Assuming that the horns are seated to the right of the conductor, the next *sfz* requires a downward move to the left to include the diagonally seated bassoons, flutes, and first violins. The final cue is given to the two remaining woodwind pairs, the clarinets and oboes.

Beethoven, Symphony no. 3, second movement, bar 145

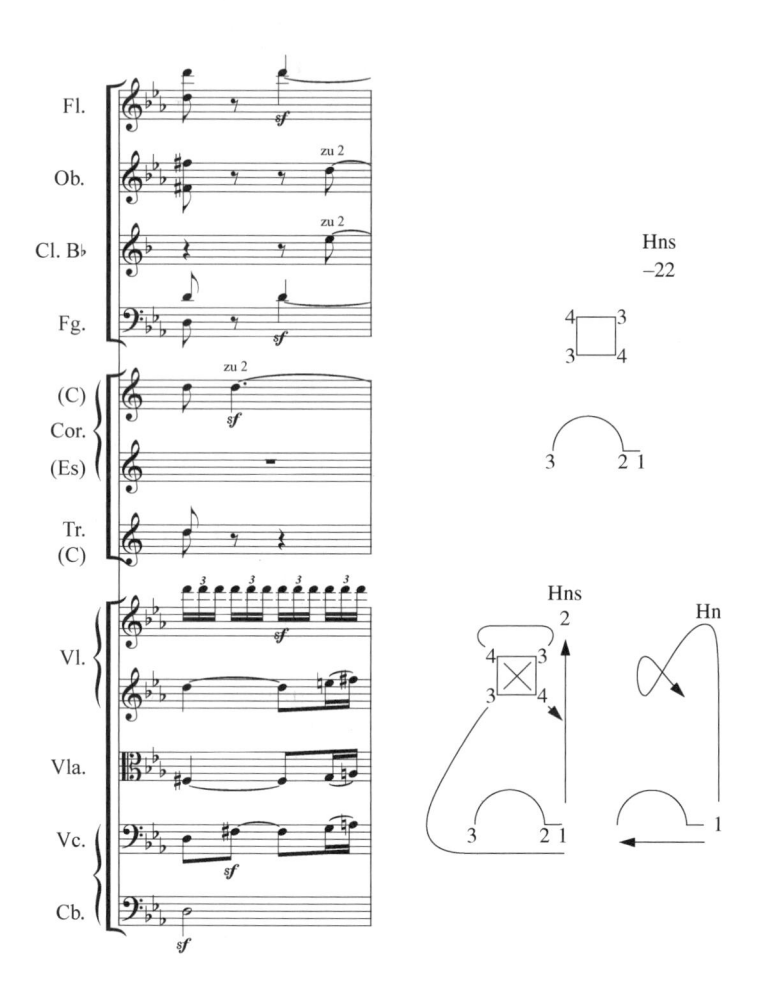

The following passage consists of two phrases of two bars each. The series of *sf*s in the woodwinds is the same both times; however, the choreography is altered significantly by the theme's being played by different instruments, first the lower strings, then the violins.

Beethoven, Symphony no. 2, first movement, bars 146–149

The first two *sfz* ♩s form a minor sixth as do the second two *sfz*s ♩s. The sixth in ♩ is twice as fast. The cue pivots to the woodwinds. Three motives of three notes each follow, the first two motives overlapping. The third motive adds a 𝄽 before moving to the flutes and bassoons. The oboes do not need cuing because they are continuing their line.

Beethoven, Symphony no. 3, fourth movement, bars 163–166

Beethoven, Symphony no. 3, fourth movement, bars 167–170

In this example, again from the fourth movement of Beethoven's Symphony no. 3, the *sf* pattern in the strings includes two identical horizontal moves from left to right on the back row. The traffic pattern continues to the cellos and double basses, at which point the winds join them.

Beethoven, Symphony no. 3, fourth movement, bars 309–314

This example from Stravinsky's *Firebird* Suite consists of three moves, each ending with the clarinets. The first and third moves from trumpets to clarinets are identical; the second move starts with the bassoons.

Stravinsky, *Firebird* Suite (1919 version), Introduction, bar 8*

---

*With kind permission of European American Music Distributors LLC, sole U.S. and Canadian agent for Schott Music.

When studying fugues or fugatos, the choreography of the cuing patterns for each entrance of the theme or motive facilitates the process of memorization.

Bizet, Symphony no. 1, second movement, bars 61–66

mm. 61-67

(continued in the next example)

+ = extra bar

Bizet, Symphony no. 1, second movement, bars 67–69

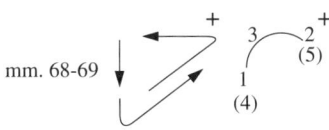

mm. 68-69

+ = extra beat

Bizet, Symphony no. 1, second movement, bars 70–71

mm. 70-71

simultaneously

220 THE SCORE, THE ORCHESTRA, AND THE CONDUCTOR

Bizet, Symphony no. 1, second movement, bars 72–74

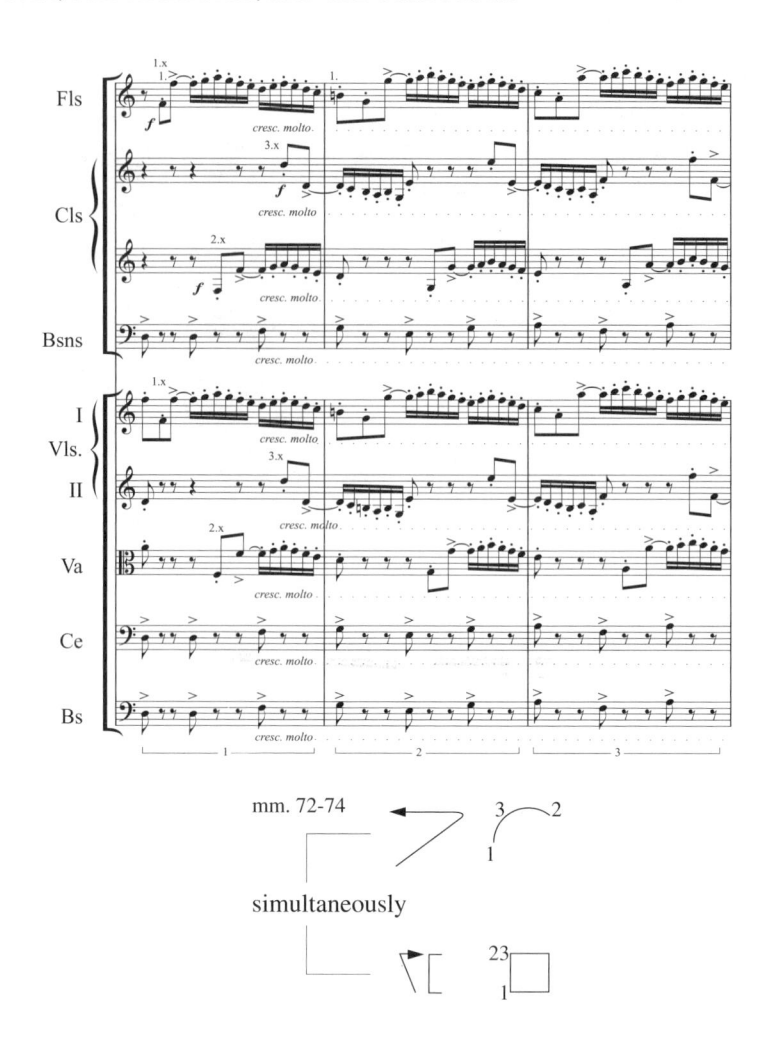

mm. 72-74

simultaneously

In the finale of Beethoven's *Eroica* Symphony, the theme enters with the first and second horns and bassoons. A move to the left adds the clarinets and the third horn, a shift to the front row brings in the flutes and oboes, and a motion to the right cues in the lower strings.

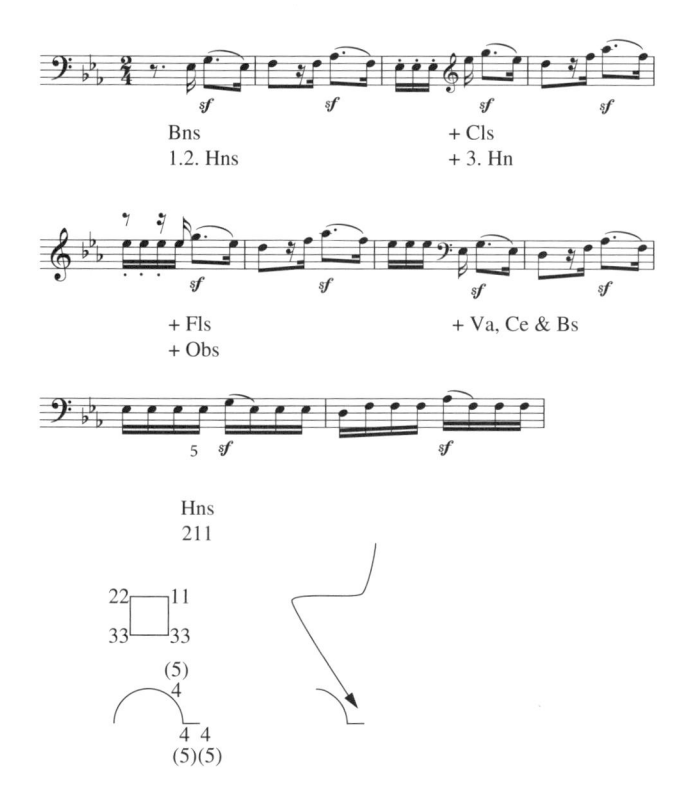

Beethoven, Symphony no. 3, fourth movement, bars 435–444

This notational system can be extended to encompass any combination of entrances. Just as an instrumentalist will practice a complicated technical passage, a conductor should practice these traffic patterns until they become second nature. The graphic illustrations are tools for score study and serve merely to demonstrate cuing patterns. They may be erased when the information has been absorbed.

---

5. The rhythmically activated theme may be thought of as the fifth entrance of the theme.

CHAPTER FIVE

Sorting the Orchestration

Analysis of the orchestration is an important part of score study. In the final creative phase the composer orchestrates the musical material for a variety of instruments. The conductor must reverse this process by identifying the original melody, harmony, and any other independent compositional segments from the finished score. The examples in this chapter illustrate how to sort the composition's orchestration into its various components.

In addition to facilitating in-depth understanding of the orchestration, sorting enables the conductor to single out and rehearse separately all the instruments that represent a particular component. Each component is important; even single notes (including nonpitched ones) may be part of a particular line or segment. Some instruments or sections continue in a straightforward fashion, while others may enter and exit at different points or shift back and forth from one function to another. The musicians may play in unison or in octaves, and the rhythm and nature of doublings may vary within a passage or be camouflaged by tremolos, syncopations, trills, ornamentations, and embellishments.

The following examples show a gradual build-up of sound in the melodic line. As the line progresses, new instruments are added, each playing identical notes and rhythms either in unison or in a different octave. After these instruments have joined in, they remain with the melodic line to the end of the passage.

Brahms, Symphony no. 4, second movement, bars 1–2

Beethoven, Symphony no. 5, first movement, bars 335–340

Beethoven, Symphony no. 6, first movement, bars 308–311

The musical line in the following example is woven through an ever-changing combination of instruments that enter and exit at different points. Dynamic changes, such as crescendos and diminuendos, are often achieved by the addition or removal of instruments. This changes the volume of sound and alters orchestral texture.

Beethoven, Symphony no. 5, third movement, bars 224–232

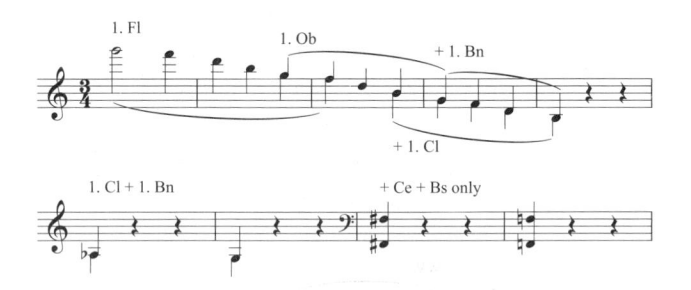

The next four examples illustrate the reinforcement of segments of a melodic line by the momentary appearance of other instruments.

Brahms, Symphony no. 1, second movement, bars 11–12

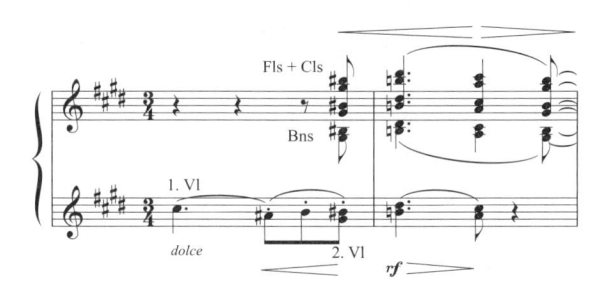

Debussy, *Prelude to the Afternoon of a Faun*, bars 53–54

Beethoven, Symphony no. 5, second movement, bars 23–24

Bartók, *Concerto for Orchestra*, first movement, bars 76–81

The next five examples illustrate rhythmic variations in doublings.

Brahms, Symphony no. 1, first movement, bars 206–207

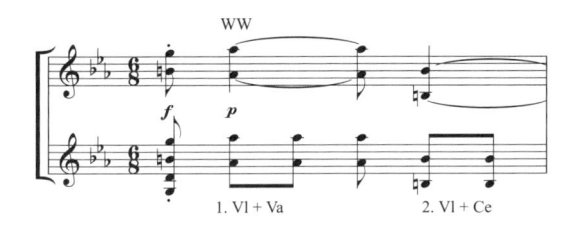

Brahms, Symphony no. 1, first movement, bar 9

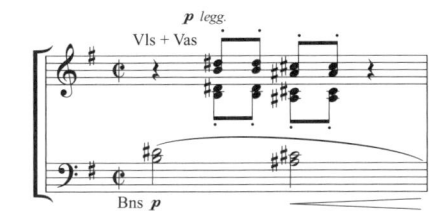

Brahms, Symphony no. 4, first movement, bar 95

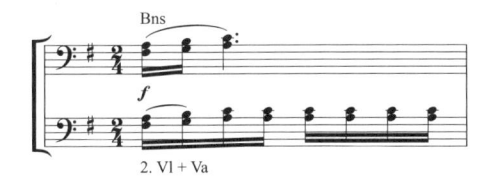

Dvořák, Symphony no. 9 (*From the New World*), first movement, bar 47

J. C. Bach, Symphony, op. 18, no. 4, first movement, bar 96

Occasionally instruments, such as the violas in the following example, shift from one function to another. Here they join the cellos' melody for a few bars; then move to the harmony provided by second violins, woodwinds, and horns; and finally, one bar later, rejoin the cellos, to which the basses have been added.

Beethoven, Symphony no. 2, first movement, bars 34–38

In the next example the violins and violas carry the two-part melody. The horns, cellos, and double basses provide a pedal point, and the cellos embellish it with pitches borrowed from the opening bar of the first movement. The last two eighth notes of each four-note segment connect briefly with either the pedal point or the harmony. In the second half of bar 285 the violas switch from the two-part melody to the first horn for a few beats, then fuse with the cellos for three eighth notes.

Brahms, Symphony no. 2, fourth movement, bars 281–286

In Beethoven's Symphony no. 6, most of the strings and woodwinds play the theme in parallel thirds, while the first violins (rhythmically activated), oboes, and horns sustain the pedal tone C.

Beethoven, Symphony no. 6, first movement, bars 263–266

In Bartók's *Concerto for Orchestra,* the violins, oboes, and clarinets play the melody, while the horns, bassoons, and lower strings provide the harmonic accompaniment.

Bartók, *Concerto for Orchestra,* first movement, bars 76–78

Dvořák, Symphony no. 9 (*From the New World*), first movement, bars 47–48

The passage from Dvořák's *New World* Symphony can be separated into three different components: (1) the melody in the oboes and first violins, which have a tremolo; (2) the harmonic material in the bassoons, second violins, and violas, with the strings playing a measured tremolo; and (3) the bass line, orchestrated for the cellos and double basses.

Sorting the Orchestration 229

In this example the harmony can be divided into three parts: (1) the major second in the upper woodwinds, upper horns, violins, and violas, with the strings moving back and forth from pitch to pitch in a measured tremolo; (2) the two trumpets and timpani, which provide rhythmic punctuation in quarter notes; and (3) the lower strings, bassoons, and third and fourth horns.

Dvořák, Symphony no. 9 (*From the New World*), first movement, bars 53–54

Shifting to a new key was difficult for the timpani and the brasses during the classical period. The valve had not yet been invented, and tuning pedals were not available for the timpani. Changing crooks and retuning timpanis were time-consuming, and the number of notes that could be played by the brasses was limited to pitches that occurred in the overtone series. For these reasons, the horns, trumpets, and timpani were frequently used together as a single unit.[1] Their functions varied considerably:

---

1. Note the long passages in which these instruments do not participate; the rests allow for crook changes in the horns and trumpets and the lengthy tuning procedures needed by the timpani.

230 THE SCORE, THE ORCHESTRA, AND THE CONDUCTOR

they supported the harmonic foundation, accented sustained chords or provided rhythmic punctuation, and occasionally carried a motive or even the theme itself.

In the second movement of Haydn's Symphony no. 103, the melody is played by the violins, with flutes and oboes doubling in the first and third bars. The lower strings and the bassoons provide the bass line. The brasses and timpani use their available pitches for fanfarelike statements. They are joined by the flutes and oboes, who abandon the melody temporarily.

Haydn, Symphony no. 103, second movement, bars 109–111

In the first movement of the same symphony, the trumpets and timpani, together with the bassoons and double basses, punctuate the E♭ in a fanfarelike fashion, while the horns sustain the same pitch as a pedal point. The melody is played by the flute(s), clarinets, first violins, and violas. A secondary line is given to the oboes, second violins, and cellos, the strings ornamenting the E♭ with a mordent, then shifting back and forth between the secondary melodic line and the pedal point in quick succession.

Haydn, Symphony no. 103, first movement, bars 48–49

In the following example, the violins and the woodwinds play the melody. The rhythm is reinforced by a pedal point in the brasses, timpani, cellos, and double basses, and the harmony is orchestrated sparsely for the divisi violas.

232 THE SCORE, THE ORCHESTRA, AND THE CONDUCTOR

Beethoven, Symphony no. 4, first movement, bars 53–55

Proper analysis of the orchestration takes into account not only the horizontal components of a work (melody, accompaniment, bass line, etc.), but also the vertical sonorities of the chords. The conductor must carefully study the layout of each chord to determine the distribution among the instruments for each partial of the chord.

The following shorthand can be used to identify the way a chord is orchestrated. Each pitch is listed on the left, and each row lists the instruments that play that note, starting with the flutes and ending with the double basses on the right. Vertical lines can be used to separate the various families of instruments.

In the opening chord of the overture to Mozart's *The Magic Flute,* the root of the E♭ chord is played by two upper woodwind pairs, two bassoons, second horn, second trumpet, first and third trombone, timpani, and all strings, while the third of the chord is covered only by the second clarinet, the second trombone, and the open G string of the violins as part of a double stop. The fifth is played by only three instruments: the first clarinet, first horn, and first trumpet.

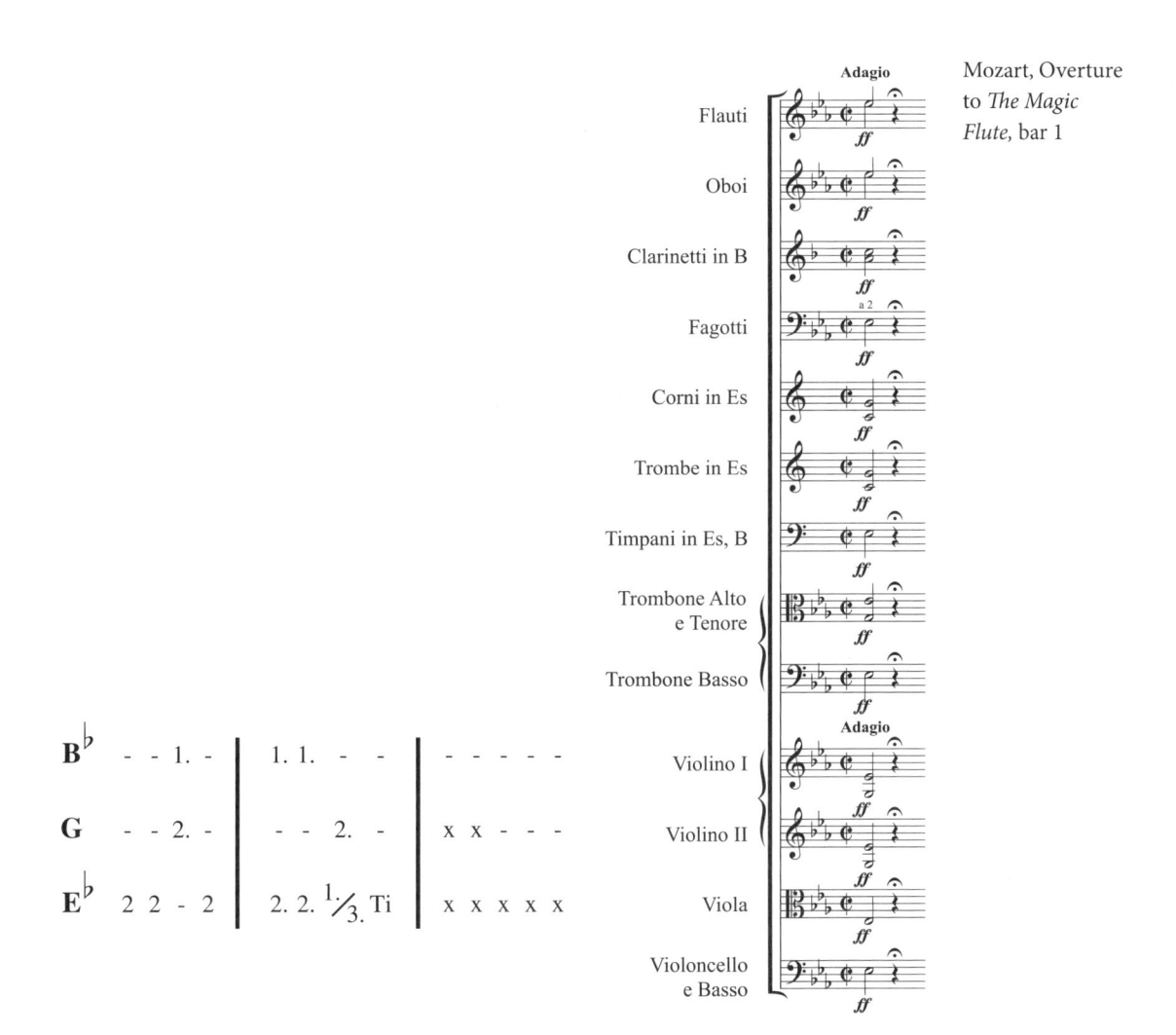

Mozart, Overture to *The Magic Flute*, bar 1

Brahms,
Symphony no. 2,
fourth movement,
bar 429

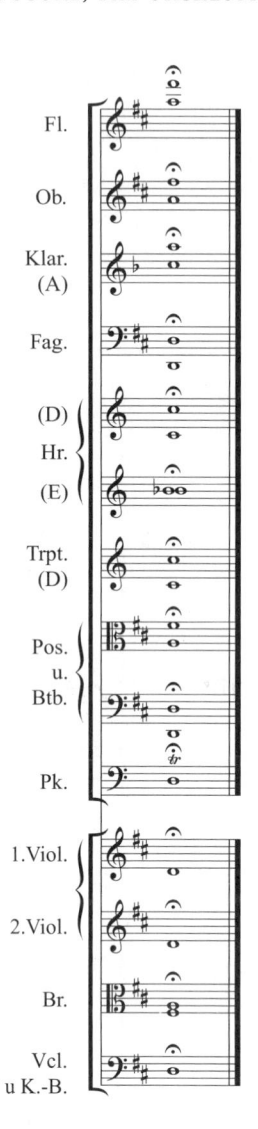

A	2. 2. 2. -	- - 2. -	- - o.s.*- -
F♯	1. 1. 1. -	- - 1. -	- - i.s.*- -
D	- - - 2	4 2 3. 1 Ti	x x - x x

*Outside/Inside, the violas playing these two notes divisi.

Note the small number of instruments playing the third and fifth of the chord.

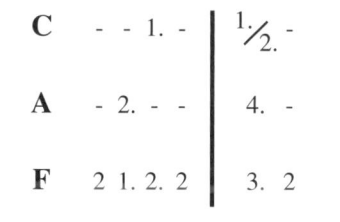

Brahms, Symphony no. 3, first movement, bar 1

```
C   - - 1. -    | 1./2. -
A   - 2. - -    | 4. -
F   2 1. 2. 2   | 3. 2
```

In this example one must be aware of the lowest note in the chord, which is played by the second trumpet. This pitch is only a half step above the bottom of the B♭ trumpet's low range, and expertise is required to play it in tune and with sufficient volume.

Beethoven, *Egmont Overture*, bar 1

These shorthand notations are suggested to identify the orchestration of each pitch or chord:

[musical staff showing pitches: CC-BB, C-B, c-b, c¹-b¹, c²-b², c³-b³]

f^3 1. - - - | - - | - - - - -

f^2 2. 1. 1. - | - 1. | - - - - -

f^1 - 2. 2. - | 1. | I. II. - - -
                     | 3. 2.|
                     | 4. |

f - - - 1. | 2. - | - - Va. - -

F - - - 2. | - - | - - - Ce. -

FF - - - - | - - | - - - - Bs.

or

f^3 1. - - - | - - | - - - - -

f^2 2. 1. 1. - | - 1. | - - - - -

f^1 - 2. 2. - | 1. | x x - - -
                     | 3. 2.|
                     | 4. |

f - - - 1. | 2. - | - - x - -

F - - - 2. | - - | - - - x -

FF - - - - | - - | - - - - x

Solving intonation problems is easier if the conductor anticipates likely trouble spots. In this example, only four instruments play f^2 (second flute, first oboe, first clarinet, and first trumpet), making a proper blend difficult to achieve. The isolated f^3 of the first flute may be out of tune. Notating the layout of the chord is useful for singling out instruments playing the same pitch. The conductor may also ask the musicians involved to play a particular note at concert pitch.

A final set of examples will further illustrate the difficulty of sorting complex orchestrations into separate components. In the following example, the melodic line (violins and cellos), pedal point (contrabassoon, timpani, double basses, and upper horns), and descending two-part line (woodwinds, lower horns, and violas) form three separate components. Note the delayed entrance of the third and fourth horns: the lower a^1 is not available on the instrument, and Brahms is evidently concerned about writing an a^2, which is a high note for the E♭ horn. The trumpets substitute for the missing downbeat of the third and fourth horns and promptly exit after the horns enter on the 4th eighth note.

Brahms, Symphony no. 1, first movement, bars 1–2

The next example contains three separate units: the melody, in parallel thirds orchestrated for oboes, bassoons, first violins, and violas; the bass line in the cellos and double basses, supported by the second horn and joined by the first horn in the second bar; and the independent melodic fragment in the second violins that arpeggiates within each chord.

Mozart, Symphony no. 35, third movement, bars 25–26

Brahms, Symphony no. 3, first movement, bars 3–4

This example also contains three components: the melody, played by the violins; the harmonic material, provided by the first and the second trombones, timpani, violas (rhythmically varied), and divisi cellos in the repeated upper notes; and the bass line, played by the lower notes of the cellos and the double basses, third trombone, and contrabassoon.

In the next example, the melody is carried by the second flute, first oboe, second clarinet, second violins, and violas (the strings with a measured tremolo). The bass line is represented by the trombones, with the bassoons and lower strings moving back and forth between the pitches of the bass line and a sustained F. The sustained F is further supported by the first flute, second oboe, first clarinet, horns, trumpets, and first violins (rhythmically activated with syncopations).

Mozart, Overture to *The Magic Flute*, bars 88–89

240 THE SCORE, THE ORCHESTRA, AND THE CONDUCTOR

In the fourth movement of Beethoven's *Eroica* Symphony, the theme is heavily orchestrated for two clarinets, two bassoons, first horn, cellos, and double basses. Alternating with the notes of the theme is a rhythmic, fanfarelike counterstatement orchestrated for the remainder of the winds and the timpani. The harmony is provided by the second violins and violas in a slow and measured tremolo, complemented by the arpeggiated figure in the first violins, which moves within each chord in the same rhythm as the measured tremolo of the inner strings.

Beethoven, Symphony no. 3, fourth movement, bars 381–382

The texture is considerably more complex in the following passage than in the fourth movement of the same symphony, as seen in the previous example. The theme itself is thinly orchestrated in octaves for the first oboe and first clarinet. The harmony is provided by a measured tremolo in the second violins and violas. The C minor chord is reinforced by the sustained notes of the two trumpets, the timpani's downbeats, and the subtle rhythmic fanfare of the horns and second bassoon, which brings back part of the marching motive of the opening bar. The bass line is played by the first bassoon, cellos, and basses and doubled in a rhythmically varied fashion by the first flute and first violins.

Beethoven, Symphony no. 3, second movement, bars 173–174

In this last example, the two solo cellos, second violins, and violas provide the harmony as they oscillate between notes of the chords. The melody is played by the first violins alone, while the flutes, oboes, clarinets, and bassoons participate in harmonic punctuations, emphasizing the cadenzalike feeling of this passage. The bass line in the tutti cellos and double basses (plus the second bassoon) is joined by the pulsating eighth notes of the horns.

Beethoven, Symphony no. 6, second movement, bar 6

CHAPTER SIX

The Zigzag Way

A. LEADING THE ORCHESTRA

Each composition presents a complex rhythmic and aural maze. Eleazar de Carvalho, a wonderful Brazilian conductor and teacher at Tanglewood and Yale from the 1960s to the 1980s, approached the score with a method of study he called the "zigzag way": when preparing a score for the first rehearsal, the conductor identifies—bar by bar—the instruments or sections needing the most guidance and attention. The zigzag way is a tool for choosing priorities; it does not exclude awareness of what is happening in the orchestra around the chosen points of attention. At rehearsal the plan is put into effect, but the well-prepared conductor abandons it as necessary to solve problems as they emerge and then returns to it when possible.

What exactly is the zigzag way? As a conductor studies a work, decisions are made about the predominant need for direction at every point, from the beginning to the end, and a mental or written map is created. The name "zigzag" is appropriate because the conductor singles out a specific group of musicians for any one of the many reasons discussed later. He or she may leave them to focus on another section of musicians in need of direction, return to the first group, turn to a third section, go back to one of the previous groups, or move on to a different section. As if following a road map, the conductor goes back and forth—zigzags—from point to point.

The zigzag way is very helpful during the middle stages of score preparation and early rehearsals. With practice, it can be integrated as one of many facets of preparation and becomes the tool it was intended to be. The conductor continues to use it but no longer consciously thinks about it. Instead, knowing where problems may arise and how to fix them, he or she is free to concentrate fully on the composer's emotional and spiritual intent and the best means of communicating it to the orchestra and the audience.

How does the conductor choose the points of attention that make up the zigzag way? First, the score is broken down into important areas for study. Then the most important priority at any given time is selected. When several seemingly equal priorities, such as rhythm, orchestration, and cuing, compete for attention, the conductor establishes a hierarchy among them.

244 THE SCORE, THE ORCHESTRA, AND THE CONDUCTOR

Understanding rhythm is a priority in score study. Control of the orchestra depends on the conductor's ability to lead the rhythmic activity of any number of musicians through the use of signals. The conductor must be aware not only of when and where rhythmic changes occur, but also of how much monitoring of such changes is required. Anticipating these shifts allows for timely messages to the orchestra through inhalation, facial expressions, or preparatory beats. When multiple layers of differing rhythms occur simultaneously, the conductor decides which of them requires attention and which might actually function better if left alone.

The fastest-moving rhythmic material (labeled **F** in the following examples) has a crucial effect on an ensemble even when only a few instruments are involved. These players need guidance; without it, they may adversely affect the rest of the orchestra. When the conductor is in sync with the fastest moving rhythmic sections, a stable foundation is established for all the interlocking sections.

Beethoven, Symphony no. 5, second movement, bars 72–73

Brahms, Symphony no. 4, fourth movement, bars 225–226

Tchaikovsky, Symphony no. 5, fourth movement, bars 107–110

Brahms, Symphony no. 4, first movement, bars 1–3

Beethoven, Symphony no. 2, fourth movement, bars 282–283

The compositional material that involves a majority (labeled **M**) of the orchestra is another priority for study. These segments have a great impact upon the cohesiveness of the ensemble. The "majority" is the actual number of individual players who participate in a particular place, not the number of sections involved.

Brahms, Symphony no. 4, first movement, bars 317–319

Tchaikovsky, Symphony no. 2, second movement, bars 57–60

Brahms, Symphony no. 1, fourth movement, bars 118–119

Violins: 14/12 (total: 26)
Violas/cellos/basses: 12/10/8 (total: 30)

Tchaikovsky, Symphony no. 4, second movement, bars 142–148

Often the fastest rhythmic material (**F**) is also played by a majority (**M**) of players.

Bartók, *Concerto for Orchestra*, fifth movement, bars 209–211

Beethoven, Symphony no. 7, second movement, bars 77–80

Brahms, Symphony no. 4, first movement, bars 309–310

The Zigzag Way 255

Brahms,
Symphony no. 4,
fourth movement,
bars 217–220

256 THE SCORE, THE ORCHESTRA, AND THE CONDUCTOR

Brahms, Symphony no. 4, fourth movement, bars 177–178

Brahms, Symphony no. 1, third movement, bars 144–149

The study and sorting of the orchestration are also essential in the preparation of the zigzag way. The conductor identifies the players and sections of the orchestra that need special attention if the ensemble is to play together successfully. Remembering that the lower instruments and those playing in extreme ranges may respond slowly to signals, the conductor notes these, as well as other passages that present special technical demands. In consideration of the physical distance between the players and the conductor, he or she devises signals that will offer clear communication to the musicians on the periphery of the stage.

Special attention is given to the bass line because it anchors most of the compositional material and is harmonically and rhythmically of crucial importance to the entire orchestra. The cellos and basses, along with selected winds, carry the bass line;

their powerful presence can hold the ensemble together, but only if the conductor is in sync with them.

Everything implicit and explicit in the score is worthy of study. Deciding on cuing, cutoffs, and beat patterns is part of the preparation for the zigzag way. The responsiveness of individual musicians must also be taken into account. In fact, if the conductor hopes to control the ensemble, consideration must be given to how individual players or sections will relate to and interact musically with the rest of the ensemble.

The successful flow of the ensemble can be interrupted easily by a range of issues, including complex rhythmic demands, sudden or unusual changes in dynamics or tempos, rhythmically active material that unexpectedly follows a long period of sustained pitches, unexpected or wide melodic skips, passages in extreme ranges, extremely rapid successions of pitches, uncommon transpositions, special effects such as rapid pizzicato and *col legno,* pizzicato alternating with arco, unusual bowings, use of different mutes, and difficult harmonics.

As the conductor studies the score, he or she will begin to formulate a musical concept for the work. Knowledge and understanding will have grown, and, as a result, some earlier decisions may need to be changed. Eventually, however, the conductor must finalize a vision of the work, trust the choices made, and decide how to communicate the interpretive concept.

Now that the conductor has studied all the basic components necessary for constructing the zigzag way, it is clear—for a time, at least—which individuals or sections of the orchestra are to be singled out for primary attention at each point in the score. The conductor now has a road map leading from one function to another, one assignment to the other.

The study leading to the zigzag way, the use of the method, and the music making are in constant flux. Obviously, in spite of previous planning, a conductor cannot give exactly the same attention to each orchestral musician in each rehearsal or performance; however, by first identifying the compositional material that provides security and cohesion, the conductor can often let go and give the musicians great latitude to express themselves. In fact, control of the orchestra can often be relinquished. At this point the conductor has achieved a collaboration with the orchestra based on listening and gentle guidance.

B. THE ZIGZAG WAY

Examples (scores are not provided):

> Beethoven, Symphony no. 2
> Beethoven, *Egmont Overture*
> Sibelius, Violin Concerto

Debussy, *Prelude to the Afternoon of a Faun*
Bartók, *Concerto for Orchestra*
Copland, *Appalachian Spring* Suite
Tchaikovsky, *Romeo and Juliet* Fantasy-Overture

1. Beethoven, Symphony no. 2, First Movement—
   Adagio molto (♪ = 84)

UPBEAT: The preparatory beat to the first bar must begin with a strong ictus. The preparatory beat may be preceded by an additional neutral beat without ictus to ensure a ♪ of exact duration. Both preparatory beats must contain the speed of ♪ = 84 and project an inner feeling of four ♪s.

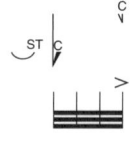

The conductor may want to dictate the ♪ in the final preparatory beat.

The ♪ can be shorter than printed, in which case the ♪ upbeat to bar 5 should be of identical length. This leads to a discrepancy with the duration of the woodwinds' ♪ unless their ♪ is shortened as well. The orchestration of the upbeat poses no challenges. All instruments play in a comfortable range.

BAR 1: With the start of the *ff* ♩., the downbeat stops without rebound.

The left hand supports the fermata with a slow forward motion that reflects the sustained pitch. Assuming that the introduction is conducted in six, the conductor does not need to mark counts 1, 2, and 3 because all instruments are participating in the fermata. If, for reasons of clarity, the conductor wishes to mark each count, the second and third ♪s should be given discreetly. The third count serves as the holding point for the fermata.

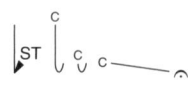

The woodwind quartet continues without a break after the fermata; therefore, the cutoff for the fermata serves as a preparatory beat for them. To show the two opposite dynamic requirements, concluding the *ff* tutti and then bringing in the *p* solo quartet, the conductor must divide the cutoff into two parts: the large upbeat motion serves as the *ff* cutoff, and the concluding reduced downbeat motion sets up the *p* woodwind entrance. An ictus, if given, might be understood as a cutoff and create an unwanted *Luftpause* before the woodwind quartet begins to play.

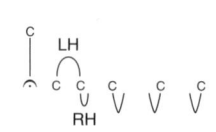

There are two reasons for making a break before the woodwind quartet begins to play: (1) the reverberation of the *ff* fermata clouds their entrance, and (2) one or more of the four wind players may not be able to sustain the forthcoming phrase until the natural breathing place in bar 4 after the ♪. A compromise solution is for the quartet to take a quick breath before the fermata ends. If a short break between the *ff* D and the woodwind quartet's entrance is preferred, the left hand gives a full *ff* cutoff to end the fermata, while the right hand remains stationary. At the conclusion of the cutoff, the left hand stops for a split second. The right hand continues with a *p* preparatory beat for the oboes and bassoons. If more of a break is wanted, the conductor waits before starting the upbeat.

To implement a *Luftpause* rather than a full ♪ pause, the *ff* sound is pushed away, creating a cutoff, a break, and a preparatory beat for the quartet as well.

Because the instruments in the woodwind quartet are double reeds, assertive beats are required. In contrast, the repeated passage in bar 5 is orchestrated for more than half of the orchestra, yet much less concise beat information is possible because the orchestration is for strings only.

BAR 2: Ideally this bar should be conducted in three. If not, each ♪ must be given. Beats 2, 4, and 6 need to be slightly more assertive than the other beats to emphasize pitch and harmony changes. Among these three, the preparatory beat to count 3 is the least assertive, because only one pitch changes. The preparatory beat to count 5, however, must be more assertive because the harmony modulates. In addition, the second oboe ascends a full fifth, while the first oboe makes the harmonically significant ascension to the D♯. Beat 6 serves as a preparatory beat to bring about the resolution of the B^4_3 in the next bar. All instruments except the second oboe move stepwise; therefore, they do not require much attention. It is important, however, for the bassoonists to be aware that the first player's seventh is resolved by the second player. The conductor can help by slightly increasing the ictus of beat 6, the preparatory beat to the e^6, and signaling to the second bassoon player the importance of the G.

BAR 3: Because the ♩. must crescendo, it is advisable to beat every ♪, each one reflecting the growth of the sound. The middle of the fourth beat represents the crescendo's maximum volume; the decrease starts thereafter and is shown in the rebound. The instruments to watch are the first bassoon, playing in its upper register, and the first oboe, carrying the melody: both instruments ascend and decrease in volume.

BAR 4: There is no rebound after the downbeat. The beat continues with the arrival of count 2 (the second ♪). During the $^6_4$ resolution to $^5_3$, the bassoons need attention. The first bassoon is playing in a high register, and the second has to maneuver an octave skip. A *Luftpause* can be implemented by stopping the third beat for a split second before continuing with the rebound, which serves as preparatory beat and cue for the entrance of the flutes and clarinets. During the last three beats of the bar, a gesture with the left hand can help prevent the descending woodwinds from making a crescendo into the forthcoming tutti *ff*. Using a powerful ictus for the sixth beat brings back the brasses, timpani, and strings at *ff*.

The flutes and clarinets join the woodwinds on count 4 and introduce a new rhythmic pattern; therefore, it is helpful to retain full ♪ beats throughout the remainder of the bar.

BAR 5: This bar is conducted in neutral ♪s of medium size and with *ff* intensity. The rebound of the third beat must maintain the *ff* while the concluding downbeat motion reflects the subito *p*. There may be a slowdown in the bass line because of the octave skip and the D to A♯ interval.

BAR 6: From a musical point of view, this bar should be conducted in three. In order to show the crescendo, however, full, smoothly connected ♪ beats are recommended, with an increase in the size of each successive beat. Rebounds of ♪ beats 1, 3, and 5 can be reduced or dropped altogether. Counts 4 and 6 serve as forceful preparatory beats for the benefit of the two *sfz*s on count 5 and count 1 of bar 7. The winds must be cued.

BAR 7: First, the conductor has to decide whether the staccato markings in the downbeats of the winds should also apply to the lower strings. The shortness of the ♪ can be demonstrated by a quick rebound, with the motion thereafter coming to a brief halt before continuing with the second beat. Should the conductor want the lower strings to play a full ♪ on the downbeat, the rebound is used as the cutoff. Each conductor has to decide how Beethoven would have wanted the violins to execute the first half of this bar. The most common version is:

The preparatory beat to count 4 must contain a strong ictus for the benefit of the *sfz* in the violins. Beat 4 rebounds strongly and provides an equally secure preparatory beat for the *sfz* in the lower strings. Anticipating the forthcoming triplet figure, this preparatory beat (count 4) should contain a feeling of inner ⌐3⌐s.

BAR 8: The downbeat rebound must contain a clear ictus to serve as the cue for the two horns. The duration of the first ♩ must also be clarified.

BAR 9: A decision must be made about the downbeat ♩ (F♯$^6_5$) . If played at its full notated value, this chord will cover the woodwind ♪s, which are marked *p*. Some conductors shorten the ♩; others use a *sfp* or introduce a decrescendo at some point. Beat 2 needs an articulated ictus for cuing the double reeds. Beat 3 requires little or no rebound. A discreet preparatory beat on count 4 with a mild ictus suffices for the resolution of the F♯$^6_5$. Creating a small *Luftpause,* a short stop on count 5, is desirable before cuing the flutes and violins.

BAR 11: This bar is similar to bars 9 and 10. The difference lies in the crescendo for the woodwind quartet, which leads to a tutti *ff* on count 6 and an early entrance of the lower strings on count 5.

BAR 12: All the ♪ beats rebound fully for the benefit of the majority of the strings, which are playing ♪s. An articulation (on or off the string) must be chosen for the ♪s. The *fp* B♭ in the first violins is maintained with a sustaining motion of the left hand. Beat 2 must also show a preparation for the first violins, which begin their scale immediately after the third count. No cutoff is necessary for the wind instruments.

BAR 13: Similar to bar 12. The principal flute and bassoon repeat the first violin statement from the previous bar and must be cued. The ascending line of the first violins is given priority even though the conductor must stay strongly connected with the ongoing ♪s of the lower strings and the scale of the woodwinds.

BAR 14: Similar to bar 12. The second violins shift from an accompanying function to join the melody in the first violins with a *sfz* entrance on count 2 (second ♪).

BAR 15: Similar to bar 13.

BAR 16: The primary musical event occurs in the bass-line scale. Only the second violin section continues to play the ♪ rhythm. The second bassoon and violas start the scale on the beat. A strong second beat must be given for the beginning of the chromatic line of the first oboe, first bassoon, and first violins. The F♯ is important for harmonic reasons because it serves as a modulation. Throughout the section, the intonation and blend must be monitored. The first flute is cued discreetly. The main focus remains with the second violins to ensure the execution of a steady rhythmic pulse that will affect the entire orchestra. Note the crescendo buildup to a *sfp* on the downbeat in the next bar.

BAR 17: Special attention must go to the second violins and violas, which are responsible for setting up rhythmically secure ♪₃s. It is easier for the second violins than for the violas to move from regular ♪s to ♪₃s, because the violas had previously participated in a passage of fast-moving ♪s. The violas, therefore, should watch the second violins, rather than seeking reassurance from the conductor, who should give a strong ictus for the first violins on count 2 and on count 6 for the *sfp* on the downbeat of bar 18.

BARS 17–22: Attention goes to the cellos, basses, horns, first violins, first flute, oboes and bassoons, which are splitting up seven-note motives. Each motive ends with the last note overlapping with the first note of the next one. The first three notes are always given a *sfz* articulation. The string cues are identical throughout the five bars. The wind cues vary.

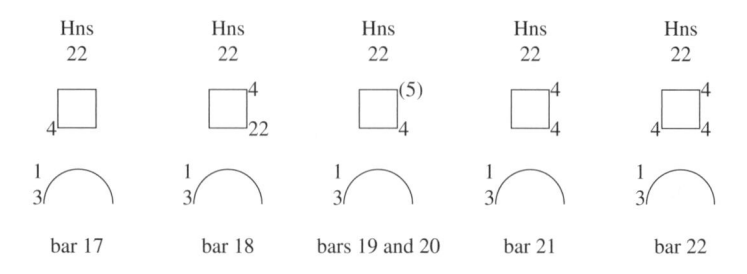

BAR 22: Several changes and additions differentiate this bar from the preceding one: (1) there is no *sfp* on the downbeat and count 3; (2) a crescendo is added throughout the entire bar; (3) the first flute joins the first oboe and bassoon; (4) the first violins repeat the scale on the sixth count; and (5) at the end of the bar, the clarinets, bassoons, horns, trumpets, timpani, and lower strings burst in with a ♪ upbeat to the next bar.

BAR 23: How would Beethoven have wanted to articulate this unison passage? The options are (1) play the identical pitches as printed with no break between them; (2) add a small break (*Luftpause*) between them; and (3) play the ♪ shorter than printed. The held ♪..s are sustained with the left hand. Short rebound beats are used for the fifth and sixth ♪s to show their staccato articulation.

BAR 24: The downbeat stops with no rebound. No cutoff is needed unless a full-length ♪ is desired. A pull-back motion is used to show the *sfp* in the horns and basses. Count 2 continues with a preparatory beat for the viola and cello A. Both ♩ beats on counts 3 and 5 are without rebound. The beat is stopped and then continues with the fourth ♪ beat bringing in the C. The forthcoming triplets in the violins, which enter after the downbeat, are anticipated and projected in count 6.

BAR 25: Until bar 34 straight ♪ beats are given. Count 3 contains the first warning sign for the forthcoming ♪s in the violas and cellos. A discreet subdivision is helpful (in ♪s) from count 4 on. The ♪s, the smallest rhythmic unit, are important. Flexibility in shifting back and forth between the upper and lower strings is necessary to accommodate the different rhythms. The ♪ beat on count 6 must anticipate the after-the-beat entrance of the violins in the next bar.

BAR 26: With the beginning of count 2, the entrance of the violas and cellos must be anticipated. The horns have sustained their octave for two and a half bars, or fifteen full ♪ counts. The rearticulation of the horns' octave needs a cue. Subdivisions tend to cause rhythmic mistakes.

BAR 27: Same as bar 25, except for the reversal of the two figures. Add cues for the principal oboe and bassoon.

BAR 28: Same approach as in the previous bars. Add the crescendo.

BAR 29: Decide on the length and dynamic level of the first ♪ in the brasses and strings. If the ♪ is sustained for its notated duration at *f* or even *mf*, the woodwind sextet's first two ⌐³¬s will be covered. The solution is for the downbeat of the rest of the orchestra to be played staccato. An articulation for the oboes, clarinets, and bassoons must be chosen. Also, a decision must be made about the duration of the first flute's upbeat (♪). Should it be played as printed, or shorter, or longer? A similar question applies to the turn after the trill. Should it be played as printed or faster? Finally, should the trill be started on the main note or on the upper note?

After the downbeat the zigzag way travels from the *sfp* in the woodwinds to the first flute, and finally to the horns and strings. The horns must match the ⌐³¬s of the woodwinds in tempo, articulation, and dynamics.

BARS 30–32: Same as above.

BAR 33: Striving for smooth rhythmic consistency, the conductor zigzags from the woodwind and horn triplets in the previous bar to the ⌐³¬s in the strings. Whether or not the strings play the triplets on or off the string is a matter of choice. A simultaneous crescendo occurs in all instruments. The oboes need a cue for their pitch change on count 5. Beat 4 is used to prepare the first violins' run beginning after count 5. Beat 6 should reflect the crescendo buildup to the *f* of the Allegro.

BAR 34: The rebound of the first beat establishes the new, slightly faster tempo (♩ = 100 versus ♪ = 84). Some conductors achieve a common denominator by introducing an accelerando throughout bar 33 (♪ = ♩). Beethoven's subito tempo and musical change should be conveyed convincingly. The first violins have just managed a difficult extended run of ♪s before settling into the new tempo. The second violins only have to shift from ⌐³¬s to regular ♪s; therefore, the first violins rely on them to set the new tempo.

BARS 34–43: Throughout these bars, top priority goes to the violins, whose ♪s serve as the rhythmic stabilizer. A subtle mini-subdivision of the second half of the first two bars is recommended, for it reflects the rhythmic outline of the melody. A slight ictus on count 2 can help to move along the ♪ figure of the violas and cellos. The articulation of the ♩s of the lower strings in bars 36, 40, and 42 require attention. Small subdivisions for each ♩ may be given. In bar 37, the violas abandon the tune briefly in order to join the accompaniment. Synchronization of the violas with the ongoing ♪s of the second violins calls for careful listening. The string crossing may cause rhythmic instability. In the same bar, because of the involvement of the double reeds and horns, the cue for the wind sextet (double reeds and horns) requires a focused preparatory beat. The extent of the crescendo is a matter of choice. The subito *p* in bar 38 is accomplished by almost stopping the downbeat, or at least reducing the motion to a minimum.

BARS 49–50: In bar 49, conductors are often tempted to stop on count 2 in order to mirror the sustained 𝅗𝅥—♩ for all instruments except the timpani. Beating is generally resumed at the next downbeat, where the ictus helps to reactivate the rhythm. This choice of a beating pattern, however, can easily lead to a rhythmic disturbance for the second violins' measured tremolo. A better way is for the conductor to remain with the second violins, give a strong preparatory beat for the timpani, and then pivot to the full orchestra after the downbeat.

BAR 61: The downbeat and rebound must not only address the ♪ pattern of the lower strings, but also serve as a preparatory beat for the continuation of the violins after the second count. Utmost attention has to be given to the bass line. The violins must listen to the basses carefully to guarantee a perfect takeover of the staccato ♪s after the 𝅗𝅥—♪.

BARS 90–91: The rebound of each downbeat is directed at the first violins, lower strings, and upper woodwinds to help them retain the proper speed after getting off the tied-over ♪. More attention goes to the lower strings, which tend to move at a slower pace. Ignore the syncopations of the second violins.

BARS 98–99: The conductor must lead the on-the-beat strings. A strong synchronization between the conductor and strings allows the winds to fit in their offbeat ♩s more easily.

BARS 102–104: All downbeats stop, omitting the rebounds, thus confirming the rests. Each second beat begins with a small ictus, reinforcing the *pp*.

BARS 105–107: Regular beats resume.

BARS 108–109: Each downbeat stops without a rebound, followed by a strong but ictusless preparatory beat for the benefit of the *sfz* and the *ff* bars. An ictus could lead to an uncalled-for *Luftpause*. The *sfz* in bar 109 is indicated by a gesture as it happens.

BARS 114–115 AND 118–119: Here the downbeat may halt to reflect the sustained 𝅗𝅥.s. The last 𝅘𝅥 can utilize a fully subdivided beat, and so may all 𝅘𝅥s in the next bar.

BARS 120–123: The downbeat on count 1 stops, while count 2 is subdivided minutely, with the second 𝅘𝅥 beat showing the *sfz*.

BARS 124–125: One beat moves to the next without any rebound, and each *sfz* is marked with a small gesture.

BARS 126–129: The focus is on the measured tremolo of the upper strings. A full preparatory beat is given for the woodwinds in bar 126, followed by a pivot to the second violins.

BARS 181–187: The downbeat does not rebound unless a fast mini-rebound is used to show the shortness of the D⁷ chord. The preparation for bar 182 must be directed to the violas and cellos, because they establish a steady ♪ pattern for several bars to come. The bassoons in bar 183 should be cued and monitored, since they may slow down a bit to enjoy one of their few solo moments. Because they are doubled with the violins, however, they must be in sync with them.

BARS 187–195: Circular beats are given for the violins.

2. Beethoven, Symphony no. 2, Second Movement—Larghetto

BARS 1–2: A preparatory beat with no ictus brings in the strings. The rebound must be quick and press forward to count 2; otherwise, the upper strings will sit too long on the first ♪, and the movement will become an Adagio. In bar 2, the cello C♯ on count 2 must be given a forceful but nonaggressive preparatory beat to secure the continuation of the tempo established in the first measure.

BAR 7: The subito *p* is confirmed by a small, barely moving downbeat that turns, however, into an emboldened preparatory beat for the double basses, which join the orchestra for the first time in this movement. (Their B is the only pitch moving on count 2.) The tempo should not slow down, but, because of the subito *p* and the isolated entry of the basses, it often does.

BAR 8: Beats 1 and 2 must feature full rebounds to ensure accurate entrances of the second violins and violas. The crescendo must be of limited strength; otherwise, the principal clarinet and oboe will be covered on their upbeat, which is only marked *p*.

BAR 9: The ♪s of the violins demand close observation. Dynamic changes to subito *p*s often upset the steadiness of the ongoing rhythmic motion.

BAR 10: After a cue for the viola entry, a good preparatory beat for the C♯ in the bass line follows.

BAR 12: After attending to the melody in the previous bar, the conductor shifts to the bass line. It is important to ignore the syncopations and allow the basses to move along gently. If the violins sense well-coordinated teamwork between the basses and the conductor, they can play their syncopations effectively. The basses tend to slow down in their descending passage because it is in a high register.

BAR 13: The conductor is still preoccupied with the bass line, but the melody in the woodwinds joining the ♪ motion needs to be monitored as well.

BAR 15: Even though the tune shifts to a sustained subito *p*♩, beats 1 and 2 have to be marked well, keeping the pulse alive, so that the violins may comfortably continue with their syncopations.

BAR 16: The conductor should subdivide the first beat, dictating each ♪. A minuscule stop on the E shows the end of the phrase. A gentle ♪ upbeat is then given for the first violins.

BAR 31: Rhythmic security is accomplished by leading the bass line. Because the articulation requires short notes, the conductor must use a staccato beat motion, even though it contradicts the legato of the melody. The left hand could come to the rescue here, leading the woodwinds with a legato beat.

BAR 32: Decide how to handle the final note A which for some instruments is an ♪, for others a ♩. At the same time, the harmony is introduced in repeated ♪s in the second violins and violas, and it is through these inner strings that rhythmic stability is achieved. The left hand should discreetly take care of the two cutoffs (♪s and ♩s). An unusually slow rebound motion on beat 3 will secure a tenuto ♪ upbeat for the first clarinet and bassoon.

BARS 33–40: Although the conductor wants to travel from the woodwinds to the first violins to associate closely with their melodic dialogue, contact must be maintained with the inner strings.

BAR 40: A strong ictus on the third beat is necessary in order to establish the first *ff* in the movement. A subdivision for all ♪s is also an option.

BAR 41: A full rebound of the first beat is recommended. Beats 2 and 3 should be subdivided (small motions).

BAR 42: No second-beat rebound is necessary. On count 3 the beat continues and serves as the preparation for bar 43; a small beat with a convincing ictus is essential for a precise entry of the woodwind quartet.

BAR 45: The upbeat to bar 45 would need little energy or no ictus were it not for the two horns, which require a precise preparatory beat. Some conductors eliminate one player, in which case the ictus could be less pronounced. However, Beethoven wrote these chords for two horns to share the string entrance so both horns should play. Only if there are serious intonation, balance, or response problems should the conductor decide to use one horn player.

BARS 154–159: See the section in chapter 3 on notation problems.

BARS 261–262: The downbeat must include a full rebound for the strings on count 2. The second beat should be stretched to achieve a full-length ♪ chord and help the first violins to get off the tied-over ♪. It also serves as a cutoff for the lower strings.

BARS 264, 266, AND 268: All three of these bars need a preparatory beat with a fairly strong ictus for the bassoons and horns.

BARS 265 AND 267: Both downbeats should stop; the rebound is eliminated. The first flutist is a soloist and should be left alone. As the flutist arrives at the final ♪, a preparatory beat is given for the downbeat of the next bar.

BAR 269: In this bar, the downbeat has to rebound fully, in spite of the subito *p*, for which a small nonrebound beat would have been preferable. Without the rebound, however, the entrance of the violins on count 2 will be late.

BAR 273: An exaggerated rebound and ictus of the first beat will secure a strong *sfz* on count 2. The beat on count 2 must stop without rebound until the arrival of count 3, at which point a pickup to the next bar is given.

BAR 275: The downbeat stops. The second beat has limited strength but must have a focused ictus in order to bring in the *p* ♪. A slight delay follows before the upbeat to the final ♪ is given.

3. Beethoven, Symphony no. 2, Third Movement—Scherzo (Allegro)

All bars are beaten in one. The large rebound of each *f* bar is followed by a small downbeat for the *p* bar. The rebound then explodes into a full preparatory beat for the next *f* bar. The *p* horn entrance requires a strong ictus.

BAR 7: The downbeat is small, but the rebound grows rapidly, preparing the *ff* in bar 8.

BAR 21: After the downbeat, the rebound moves to count 2 (second ♩), followed by a stop and a pull-back motion to show the *fp*. No preparatory beat is given for the next bar.

BAR 22: With the arrival of bar 22 the beat moves upward, turning into a preparatory beat for bar 23. An affirmative upbeat with an equally affirmative ictus helps the first violins to securely establish their first ♪ phrase. Even more important, this upbeat serves as the preparatory beat for the second violins, which establish the new harmony.

BAR 83: Use a subdivision ♩ for the staccato A seventh chord.

BAR 84 (SECOND ENDING): There is a split-second's stop on the downbeat, followed by a gentle preparatory beat for the woodwind entrance.

4. Beethoven, Symphony no. 2, Fourth Movement—Allegro molto

BARS 1 AND 2: In two. The conductor starts with the baton placed in an upper position, gently gives a downbeat moving to the right, then returns for the second beat, which contains a nonaggressive ictus as a preparatory beat for the violins and woodwinds. The following downbeat (bar 1) explodes into a full preparatory beat with a strong ictus for the *sf* on the second count.

BARS 94–98: The conductor's first concern is to maintain perfect rhythmic coordination between the violins and the timpani. The power of the timpani can easily upset the security of the ensemble. The bass line, for low strings doubled by the bassoons, is musically dominant at this point. Notice the canon in the upper woodwinds. In bar 98, the conductor connects with the first bassoon. Neither the first nor the second violins will have difficulty fitting in their ornamented A^7 if they know that the bassoonist and the conductor are in accord.

BARS 334–338: The downbeat stops without rebound. It is not necessary to mark bar 335 because everybody participates in the fermata. A large preparatory beat serves as cutoff for the *ff* A^7. The concluding downward motion in bar 336 must, however, be of the smallest size, reflecting the subito *p*. There is no break. Bar 336 may be marked. As the second fermata comes to an end, the conductor gives a preparatory beat with no ictus, in order to reset the tempo. The horns would prefer a preparatory beat with an ictus, but by giving one an unwanted break could occur, separating the *p* chord from the *pp* continuation.

5. Beethoven, *Egmont Overture*

BAR 1: The upbeat to bar 1 may be of any duration, because no tempo has to be established. A slow upbeat is preferable in order to convey the dramatic impact of this opening. The dynamic level is only *f*. The downbeat resembles a downbow motion. It is important that no rebound takes place. After a short stop the beat continues downward or toward the body, reflecting the diminuendo of the F. The duration of the note should be the equivalent of at least eight ♩s of the upcoming tempo. A small break between bars 1 and 2 is necessary because the strings need time to retake the bow before the *f* F minor chord. A push-away motion at the end of the downbeat causes the desired break. That motion becomes the preparatory beat for the second bar and sets the speed of the forthcoming tempo.

BARS 2–4: Again, the downbeat resembles a downbow motion, with no rebound. On count 2 the conductor uses a push-away motion, and that provides the strings with enough time for the retake. This push-away motion, which is also the upbeat for the next ♩, makes it possible to prevent each ♩ from ending up a ♩ followed by a 𝄾. The staccato ♩ should have a duration of approximately five ♪s. Clearly the downbeat and the push-away motion must contain the speed of the ♩ of the *Sostenuto ma non troppo*. The above process is duplicated for the second ♩. It is important that the push-away motion beat be duplicated as if there were a third identical ♩ concluding the bar (on count 3). Often the second ♩ is held longer than the first one; this should be avoided. The two ♩s should be of equal duration. (The same principle applies to the opening bars of Verdi's *La Forza del Destino*.) Bars 3 and 4 are identical to bar 2, except for the end of bar 4. Count 5 should be discreetly marked. With the arrival of count 6 an upbeat brings in the pickup to bar 5. Count 6 is subdivided for the benefit of the ♪.

Bar 5 is in six. The rebound of the downbeat serves as a cutoff of the C chord, minus the third. On count 2 the conductor's motion stops briefly. This lack of rebound reflects the silence. Count 3 serves as a preparatory beat for the first oboe. All subdivided ♩s are given as smoothly as possible. Some conductors create a feeling of three ♩s per bar using a three-beat pattern. The ascending seventh in the oboe upbeat phrase must be given emotional weight.

BAR 6: Beats 1, 3, and 5 cue in the first clarinet, the first bassoon, and finally the second bassoon. It must be remembered that each cue (except for the second bassoon's) prepares an appoggiatura (C and A♭). The preparatory beat for count 6 must have a stronger ictus, because it is the first time that all four woodwinds move simultaneously. The G_5^6, with its natural tension, is repeated on the downbeat of the next bar. The cuing pattern is:

BAR 7: The downbeat stops without rebound. Beat 2 becomes the preparatory beat for the resolution of the G_5^6 chord. Beat 3 serves as a cutoff for the woodwind quartet and a preparatory beat for the first violins. Beats 5 and 6 should have a ♩ feeling.

BAR 8: Cuing pattern after the upbeat for the first violins:

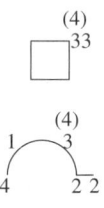

The downbeat serves as an upbeat for the second violins. The lower strings, violas, and bassoons are cued. The beat on count 4, with its appoggiatura, shows a crescendo, which reaches its climax with the arrival of count 5. Beat 5 shows the decrescendo. This beat can be extended a bit before the arrival of the last ♩ in the bar. It makes musical sense to take a bit of time before delivering the preparatory beat for the next bar. Beat 6 transforms into a powerful preparatory beat for bar 9. The duration of the upbeat does not need to be in the tempo of the basic pulse.

BAR 9: With the arrival of the first 𝆑𝆑, the six ♩s are in tempo. There is no rebound of the downbeat. The conductor moves through the $\frac{3}{2}$ pattern with small motions. Beat 5 becomes a cutoff, creating a 𝄽. Beat 6 prepares the next bar's downbeat.

BARS 10–11: The same as bars 3–4, except that in bar 11, after the second push-away motion on count 4, the beat stops. The upbeat patterns of beats 5 and 6 are extremely small. However, it is important for the baton to be high enough for the downbeat motion for count 1 in the next bar to be clearly visible.

BAR 12: Beginning with bar 12, five successive entrances follow each other, all entering after each main count (1, 3, 5). Starting with the first clarinet, the traffic pattern moves to the right, bringing in the first bassoon, followed by cues for the second bassoon, the first oboe, and the second clarinet. The next move shifts to the first flute in bar 13, then leads to the right for the entrance of the first oboe.

BAR 13: ₁⌐⌐₂

BAR 14: ¹¹⌐¹¹ ¹¹⌐¹ ¹²⌐¹¹
       ₁   ₂ ₁   ₁ ₂   ₂
       ♩ ♩   ♩   ♩ ♩
                    + Strings

Bar 14 is still in six, conducted with a ♩ feeling. The strings are cued, after which comes a clear preparatory upbeat for the last ♩ in the bar. Special attention must be given to the high G♭ of the first bassoon.

BAR 15: All of the conductor's attention goes to the ♪s of the second violins and the violas. The downbeat serves as a gentle preparatory beat for the first violins (A♭). The second ♩ beat must contain an ictus for the wind entrance on the important count 2. Beat 5 must lead to beat 6 to make sure the cellos and basses are not late with their entrance.

BAR 22: Beat 3 must lead to beat 4 to make sure the horns are on time with their entrance. Beat 5 must lead to beat 6 for the benefit of the string ♪ entrance.

BARS 24–25: The tempo of the ♪ in the introduction equals the ♩ in the forthcoming Allegro; in other words, the ♪ equals the ♪.

If the two chosen tempos do not have a common denominator, the conductor may want to speed up or slow down in bar 24 to make a tempo relationship possible.

BAR 25: Depending on the tempo, this Allegro can be either in one or in three. Because of the hidden $\frac{2}{4}$ bars in the first ten bars, it is better not to exaggerate the downbeats of each $\frac{3}{4}$ bar.

BARS 42–57: These bars are anchored by the bass line (cellos and basses); therefore, strong and convincing upbeats are needed. After the downbeat, the conductor should pivot to the upper strings, which enter after the second ♩ count. Beginning with bar 43, the downbeat on count 1 serves as an upbeat for the wind ♩s as well.

BAR 47: Some conductors have the last stand of the cellos play the same rhythm as the basses.

BAR 81: The beat stops with no rebound. On count 3, a powerful ♩ upbeat is given for the next bar's A♭ major chord.

BAR 82: The conductor must decide whether the ♪ should be shorter than printed. (Note rhythmic proportions: 3/8 ♩ ♩ ♪ ♪| versus 3/8 ♩ ♩ ♪ ♪|) . The bar is conducted in small but strong ♩s. The second beat stops without a rebound. On count 3, a preparatory beat emerges for the downbeat of the next bar.

BARS 83–85: The same as bar 82. On count 3 a *p* preparatory beat is given with a focused but discreet ictus for the winds. The next two bars are conducted in one. A *ff* ♩ preparatory beat on count 3 is given for the return of the strings.

BAR 104: The conductor must listen to the ♪s in the bass line and remain in constant contact with them. All of the three-♪ upbeat figures require a strong ictus on count 2; otherwise, the entrance of the scale will be late. Leading the rebound of the first beat to the second in a connected fashion prevents late entrances.

Bars 116–124 are in one. While remaining aware of the ♪s in the upper strings, the conductor travels from one five-note motive to the next. As the motive breaks up, the conductor cues the third and fourth horns. The downbeat stops in bar 123. A strong ♩ preparatory beat is given on count 2 for the *f* ♩. After the entrance of the ♩ on count 3, the conductor gives a strong ♩ upbeat (the rebound of beat 3) for the forthcoming *f* downbeat, then returns to beating in one. A pull-back motion should indicate the *p*.

BARS 152–159: On all third counts a strong ♩ upbeat is given for each of the following bars. The conductor goes into three. All of the subsequent bars must contain a strong ictus for each downbeat entrance of the winds. Beats 1 and 2 are small and without rebounds.

BARS 259–274: The *ff* chords are given with small but powerful ♩ beats. The rebound of the second beat is stopped. On count 3, a ♩ upbeat for the ♪ upbeat is given. The strings are brought in with a gentle ♩ upbeat. The next four bars are conducted in one with circular motions. A strong ♩ preparatory beat brings the brasses back.

BARS 278–286: Beat 1 stops without a rebound. With the arrival of count 2, an aggressive preparatory beat with no rebound is given for the benefit of the G (♪). The remainder of the bars are conducted in one until the arrival of the Allegro con brio. It is not necessary to mark each bar. No rebound should be given after the first clarinet and second bassoon enter. The beat stops until the arrival of the following bar, at which point an upbeat (of ♩. duration) is given for the D♭ major chord. After the fermata bar, a ♩ or ♩ upbeat is given for the next section, depending on whether the conductor does the Allegro con brio in two or four. If the conductor wants to make a break between the two sections, the cutoff movement with the left hand stops before an upbeat is given for the new tempo.

6. Sibelius, Violin Concerto, First Movement—Allegro moderato

BARS 1–33: This passage is in two. Listening to the upper A played by the outside players in the second violin section provides stability. Cue the first clarinet and viola entrances, and minimize the crescendo. Often the viola entrance causes an unwanted dynamic build-up. The tempo in the strings must remain steady even if the soloist takes liberties with the rhythm.

BAR 43: At this point the conductor may either stay in two or go into four.

BAR 48: Count 1 does not have a rebound. A preparatory ♩ beat is given to count 2. Continue with a ♩ beat on count 2.

BAR 49: There is no rebound on count 1. The downbeat stops for a split second. A quick rebound beat (♪) follows, cuing in the chord on count 2. Continue beating in four. Separate cutoffs are recommended for the winds and strings.

BARS 50–51: After bringing in the brasses with a ♩, ♩, or any unmeasured upbeat, return to regular ♩ beats with no rebound on the downbeat.

BARS 53–54: The horns and timpani need to be cued in and cut off.

BARS 71–74: The preparatory beats contain a light ictus for the clarinet cue and a strong ictus for the horn cue. Until the double bar these four bars are conducted in two. However, the second half of each bar, except for bar 73, is subdivided discreetly into two ♩s for the benefit of ♩s or triplets on count 4.

BARS 74–75: When the clarinet triplets are taken over by the violas, a common denominator is created. Continue in two.

BARS 91–100: As the music slows down, the conductor should at some point go into six. The entrances of the fourth, second, first, and, finally, the third horn are cued in gently.

BAR 99: A preparatory beat with a strong ictus is required for the clarinets and the third and fourth horns on count 6.

Bars 99, 102, 104, 107, 109, and 111 are in six. The soloist, first clarinet, bassoons, solo viola, and conductor must mentally reset the quadruplets so that they fit into the $\frac{6}{4}$. Each half of the bar presents a 4:3 pattern. The accuracy of the second ♪ is important. If it is correctly placed, the other ♪s will fall into place. After synchronizing the beats on counts 1 and 4 with the soloist, the conductor articulates each of the ♪s so that whoever has the quadruplet figure can play against them with confidence.

BAR 100: The conductor leads.

BAR 116: The conductor gives a cue to the soloist, timpanist, and bass players.

BAR 118: In two.

BARS 319–323: In each bar, the downbeat stops. Beat 2 starts with a strong ictus that brings in the orchestra. On count 3, the beat stops. On count 4, the basses are given a strong upbeat.

Bars 365–366 are in two. Thinking ♩-3-s results in rhythmic accuracy.

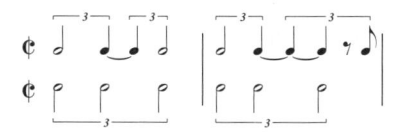

BAR 368: Rhythmic accuracy is achieved by mentally setting up three ♩-3-s in the second half of the bar.

BARS 369–371 are in three ♩-3-s. In these bars, the conductor leads, with the soloist playing the syncopations against the ♩-3-s in the clarinets.

BAR 372: In two.

---

1. Set up 3 ♩-3-.

BARS 373–378 This passage stays in two. Feel ⌞³⌟s in each ♩ throughout these bars, and think of the solo violin's ⌞³⌟s as:

[musical notation]

BAR 381: Even with more and more instruments joining the soloist's ⌞³⌟s, the conductor remains in two. It is helpful to think of each bar as a $\frac{6}{4}$.

BAR 399: The horns need a cutoff.

BAR 407: The conductor may be tempted to go into three for the benefit of the pizzicato, but remaining in two makes it easier to achieve a gradual accelerando.

7. Debussy, *Prelude to the Afternoon of a Faun*

BARS 1–4: The preparatory beat begins as the flutist is about to inhale. The flute solo is accompanied discreetly and marked with neutral beats. If the beats are small enough, each individual ♪ can be given. Count 1 in both the second and third bars should be clearly recognizable to the musicians. All ♪s are given within the subdivided three-beat pattern. The fifth and the eighth ♪ beats may contain a mini-ictus to prepare the beginning of the ♪ scale. Breathing places may require negotiation between the flutist and the conductor.

BAR 4: An enlarged downbeat is recommended. Its rebound is tentative, because the flutist may need to take a breath that could delay the timing of the second ♪ count. A strong, ictus-charged ♪ preparatory beat on count 3 will secure a precise woodwind quartet and harp entrance. The fourth beat has a strong ictus and a full rebound for the benefit of the accentuated horn. A gentle ictus for beat 7 helps to show the retonguing of the B by the horn.

BAR 5: The downbeat rebounds fully, serving as both a cutoff for the woodwinds and a preparatory beat for the third horn. The decrescendo in the horn is shown with the beginning of count 4. Beat 6 becomes the cutoff for the entire orchestra and sets up a bar of silence.

BARS 6–7: If the harp chord rings over into bar 6, the harpist can dampen the strings. Not visible to the audience, a small neutral beat in the pattern of six marks each ♪. Beat 6, the preparatory beat for the violins, is as gentle as possible to affirm a *pp*. The downbeat in bar 7 rebounds with a small ictus for the benefit of the accent in the first horn.

BAR 9: The lower strings' ♩s are cut off discreetly. Clarity of the $\frac{6}{8}$ pattern must prevail. Beat 2 is the preparatory beat for the third horn, and beat 4 is the preparatory beat for the pitch change in the first horn.

BAR 10: Beat 6, the preparatory beat for bar 11, cautiously brings back the solo flute, which now has harmonic support. A discreet cutoff is used for the first and third horns.

BARS 30–31: The easy, flowing ♪ motion ends with the upbeat to the fourth ♩. (the tenth ♪ count). It also serves as the cutoff for the strings. The tenth ♪ beat rebounds for the third horn tenuto, whereupon the conductor returns to the ♪ of the clarinet. This last beat of bar 30 contains a strong ictus for the next downbeat, which is orchestrated for the first clarinet, the *sfz* of the four horns, and the pizzicato in the basses. Staccato beats are utilized for the harp notes. A legato beat with circular motions is used for the off-the-string ♬s of the cellos. After bringing in the second violins and violas, beat 8 must serve as a preparatory beat for count 9 to help the cello and clarinets get off the tied-over notes from the previous count.

BAR 32: Depending on the tempo, the conductor may want to go into three (beating ♩s) or remain in ♪s. For greater security, the first ♩ can be subdivided, followed by ♩ beats. Conducting the clarinet melody with a legato motion would be natural, were it not for the entrance of the harp, the two pizzicato entrances in the strings, and the *sfz*, which require beats with an aggressive ictus.

BARS 49–50: Attention goes to the first horn, then to the second harp. The flutes can be left alone. A subdivided ♪ beat can be introduced at any time. The harmonics in the first harp tend to slow the tempo. The last ♪ in bar 50 must contain a strong ictus for the benefit of the four horns.

BARS 51–54: Either ♪ or ♩ beats are suitable. If this passage is conducted in ♩s, the rebound of the first ♩ beat must be assertive to help the change of harmony in the violins. Throughout these two bars, the violins (and the flutes and third horn in the bar 52) play on-the-beat ♩s. If the violins are not in sync with the conductor in bars 53 and 54, the second flute, first oboe, and first clarinet will have difficulty playing the offbeats. It may be safer to beat bar 54 in six. A ritardando at the end of that bar is recommended. It should be noted that the woodwinds, horns, and strings have differing dynamics.

BARS 55–78: The word *soutenu* suggests a slow ♩ beat. If the conductor leads the melody in the woodwinds without addressing the syncopation in the upper strings, successful coordination is possible. It is important that the rebound of the first beat function as an upbeat to an imaginary pulse on count 2. Musically this contradicts the ♩ of the tune; however, the strings need a clear basic pulse for rhythmic security.

BARS 59–60: Because of a tied-over ♪ in the upper strings, a subdivision of ♪s is recommended for count 2.

BARS 61–62: These bars are in full ♩ beats. The first bassoonist, joining the tune in bar 61, may have intonation and balance problems because of the passage's high range.

BARS 63–64: Although the conductor may want to associate with the melody in the strings, the focus should be on the winds and the harps. The double hemiolas (three 2/4 bars over two 3/4 bars and three ♩³s over two ♩s) need careful monitoring. The rhythmic meeting-places occur on counts 1 and 3 in bars 63 and 65 and on count 2 in bar 64.

BAR 63: The harp must group the ♪s into three (3 × 2) to match the woodwinds. If the conductor is in sync with the woodwinds and harp, the melodic line in the strings will fit in well. The basses and bassoons need little help in these bars.

BARS 79–81: These bars are conducted in four. If necessary, the first ♩ beat can be subdivided to help the harpist set the desired tempo by dividing the ♪s into two groups (2 × 3).

BARS 83–85 AND 90–91: Although the tempo gets faster here, it is better to beat these bars in ♪s to match the rhythmic architecture of the theme played by the first oboe. This beat makes it possible to emphasize the tenutos and *sfz*s. To establish a subito tempo change, the three horns group their ♪s into two (2 × 3). Throughout these bars, the strength of the ictus of the ♪ beat should be varied according to the desired musical effect or for ensemble precision. The sextuplets in the winds remain the rhythmic stabilizer; however, one must listen carefully to the introduction of a succession of ♪s in the strings in bar 85. Maintaining focus on the winds is important because the orchestration changes constantly, and different groups play on each count.

BAR 92: The violas unexpectedly take over the ♪ figuration. The second violins join them in the middle of the bar. During the triplets of the clarinets over counts 3 and 4, the regular ♪ beat is maintained. Full support and attention are given to the figuration in the middle strings. The clarinets fit in their triplets against the regular ♪ beat being given by the conductor. Unless the clarinetists are experienced in playing cross rhythms, the conductor may need to explain how this is done.

BAR 93: The ♩ counts can be subdivided into ♪s. Beginning with count 4, the second bar of the *retenu*, the beat shifts to subdivided triplet beats (three per ♩), further slowing the tempo. The conductor must scrupulously lead the ritardando with the clarinets, grouping their last six notes into three pairs of two. The first triplet downbeat must show a strong ictus as a preparatory beat for the first horn player's retonguing of the C♯. The last triplet beat serves as a preparatory beat with a small but strong ictus for the forthcoming antique cymbals and the low third and fourth horns. Attention must be paid to the rhythmic accuracy of the first horn, which shifts from *bouché* to natural.

BAR 94: This bar is conducted in twelve with extremely small motions as though it were a $\frac{12}{8}$ bar. It can also be conducted in four. The ♪s on both sides of the double bar are of the same duration; they connect the sections as a common denominator. By convention, the trills and tremolos are unmeasured.

BAR 95: The beat returns to a subdivided $\frac{4}{4}$ (eight ♪ beats) for the benefit of the solo violins and flutes. To secure the proper rhythmic relationship between bars 94 and 95, each ♪ in bar 95 must contain three s.

With the arrival of the second beat, the conductor may change to full ♩ beats and return to ♪ beats when the need arises.

BARS 96–97: These are conducted in ♩s, with each beat projecting either an inner three for the first and second flutes and first oboe or an inner two for the clarinets, solo violins, and solo cello, depending on which group the conductor chooses to address. If subdivision becomes necessary, the conductor should go with the majority and choose the five musicians playing regular ♪s over the three musicians who are playing triplets. Both ♩s on count 4 should be subdivided into two ♪s.

BAR 99: Counts 1 and 2 are conducted in ♩s. Subdivision begins on count 3 (two ♪s per ♩). The inner $\overset{\text{♪}}{\underset{6}{\rule{1em}{0.4pt}}}$s cannot be ignored. They continue throughout this bar and last until the return to the $\frac{12}{8}$ in the next bar.[2]

BARS 100–101 are in twelve ♪ beats. A $\frac{12}{8}$ ♪ preparatory beat is necessary for the instruments that change harmony on count 4.

BAR 102: This bar is conducted in nine ♪s or in three ♩.s.

BARS 103–105: These move in three ♩. beats. The main line is carried by the first flute and first oboe. The top voice of the accompanying chords in the rest of the orchestra evolves into a countermelody in bar 105.

BAR 104: Subdivision (in ♪s) of the last beat on count 3 is recommended.

BAR 105: The majority of the musicians who play the ascending top line (two solo violins, tutti first violins, and cello) are moving in a $\frac{3}{4}$, which is subdivided into six. The first flute and first oboe remain in $\frac{9}{8}$. More musicians are playing in $\frac{3}{4}$, so it is logical to focus on them and leave the two woodwinds alone to fit their three notes against the duplet ♪s on counts 1 and 3. The *très retenu* in this bar, however, is easier to achieve when the conductor remains with the fastest rhythmic unit, the ♪ of the $\frac{9}{8}$ bar played by the first flute and first oboe. Bars 105 and 106 are connected by a common

---

2. $\overset{\text{♪}}{\underset{6}{\rule{1em}{0.4pt}}}$ in $\frac{4}{4}$ bar; ♪ in $\frac{12}{8}$ bar.

denominator: the ♪ of the 9/8 bar and the 𝅘𝅥𝅮 of the 𝅘𝅥𝅮 in the harp are of the same duration.

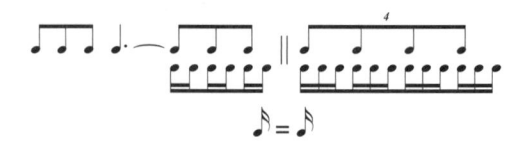

BAR 106: This bar is conducted in eight 𝅘𝅥𝅮 notes (subdivided into 4), each containing three 𝅘𝅥𝅮s.

The horns' rhythmic notation can be thought of as follows:

BARS 105–107

BARS 107–110: This passage returns to a twelve-♪ beat (two ♪s for each), until the end of the piece. In bar 107 the horns command attention. There should be small but full rebound ♪s for counts 4, 5, 10, and 11. The rebounds serve as double preparatory beats. Beats 5 and 11 contain a discreet but firm ictus for the purpose of moving the horns along. Preparatory beats are needed for the antique cymbal and harp harmonics and for the final pizzicatos. Some conductors let the last pizzicato ring and hold the flutes for a few beats longer than their written notation to effect a gradual fading away.

8. Bartók, *Concerto for Orchestra,* First Movement (Introduzione)—Andante non troppo and Allegro vivace

BAR 1: A most delicate preparatory beat with no ictus is given for the lower strings. Focus is on the basses. With the exception of the preparatory beat for each change of pitch, the beats are small and reflect the sustained notes.

BARS 3 AND 4: These bars can be beaten in three half notes without showing a three pattern (hemiola). Each half note receives a ♩ preparatory beat with a barely visible rebound, followed by a larger preparatory beat for the next half note. The conductor must insist on legato playing with no crescendo. Dictating is effective for this beginning section. (See the section in chapter 1 on dictating.)

BARS 6–9: The preparatory beats for each entrance or pitch change are without ictus.

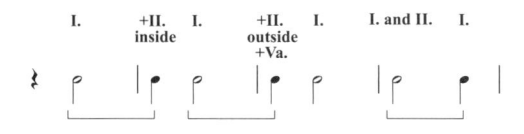

This *pp* section should be conducted with small but clear patterns.

BAR 10: The downbeat should contain an inner feeling of three ♪s to help the flutist enter with even and steady ♪s. The inner rhythmic division is 3 × 2 ♪s.

BAR 11: One cutoff is given for the flutes, first violins, and violas, then another one for the lower strings. This second cutoff will also serve as a preparatory beat for the cellos and basses in the next bar.

BARS 22–33: Some conductors add a C♯ and a low D♯ for the basses. The conductor must also decide how much of a crescendo is appropriate. If there has been no crescendo before the beginning of this phrase, the crescendo should not go beyond *mf*. A sudden build-up is created by the accelerando, the ascending pitches, and the addition of the violas to the texture. The flute solo is led with small beats in the $\frac{3}{4}$ pattern.

BAR 34: The first beat is subdivided. The second ♪ beat stops without rebound to show the interruption of the flute line and serves as a cutoff for the violins. Count 3 should function as a cutoff for the violas and cellos.

BARS 35–46: The preparatory beat is without ictus. The rebound of beat 1 moves to the second count with clarity and conviction; otherwise, the tempo will lose momentum. When divisi is required, ensemble problems occur; focusing on the inside players steadies the rhythm. The beat must communicate a sustained *pp*. However, in spite of the *pp* dynamic level, a preparatory beat with a strong ictus is given to ensure a precise entrance for the trumpets. The rebound on count 1 is barely visible, as is the beat on count 2. A strong ictus is used again on count 3 for the trumpets.

BAR 47: The first trombone must be cued without ictus to ensure a smooth entrance. The second trumpet runs out of pitches at the bottom of its range, so the first trombone takes over. A left-hand signal secures the *p* level.

BAR 51: In order to create a sudden, explosive *f* entrance, the upbeat to this bar is one *f* ♪ in duration. The duration of a *f* ♩ upbeat would weaken the surprise of the downbeat *f* entrance. Although this section has a legato feeling, the instrumentation requires strong ictuses for almost all the beats. The beats that include the ♩.s and ♩s should not rebound. These beats stop until a preparatory beat is given for the following count; however, the sustaining of the notes must be projected strongly.

BAR 63: At the beginning of the bar, the dynamic level drops to *mf*; the tempo and dynamics increase steadily thereafter. The "Morse code" punctuations in the trumpets should dominate.

BARS 63–75: The bar phrasing here is 22333.

BAR 70: From here on the bars are conducted in one.

BAR 75: This bar can be conducted in small but powerful ♩s with no rebound on count 3. Another possibility is to conduct the bar as though the rhythm is a ♩ followed by a ♩. After a split-second stop on beat 3, an ♪ or ♩ upbeat is given.

BARS 76–89: The bar phrases are 332-332-3333-3333. The oboes and clarinets join the melody periodically, while the horns and bassoons double the lower strings. Each rebound must serve as a preparatory beat for the following bar.

BAR 90: This bar is generally played *doppio movimento* (♪ = ♩).

BARS 92–95: Use ♩ and ♪ beats for bars 92 and 93 for the benefit of the tuba, cellos, and basses. In bar 93, on the third ♪, the beat stops without rebound. A ♩ beat is given for bar 95.

BARS 149–153: The *poco a poco più* moves into the *tranquillo* in an organic fashion. Each bar is slower than the previous one. (A "Rorschach" mirroring occurs in bars 149–150 and 151–152).

BAR 154: Under no circumstances should the oboe slow down in this $\frac{4}{8}$ bar. Often the E ♩ is stretched a bit, but this is unnecessary because the elongation is written out.

BAR 157: The conductor needs to be in touch with the harpist throughout this section. Note the *distinto* marking.

BARS 192–197: The unusual bowing request of *punta d'arco* for the ten solo violins often causes a slowdown.

BARS 206–207: A full rebound beat in bar 205 serves as a preparation to the downbeat of bar 206. This helps the second violins to get off the tied-over ♪. The ritardando is controlled by the second violins. Bar 207 may be subdivided into three with very small nonrebound beats.

BAR 209: A clear ictus is needed for the benefit of the third flute, second clarinet, and first horn.

BAR 230: Beat 1 does not have a rebound. On count 2 an ♪ upbeat is given for the final G. Count 3 explodes into a strong preparatory beat for the entrance of the *f* violins.

BAR 271: This bar is beaten in three. There is no rebound on the third beat. After a split second, a smooth ♪ upbeat is given on count 3 for the first clarinet. Bars 272–310 are beaten in one.

BARS 311–312: These bars can be conducted as a hemiola in $\frac{3}{4}$ with the last ♩ equaling the ♩. of Tempo I. Thinking triplets in the ♩ upbeat to bar 313 sets up the rhythm.

BAR 396: The *Luftpause* emerges naturally because of the string crossing in the violins. No rebound should be given. With the entrance of the fifth, a ♩ upbeat with a slight ictus is given for the third and fourth horns, harp, and violins.

BAR 456: This bar can be a problem because the leadership in the violins is taken over by the third stand of the first violins. The outside player is responsible for leading the remaining three first violinists and the four second violinists unless the principal second violinist takes over. Because they have the smallest rhythmic unit, the players on the first and second stands of the first violins must listen to the players in the back when all join the ♪ figure at the end of the sustained C♯. Some conductors switch parts and have the first and second stands of the first violins play the ♪s. The sustained C♯ is played by the third and fourth stands.

BARS 470–487: The ritardando begins in bar 470 and concludes at the end of bar 475, at which point the tempo gradually begins to accelerate until Tempo I is reached.

Often bar 475, the end of the phrase, slows down below ♩ = 60 and continues with a tempo much slower than the one notated. As the *con sordino* first horn doubles the bass line, it tends to slow down. Except in bars 470, 471, 474, and 475, attention goes to the bass line.

BARS 494–508: The brasses, with their irregular entrances, should be rehearsed separately.

BARS 494–END: The bar phrasings are 332-332-232-232-5×3-6×3-2×3.

9. Copland, *Appalachian Spring* Suite

PAGE 20, SIX BARS BEFORE REHEARSAL NUMBER 16: This passage is conducted in two or four. The cue pattern is ⁴□³ ²¹. Each ♩ should show the tenuto. In the fifth bar before rehearsal number 16, the beat stops on the fourth ♩ with no rebound. The silent bar is conducted lightly.

The next cue pattern is ⁴□² ⁽³⁾¹. In the second bar before rehearsal number 16, the beat stops on the second ♩ with no rebound. A barely visible third beat is given before an ictusless upbeat on count 4 brings back the first flute. The beat stops on count 2; counts 3 and 4 are not conducted. It is important to bring out the three dynamic levels.

The upbeat to rehearsal number 16 should contain a strong ictus for the benefit of the first trombone and harp. The second beat stops without rebound. On count 3, a preparatory beat brings in the next bar.

In the third bar the conductor's attention goes to the second bassoon until the first trombone takes over again in the fifth bar after rehearsal number 16. In the seventh bar a cue must be given for the second clarinet, which has not played for twenty-six bars. There is a common denominator at rehearsal number 17.

At rehearsal number 17 a clear downbeat must be given for the benefit of all the musicians who are not playing. In the third bar after 17, the last ♩ is divided mentally into two ♪s. The ♪ becomes the new ♩ of the *a tempo primo* section. Attention shifts to the first trombone and harp. At rehearsal number 18 the downbeat stops, then moves to beat 2, which serves as an upbeat for the first oboe.

On the second count in the sixth bar after rehearsal number 18, the conductor mentally divides the second ♩ into three ♪s. As the "Slower" section begins, the first ♩ of the ¾ bar is mentally divided into four ♪s, making the ♪ and the ♪ a common denominator (♪³ vs. ♪).

PAGE 28: At rehearsal number 26 the second bassoon and viola need all the attention.

PAGE 45, 1 BAR BEFORE REHEARSAL NUMBER 37: Because the accelerando from ♩=132 to ♩=184 takes place in the space of a single bar, the conductor may want to begin it earlier.

With the ♩ beat going beyond 150 very quickly, it is helpful to go into ¢ one and a half bars before the ¢ Presto begins. The shift to ¢ can begin after the violas' *sfz*. The first ♩ is subdivided. The second half of the bar is in one. The musicians who do not play at this point may easily mistake the first full ¢ bar at 1 bar before rehearsal number 37 for the beginning of the Presto and at a later time reenter a bar too soon. Announcing the change before rehearsing this section will eliminate this possible problem.

The chapter on the common denominator applies to page 63, 1 bar before rehearsal number 50 and 2 bars after rehearsal number 50.

10. Tchaikovsky, *Romeo and Juliet* Fantasy-Overture

BAR 1: Two ♩ preparatory beats are given on counts 3 and 4, the first with no ictus and the second with a moderately strong ictus for the benefit of the two bassoons.

There are two alternatives for bars 1 and 2. One is to conduct in straightforward ¢. The other is to stop at the downward motion of each half note and continue at the next quarter note count, with both an upbeat to each following ♩.

BAR 3: A ♩ beat is given, followed by two ♩ beats.

BAR 4: A four-beat pattern is given for the benefit of showing the —— and cutoff. A subdivided ¢ is possible as well.

BAR 5: This bar is conducted in four.

BAR 6: This bar is in ¢.

BARS 7–8: The downbeat serves as a cutoff and stops to emphasize the silence. On the second count a ♩ preparatory beat is given for the B minor chord. Continue in ♩ beats.

BARS 9–10: These bars are in ¢.

BAR 11: This bar begins in four. The rebound of the downbeat ♩ serves as the cutoff for the C♯ chord, and beat 2 becomes an upbeat for the ♩ in the lower strings. From the second ♩ of this bar until bar 21, it is best to beat in ¢. A clear distinction should be made between the accentuated and nonaccentuated ♩s. The preparatory beat for the two horns requires a strong ictus.

BARS 15 AND 19: If a break before the F♯ of the first violins and the A of the cellos and basses is desired, the downbeat stops without a rebound. A push-away motion on the second ♩ count serves as both a cutoff for all strings and horns and a preparatory beat for the first violins and the lower strings respectively.

BARS 19–20: The conductor gives ♩ upbeats for each ♩ without rebound. This makes it possible to take time.

BAR 21: This bar begins in four for the cellos, then goes into two when attention shifts to the woodwinds.

BAR 27: The second half of this bar is subdivided, with the last ♩ in the bar containing a strong ictus for the double reeds and horns in bar 28.

BAR 28: Conducting in four reflects the harp's ♩ motion.

BAR 29: A strong ictus on beat 4 helps to create a *Luftpause* before the next phrase and will assist the double reeds and horns in entering securely in bar 30.

BAR 30: This bar returns to ¢ with no rebound on the downbeat. The beat simply stops. In the second half of the bar, a gentle ♩ pickup is given for the flutes.

BAR 31: As in bar 27, the second half of this bar is subdivided, with the last ♩ containing a strong ictus for the benefit of the double reeds and horns in bar 32.

BARS 32–33: Similar to bars 28–29.

BARS 34–35: Similar to bars 30–31. In spite of the *pp* dynamic level, a strong preparatory beat must be given for bar 34. Achieving precision in entrances is difficult for the winds when the dynamic level is *p* or softer.

BAR 36: Similar to bar 28.

BAR 76: After resting for seventy-five bars, the timpanist is cued for the first entrance.

BARS 78–85: These bars are in ¢. ⌒. The two ♩s must be indicated in bars 80, 81, 84, and 85. The second ♩ stops for a split second to show the written-out silence. A ♩ upbeat is given for the next bar.

BARS 86–95: These bars are in two. When practical, subdivided ♩s, preferably small beats with no rebound, should be given.

BARS 97–108: These bars are in ¢. The cuing patterns are:

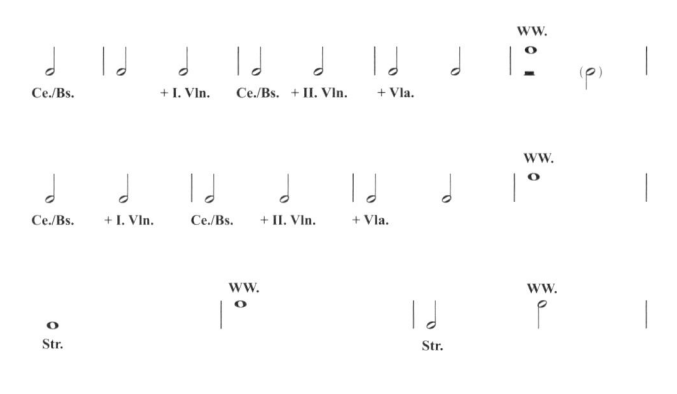

BAR 101: There is no rebound here.

BARS 105–107: The downbeat of each 𝅝 stops. The beat continues on the second count with a preparatory beat for either the woodwinds or the strings. The ictus varies significantly: no ictus is necessary for the strings, but a strong one is required for the woodwinds.

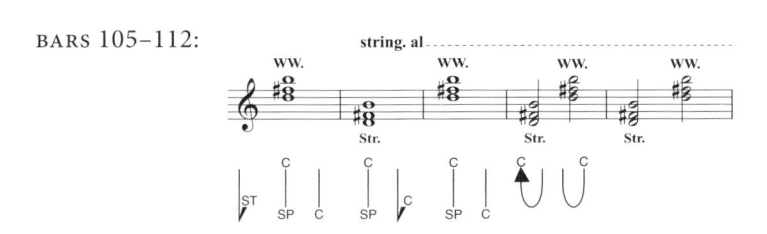

BARS 105–112:

[musical notation excerpt]

The stringendo causes the 𝅗𝅥 to reach the 𝅘𝅥 speed of the Allegro giusto (𝅗𝅥 = 𝅘𝅥).

BAR 112: This bar is in four. The horns and timpani are cued.

BARS 112–114: Here, count 2 always stops. No rebound is given to show the 𝄼 pause. Beating resumes on count 3.

BAR 115: It is recommended that the scales be played *f*, while the chords are reduced to *mf*.

BARS 122–143: Focus remains with the first violins and woodwinds [rhythmic figure] figure. The syncopations are ignored, and attention is given to each 𝅘𝅥 pulse.

BARS 143–147: These five bars can be regrouped rhythmically. The musically realized fencing strikes become faster and faster.

[musical notation excerpt]

No pattern should be revealed. Listening focuses on the [rhythmic figure] figure.

BARS 164–175: The first half of each bar is in 𝅘𝅥s; the second half is in 𝅗𝅥s. The last 𝅘𝅥 in each bar, played by the bassoons, should be reflected in the beat with a minimal non-rebound subdivision.

BARS 176–183: These bars are in 𝅗𝅥s except for bars 177 and 179, where the first half of the bar is beaten in two 𝅘𝅥s. A strong ictus is needed for the horns.

BARS 212, 387–388, AND 434–435: These bars are in four.

BARS 280–284: These bars are in four. Attention goes to the strings. Beat in two when addressing the horns.

BARS 285–292: These are in ¢. Each ♩ should be shown with small subdivisions.

BARS 463–466: In order to help the woodwinds and strings get off the tied-over ♩ ♪ (♩ ♬) , the second beat must lead to the third beat as though it were an upbeat. This is illustrated in the following example of Beethoven's Symphony no. 5, first movement, bars 1–2.

BARS 467 TO 470: The conductor must focus on the violins, violas, cellos, and single reeds. Each ♩ rebounds strongly. The rest of the orchestra, especially the timpani, cymbals, and bass drum, should be left on their own.

BARS 494–503: This passage is in two, *doppio movimento:* ♩ = ♩.. The ♩s are conducted with small beats in bars 499 and 502, including the upbeats. From bar 504 back to $\frac{4}{4}$.

BARS 519–END: After the first count conduct four $\frac{2}{4}$ bars and one $\frac{3}{4}$ bar:

BAR 518: This bar begins with a cutoff of the ♩ downbeat. Immediately thereafter, indicate the *p* dynamic marking and continue with small gestures for the timpani. Following this, expand into full ♩s showing the crescendo. In bar 519 the first count turns into a $\frac{1}{4}$ bar. An upbeat is given for the *ff* (2♪ chord) with no rebound. In the second $\frac{2}{4}$ bar and the identical bar after the tacet bar, the downbeat moves to the second count with the intensity of a crescendo. The second beat uses a small but powerful subdivision for the benefit of the offbeat ♪. It should not have a rebound. The tacet bar between those two bars is not conducted. In the second half a full preparatory beat is given for the next bar.

290   THE SCORE, THE ORCHESTRA, AND THE CONDUCTOR

The following examples show scores marked for study purposes.

Bartók, *Concerto for Orchestra*, first movement, bars 264–267

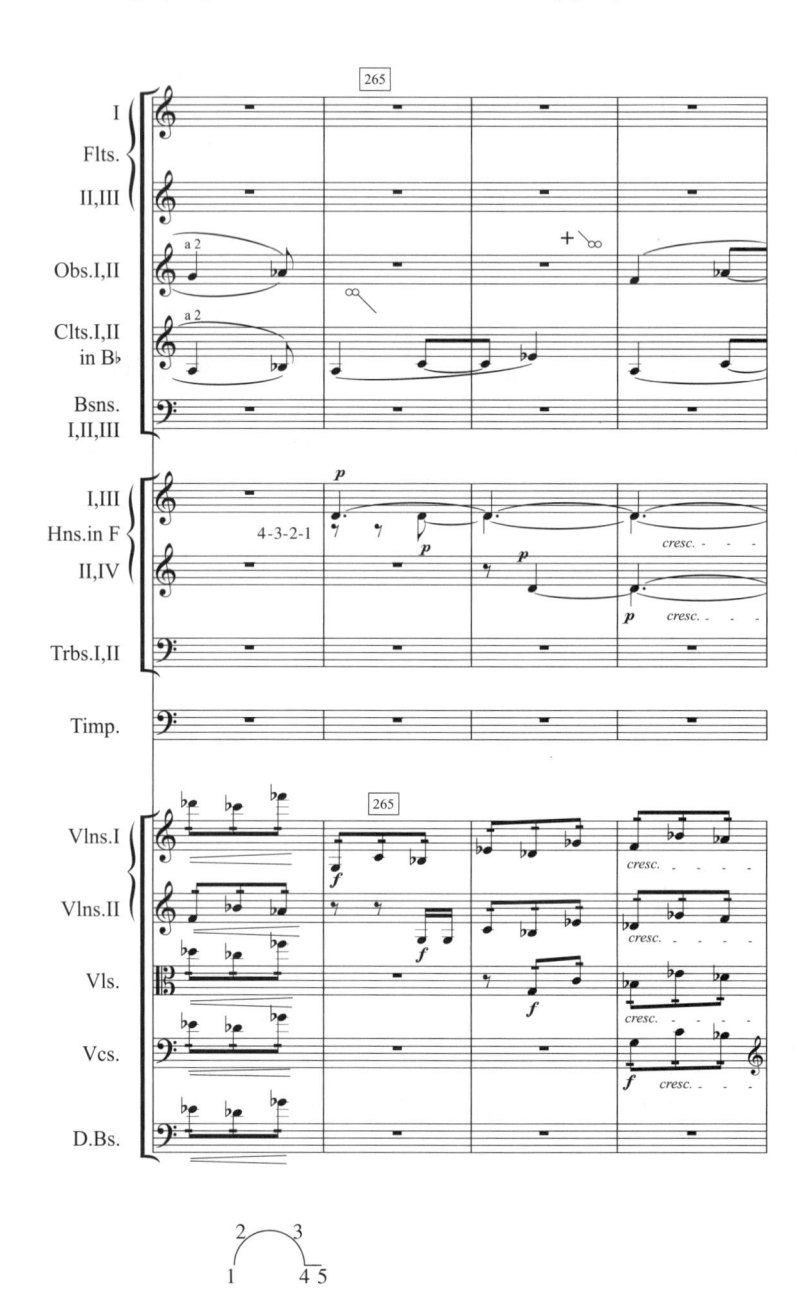

Bartók, *Concerto for Orchestra*, first movement, bars 268–271

Bartók, *Concerto for Orchestra*, first movement, bars 465–469

Bartók, *Concerto for Orchestra*, first movement, bars 470–474

Bartók, *Concerto for Orchestra,* first movement, bars 475–479

Bartók, *Concerto for Orchestra*, first movement, bars 480–484

Bartók, *Concerto for Orchestra*, first movement, bars 503–506

Bartók, *Concerto for Orchestra*, first movement, bars 507–510

Berlioz,
Symphonie fantastique,
first movement,
bars 1–2

Berlioz,
Symphonie fantastique,
first movement,
bars 7–10

After a conductor studies the score in depth and makes decisions about the course of each bar, the composer's tempo markings, dynamics, and articulations and the conductor's markings of cues, patterns, phrases, and conducting symbols become absorbed and integrated into an overall view and understanding of the composition.

CHAPTER SEVEN

Special Techniques

A. ACCOMPANYING

The orchestral accompaniment to a concerto or aria is an integral part of the composition. A soloist and conductor may differ about tempo, articulation, mood, and overall concept, but hopefully they will be able to coordinate their views amicably. If they cannot agree, controversial negotiations should take place in private, not in front of the orchestra. Concertos and arias were written as vehicles for soloists, sometimes particular performers; therefore, soloists have the final word if disagreements persist, and the conductor must honor their artistic vision unconditionally.

Tempos are set by the soloist, and any requested adjustments, whether technical or musical, are incorporated by the conductor without resistance. If the artist asks for a tutti in a different tempo, or particular phrasings or articulations, the conductor agrees. The soloist may also specify the degree of ritardando into the traditional $^6_4$ chord before the cadenza.

During rehearsals and performances, the conductor focuses on the soloist and concentrates on the rhythmic outline of the solo part, synchronizing it with the ongoing pulse in the rest of the orchestra.

Beethoven, Piano Concerto no. 4, first movement, bars 243–244

The conductor will assume leadership when the main material is in the orchestra and the soloist is assigned ornamental figures.

Rachmaninoff, *Rhapsody on a Theme of Paganini,* var. XI, 2 and 3 bars after rehearsal no. 31

(Cue #2 includes string cutoff)

Orchestra entrances following a cadenza can be hazardous; they require careful listening and collaboration with the soloist. Rather than relying on a written-out cue of the last few bars, the conductor should request a copy of the complete cadenza from the soloist. The orchestra needs a warning gesture prior to the final cue. Organizing cadenza passages into rhythmic patterns or finding pitch reference points helps the conductor to bring the orchestra in at the correct moment.

Liszt, *Totentanz*, bar 15

When the cadenza ends with free, unmeasured musical material, some soloists signal a preparatory beat to the conductor, who then cues the orchestra; other soloists decline the responsibility for cuing. The preparatory beat must be timed so that the orchestra reenters the moment the cadenza concludes. When accompanying a pianist, the conductor can watch the soloist's hands and begin the preparatory beat as the fingers move past a specific spot on the keyboard.

Special Techniques 303

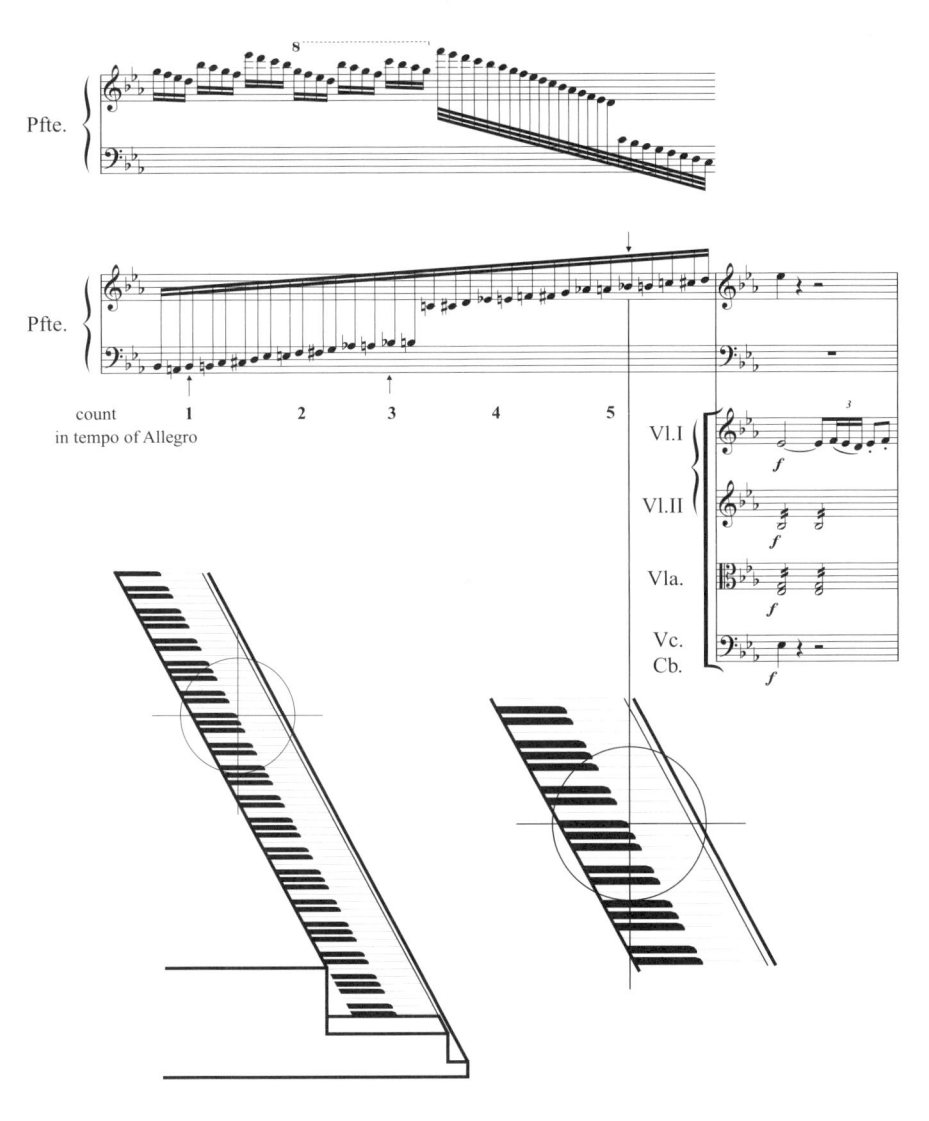

Beethoven, Piano Concerto no. 5, first movement, bars 372–373

count in tempo of Allegro

Beethoven, Piano Concerto no. 4, third movement, bars 155–159

Beethoven, Piano Concerto no. 4, third movement, bars 159–160

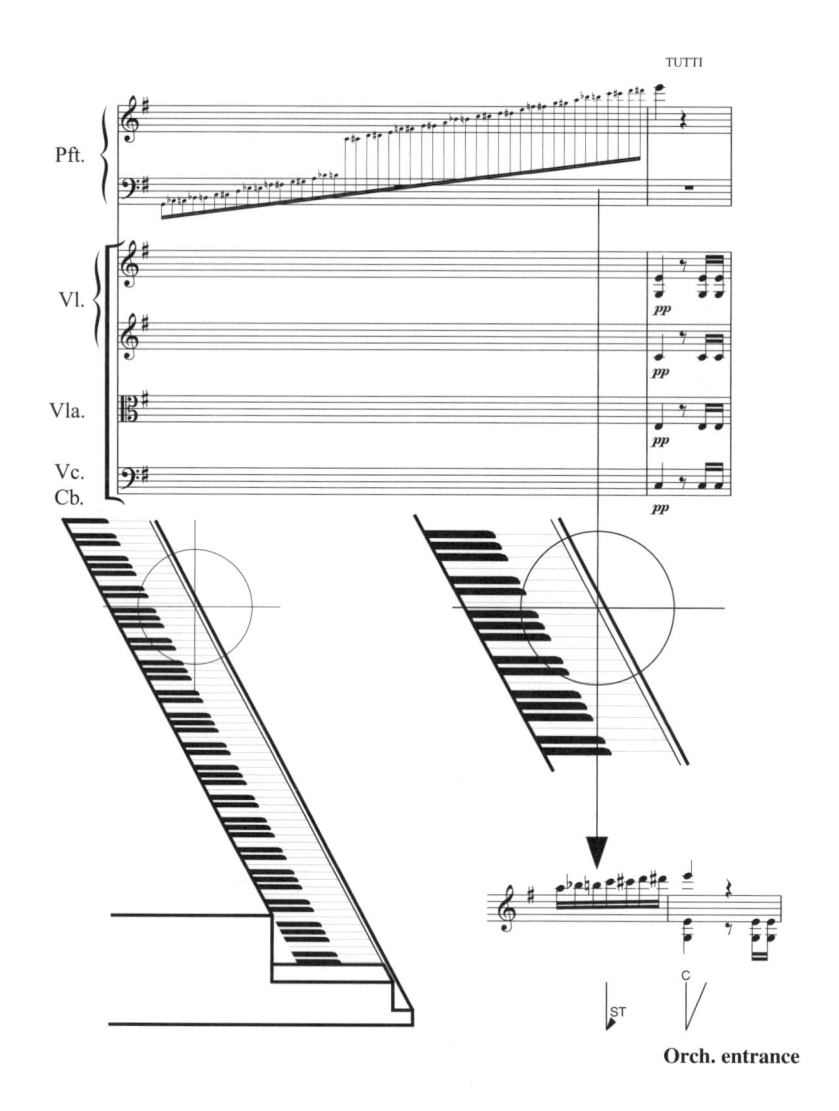

Pft.

Vl.

Vla.

Vc.
Cb.

TUTTI

Orch. entrance

Observing the bow or the left hand of string players as it shifts from string to string is helpful. A good example is the passage in Strauss's *Till Eulenspiegels lustige Streiche* where watching the shift from the E string to the A, D, and finally the G string helps determine when the concertmaster is about to reach the end of the scale.

R. Strauss, *Till Eulenspiegels lustige Streiche,* 12 bars before rehearsal no. 15

In piano concertos, fast improvisational passages in the right hand would be difficult to follow were it not for the regularity of the bass line in the left hand and the harmonic changes.

Chopin, Piano Concerto no. 1, first movement, bar 532

Chopin, Piano Concerto no. 1, second movement, bar 94

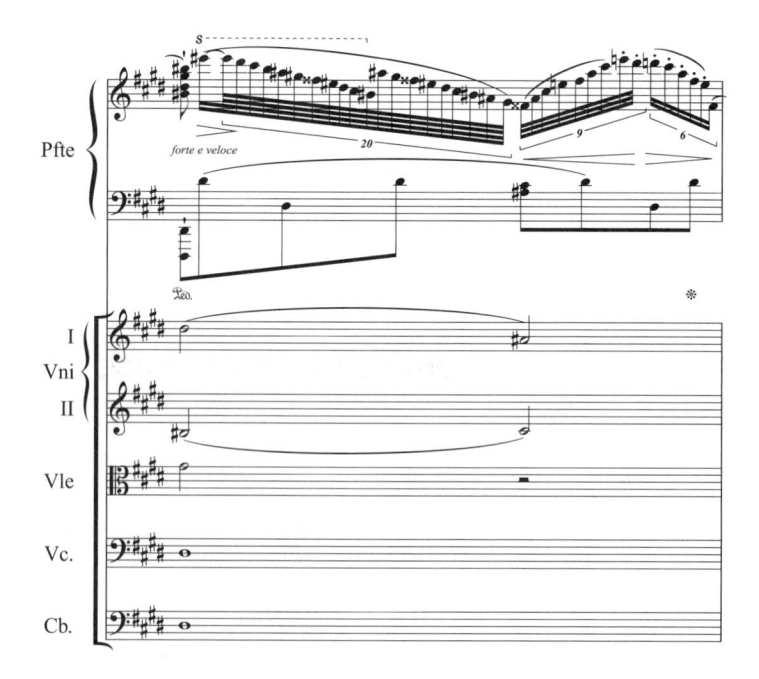

In fast passages certain audibly distinctive parts of a phrase (such as the beginning notes of runs or arpeggios) can serve as guidelines or markers. If they produce a recognizable and useful compound rhythm, the conductor may find it easier to accompany the soloist by following the compound rhythm rather than the individual notes.

Beethoven, Triple Concerto, first movement, bars 382–385

Beethoven, Piano Concerto no. 5, third movement, bar 325

Brahms, Piano Concerto no. 2, first movement, bar 256

When sustained chords in the orchestra serve as accompaniment for the soloist who is carrying the main musical material, the conductor's beat is neutral and without ictus. A preparatory beat is needed before a rhythmic shift, a change of harmony, or an entrance of one or more instruments.

Beethoven, Piano Concerto no. 5, second movement, bars 18–21

The addition of text facilitates accompanying singers, for the meaning and drive of the text give predictability to the flow of the musical line. On the other hand, challenges are often posed by vocal ornamentations and embellishments; unexpected breaks for breathing; complicated recitatives; ensemble problems in duets, trios, and other combinations; and difficult *colla voce* and *colla parte* passages.

Conductors must work with soloists prior to the first rehearsal with the orchestra. Some soloists prefer to go over only the few passages that have caused them problems in past performances. The conductor, however, may want to become better acquainted with the soloist's playing or singing and, if so, should insist on hearing the soloist play or talk through the entire work if necessary. The use of an accompanist during rehearsals with the soloist is not always desirable because focusing on the soloist may be more difficult. Communication problems with the accompanist may further complicate matters.

B. OPERATIC CONDUCTING

1. General Procedures

For many conductors, leading an operatic work seems daunting from both a musical and a technical standpoint; however, the increased rehearsal time offsets the complexities. In terms of study and conducting, operatic works differ little from their symphonic counterparts. Both disciplines utilize an orchestra of similar instrumentation, and their conductors share similar means of communication. The main differences are the addition of text and the formidable number of people involved in making the opera production come together. The beginning opera conductor learns quickly that the stage director, singers, and coaches have their own, often differing viewpoints about many aspects of the production.

As a primary obligation, the conductor keeps the text in mind throughout rehearsals and performances, remembering that each note, chord, and musical segment was composed and orchestrated in response to text. The opera conductor follows the singers and shares their dramatic and emotional involvement. Just as the orchestra conductor is conscious of each instrumentalist's struggle with the composer's demands, the opera conductor must be aware of each singer's strengths and limitations, anticipating where a singer may need special consideration, such as extra time for a breath, and making accommodations when musically justified (e.g., incorporating unwritten tempo changes, accelerandos, ritardandos, pauses, and dynamic changes).

The physical separation between pit and stage puts a great strain on ensemble precision and dynamic balance. To begin with, singers are separated from the conductor by a considerable distance, and furthermore, they often move about the stage continuously. They may sing facing away from the conductor or from other positions that make listening to one another very difficult. Also, the orchestral sound may engulf the conductor in the pit. Although lip reading and careful observation of body language help, nothing substitutes for hearing the vocal line clearly. And just as conductors have difficulty hearing singers, the singers may not be able to hear a balanced orchestral sound. Conductors can support the singers by emphasizing audible rhythmic elements in the orchestra and by giving special attention to rhythmic or melodic doublings of the vocal lines. Reinforcement of the bass line helps the singers and orchestra stay together.

Today, sophisticated amplification of the orchestral sound through backstage speakers is a helpful tool. Some conductors also utilize a small speaker next to the podium that discreetly amplifies the singers.

The natural flow and drive of the text are musically reinforced by the setting of the vocal line and its accompaniment. Proper accompaniment of the vocal line requires synchronization between singer and conductor. The singers' responses to signals parallel those of orchestra members: larger voices tend to have limited mobility and difficulty with excessively fast passages, extreme intervals, sudden changes in dynamics, and pitches in extreme registers. Their responses to signals may be delayed.

Rehearsals for the singers in an opera production are generally spread over relatively long periods of time. In the beginning, singers, coaches, and conductor work together closely, concentrating on the vocal line and the condensed orchestral version played on the piano. Tempos, dynamics, articulation, and dramatic characterization are negotiated between singers, coach, and conductor.

The next rehearsal period is primarily devoted to blocking[1] and staging, although musical rehearsals are interspersed with staging rehearsals at regular intervals. When the singers are focusing on dramatic interpretation and staging, the conductor's role is secondary. If possible, the conductor should attend some staging rehearsals, listen for musical errors, and give corrections or changes at the end of the rehearsal or at a separate time scheduled with the singers. Unless the conductor attends stage rehearsals regularly, cuing the singers, whose physical positions change often and rapidly, becomes a challenge. Marking the score as illustrated below is helpful for identifying positions of singers.

Verdi, *La Traviata*, act 2, no. 7, 2 bars after rehearsal no. 33

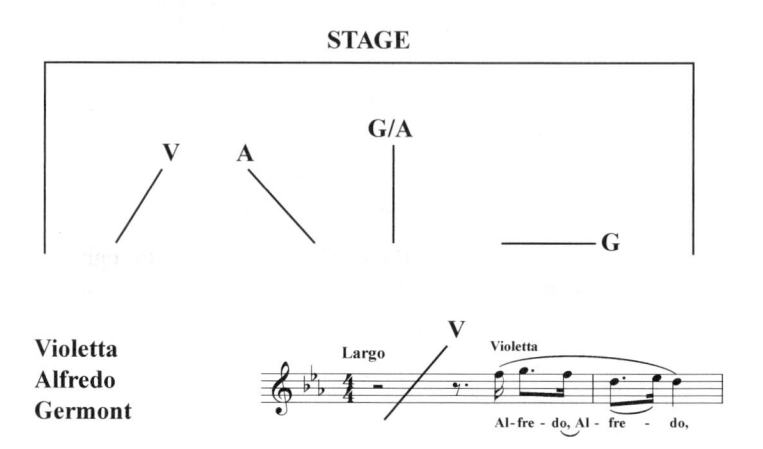

STAGE

V   A   G/A

G

Violetta
Alfredo
Germont

Largo   V Violetta

Al-fre - do, Al - fre - do,

Stage rehearsals should be interrupted by the conductor or coach/accompanist only when musical mistakes are repeated and may become habit-forming. During the final run-through and piano dress rehearsal, the conductor avoids stopping the music so that the singers can pace themselves and simulate a performance. Only emergency interruptions for major mishaps or complete musical breakdowns are made by the stage director at the piano dress rehearsal or by the conductor at the orchestra dress rehearsal. When minor musical breakdowns occur, the conductor attempts to repair the situation while the music continues. Mishaps can occur during performances; fixing them without stopping in rehearsals is good training.

The initial orchestra rehearsals are for orchestra alone; singers are added after the ensemble has been properly prepared. After a period of stage rehearsals and occasional musical rehearsals, a *Sitzprobe*[2] (or two) is highly recommended if it can be afforded.

In contrast to the three or four intensive orchestra rehearsals before a symphonic concert, the operatic forces work together for weeks before opening night. This extensive preparation should lead to the security achieved in chamber music or recitals;

---

1. Blocking is the choreography of the singer's physical whereabouts at any given moment in the opera.
2. A *Sitzprobe* is an orchestra rehearsal with the cast sitting onstage singing, but without any stage action involved.

however, in spite of lengthy rehearsal periods, conductors today often have to cope with singers who miss rehearsals because of other commitments and with cast changes in later performances.[3]

In a successful operatic work, the composer's musical language confirms and complements the intention of the librettist. The composer has made crucial decisions about characterization, timing, mood, and atmosphere through the setting of the vocal line and the accompaniment.

Because of the many variables in opera, arriving at artistic solutions that do justice to the librettist and, above all, to the composer is not easy. Careful study of the libretto and score resolves most issues. When stage director and conductor disagree, conflicts should be worked out before the first rehearsal. Some stage directors embrace the librettist's and composer's artistic vision. Others change the place of action or shift the entire work to a different time period. When a contemporary translation is added, the original intent of librettist and composer is often left far behind.

A case can be made for performing opera in the language of the audience rather than the original language. The problem is finding a decent translation where words, vocal line, and accompaniment retain their original fusion. Although controversial, the use of supertitles, projected above the stage or on the back of seats, is becoming increasingly popular; however, depending on the seat location and the physical whereabouts of the supertitles, the listener inevitably misses some of the proceedings on stage.

2. Casting an Opera

Generally, the music director or conductor casts the singers in collaboration with the stage director and the general manager. In small opera companies the conductor or music director alone may be responsible for the casting. Both conductor and stage director will have conceived a specific dramatic concept for the characters and will attempt to find singers who best approximate their combined image. Evaluations of singers are based on several attributes:

- the sound of the voice (color, timbre, beauty)
- the level of vocal technique (agility, dynamic variety, intonation)
- vocal evenness and flexibility
- range (reliability of top and bottom notes)
- the size of the voice
- good diction (enunciation and projection)
- understanding of the text
- skill in languages

---

3. The star system and the ease with which singers can commute between opera houses can lead to unrehearsed performances, often jeopardizing finely tuned ensemble work.

- rhythm (accuracy and steadiness)
- articulation and dynamics (observing the composer's instructions)
- the ability to act and communicate the meaning and emotions of the text

Both conductor and stage director want singers who are able to fit into and complement a unified and balanced cast. If several singers auditioning for the same role fulfill the vocal and musical requirements equally well, the conductor may defer to the stage director. Generally, final casting decisions are made by the general director or general manager, who takes into account the singer's fee, career history, personal reliability, reported musical accuracy, collaboration and cancellation record, and box-office appeal.

The artistic complexities and responsibilities are manifold in opera. A singer who, for instance, demonstrates a fine voice and full range during a short audition may be unable to sing the entire role or may lack the vocal stamina to survive a highly concentrated rehearsal period with two or three performances following opening night. Replacing a singer on short notice can be a major problem unless a double cast or cover cast is in place.

3. Voice Categorization

Voice categorization reflects a sorting basically adhered to in the United States and Europe, though some minor disagreements persist between the two. The categorization, called the *Fach* system, is based on range, volume, vocal demands, and type of role and is accepted as a guideline by composers, singers, directors, and managers. Although singers sometimes fluctuate between two categories (as do composers in their vocal writing), most singers remain in one category. Innate vocal ability or training may extend a voice outside a particular category, and some roles may not fit precisely into a *Fach* because the composer has written the part for a specific singer with specialized vocal skills.

Sometimes singers audition for a role outside their *Fach*. When casting, the conductor must be certain that the singers are firmly established by prior work in the *Fach* of the roles for which they audition. Often audition arias, even those taken from the opera to be performed, do not reveal whether or not the singer can carry an entire role, because extremes in range and flexibility may occur in other parts of the score.[4] Conductors often ask singers to audition with those passages, score in hand if necessary. Recitatives or spoken dialogue may also be requested. If doubt remains about a singer's qualifications and suitability for a specific part, the singer should be recalled for a second audition.

Selecting soloists for oratorios or works for voice and orchestra is simpler than choosing opera singers because only the conductor is involved in the auditioning, and

---

4. For example, in Mozart's *Marriage of Figaro*, neither of Susanna's arias encompasses the range required in other sections of the opera.

because the audition arias generally include the most difficult vocal demands of the entire score. When challenging passages occur in parts other than arias (for example, the soprano part in Haydn's *Creation*), the conductor may ask to hear them at the audition.

4. Voice Charts

All charts of voice categorizations, ranges, volume, technical facility, and role identifications are approximations.

Classification of Female Voices

Fach (Other Names)	Range (approx.)	Volume	Agility
Dramatic Coloratura Soprano Hoher Sopran		Medium to Large	Good to Excellent
Lyric Coloratura Soprano Koloratursoubrette, Soprano leggiero, Hoher Sopran		Small to Medium	Excellent
Soubrette Light Soprano, Ingenue		Small to Medium	Excellent
Lyric Soprano Soprano Lirico, Ingenue		Medium	Good to Excellent
Spinto Soprano Jugendlich-Dramatischer Sopran, Zwischenfach		Medium to Large	Good
Dramatic Soprano Hoch Dramatischer Sopran, Soprano Drammatico		Large	Fair
Dramatic Mezzo-Soprano		Large	Fair
High Mezzo-Soprano Coloratura Mezzo-Soprano, Lyric Mezzo		Medium to Large	Good to Excellent
Lyric Mezzo-Soprano Mezzo-Soprano		Medium to Large	Good
Pants Role (Mezzo-Soprano) Hosen Rolle, Trouser Role		Medium to Large	Good
Spielaltistin Komische Alte, Alto		Medium	Good to Fair
Alto		Medium to Large	Good
Contralto		Large	Fair

Female Voice Classification Overlap Chart

CS	**Dramatic Coloratura Soprano**	Lyric Coloratura Soprano Lyric Soprano Spinto Soprano
CS	**Lyric Coloratura Soprano**	Dramatic Coloratura Soubrette Lyric Soprano High Mezzo-Soprano
S	**Soubrette**	Lyric Soprano
S	**Lyric Soprano**	Soubrette Spinto Soprano Pants Roles
S	**Spinto Soprano**	Lyric Soprano Dramatic Soprano
S	**Dramatic Soprano**	Spinto Soprano Dramatic Mezzo-Soprano
M	**Dramatic Mezzo-Soprano**	Dramatic Soprano High Mezzo-Soprano Lyric Mezzo Soprano
M	**High Mezzo-Soprano**	Dramatic Mezzo-Sop. Lyric Mezzo-Soprano Pants Role
M	**Lyric Mezzo-Soprano**	Dramatic Mezzo-Sop. High Mezzo-Sop. Pants Role Spielaltistin Alto
M	**Pants Role (Mezzo-Soprano)**	High Mezzo-Soprano Lyric Mezzo-Soprano Spielaltistin Alto
A	**Spielaltistin**	Lyric Mezzo-Soprano Alto
A	**Alto**	Lyric Mezzo-Soprano Pants Role Spielaltistin Contralto
A	**Contralto**	Spielaltistin Alto

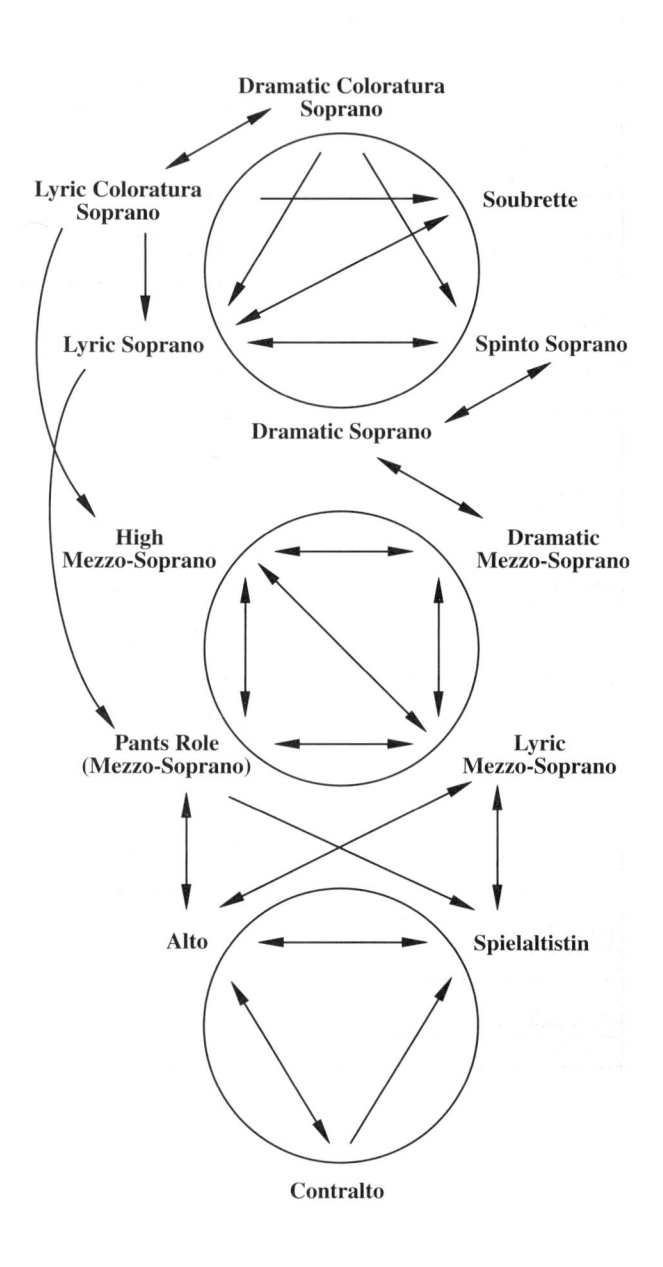

Classification of Male Voices

Fach (Other Names)	Range (approx.)	Volume	Agility
Buffo Tenor Spieltenor, Charakter Tenor		Medium to Small	Excellent
Lyric Tenor Mozart Tenor, Tenore di grazia, Irish Tenor, Hoher Tenor		Medium	Excellent
Italian Tenor Higher Tenor, Charakter Tenor		Medium to Large	Good
Spinto Tenor Jugendlicher Helden Tenor		Medium to Large	Fair
Helden Tenor Dramatic Tenor, Heroic Tenor		Large	Fair
Helden Baritone Dramatic Baritone, Heroic Baritone		Large	Fair
Italian Baritone Charakter Baritone, Hoher Baritone		Medium to Large	Fair to Good
Lyric Baritone Spiel Baritone, Lyrischer Baritone, Kavalier Baritone		Medium	Good
Baritone / Buffo Baritone Kavalier Baritone / Spiel Baritone / Hoher Baritone / Lyric Baritone		Medium	Good
Bass-Baritone Charakter Bass, Basso Cantante		Medium to Large	Good
Lyric Bass		Medium	Good
Basso Buffo Spielbass, Bass		Medium	Good
Dramatic Bass Schwerer Spielbass, Basso Profundo, Seriöser Bass, Schwerer Bass		Large	Fair

Male Voice Classification Overlap Chart

T	**Buffo Tenor**	Lyric Tenor
T	**Lyric Tenor**	Buffo Tenor Spinto Tenor Italian Tenor
T	**Italian Tenor**	Lyric Tenor Spinto Tenor Buffo Tenor
T	**Spinto Tenor**	Lyric Tenor Helden Tenor Italian Tenor
T	**Helden Tenor**	Spinto Tenor Helden Baritone
BAR	**Helden Baritone**	Helden Tenor Italian Baritone
BAR	**Italian Baritone**	Helden Baritone Lyric Baritone Bass-Baritone Baritone / Buffo Bar.
BAR	**Lyric Baritone**	Italian Baritone Bass-Baritone Baritone / Buffo Bar.
BAR	**Buffo Baritone**	Lyric Bass Bass-Baritone
BASS-BAR	**Bass-Baritone**	Basso Buffo Italian Baritone Lyric Baritone Lyric Bass Baritone / Buffo Bar.
BASS	**Lyric Bass**	Bass-Baritone Basso Buffo Dramatic Bass
BASS	**Basso Buffo**	Bass-Baritone Lyric Bass
BASS	**Dramatic Bass**	Basso Buffo Lyric Bass

---

5. The term *buffo* is put either before or after the voice categorization. Identification is determined by range, tessitura, and character.

	Voice	Agility*	Operatic Roles
CS	Dramatic Coloratura Soprano	EX	Queen, Norma, Lucia, Konstanze
CS	Lyric Coloratura Soprano	EX	Blondchen, Olympia, Zerbinetta
S	Soubrette	EX	Musette, Marzelline, Gretel
S	Lyric Soprano	VG	Pamina, Mimi, Liu, Lauretta
S	Spinto Soprano	G	Elsa, Agathe, Magda
S	Dramatic Soprano	L	Isolde, Turandot, Elektra
MS	Dramatic Mezzo-Soprano	L	Ortrud, Eboli, Amneris
MS	High Mezzo-Soprano	EX	Rosina, Cenerentola
MS	Lyric Mezzo-Soprano	VG	Carmen, Maddalena, Dorabella
MS	Pants Roles (Mezzo-Soprano)	G	Cherubino, Siebel, Orlofsky
A	Spielaltistin	L	Berta, Quickly, Marcellina
A	Alto (The term is mostly used in the Lieder and Oratorio repertory.)	G	
A	Contralto	L	Erda, Dalila, Principessa

	Voice	Agility*	Operatic Roles
T	Buffo Tenor	EX	Basilio, Vasek, Jacquino, Dr. Blind
T	Lyric Tenor	EX	Ottavio, Ferrando, Fenton, Belmonte
T	Italian Tenor	VG	Duke, Alfredo, Turiddo
T	Spinto Tenor	G	Cavaradossi, Max, Walther
T	Helden Tenor	L	Tristan, Siegfried, Peter Grimes
BAR	Helden Baritone	L	Wotan, Scarpia, Boris, Telramund
BAR	Italian Baritone	G	Germont, Marcello, Escamillo
BAR	Lyric Baritone	VG	Guglielmo, Papageno, Harlequin
BAR	Baritone / Buffo Baritone	VG	Alberich, Beckmesser, Sportin' Life
B/BAR	Bass-Baritone	G	Figaro, Don Giovanni, Horace Tabor
B	Lyric Bass	G	Schaunard, Commendatore, Simone
B	Basso Buffo	VG	Rocco, Osmin, Bartolo (Barber), Leoporello
B	Dramatic Bass	L	Philip II, Sarastro, Gurnemanz

* EX = Excellent
VG = Very Good
G = Good
L = Limited

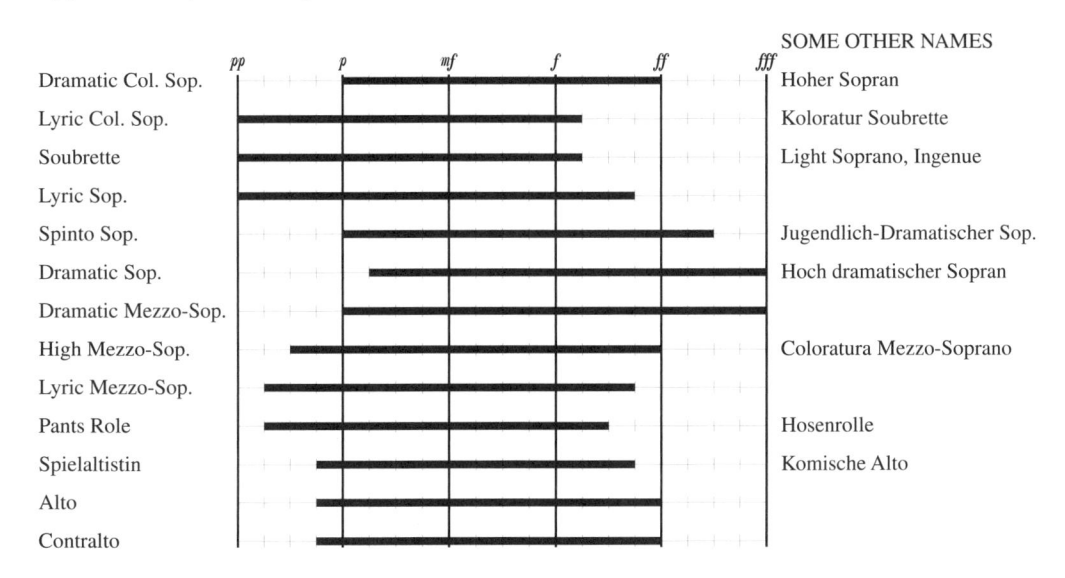

Approximate Dynamic Range—Female

Voice	Dynamic Range (pp – fff)	SOME OTHER NAMES
Dramatic Col. Sop.	p – ff	Hoher Sopran
Lyric Col. Sop.	pp – mf	Koloratur Soubrette
Soubrette	pp – mf	Light Soprano, Ingenue
Lyric Sop.	pp – ff	
Spinto Sop.	p – ff	Jugendlich-Dramatischer Sop.
Dramatic Sop.	p – ff	Hoch dramatischer Sopran
Dramatic Mezzo-Sop.	p – ff	
High Mezzo-Sop.	pp – ff	Coloratura Mezzo-Soprano
Lyric Mezzo-Sop.	pp – ff	
Pants Role	pp – f	Hosenrolle
Spielaltistin	pp – ff	Komische Alto
Alto	p – ff	
Contralto	p – ff	

Approximate Dynamic Range—Male

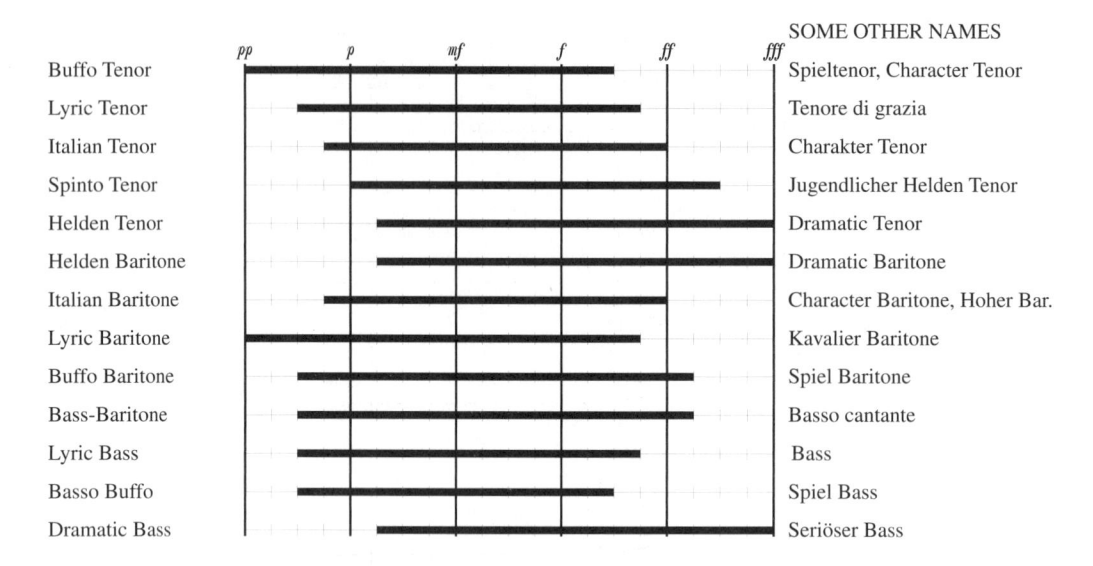

Voice Type	pp	p	mf	f	ff	fff	Some Other Names
Buffo Tenor		●━━━━━━━━━━━━━━━●					Spieltenor, Character Tenor
Lyric Tenor		●━━━━━━━━━●					Tenore di grazia
Italian Tenor		●━━━━━━━━━●					Charakter Tenor
Spinto Tenor		●━━━━━━━━━━━━━●					Jugendlicher Helden Tenor
Helden Tenor		●━━━━━━━━━━━━━●					Dramatic Tenor
Helden Baritone		●━━━━━━━━━━━━━●					Dramatic Baritone
Italian Baritone		●━━━━━━━━━━━━━━━●					Character Baritone, Hoher Bar.
Lyric Baritone	●━━━━━━━━━━━●						Kavalier Baritone
Buffo Baritone		●━━━━━━━━━━━●					Spiel Baritone
Bass-Baritone		●━━━━━━━━━━━●					Basso cantante
Lyric Bass		●━━━━━━━●					Bass
Basso Buffo		●━━━━━━━●					Spiel Bass
Dramatic Bass		●━━━━━━━━━●					Seriöser Bass

5. Opera Chart

During rehearsals and at performances, the opera conductor should have at hand a detailed layout of the work's musical numbers and sections.[6] Every aria, ensemble, and choral and orchestral section should be listed with corresponding page numbers for the piano-vocal and orchestral scores, as well as the name of each character, the first sentence of the text, and the duration, instrumentation, and setting of each number. The chart helps to give an overview of the participation of the cast, chorus, ballet, and orchestra members at a glance.

---

6. Similar charts can be created for oratorios or other works for orchestra, soloists, and chorus.

Title: Cosi Fan Tutte | Composer: W. A. Mozart | 1st perf.: 1/26/1790 Setting: Vienna | Others:

Location	Number	Vocal Score Page	Orch. Score Page	Duration	Form	Fiordiligi	Dorabella	Despina	Ferrando	Guglielmo	Don Alfonso	CHORUS	Harpsichord	Flute	Oboe	Clarinet	Bassoon	Horn	Trumpet	Trombone	Tuba	Timpani	Percussion	Harp	Keyboard	1st Violin	2nd Violin	Viola	Cello	Bass	First line
Bottega	1	5	1	5	Overture									1	2	2	2	2	2			1									
12 min		11	17	2	Trio				✓	✓	✓				2	2	2	2									La mia Dorabella
		17	23	1	Rec				✓	✓	✓		1														Fuor la spada
	2	18	24	1.5	Trio				✓	✓	✓			1			1										E la fede
		21	27	1	Rec				✓	✓	✓		1														Scioccherie
	3	25	29	2.15	Trio				✓	✓	✓				2		1	2				1					Una bella
Giardino	4	29	37	4.5	Duet	✓	✓								2	2	2	2									Ah guarda

Title: La Traviata				Composer: G. Verdi			1st perf.: 3/6/1853 Setting: Venice											Others:														First line
Location	Number	Vocal Score Page	Orch. Score Page	Duration	Form	Violetta	Alfredo	Germont	Annina	Flora	Gastone	Giuseppe	Douphol	Marchese	Dottore	Domestico	Comnision	CHORUS	Harpsichord	Flute	Oboe	Clarinet	Bassoon	Horn	Trumpet	Trombone	Tuba	Timpani	Percussion	Harp	Keyboard	1st Violin / 2nd Violin / Viola / Cello / Bass
Act I	1	1	1	3	Preludio															1	1	1	2	4								
Salotto	2	3	7	4	Intro	✓	✓			✓				✓				STB		2	2	1	2	4	2	3	1	1	1			Dell'invito
	2/3*	18	31	2.5	Brindisi	✓	✓			✓				✓						2	2	2	2	4	2	3	1	1	1			Libiamo
	2/4	29	48	2.5	Valzer	✓	✓			(✓)(✓)		(✓)		(✓)(✓)						1	2	2	2	2						Banda		Che è ciò?
	2/5	47	65	1.5	Stretta	✓	✓			✓		✓		✓				STB		2	2	2	2	4	2	3	1	1	1			Si ridesta
	3/6	58	80	1	Scena	✓																										E strano
	3/6	59	82	3.5	Aria	✓														1	2	2	2	2								Ah, fors'e
	3/6	64	89	4	Allegro	✓	(✓)													2	2	2	2	4	2	3	1					Follie!

*vocal score/orchestra score

Strings: active tacet

6. Recitative Conducting

a. Opera

In recitatives, whether accompanied by harpsichord or orchestra, the singer shapes the vocal line freely according to his or her interpretation of the text. The singer uses the score's rhythmic notation as a guideline but may change note values or tempos, ignore or prolong rests, add or omit ritardandos and accelerandos, and delete or change appoggiaturas. These alterations are acceptable when motivated by the text.

The two basic types of recitative are *recitativo secco,* which has keyboard accompaniment; and *recitativo accompagnato,* which has orchestral accompaniment.

If a keyboard instrument is accompanying, no conducting is necessary except at the end of a recitative as it leads into the orchestral entrance, usually with a dominant or dominant seventh chord or a V–I cadence. Here the conductor coordinates the resolution of the recitative with the entrance of the orchestra. The conductor may also be needed if a low string instrument doubles the voice line; however, when the vocal line and text are included in the string part, the continuo player can follow the singer without assistance from the conductor.

During a recitative, the vocal line is punctuated or interrupted by single or multiple chords of various durations or by short musical segments. In between them the singer is free from musical constrictions. At the beginning of unaccompanied passages or sustained chords, the conductor forges ahead through the tacet counts and bars using a neutral beat in the appropriate beat pattern, enlarging the first downbeat of each bar for the benefit of the orchestra, and stopping where the preparatory beat to the next orchestral entrance begins. There are three reasons for rapidly conducting through the tacet sections:

1. The conductor will be ready for the next chord change or orchestral entrance when the singer reaches that point.
2. To follow the freely interpreted vocal line is confusing to the orchestra musicians because the beat pattern will be unsteady.
3. Musicians who are not playing can verify the tacet bars.

Mozart, *The Marriage of Figaro,* act 4, no. 26, bars 7–10

In most recitatives the conductor decides on the duration of each chord. If the composer uses staccato signs for some chords, the unmarked ones are tenuto. The approximate duration of any chord is influenced by the basic tempo in which the recitative is written and the surrounding dramatic circumstances. A single tenuto chord is cut off with the rebound leading to the next count. Tempo indications for musical segments are strictly observed.

The traditional cadential chord (V or V^7) at the end of most recitatives is followed by the entrance of the orchestra. The timing depends on the dramatic pacing at the conclusion of the recitative, the musical character of the orchestral entrance, and the events happening on stage. If an actual break between two cadential chords (V–I) is desired, a left-hand cutoff is given, followed by a new preparatory beat for the final chord. If no break between the two chords is desired, the rebound of the first beat serves as a preparatory beat for the second chord. With only a short break between the two chords, the first beat stops at its conclusion, then continues with a strong ictus, using a push-away motion, which will be understood by the orchestra musicians as a quick break before the final chord. Should the final chord be sustained, the conductor does not rebound, but rather stops the beat before continuing.

---

7. Orchestra musicians appreciate seeing a larger upbeat to the first count of every bar and a larger downbeat motion.

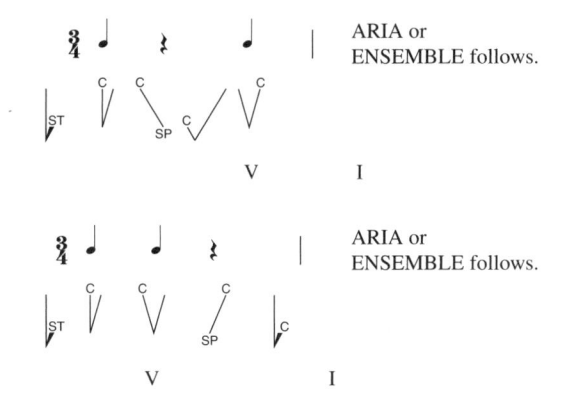

```
3/4  ♩  𝄽  ♩  |    ARIA or
                   ENSEMBLE follows.
 ST  C  C    C
  |  V  \  C / V
        SP  /
         V        I


3/4  ♩  ♩  𝄽  |    ARIA or
                   ENSEMBLE follows.
 ST  C  C    C
  |  V  V  /   |C
          SP
         V        I
```

Any musical insert or segment containing a measured pulse is cued with a preparatory beat to set the tempo. After the preparatory beat has been given, no last-second adjustments should be made. The preparatory beat establishes the tempo of the orchestral insert; therefore, the slightest hesitation to accommodate the singer will cause an unsteady tempo. The better choice is to establish a secure tempo, even if the orchestra is slightly out of sync with the singer when it enters.

Compositional circumstances determine whether one or two preparatory beats are necessary for *a tempo* musical inserts. The following example illustrates that, rather than stopping on count 2, a nondurational upbeat serves as a preparatory beat to count 3 and is followed by an assertive move to count 4. These steps establish the tempo of the rhythmic segment.

Mozart, *The Marriage of Figaro,* act 3, no. 19, bars 5–7

If a *p* string chord of unmeasured duration is to be cued in and the singer moves ahead faster than expected, the conductor can terminate the preparatory beat with a quick downbeat motion, pushing the orchestra to enter sooner. When a singer unexpectedly delays an entrance, the conductor stops in the middle of the preparatory beat and arrives at the downbeat with the singer; or, if there is time, the conductor renews the preparatory beat. This approach does not work if winds are involved, because they require a distinct preparatory beat.

In passages where several bars of singing are unaccompanied, the conductor usually marks each bar by lightly touching the score with the tip of the baton. In Puccini's *La Bohème,* where up to thirty bars pass without any orchestral participation, the conductor usually announces in rehearsal that one motion or one touch of the baton on the score represents a specific number of bars, so that all musicians know the bar to which the next preparatory beat will be addressed. The exactness of this information is especially important to musicians who have many tacet bars and need to keep track of their whereabouts within the work.

b. Sample Zigzag Way: Mozart, The Magic Flute

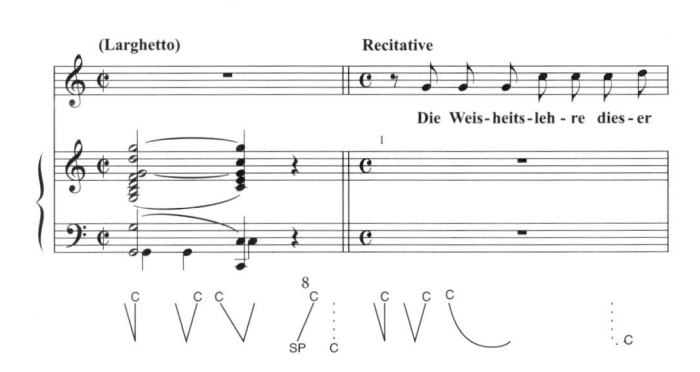

BAR PRIOR TO THE RECITATIVE: In this bar, the orchestral passage concludes with beat 4, which serves as a cutoff. With the arrival of the silence, the beat motion stops.
After a short pause the conductor moves calmly upward with a neutral beat.

BAR 1: The conductor continues to mark off counts 1 to 3. The motion continues with beat 4, which is unmeasured and moves slowly upward. Beat 4 must move high enough so that a sudden downbeat can be given if Tamino finishes his line sooner than anticipated.

BAR 2: As the singer reaches the syllable "Kna-," the conductor delivers a downbeat with a strong ictus that serves as a preparatory beat for the first chord on count 2. A preparatory beat for the second chord is given. Because no action takes place on count 4, beat 3 stops without rebound. Consider pulling back beat 3 to indicate the shortness of the C^6_5 chord. A mini-cutoff may also be used.

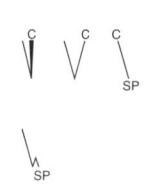

---

8. Cutoff motion.

After a short moment of rest, the conductor continues with beat 4 (unmeasured), moving slowly upward.

BAR 3: The conductor continues into count 1 in the third bar. Beat 2 is extended while the conductor waits for the singer to conclude the first sentence. The beat motion must continue on count 2 (unmeasured) (c) and change direction only when the singer reaches "gra-" on the arrival of count 3. Beat 3 becomes a preparatory beat for the next chord, which enters on count 4. Beat 4 rebounds quickly to deliver a preparatory beat for the following downbeat.

BAR 4: The downbeat stops. Use a pull-back motion or mini-cutoff to show the staccato.

The conductor then moves quickly through the pattern of count 2 in order to be ready for the next beat on count 3.

Beat 3 is the preparatory motion to count 4. The singer may deliver his line quickly; if so, the conductor must be ready to come in immediately with the next chord. The preparatory beat begins with the word "nun."

c. Oratorio

Technically, oratorio and opera conducting are alike; the conductor's approach toward the vocal line and the singer are the same, whether in a Verdi opera or a Haydn oratorio. In opera, rhythmic alterations of the vocal line are acceptable common practice; in contrast, the oratorio singer will rarely move beyond the notation in the score by changing durations of notes or rests for declamation or other dramatic considerations. This stricter interpretation simplifies matters for the conductor. Should an oratorio singer decide that slight alterations would enhance understanding of the words or heighten dramatic delivery, the conductor accommodates him or her as in opera. When translations are used, oratorio singers may need to make minor changes in some vocal lines, rhythms, and pitches to match the inflections in the translation. This is acceptable when done responsibly and not to excess.

Haydn, *The Creation*, Introduction, bars 60–61 [Recitative]

d. Orchestra

In orchestral recitatives, when the solo line is played by a single instrument, the musician is given a certain amount of rhythmic freedom. The conductor accompanies the musician as the singer is accompanied in opera.

Haydn, Sinfonia concertante, third movement, bars 25–27

Haydn, Sinfonia concertante, third movement, bars 28–34

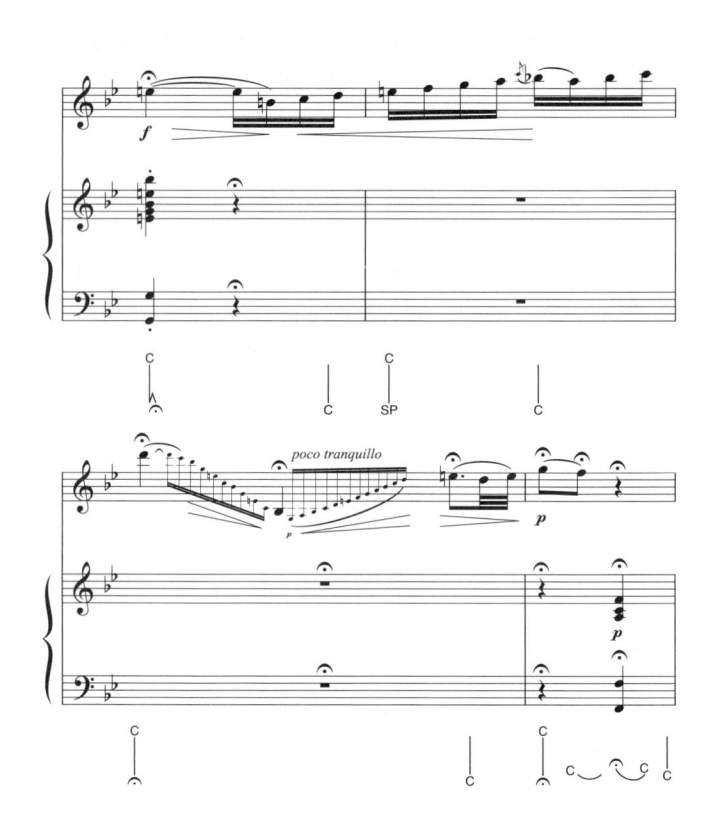

Haydn, Sinfonia concertante, third movement, bars 286–293

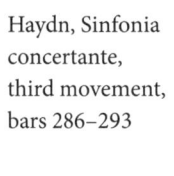

If the solo line is played by several musicians, the conductor leads and takes responsibility for the musical shaping of the line (see Beethoven, Symphony no. 9, fourth movement).

C. CHORAL CONDUCTING

The study and performance of choral and orchestral works are based on the same technical rules and principles of communication. The orchestral conductor deals with works written for a certain number of different orchestral instruments, while the a cappella choral conductor deals with only one type of instrument—the human voice.

The initial tasks for the choral conductor are studying the text separately from the music, searching for a dramatic concept, and seeking an interpretation based on the composer's setting of the text. Although conductors will interpret the meaning of the text differently, commitment to the text unlocks doors to the composer's intent.

In a cappella singing, achieving accurate pitch is a necessary and major accomplishment. In addition, blending a number of voices into a unified sound is extremely difficult, for each voice has its unique timbre. Unifying the shading of each vowel and synchronizing the pronunciation of each syllable requires a highly sensitive ear and excellent teaching skills.

New priorities emerge when a chorus and orchestra are combined. The choral conductor must know what information the orchestral musicians expect and how to distribute attention between orchestra and chorus to secure the best coordination and balance of the two ensembles. This kind of knowledge is essential for the choral conductor in preparing a zigzag way.

With the exception of a few professional choruses, the preparation for a choral concert is spread over a period of several months, with one or two rehearsals each week. Because amateur choruses often include members with limited musical backgrounds, the conductor may feel compelled to drill the singers and overconduct during the early rehearsals. This may stifle the conductor's musical expressiveness, and even if the conductor puts aside exaggerated conducting in later rehearsals, by that time the singers may have become dependent on it. Last-minute transformations from taskmaster to sensitive and musical conductor are rarely successful.

The text of a choral work in any chosen language is generally set for female and male singers with two categories for each: soprano and alto, tenor and bass. The low voices, adult male singers, are sometimes divided into three sections: basses (lowest voices); tenors (highest); and baritones (those in between). Similarly, female voices may be divided into sopranos, altos, and mezzo-sopranos (those in between). Occasionally an extremely low part for alto may be labeled "contralto." Parts written for countertenors encompass the range of altos or mezzo-sopranos.

Each voice category may be further divided (soprano I, soprano II, alto I, alto II, etc.). A composer may choose to write for men's or women's choirs or decide to omit one or more voice categories in a mixed choir. Works may contain single or multiple parts, single or multiple choirs, or combinations thereof. The score may include children's voices, divisible, like those of adults, into categories ranging from low to high.

Vocal parts are written at actual pitch; individual clefs are used for each of the major categories:

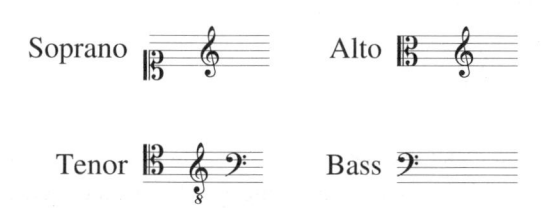

Eventually the treble clef replaced the soprano, alto, and tenor clefs. The tenor line was sung an octave lower than the notated pitch. Today, most composers write all women's voices in the treble clef and all men's voices in the bass clef.

The approximate vocal ranges are

[Musical notation showing vocal ranges in treble clef labeled: Alto, 2. Alto, 1. Alto, Mezzo Soprano, Soprano, 2. Soprano, 1. Soprano, with Children bracket]

[Musical notation showing ALTO and SOPRANO ranges labeled: 2. Alto, 1. Alto, MEZZO SOPRANO, 2. Soprano, 1. Soprano]

[Musical notation in bass clef labeled: Bass, 2. Bass, 1. Bass, Baritone, Tenor, 2. Tenor, 1. Tenor]

[Musical notation showing BASS and TENOR ranges labeled: 2. Bass, 1. Bass, BARITONE, 2. Tenor, 1. Tenor]

The orchestral conductor must know the technical, musical, and expressive capabilities of each instrument in the orchestra. The choral conductor must know the singers' capabilities and idiosyncrasies, vocal categories, range, volume, breath control, endurance, agility, and dynamic and technical abilities, as well as the correct pronunciation and translation of each language to be performed, including Latin as performed in Europe and the United States.

Signals are altered depending on whether a word begins with a vowel or a consonant, an extreme *pp* is required, or some problematic pitch progression is requested. Singers need special consideration when the score demands wide skips or unusual agility or vocal endurance, and when passages have inadequate breathing places (staggered breathing may help) or are in extreme ranges. When a work is written in four parts (SATB), range problems may occur for the mezzo-soprano and baritone, because neither fits comfortably into those categories.

The choral conductor focuses on the main musical thrust of each passage and the fastest-moving segments in order to maintain control. Cuing depends on the requirements of the individual sections. Preparing a physical layout of cuing patterns may prove helpful. The following example from Verdi's Requiem illustrates notation of cuing patterns:

```
CHORUS II    S  A | T  B
CHORUS I     S  A | T  B
```

The cuing pattern for the succession of entrances in the following double fugue is simplified and retained easily when conceptualized in physical terms.

```
       (7)(10)
     2   4 | 6   9
     1   3 | 5   8
```

Verdi, Requiem, Sanctus, bars 9–13

Verdi, Requiem, Sanctus, bars 14–18

Verdi, Requiem, Sanctus, bars 19–23

In conclusion, the choral conductor encourages emotional involvement by refusing to allow early rehearsals to be reduced to mechanical drilling of notes and rhythms. From first rehearsal to actual performance, the conductor's communication should be expressive, always relating to a musical concept. Calm and thorough work and physical language that corresponds to the music will result in excellent performances.

D. BAND CONDUCTING

Preparing the score and performing are the same for band and orchestra conductors. Both require the same technical, musical, and analytical skills and score preparation; signals are influenced by the same factors of instrumentation, dynamics, and articulation. Both require sorting of instrumentation, knowing the position of each player and section, and identifying musical and functional priorities that establish a zigzag method. Repertoire is the basic difference between them.

The band repertoire is written for wind and percussion instruments; the only exception is the string double bass, which is frequently added to symphonic bands and wind ensembles. A choir of clarinets and flutes most closely resembles a string section in terms of manageability and responsiveness to the conductor's beat. These instruments can begin a tone almost inaudibly and let the tone emerge gradually. If the pitches are in a comfortable range, a *pp* entrance can be achieved by having each instrument enter at a slightly different moment. Exactly as for a string *ppp* entrance, the conductor's preparatory beat must be without ictus. A choir of tubas, similar to the double bass section in the orchestra, may enter with a slight delay because of the size of the instruments and the distance between conductor and section.

Maintaining a good balance between woodwinds and brasses is achieved through a thorough knowledge of each individual instrument, each player's abilities, and the acoustics of the hall in which the ensemble will perform. Like that of the choral conductor, the band conductor's preparation and rehearsals generally extend over a long period of time before the concert. Because many bands are made up of amateur musicians, the conductor may try to speed the learning process in the early stages of rehearsal by excessive dictation. This may lead to the musicians' reliance on overconducting and create an inflexibility that will later limit artistic subtleties. To prevent this, the musical message must prevail from the very first rehearsal.

E. BALLET CONDUCTING

The ballet conductor supports dancers' artistry with musical accompaniment. The composer's proper interpretation can be fully realized only if early and continuous communication takes place between the conductor, choreographer, and dancers. Before the choreographer and dancers begin their work, the ballet conductor arrives at the ultimate musical concept. The choreographer uses the conductor's tempos to set the dance to each bar of music. Because the dancers depend on hearing the music the same way every time, identical tempos are required for all rehearsals and performances. Imbalances caused by variations of tempo and arbitrarily timed fermatas or silences will lead to serious problems.

The conductor's approach to accompanying is very much the same whether the artists are singers or dancers. Just as vocal lines have a life and momentum of their own, so do dance movements (steps, jumps, turns, stops, etc.). A ballet conductor makes minor tempo adjustments while observing the dancers' motions.

Dancers often rehearse with a piano accompanist, who must be in complete accord with the conductor. The importance of tempo continuity demands that contact between accompanist and conductor be maintained throughout the entire preparation period. The pianist reflects the orchestration as much as possible by observing dynamics and articulation, the texture of the instrumentation, and the mood and character of the music. Mechanical, monotonous playing is not acceptable. If the dancers work with recordings, the conductor should have a say in which recording is chosen. If a specific recording has already been selected by the choreographer, the conductor makes an effort to duplicate that interpretation.

F. BACKSTAGE CONDUCTING

When conducting offstage instrumentalists and/or singers, a backstage conductor watches and follows the main conductor on a monitor and pushes tempos ahead to accommodate time delays created by the distance between the orchestra and the offstage musicians. The backstage conductor leads when the orchestra is accompanying or when the passages performed backstage are technically demanding and musically dominating. Examples can be found in Mahler's Symphony no. 2, Puccini's *Turandot*, Verdi's *Il Trovatore*, and Bizet's *Carmen*. Some passages with a steady rhythm can be conducted directly by the main conductor. Earphones and small loudspeakers that transmit the music from the main stage or pit to the backstage musicians are additional tools for improving collaboration.

G. CROSS-RHYTHMS

Many musicians are baffled by cross-rhythms, which are a number of notes of equal duration placed against a different number of notes of equal duration (such as two against three, three against four, four against five, etc.). In a $\frac{2}{4}$ bar conducted in two, even-numbered groups of equal notes (4, 6, 8, etc.) distributed over the entire bar are directly related, since they can be equally divided between the two pulses. Unless corresponding subdivisions are applied to each pulse, odd-numbered groupings such as 3, 5, or 7 do not have any direct correlation except for the first note in the bar, which coincides with the downbeat. A grouping of three ( ) against two quarter notes can be executed by dividing each quarter note into three inner units. The total number (six) can then be compounded into three units:

When cross-rhythms are used by composers, the conductor's beat usually follows the basic time signature. If there are five equal beats in a $\frac{2}{4}$ bar, each quarter note should first be divided into five equal quintuplet sixteenth notes, making a total of ten quintuplet sixteenth notes. These ten equal notes can then be divided into five equal units, each containing two quintuplet sixteenth notes.

If a $\frac{3}{4}$ bar at $\quarternote$ = 60 has five equal beats, each quarter note should be divided into five equal quintuplet sixteenth notes, producing a total of fifteen quintuplet sixteenth notes. These fifteen equal notes can then be divided easily into five equal units, each containing three quintuplet sixteenth notes.

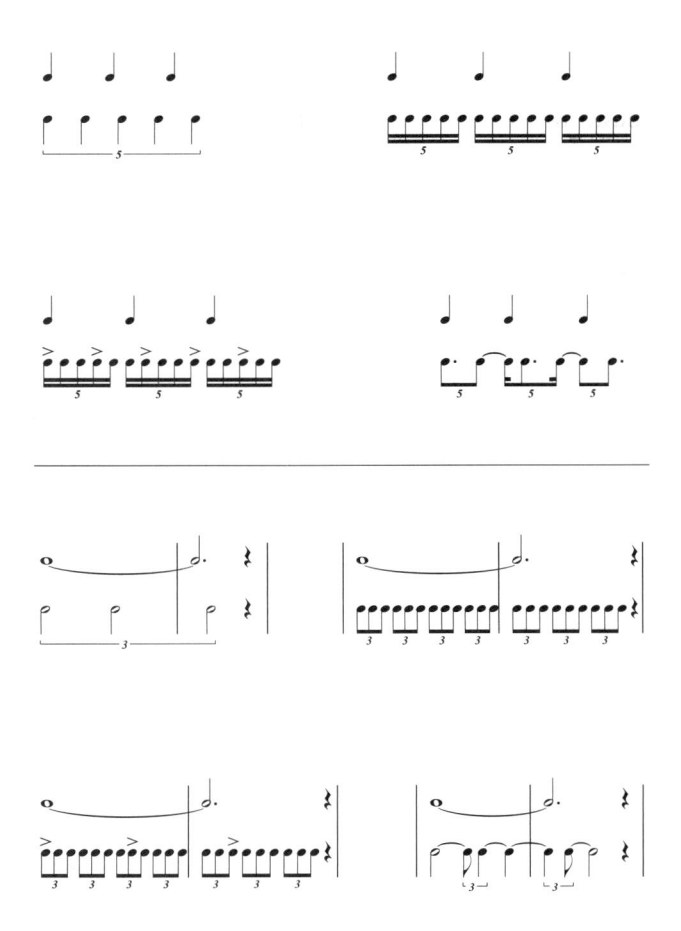

If the second note of the counterrhythm is perfectly placed, the remaining notes of the counterrhythm will fall into place easily.

338 THE SCORE, THE ORCHESTRA, AND THE CONDUCTOR

A musician sometimes is required to count a number of notes of equal duration unrelated to the ongoing pulse or beat pattern given by the conductor. In such instances the musician must look for a smaller subdivision. When the tempo is moderately slow, the conductor may mark each note of the counterrhythm with a small signal of the left hand. If the basic pulse is too slow to allow a new rhythm to be extracted reliably, the musician or conductor may want to set up the notes of the new rhythm within the previous bar. Doing so can establish the counterrhythm securely in the mind.

Stravinsky, *Movements for Piano and Orchestra*, third movement, bars 82–84

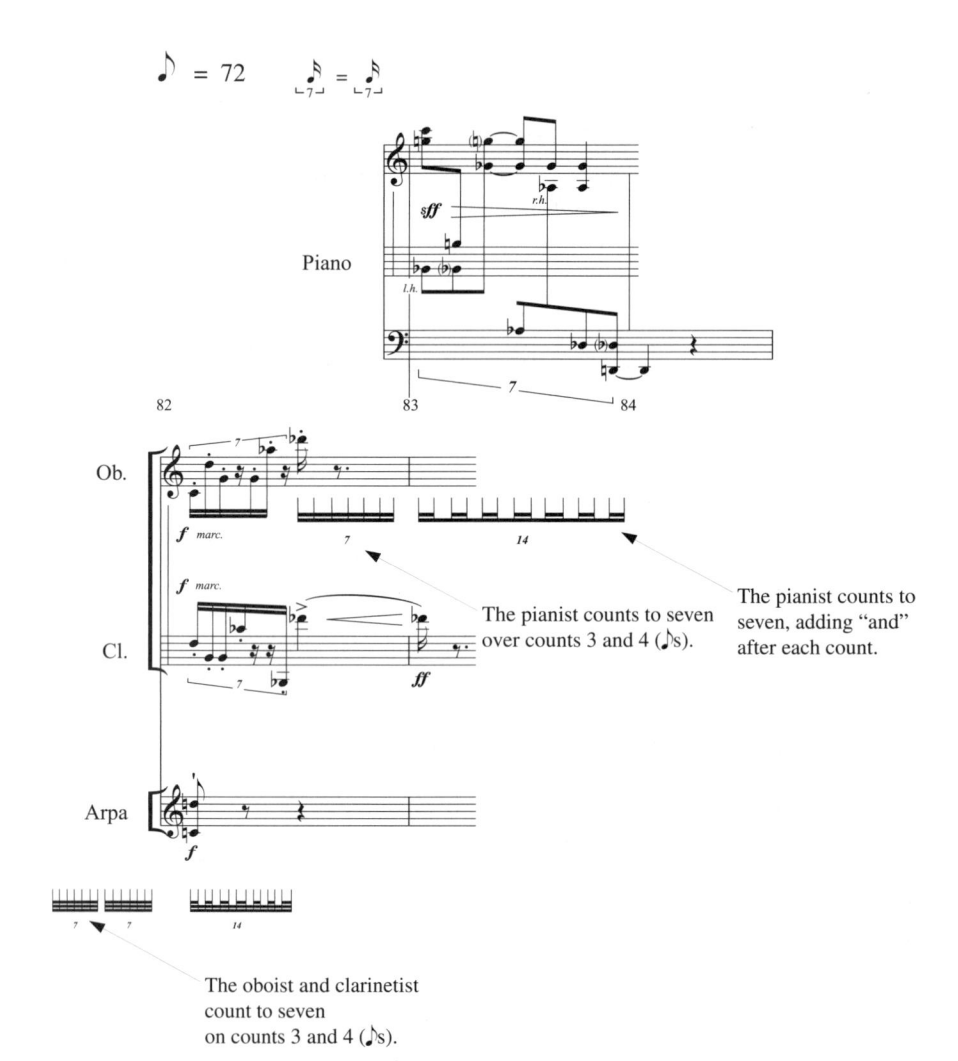

The pianist counts to seven over counts 3 and 4 (♪s).

The pianist counts to seven, adding "and" after each count.

The oboist and clarinetist count to seven on counts 3 and 4 (♪s).

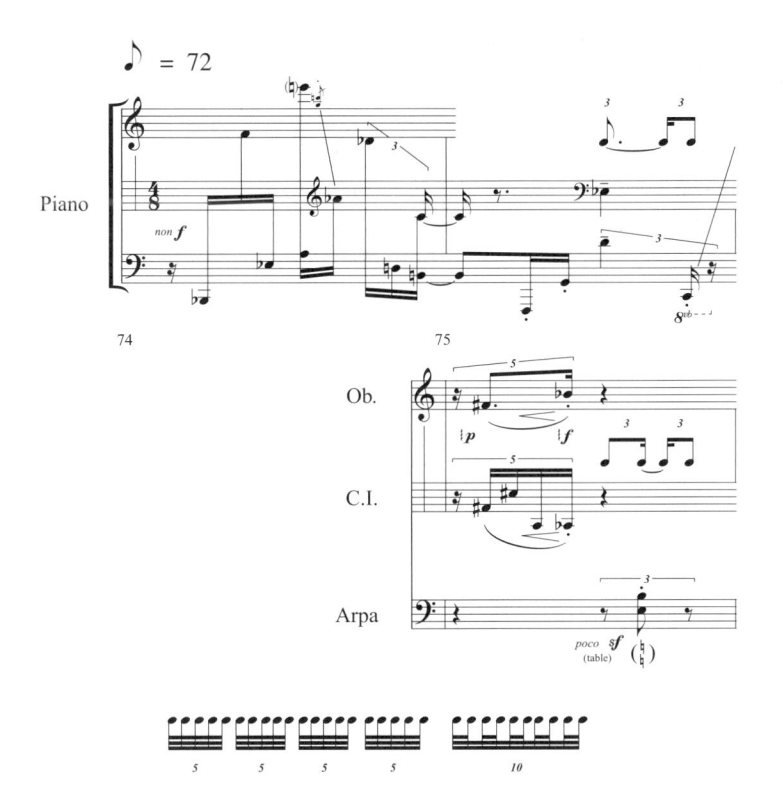

Stravinsky, *Movements for Piano and Orchestra*, third movement, bars 74–75

The same counting procedure applies to the above example for oboe and English horn.

In order to practice multiple rhythms, the conductor must be able to count 1, 2, 3, 4, 5, 6, 7 at a very fast pace ("ua, too, tee, fo, fi, see, se"). Some musicians pick one-syllable patterns that can be used in different combinations: "sana" (2), "sanama" (3), "sanamari" (4), "sanamarina" (5), "sanama-sana" (3 + 2), "sana-sanama" (2 + 3), "sanama-sanama" (3 + 3), "sana-sana-sana" (2 +2 +2), "sanamarinasana" (5 + 2), and "sanamari-sanama" (4 + 3). Other rhythmic combinations can be handled similarly. The brasses' double tonguing can be used by combining double and triple tonguing: *tu-ku tu-tu-ku* (2 + 3), *tu-tu-ku tu-ku* (3 + 2), or *tu-tu-ku tu-ku-tu-ku* (3 + 4 or 3 + 2 + 2), and so on.

CHAPTER EIGHT

Additional Concerns

A. EAR TRAINING

Except for improvisation, most music making begins with compositional material in musical notation waiting to be realized in sound by performers. Without adequate ear training, one cannot recognize the sounds and rhythms notated in the score. Conductors must be able to recognize and correct any notes, chords, or rhythmic configurations in the orchestra that do not match the score.

Aural skills must be pursued and nurtured. Aspiring conductors should seek out teachers who will instill pitch and chord recognition. In addition to the ear-training classes offered in music schools, *solfeggio* and advanced ear-training courses are essential. Playing a score at the piano, singing individual lines and arpeggiated chords, and practicing complex rhythmic figurations are all helpful.

B. MEMORIZATION

Hearing live or recorded performances often precedes learning a score; therefore, depending on a conductor's recall, certain portions of a work may have been memorized before serious study begins. Although the natural flow of music serves memory well, study and analysis provide the security and knowledge needed to conduct without a score.

A positive argument for memorization is the additional time required with the score. As each bar, phrase, and detail receives closer scrutiny, understanding of the composition grows and solidifies and new insights emerge. Conducting from memory also allows for increased eye contact with the musicians, which facilitates sharing the emotional impact of the music. However, conducting without a score is not acceptable if the conductor, after thorough preparation, remains preoccupied with the reliability of his or her memory.

With or without a score, the conductor must be free to focus on leading the orchestra and listening to the musicians so that unplanned occurrences can be resolved immediately. One must be prepared to shift unexpectedly to different tasks at any point as the need arises.

Regardless of when and how the practice of conducting without a score emerged, whether the orchestra musicians approve of it or object to it, and whether or not it appeals to the audience, the important question is: will memorization result in a better performance?

C. SPECIALIZATION

Whether for reasons of genuine preference, opportunity, or practicality, conductors as well as instrumentalists or singers may choose to specialize in a particular field or narrow period, school, style, or specific composer; chamber or orchestra music; opera, oratorio, or recital work; new or early music; and classical or pop and film music. Although focusing on a specific area leads to expertise and may increase performance opportunities, the conductor who specializes may face other career difficulties. For instance, a conductor working predominantly with new music may not be considered a qualified conductor of the standard repertoire. The shift from opera to symphony conductor is considered a natural development in Europe. In the United States, however, operatic conductors are rarely engaged by symphony orchestras, although that seems to be changing.

A preference for a particular period, composer, or type of ensemble may evolve quite naturally and early; however, the wise conductor establishes a broad musical foundation and becomes familiar with and performs in as many different periods and styles of musical re-creation as possible before specializing.

D. COSMETICS

The term *cosmetics* generally refers to the physical appearance of a conductor's signals, facial expressions, and posture. Many believe that a conductor needs to concentrate only on a clear beat pattern, because if music is felt strongly, the body will respond properly and produce natural and effective physical messages. However, attention to one's physical gestures, posture, and appearance is advisable. Personal observation may reveal contradictions between feelings and their physical expression; misleading messages can be modified and changed through constructive feedback by trusted colleagues and orchestra musicians.

Regular checks on the physical aspects of one's conducting are highly recommended. Watching videos of oneself may reveal an accumulation of undesirable habits: the beat gestures may have become too large to be effective, or the baton may occasionally travel beyond the center of the body, moving too high, too low, or too far forward for cohesiveness to be maintained. The patterns may have become unclear or distorted.

Posture is important. Communication from an erect position is the most effective. Solid positioning gives the entire body security and support. Leaning forward or sideways, bending knees, or shifting one's weight from one leg to the other weakens the strength and effectiveness of a conductor's signals.

The grounded conductor experiences a feeling of being connected to terra firma. Any excessive bending or straying is equivalent to breaking a pipeline carrying essential fuel; the interruption of flow prevents energy and intensity from reaching the musicians. Bad posture will also inhibit proper breathing and relaxation by preventing sufficient expansion of the lungs. Continually changing one's placement on the podium must be curtailed, because it forces musicians to search for beat information from a moving source, which is not an easy task.

The baton should be visible to all musicians at all times, never disappearing behind the conductor's back or below the music stand. Turning too often or too far to one side or the other hides the baton from some musicians and deprives them of essential information.

It is acceptable to be physically excessive at times, as long as the motions are musically motivated; however, when a conductor genuinely projects the composer's wishes, making music the prime source of communication, musicians will comply without the use of exaggerated gestures. Ideally, facial expressions mirror genuine musical involvement, but conductors must take care not to sing or hum along or mouth words or rhythms. Motions of the non-baton hand must be integrated and based on strong musical backing and motivation.

After the conductor has spent months or years learning a score and preparing for rehearsals and a final performance, one ultimate responsibility remains: total commitment to the composition(s) to be performed. During a performance, the listener should not for a single moment be distracted from the music by the conductor's nodding or smiling, acknowledgment of a successful rendition of a difficult passage, or physical disapproval of a mishap. No event should interfere with the conductor's musical involvement with the composition as it unfolds.

A final thought about a nonmusical matter. Each performance is surrounded by rituals that may seem unconnected to the composition about to be presented. For the conductor, these rituals include silently greeting the orchestra, shaking hands with the concertmaster, bowing and acknowledging the applause, acknowledging individual musicians or sections, asking the orchestra to stand and share the applause, and calling the composer, narrator, soloists, or other participants to the stage. These rituals are significant in either setting the tone for opening or concluding a performance. Conductors are encouraged to reflect on their significance and consider variations, changes, and improvements.

E. GENERAL ATTITUDE AND BEHAVIOR

A conductor's general behavior and attitude communicate important information to the orchestra before a word is spoken or an upbeat is given. During the introduction to the orchestra, the musicians are registering the conductor's projected level of energy and eagerness and dedication to the job at hand.

Although most musical intentions and wishes can be expressed through the actual conducting and body language, some verbal communications, such as announcements or starting points, are unavoidable during rehearsals. Clarity, brevity, the decibel level of the voice, and the pacing of the message's delivery are important. Speaking too slowly or too quickly may irritate the players. The layout of the orchestra requires a vocal level that will reach the musicians farthest away without offending the ones in close proximity.

Energy, fueled by a felt and visible dedication to the score, is the essential ingredient and must be present at all times during rehearsals and concerts. A positive attitude must prevail. Politeness, appreciation, praise, and encouragement are welcome indeed. There is no room for negativism, sarcasm, indifference, showing off, belittling, lecturing, embarrassing, or preaching. All are unacceptable. Also, stories or anecdotes, even those related to the work being rehearsed, are rarely appreciated. Only the motivation of serving the composer better can justify asking the musicians to "work harder."

Calling musicians by name, if a list has been provided in advance of the first rehearsal, may impress some and turn off others. The ability to memorize a few selected names does not endear a conductor to the nameless others, who may feel deprived of this special attention.

How much socializing between conductor and orchestra members is welcome, acceptable, overdone, unwise, or unacceptable? Special relationships do exist between the conductor and the concertmaster, the personnel manager, the union representative, and the librarian, and they require one-to-one communication from time to time. However, if musicians sense special relationships between the conductor and certain players, distrust, anxiety, or jealousy may arise. Discretion is important. The conductor may feel affinity with some players, but similar treatment of all musicians is wise and will be appreciated.

Because musicians will rarely volunteer criticism to the conductor directly, regular consultation with the orchestra committee, a cross-section of the musicians, is recommended for taking the pulse of the relationship between the orchestra and conductor. In the committee meetings, the musicians' representatives should be encouraged to express concerns and pass on criticism without having to fear possible repercussions.

Orchestra musicians have valuable insights and can offer excellent suggestions. They may comment that the conductor talks too much; ignores details such as intonation, balance, articulation, and rhythmic accuracy; continually interrupts musicians; fails to give them a sense of what the piece is all about; underrehearses some spots while overrehearses others; and never goes over difficult passages slowly or does so too often. These criticisms merit serious consideration.

A conductor may have grievances also. Speaking directly to the musician(s) involved may resolve the problem. However, if direct conversation or consultation with the orchestra committee does not resolve the problem, a mediator or other go-between, such as the manager, artistic administrator, personnel manager, or trusted board member acceptable to both parties can be requested by either the musicians or the conductor. The union contract may dictate dispute resolution.

F. ORCHESTRA MUSICIANS ON PROBATION

An orchestra member's playing may become a concern to fellow musicians and the conductor. If so, the conductor speaks directly to the musician, expresses the specific complaint, and requests improvement. If the playing does not improve, an audition is set for a later date. The audition repertoire is chosen by the orchestra committee and conductor and made available to the musician well in advance of the actual audition. The audition is attended by a representative of the orchestra committee, a union official, an administrative staff member, and the conductor. A decision to dismiss a musician is based on appropriate discussions and established, written guidelines and voting procedures. A written record of all communications and procedures must be maintained in the event of litigation.

G. PROGRAMMING

Programming concerts requires time and creativity. The duration of concerts and inclusion of soloists have remained consistent over time. A full-length concert generally lasts from sixty-five to ninety minutes, with an intermission dividing the concert into two more or less equal halves. Ideally, each program keeps the audience involved and interested throughout and builds to a satisfactory conclusion.

A short orchestral work usually opens the concert, with a soloist ending the first half. The opening piece should set up the concerto without overwhelming it; a work with large orchestration, loud dynamics, or rich sonority dwarfs a Mozart or Chopin concerto. As a rule, the second half comprises a major symphonic work or a selection of shorter pieces.

Putting the soloist in the second half is recommended when a soloist is of exceptional stature or the concerto is very popular. (Examples are the Tchaikovsky piano or violin concertos, Beethoven's *Emperor* Concerto, and a Rachmaninoff or Brahms piano concerto). When the major symphonic work ends softly (e.g., Brahms's Symphony no. 3, Ives's Symphony no. 4, Mahler's Symphony no. 4, Bernstein's *Jeremiah* Symphony, Copland's *Appalachian Spring* Suite, Tchaikovsky's Symphony no. 6, and Schubert's Symphony no. 8), it is often placed in the first half, with the soloist ending the concert. Problems occur when single compositions last an hour or more (e.g., Beethoven's Symphony no. 9 and Mahler, Bruckner, or Shostakovich symphonies). If the program opens with a short piece, the intermission starts too soon; if a lengthy piece is chosen, the concert becomes too long.

In general, concerts are programmed from the earlier to more contemporary composers. If music of the same composer is performed, it is usually programmed in chronological order. These traditions do not have to be honored. The juxtaposition of various styles of compositional periods is very attractive if the works are compatible. Programs featuring only one composer require careful selection. The most successful one-composer concerts tend to be all Bach, Mozart, Beethoven, Brahms, or Tchaikovsky. Presenting only works of the same period is also possible, but, again, the pieces must be carefully chosen and the program well balanced. Theme programs such a "A Night in Paris" or "Romeo and Juliet in Music" are interesting, but they are often difficult to fill with appropriate works.

Occasionally a conductor chooses compositions with drastically different instrumentation, mixing heavily orchestrated works with chamber-orchestra pieces such as wind serenades, compositions for strings only, or pieces for smaller ensembles. Choral works such as oratorios, requiems, and masses are usually full-length events and present no programming issues unless the work covers only one half of the concert.

Planning rehearsal needs is integral to successful programming. Conductors must always take into consideration the strength of individual sections and players as well as the available rehearsal time. When a new work is scheduled, consideration must be given to the balance of the program; an appropriate work must precede the new composition so that it can shine. Top orchestras rarely have to worry about sufficient rehearsal time, but scheduling too many difficult works for less experienced groups in a single concert (Prokofiev's *Classical Symphony*, followed by Copland's Clarinet Concerto and Schubert's Symphony no. 2, for example) can lead to disaster.

Conductors can further the cause of new music by performing and commissioning contemporary works. Resistance must be met by making every attempt to familiarize audiences with new music. Composers will come to rehearsals and concerts, and they are usually glad to talk to the musicians, administration, board members, and audiences. Besides introducing their works at the concerts, they may be invited to give lectures to various organizations and schools by themselves or with orchestra members and the conductor. Composers-in-residence may propose new works suitable for the level of the orchestra and the available rehearsal time.

H. AUDITIONS

Auditioning musicians for employment in an orchestra begins with the selection of a committee to listen to the candidates. The committee usually consists of three to five or more orchestra members, the music director, a union official, the personnel manager, and a member of the administration (the last three nonvoting). A monitor is assigned to sit with the auditioning musician behind the screen. If the orchestra has an associate or assistant conductor, the committee may include one or both. Which particular orchestra members are selected as judges depends on the instrument(s) for which the audition is held. The following list shows the auditioning instrument on the left and the judges on the right.

Principal flute:	Principal oboe, clarinet, and bassoon plus concertmaster or principal 2nd violin
Principal oboe:	Principal flute, clarinet, and bassoon plus concertmaster or principal 2nd violin
Principal clarinet:	Principal flute, oboe, and bassoon plus concertmaster or principal 2nd violin
Principal bassoon:	Principal oboe, clarinet, and 1st horn plus principal cello or principal bass
2nd flute, 3rd flute/piccolo:	Principal flute, oboe, clarinet, and bassoon plus principal 2nd violin
2nd oboe, 3rd oboe/English horn:	Principal oboe, flute, clarinet, and bassoon plus principal 2nd violin or viola
2nd clarinet, 3rd clarinet, E♭ clarinet:	Principal clarinet, flute, and oboe plus principal 2nd violin
Bass clarinet:	Principal clarinet and principal bassoon plus principal viola, cello, or bass
2nd bassoon, 3rd bassoon:	Principal oboe, bassoon, and clarinet plus principal cello or principal bass
Contrabassoon:	Principal bassoon, 3rd trombone, and tuba plus principal bass
Principal horn:	Principal oboe, bassoon, and trumpet plus concertmaster or principal 2nd violin
Principal trumpet:	Principal horn, 1st trombone, and any principal woodwind plus concertmaster or principal 2nd violin

Principal trombone:	Principal trumpet, horn, any principal woodwind, and tuba plus principal cello or principal viola
Tuba:	Contrabassoon, 3rd trombone, and 2nd or 4th horn plus principal cello or bass
3rd horn:	Any principal woodwind, principal horn, principal trumpet, and principal trombone plus a principal string player
2nd horn, 4th horn:	Any principal woodwind, principal horn, principal trumpet, and 2nd trombone plus a principal string player
2nd trumpet, 3rd trumpet:	Any principal woodwind, principal trumpet, principal horn, and principal trombone plus principal 2nd violin
2nd trombone, 3rd trombone:	Principal bassoon, principal trombone, principal trumpet, and principal tuba plus principal cello or bass
Timpani:	Principal percussionist and principal woodwind or brass player plus a principal string player
Percussion:	Timpanist, other percussionists, principal woodwind player, and principal brass player plus a principal string player
Concertmaster:	Chosen by the conductor in consultation with other string, woodwind, or brass principals
Principal 2nd violin:	Concertmaster, principal viola, and other string or wind principals
Principal viola:	Concertmaster and any string or woodwind principals plus principal horn
Principal cello:	Concertmaster and principal viola or principal 2nd violin, plus principal bassoon and trombone
Principal bass:	Concertmaster, principal cello, principal bassoon, contrabassoon, and 3rd trombone or tuba
Section violin:	Concertmaster and principal strings plus principal oboe
Section viola:	Concertmaster and principal strings plus principal oboe and horn
Section cello:	Concertmaster and principal strings plus principal bassoon and 1st or 2nd trombone

Section bass:	Concertmaster, principal strings, principal bassoon, principal trombone, and tuba
Harp:	Concertmaster and string, woodwind, or brass principals
Piano:	Chosen by the conductor in consultation with the concertmaster, or any string, woodwind, or brass principals

The following list provides audition procedures:

1. Establish a voting and ranking system.
2. Maintain absolute silence; exchanges between the monitor and the person auditioning are permissible but must not be audible to the judges.
3. Limit audition time to six to twelve minutes.
4. Work out the logistics, set up a timetable, and make sure warm-up rooms are available.
5. Decide announcement procedures (union bulletin, newspapers, Internet, flyers to music schools, and personal calls).
6. Decide whether potential candidates who are known should be approached and invited to audition.
7. Check union guidelines.

Frequently asked questions about auditions include:

- What are the music director's options and prerogatives?
- Should recommendations be required?
- Who chooses the repertoire?
- Will the repertoire be solo pieces, orchestral excerpts, or both?
- Should auditioners be audio screened prior to live auditions?
- Will a list of excerpts and copies be provided?
- Will the candidates receive the audition parts in advance?
- Should candidates play the same orchestral excerpts in the same order?
- Should finalists (two or three) play in front of the screen?
- Who serves behind the screen as monitor and liaison between the audition committee and the candidate?
- Should rules be established about wearing high heels, perfume, or jewelry?
- Are callbacks desirable?
- Will results be announced at the conclusions of auditions or sent in writing at a later date?
- What procedures are used for a candidate who is considered unqualified to audition based on lack of experience or unfavorable recommendations?
- Can a candidate be dismissed after performing only a few excerpts when the performance level is clearly below expectations?

1. AT THE REHEARSAL

There are as many approaches to rehearsing as there are conductors. The best way to learn how to rehearse well is to observe other conductors at work. Whatever the order or style of rehearsing, the conductor must project musical involvement from the moment the rehearsal begins. Rehearsal time is extremely valuable; therefore, the allotted time must be used as economically as possible, without overrehearsing certain sections at the expense of underrehearsing others.

Although some explanation may be helpful or even essential for contemporary music, verbal explanations should be avoided as much as possible. Musical suggestions are communicated through physical motions, body language, and facial expressions—not through verbal instructions. However, some conductors enjoy talking to the orchestra; they like to provide relevant information, a bit of what they consider noteworthy history, some tidbits about the works, and perhaps a few personal anecdotes.

As a general rule, musicians deserve credit for having some acquaintance with the work and being able to resolve most problems on their own. For example, the conductor may want a particular articulation in a well-known work. If the passage is played through without prior comment, quite possibly the musicians will read the composer's notation and play it exactly as the conductor has envisioned.

Some conductors elect to run straight through a piece, while others may prefer to work out each problem as it occurs. With similar circumstances involving the same composition, orchestra, and amount of rehearsal time available, conductors will vary on how to pace the rehearsal.

Anticipating the most effective procedures for the first rehearsal depends on the repertoire. Deciding in advance on technical and stylistic principles, as well as articulations and dynamic levels, is helpful. At the rehearsal, immediate correction of intonation problems or obvious pitch and rhythmic mistakes is objectionable to the musicians. Intonation will almost always improve with continued playing, and mistakes in first readings are normally corrected when the passages are repeated. However, if mistakes are repeated, the conductor must continue rehearsing until satisfactory improvement is achieved.

Careful pre-rehearsal score study will often help the conductor to eliminate difficulties early on because the musicians will frequently have the same difficulties the conductor had with the score, such as misreading rhythms or pitches or overlooking tempo changes, accidentals, articulations, and dynamics.

The conductor's rehearsal letters and numbers and bar numberings must be synchronized with those of the musicians. Bar numberings may not be identical because of the way first and second endings are counted and because of *attacca* connections between movements. In addition, one must envision or anticipate certain places where the orchestra may need to start rehearsing. Is anything more tedious and unnecessarily time-consuming than a conductor's silently counting off many bars, followed by the musicians doing likewise?

When bar numbers are missing and rehearsal numbers are too far apart, one can insert additional numbers or letters (marking E1 at twenty-six bars after rehearsal letter E, for example) and ask the musicians to put the new information into their parts. Whenever possible, the librarian should add the new markings before the parts are given out to the musicians. This avoids irritating players who have long stretches of rests and may have to do elaborate searching to find the spots where they are supposed to add rehearsal marks.

Analyzing the orchestration helps to identify players or sections that need work at the first rehearsal. The conductor may want to hear a particular musical line shared by many instruments. Noting the names of the relevant instruments at the bottom of the score allows these instruments to be called out without hesitation.

Rehearsing at slower tempos than indicated in the score is generally useful. When time permits, giving extended attention to various individual instruments or sections of the orchestra may be necessary; however, if particular musicians or sections are rehearsed extensively, the specter of boredom will definitely arise among the other musicians. This is ameliorated somewhat when everyone, especially the nonparticipating players, hears improvements.

A conductor wants to distribute attention to as many sections as possible during rehearsals, but those without any specific problems may get little attention for several rehearsals. Sincere compliments to those who are playing well are always appreciated.

Although it is important to observe and execute dynamics as accurately as possible during rehearsals, temporarily reducing certain difficult *ff* sections to *p* or *mf* levels allows the musicians to hear each other better. This procedure facilitates ensemble playing and significantly improves intonation, especially in complex tutti sections.

Many conductors make suggestions or critical remarks while the orchestra is playing. Musicians don't like this because the information is difficult to understand and disturbs the ongoing playing. Facial expressions and body language are welcome and much more helpful. Musicians are also irritated when conductors resume rehearsing after an interruption without calling out clearly where to start.

Sectionals can be of tremendous benefit. One can work separately with the strings and the winds; divide the strings between the higher (violins) and lower ones (cellos and basses), the violas joining either group depending on the compositional context; and divide the woodwinds and brasses. The percussion section, harp, piano, celesta, organ, and any other additional instruments can be added to one or the other groups, depending on their musical contribution.

Whether sectional rehearsals are feasible depends upon the orchestra's finances and rehearsal space and on the musicians' availability. Assistant conductors can be utilized if simultaneous rehearsals are possible. Also, some sections may be rehearsed by qualified principals. (A conductor or assistant conductor may become necessary when rhythmic problems are complex.) If space, leadership, and a librarian are available and sectional rehearsals are implemented, the leaders must synchronize their musical approach with the music director before rehearsals begin. Instead of continuously rehearsing the full orchestra, splitting it into sections of sixty minutes for strings only, ninety minutes for full orchestra, and sixty minutes for winds only, for example, increases the available rehearsal time.

J. INTONATION

Playing in tune, an ever-present challenge for any orchestra, requires continuous effort by all players to master the inherent pitch problems of their individual instruments while constantly adjusting to the pitch of fellow musicians. The principal players attempt to keep their sections in tune while collaborating with the other principals. In addition to recognizing out-of-tune playing, conductors must identify the musicians who at any given time carry the prime responsibility for establishing and securing accurate intonation.

Generally the concertmaster supervises the initial tuning, with the principal oboist giving the A at a predetermined pitch negotiated between the orchestra and the conductor. Most orchestras tune onstage, the winds first, then the strings. Occasionally the woodwinds and brasses tune separately, as do the upper and lower strings (violas, cellos, and basses first, then violins, or vice versa). When a keyboard instrument is used, the keyboardist gives the A. When an electronic A is piped into the various warm-up rooms, musicians tune backstage and need only a brief moment onstage to verify and coordinate the A.

Although the oboe is considered one of the most accurate instruments in terms of pitch, many intonation problems originate within the woodwind section. Complications arise because of the construction of the various instruments, as well as their distinct timbres and various means of tone production. A unified blend is difficult to achieve. The lowest instrument in the woodwind section, the second bassoon, provides the harmonic foundation. The flutes and clarinets normally make pitch adjustments when necessary because it is easier for them than for double reed players. Horns play frequently with the woodwinds, providing a link to the rest of the brasses.

Ultimately each player is responsible for his or her pitch accuracy, regardless of the prevailing circumstances. Musicians who double (play two instruments or more), such as the flute and piccolo, oboe and English horn, bassoon and contrabassoon, and the various clarinets (E♭, D, B♭, A, and bass clarinet), often have intonation problems when they change from one instrument to another. To facilitate coordination of pitch, these players may momentarily lower their dynamic level.

In any octave doubling, the instruments in the more comfortable range set the pitch. When the first violins play in a high register and the seconds double them an octave lower, the firsts defer to the seconds. Any notes played at the periphery of an instrument's range, the lowest and highest pitches, are prone to intonation problems. (See, for example, the bassoon solo in Stravinsky's *Rite of Spring*; the D clarinet solo in Strauss's *Till Eulenspiegel*; the contrabassoon solo in Ravel's Piano Concerto for the Left Hand; the trumpet solo in the Prelude to Wagner's *Parsifal*; the French horn solos in Ravel's Piano Concerto in G and Shostakovich's Symphony no. 5; and the D♭ in the piccolo, clarinet, and harp in Bartók's *Concerto for Orchestra* (third movement, bars 19–21). Extreme dynamics (*fff* or *ppp*) also challenge good intonation.

Within the complexity of a composition, there is no fixed or inflexible pitch. Depending on its tonal function and placement within a chord or passage, the same note may vary in pitch, if ever so slightly. The conductor, in trying to identify why a certain pitch or chord is out of tune, must sort out the orchestration and consider the range of the instruments playing the chord, the dynamics, and the linear and harmonic context. If the musicians responsible for each partial of the chord are grouped together, the instrumentalists who are playing the out-of-tune notes can be identified and corrected more easily.

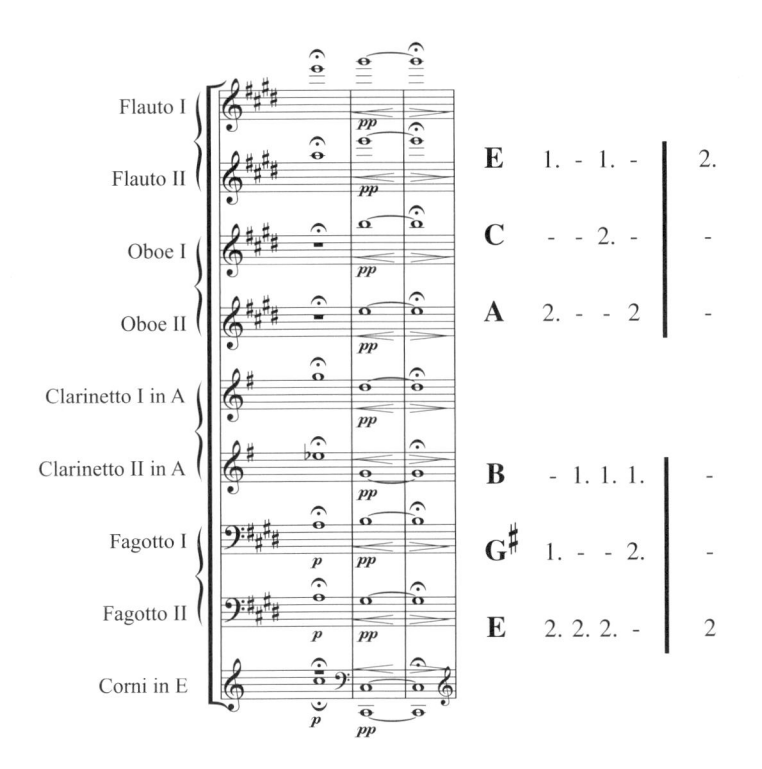

Mendelssohn, *A Midsummer Night's Dream*, Overture, bars 3–5

K. BOWINGS

Unless a conductor's background includes playing a string instrument at a high level of proficiency, the strings will present major challenges. A thorough understanding of the complexities involved in string techniques is not easily acquired, yet the conductor must understand and be able to implement suitable bowings and harmonics, advise when to utilize certain strokes and pressures or play in different parts of the bow and strings, and explain when and how to employ different kind of pizzicatos and vibratos. With professional orchestras, however, a conductor never presumes to introduce an "ingenious" or "clever" bowing. Instead, the conductor concentrates on developing the sound desired from the strings. The conductor expresses specific requests to the concertmaster and then selects a preference from the possibilities the concertmaster demonstrates.

For those conductors unfamiliar with string instruments, listening to fine string virtuosos and chamber musicians reveals the vast possibilities of each string instrument. As a practical matter, it is helpful for the conductor to have his or her own string parts marked with the desired bowings. Before making these available to the orchestra, some consultation between the concertmaster and the conductor is highly recommended.

L. ABOUT BREATHING

Proper breathing is integral to conducting. Inhalation occurs with all significant preparatory beats, exits, cues, rhythmic shifts, pitch and harmonic changes, and articulations. Exhalation takes place naturally and discreetly thereafter.

Whether singers or wind players can sustain a musical line of exceptional length without a break for breath depends on the dynamic level of the phrase and the performers' strength and sustaining power. If an interruption is necessary, an extra place for breath must be found. Deciding when to interrupt the phrase unobtrusively should be made before the rehearsal (see the oboe solo in the last movement of Beethoven's Symphony no. 3 or the flute solo in Debussy's *Prelude to the Afternoon of a Faun*).

In the second movement of Bizet's Symphony no. 1, the second oboe shares the lengthy solo with the principal, each playing only a portion of it. In the following example, Bizet manages to create a smooth connection from one player to the other by having the entering instrument overlap the last note of the one already playing. This sharing of a line rarely sounds uninterrupted because the tonal quality of two players seldom matches or blends perfectly. When numerous instruments play the same line in unison, the breathing can be staggered, with individual players dropping out for a quick, discreet breath.

[musical example: Bizet, Symphony no. 1, second movement, bars 11–12]

A conductor can request an overlap when it is omitted, as in Rachmaninoff's *Symphonic Dances*.

[musical example: Rachmaninoff, *Symphonic Dances,* second movement, bars 36–37]

Choral conductors make frequent use of staggered breathing within a phrase; this guarantees an uninterrupted level of sound.

APPENDIX A

Instrumental Charts

STANDARD SYMPHONY ORCHESTRA

The instruments are listed in score order.

1	Piccolo	28	Horn in G
2	Flute	29	Horn in F♯
3	Alto flute in G	30	Horn in F (𝄞)
4	Oboe	31	Horn in F (𝄢—new notation)
5	English horn	32	Horn in F (𝄢—old notation)
6	Heckelphone	33	Horn in F (𝄡(A))
7	Clarinet in E♭	34	Horn in E
8	Clarinet in D	35	Horn in E♭
9	Clarinet in C	36	Horn in D
10	Clarinet in B♭	37	Horn in D♭
11	Clarinet in A	38	Horn in C
12	Basset horn 𝄞	39	Horn in B (in H) (basso)
13	Basset horn 𝄢	40	Horn in B♭ (basso)
14	Bass clarinet in B♭ (𝄞)	41	Horn in A (basso)
15	Bass clarinet in B♭ (𝄢)	42	Horn in A♭ (basso)
16	Bass clarinet in A (𝄞)	43	Trumpet in G
17	Bass clarinet in A (𝄢)	44	Trumpet in F♯
18	Bassoon	45	Trumpet in F
19	Contrabassoon	46	Trumpet in E
20	Ophicleide	47	Trumpet in E♭
21	Soprano saxophone in B♭	48	Trumpet in D
22	Alto saxophone in E♭	49	Trumpet in D♭
23	Tenor saxophone in B♭ (𝄞)	50	Trumpet in C
24	Tenor saxophone in B♭ (𝄢)	51	Trumpet in B (in H)
25	Horn in B♭ (alto)	52	Trumpet in B♭
26	Horn in A	53	Trumpet in A
27	Horn in A♭	54	Trumpet in A♭

357

55 Piccolo trumpet in B♭
56 Cornet in G
57 Cornet in B♭
58 Cornet in A
59 Fluegelhorn in B♭
60 Buccina
61 Alto trumpet in F
62 Bass trumpet in E
63 Bass trumpet in E♭
64 Bass trumpet in D
65 Bass trumpet in C
66 Bass trumpet in B (in H)
67 Bass trumpet in B♭
68 Alto trombone
69 Tenor trombone
70 Bass trombone
71 Wagner tuba (tenor) in B♭ (𝄞)
72 Wagner tuba (tenor) in B♭ (𝄢)
73 Wagner tuba (tenor) in E♭
74 Wagner tuba (bass) in F
75 Wagner tuba (bass) in B♭
76 Tuba
77 Kettledrums
78 Chimes
79 Crotales (antique cymbals)
80 Marimba
81 Orchestra bells
82 Vibraphone
83 Xylophone
84 Bass drum
85 Bongo drums (timbales)
86 Castanets
87 Cymbals
88 Gong
89 Guiro
90 Side drum (military)
91 Snare drum
92 Tambourine
93 Tam-tam
94 Temple blocks
95 Tenor drum
96 Tom-tom
97 Triangle
98 Tubular chimes
99 Whip
100 Wood block
101 Celesta
102 Organ
103 Piano
104 Harp
105 Harmonium (portative organ or synthesizer)
106 Harpsichord
107 Cimbalom
108 Violin
109 Viola
110 Violoncello 𝄞 after 𝄡(T) (version A)
111 Violoncello 𝄞 after 𝄡(T) (version B)
112 Violoncello 𝄞 after 𝄢 (version A)
113 Violoncello 𝄞 after 𝄢 (version B)
114 Double bass

UNUSUAL INSTRUMENTS

The instruments are listed in score order. Instruments used in the baroque period are not included.

1 Piccolo in D♭
2 Recorder
3 Bass flute in C
4 Oboe d'amore

5	Baritone oboe	40	Finger cymbals
6	Tarogato	41	Flexatone
7	Alto clarinet in E♭	42	Musical Saw
8	Alto clarinet in F	43	Pistol shot
9	Contrabass clarinet in B♭	44	Ratchet
10	Contrabass sarrusophone	45	Rattle (wasamba)
11	Sopranino saxophone in F	46	Siren (hand-cranked)
12	Soprano saxophone in B♭	47	Siren (mouth)
13	Baritone saxophone in E♭	48	Sleighbells
14	Bass saxophone in B♭	49	Switch
15	Sopranino saxhorn in B♭	50	Tabor
16	Soprano saxhorn in E♭	51	Thunder sheet
17	Soprano saxhorn in B♭	52	Whistle (bird)
18	Tenor saxhorn in E♭	53	Whistle (police)
19	Tenor saxhorn in B♭	54	Wind machine
20	Bass saxhorn in E♭	55	Tamboritsa
21	Bass saxhorn in B♭	56	Mandolin
22	Contrabass saxhorn in B♭	57	Guitar
23	Piccolo trumpet in B♭	58	Violino piccolo
24	Piccolo trumpet in A	59	Electric violin
25	Trumpet or cornet in G♭	60	Viola d'amore
26	Alto horn in E♭ (Mellophone)	61	Accordion
27	Baritone (𝄞)	62	Prepared piano
28	Baritone in E♭ (𝄞)	63	Glass harmonica
29	Baritone (𝄢)	64	Ondes Martenot (tone generator)
30	Euphonium		
31	Contrabass trombone	65	Maracas
32	Tuba in F (C notation)	66	Wind chimes
33	Tuba in E♭ (C notation)	67	Roto-tom (tunable)
34	Tuba in BB♭ (C notation)	68	Sand blocks
35	Cimbasso	69	Chains
36	Almglocken	70	Wind controller
37	Anvils	71	Synthesizer
38	Bell tree	72	Electric piano
39	Cowbell		

APPENDIX B

Notation of Instruments

English listing of orchestral instruments, cross-indexed alphabetically with French, German, and Italian translations. Related names, substitute instruments, transposition, clefs used, and a representative example are also included.

The English-language name of each instrument is followed on the right by the clef(s) used (in parentheses) and the transposition (unless the instrument sounds as notated). Arranged directly below the instrument name is a list of translations, other names, and substitute instruments (where applicable). Standard orchestral instruments are indicated in all capital letters. A representative example (Composer, Title) of a work featuring the instrument is given directly below the transposition. The French (f), German (g), and Italian (i) translations of each instrument's name list language and transposition only, with their English-language counterpart referenced below.

STANDARD/nonstandard (𝄞 𝄢 𝄡(A) 𝄡(T)) Transposition
    translations (language)
    other names (language)   Composer, Title
    (substitute instruments)

Translation/other names (f, g, i)   Transposition
    See reference

accordéon (f)
    See accordion

accordion   (𝄞 𝄢)
    accordéon (f)
    Akkordeon (g)
    Bandoneon (g)   Hindemith, *Kammermusik no. 1*
    concertina
    fisarmonica (i)

Harmonika (g)
Konzertina (g)
Ziehharmonika (g)
(piano, synthesizer)

Aelophon (g)
See wind machine

Akkordeon (g)
See accordion

albero dei sonagli (i)
See bell tree

Almglocken (g)
See cowbell

Alpenglocken (g)
See cowbell

Alpine herd bells
See cowbell

Alt-Saxophon (g)   Sounds a major sixth lower
See alto saxophone in E♭

Altflöte (g)   Sounds a perfect fourth lower
See alto flute

Altflöte in F (g)   Sounds a perfect fifth lower
See alto flute in F

Althoboe (g)   Sounds a perfect fifth lower
See English horn

Althorn (g)   Sounds a major sixth lower
See horn in E♭

Altklarinette (in Es) (g)   Sounds a major sixth lower
See alto clarinet

Appendix B: Notation of Instruments 363

Altklarinette in F(g)   Sounds a perfect fifth lower
    See alto clarinet in F

alto (f)
    See viola

alto clarinet (in E♭)   (𝄞) Sounds a major sixth lower
    Altklarinette (g)
    clarinette alto (f)   Holst, First Suite in E♭ for Military Band
    clarinetto alto (i)
    contralto clarinet

alto clarinet in F   (𝄞) Sounds a perfect fifth lower
    Altklarinette in F (g)
    clarinette alto en fa (f)
    clarinetto alto in fa (i)   Stravinsky, *Threni*
    contralto clarinet in F
    (alto clarinet, basset horn)

ALTO FLUTE (in G)   (𝄞) Sounds a perfect fourth lower
    Altflöte (g)
    bass flute in G
    flauto contralto (i)   Stravinsky, *The Rite of Spring*
    flautone (i)
    flute in G
    flûte alto (f)

alto flute in F   (𝄞) Sounds a perfect fifth lower
    Altflöte in F (g)
    flauto contralto in fa (i)   Glazounov, Symphony no. 8
    flûte alto en fa (f)

alto horn   Sounds a major sixth lower
    See horn in E♭

alto saxhorn in E♭   (𝄞) Sounds a major sixth lower
    saxhorn alto (i)
    saxhorn alto en mi♭ (f)   Berlioz, *Les Troyens*
    (alto saxophone, horn)

alto saxophone in E♭   (𝄞) Sounds a major sixth lower
    Alt-Saxophon in Es (g)
    Sassofono alto in mi♭ (i)   Ravel, *Bolero*
    saxophone alto en mi♭ (f)

alto trombone   (𝄞 𝄡⁽ᴬ⁾)
    Altposaune (g)   Schumann, Symphony no. 3

alto trumpet in F   (𝄞) Sounds a perfect fifth lower
    Alttrompete in F (g)
    tromba alto in fa (i)
    tromba contralta in fa (i)
    trompette alto en fa (f)   Rimsky-Korsakov, *Le coq d'or*
    trumpet in F, alto
    (trombone, horn in F)

Altposaune (g)
    See alto trombone

Alttrompete in F (g)   Sounds a perfect fifth lower
    See alto trumpet in F

Amboss (g)
    See anvil

Antike Zimbeln (g)   Sound two octaves higher
    See crotales

antique cymbals   Sound two octaves higher
    See crotales

anvil
    Amboss (g)
    enclume (f)   Wagner, *Das Rheingold*
    incudine (i)

armonium (i)
    See harmonium

arpa (i)
    See harp

Autobremstrommeln (g)
　See brake drums

bagpipes	(𝄞𝄢)
　cornamusa (i)
　cornemuse (f)
　Dudelsack (g)	Janácek, *The Excursions of Mr. Broucek*
　Sackpfeife (g)
　(oboe, bassoon)

Bandoneon (g)
　See accordion

banjo	(𝄞𝄢)
	Weill, *The Rise and Fall of the City of Mahagonny*

Bariton (g)	Sounds a major ninth lower
　See baritone

Bariton-Saxophon in Es (g)	Sounds an octave + a major sixth lower
　See baritone saxophone in E♭

baritone	(𝄞) Sounds a major ninth lower
　Bariton (g)
　baritono (i)
　baryton (f)	Grainger, *Lincolnshire Posy*
　(euphonium)

baritone oboe	Sounds an octave lower
　See heckelphone

baritone saxophone in E♭	(𝄞) Sounds an octave + a major sixth lower
　Bariton-Saxophon in Es (g)
　saxophone baryton en mi♭ (f)	Gershwin, *An American in Paris*
　sassofono baritono in mi♭ (i)

baritono (i)	Sounds a major ninth lower
　See baritone

Baroque trumpet	Sounds a minor seventh higher
　See piccolo trumpet

baryton (f)   Sounds a major ninth lower
  See baritone

Baβ-Klarinette in A (g)   (𝄞) Sounds a minor tenth lower
  See bass clarinet in A   (𝄢) Sounds a minor third lower

Baβ-Klarinette in B (g)   (𝄞) Sounds a major ninth lower
  See bass clarinet   (𝄢) Sounds a major second lower

Baβ-Posaune (g)
  See bass trombone

Baβ-Saxophon in B (g)   Sounds an octave + a major ninth lower
  See bass saxophone in B♭

Baβflöte (g)   Sounds an octave lower
  See bass flute

Baβgeige (g)   Sounds an octave lower
  See bass

Baβoboe (g)   Sounds an octave lower
  See heckelphone

Baβtrompete in B (g)   Sounds a major ninth lower
  See bass trumpet in B♭

Baβtrompete in C (g)   Sounds an octave lower
  See bass trumpet in C

Baβtrompete in D (g)   Sounds a minor seventh lower
  See bass trumpet in D

Baβtrompete in Des (g)   Sounds a major seventh lower
  See bass trumpet in D♭

Baβtrompete in E (g)   Sounds a minor sixth lower
  See bass trumpet in E

Baβtrompete in Es (g)   Sounds a major sixth lower
  See bass trumpet in E♭

Appendix B: Notation of Instruments 367

Baβtrompete in H (g)   Sounds a minor ninth lower
   See bass trumpet in B

Baβtuba (g)
   See tuba

BASS   ($\mathcal{9}\colon \, \&\, \mathbb{B}^{(T)}$) Sounds an octave lower
   Baβgeige (g)
   contrabass
   contrabasso (i)
   contrebasse (f)
   double bass   Mahler, Symphony no. 1
   Kontrabaβ (g)
   string bass
   violone (i)

bass "Wagner" tuba (in F)   ($\&\,\mathcal{9}\colon$) Sounds an octave + a perfect fifth lower
   tube basse en fa (f)   Wagner, *Götterdämmerung*

bass "Wagner" tuba in B♭   ($\&\,\mathcal{9}\colon$) Sounds a major ninth lower
   tube basse en si♭ (f)   Wagner, *Götterdämmerung*

BASS CLARINET in A   ($\&$) Sounds a minor tenth lower
   Baβ-klarinette in A (g)   ($\mathcal{9}\colon$) Sounds a minor third lower
   clarinette basse en la (f)
   clarinetto basso in la (i)   Mussorgsky-Ravel, *Pictures at an Exhibition*
   clarone in la (i)

BASS CLARINET (in B♭)   ($\&$) Sounds a major ninth lower
   Baβ-Klarinette in B (g)   ($\mathcal{9}\colon$) Sounds a major second lower
   clarinette basse en si♭ (f)
   clarinetto basso in si♭ (i)   R. Strauss, *Salome*
   clarone in si♭ (i)

BASS DRUM
   big drum
   gran cassa (i)
   grosse Trommel (g)
   grosse caisse (f)   Verdi, Requiem
   tamburo grande (i)

bass flute (in C)   (𝄞) Sounds an octave lower
   Baβflöte (g)
   flauto basso (i)   Zandonai, *Francesca da Rimini*
   flûte basse (f)

bass flute in G   Sounds a perfect fourth lower
   See alto flute

bass oboe   Sounds an octave lower
   See heckelphone

bass ophicleide
   See ophicleide

bass saxhorn in B♭   (𝄞) Sounds a major ninth lower
   saxhorn baryton en si♭ (f)   (𝄢) Sounds a major second lower
   (tenor saxophone)   Gounod, *Faust*

bass saxhorn in E♭   (𝄞 𝄢) Sounds an octave + a major sixth lower
   saxhorn contrebasse en mi♭ (f)
   (baritone saxophone)

bass saxophone in B♭   (𝄞) Sounds an octave + a major ninth lower
   Baβ-Saxophon in B (g)
   saxophone basse en si♭ (f)   Strauss, *Sinfonia domestica*
   sassofono basso in si♭ (i)

BASS TROMBONE   (𝄢)
   Baβ-Posaune (g)
   trombone basse (f)   Kodály, *Háry János*
   trombone basso (i)

bass trumpet in B   (𝄞) Sounds a minor ninth lower
   Baβtrompete in H (g)
   tromba basso in si (i)   Liszt, *Missa solemnis*
   trompette basse en si (f)

bass trumpet in B♭   (𝄞) Sounds a major ninth lower
   Baβtrompete in B (g)
   tromba basso in si♭ (i)   Berlioz, *Requiem*
   trompette basse en si♭ (f)

bass trumpet in C
    Baβtrompete in C (g)
    tromba basso in do (i)
    trompette basse en ut (f)

(𝄞) Sounds an octave lower

    Wagner, *Siegfried*

bass trumpet in D
    Baβtrompete in D (g)
    tromba basso in re (i)
    trompette basse en ré (f)

(𝄞) Sounds a minor seventh lower

    Wagner, *Götterdämmerung*

bass trumpet in D♭
    Baβtrompete in Des (g)
    tromba basso in re♭ (i)
    trompette basse en ré♭ (f)

(𝄞) Sounds a major seventh lower

    Wagner, *Die Walküre*

bass trumpet in E
    Baβtrompete in E (g)
    tromba basso in mi (i)
    trompette basse en mi (f)

(𝄞) Sounds a minor sixth lower

    Wagner, *Götterdämmerung*

bass trumpet in E♭
    Baβtrompete in Es (g)
    tromba basso in mi♭ (i)
    trompette basse en mi♭ (f)

(𝄞) Sounds a major sixth lower

    Wagner, *Götterdämmerung*

bass tuba
    See tuba

BASSET HORN
    Bassethorn (g)
    cor de basset (f)
    corno di bassetto (i)
    (clarinet, English horn, horn)
    See also alto clarinet in F

(𝄞) Sounds a perfect fifth lower
(𝄢) Sounds a perfect fourth higher

    (𝄞) Mozart, Requiem
    (𝄢) R. Strauss, *Elektra*

basset oboe
    See heckelphone

Sounds an octave lower

Bassethorn (g)
    See basset horn

(𝄞) Sounds a perfect fifth lower
(𝄢) Sounds a perfect fourth higher

basson (f)
> See bassoon

BASSOON
> basson (f)
> Fagott (g)
> fagotto (i)
> See Prokofiev scores for rare use of treble clef.

Tchaikovsky, Symphony no. 6

Becken (g)
> See cymbals

Becken-Paar (Tellern) (g)
> See cymbals

bell lyre
> See orchestra bells

Sounds two octaves higher

bell plates
> campane a lastra di metallo (i)
> cloches plaques (f)
> metal plates
> Plattenglocken (g)

bell tree
> albero dei sonagli (i)
> chapeau chinois (f)
> mezzaluna (i)
> pavillon chinois (f)
> Schellenbaum (g)

Berlioz, *Symphonie funèbre*

bells
> See chimes

big drum
> See bass drum

bloc chinois (f)
> See temple block

bloc de bois (f)
> See wood block

bloc de metal (f)
　　See metal block

blocchi di carta ventrata (i)
　　See sandblocks

blocco di legno (i)
　　See wood block

blocco di legno cinese (i)
　　See temple block

blocco di legno coreano (i)
　　See temple block

blocco di metallo (i)
　　See metal block

Blockflöte (g)
　　See recorder

bombardone (i)
　　See tuba

bonghi (i)
　　See bongos

bongo drums
　　See bongos

Bongos (g)
　　See bongos

bongos
　　bonghi (i)
　　bongo drums　　Bernstein, Symphonie Dances from *West Side Story* (rev. ed.)
　　Bongos (g)

brake drums
　　Autobremstrommeln (g)
　　tambours de frein (f)
　　tamburo dei freno (i)

Bratsche (g)
   See viola

Brummtopf (g)
   See lion roar

buccina (i)
   See flicorno soprano (i)
   See flicorno contralto (i)
   See flicorno tenore (i)
   See flicorno basso (i)

bugle   Sounds a major second lower
   See Flügelhorn

bugle en si♭ (f)   Sounds a major second lower
   See soprano saxhorn in B♭

bugle à clefs (f)   Sounds a major second lower
   See Flügelhorn

bugle à pistons (f)   Sounds a major second lower
   See Flügelhorn

caisse claire (f)
   See snare drum

caisse roulante (f)
   See tenor drum

campanaccio (i)
   See cowbell

campane (i)
   See chimes

campane a lastra di metallo (i)
   See bell plates

campane da gregge (i)
   See cowbell

campane da pastore (i)
   See cowbell

campane tubolari (i)
   See chimes

campanelli (i)   Sound two octaves higher
   See orchestra bells

campanelli a tastiera (i)   Sound two octaves higher
   See orchestra bells, keyboard Glockenspiel

campanelli di vacca (mucca) (i)
   See cowbell

campanetta (i)   Sound two octaves higher
   See orchestra bells

cariglione (i)   Sound two octaves higher
   See orchestra bells

carillon (f)   Sound two octaves higher
   See orchestra bells

carta vetrata (i)
   See sandblocks

cassa di legno (i)
   See wood block

cassa rullante (i)
   See tenor drum

cassettina (i)
   See wood block

castagnette (i)
   See castanets

castagnettes (f)
   See castanets

castanets
    castagnette (i)
    castagnettes (f)
    Kastagnetten (g)   Bizet, *Carmen*
    nacchere (i)

catene (i)
    See chains

Celesta (g)   Sounds an octave higher
    See celesta

CELESTA   (𝄞 𝄢) Sounds an octave higher
    Celesta (g)
    celesta (i)
    célesta (f)   Tchaikovsky, *The Nutcracker*
    celeste (i)

célesta (f)   Sounds an octave higher
    See celesta

celeste (f)   Sounds an octave higher
    See celesta

Cello (g)
    See cello

CELLO   (𝄞 𝄢 𝄡⁽ᵀ⁾)
    Cello (g)
    Violoncell (g)
    violoncelle (f)
    violoncello (i)
    Note the inconsistency of the octave transpositions:
        After tenor clef, treble clef sounds as written
            (Puccini, *Madame Butterfly*).
        After tenor clef, treble clef sounds an octave lower
            (Berg, Three Orchestra Pieces, op. 6).
        After bass clef, treble clef sounds as written
            (Rimsky-Korsakov, *Scheherazade*).
        After bass clef, treble clef sounds an octave lower
            (Tchaikovsky, *Romeo and Juliet* Fantasy-Overture).

Cembalo (g)
    See harpsichord

ceppi di carta di vetro (i)
    See sandblocks

cetra (i)
    See zither

chaînes (f)
    See chains

chains
    catene (i)
    chaînes (f)
    Ketten (g)

chapeau chinois (f)
    See bell tree

chimes
    bells
    campane (i)
    campane tubolari (i)
    cloches (f)
    cloches tubes (f)
    Glocken (g)
    Metallröhren (g)   Berlioz, *Symphonie fantastique*
    Röhrenglocken (g)
    tiefe Glocken (g)
    tubes des cloches (f)
    tubular bells
    tubular chimes

chitarra (i)   Sounds an octave lower
    See guitar

Cimbal (g)
    See cimbalom

cimbali antichi (i)   Sound two octaves higher
    See crotales

cimbalini (i)
   See finger cymbals

cimbalom   (𝄞𝄢)
   Cimbal (g)
   cimbalon
   cymbalom
   dulcimer
   Hackbrett (g)   Kodály, *Háry János*
   salterio tedesco (i)
   typophone (f)
   tubafono (i)

cimbalo (i)
   See harpsichord

cimbalon
   See cimbalom

Cimbasso (g)
   See tuba

cinelli (i)
   See cymbals

cithara (i)
   See zither

clairon (f)
   See Flügelhorn

CLARINET in A   (𝄞) Sounds a minor third lower
   clarinette en la (f)
   clarinetto in la (i)   Tchaikovsky, Symphony no. 5
   Klarinette in A (g)

CLARINET in B♭   (𝄞) Sounds a major second lower
   clarinette (f)
   clarinetto (i)   Mozart, Symphony no. 39
   Klarinette (g)

Appendix B: Notation of Instruments

clarinet in C	(𝄞)
clarinette en ut (f)	
clarinetto in do (i)	Beethoven, Symphony no. 1
Klarinette in C (g)	
clarinet in D	(𝄞) Sounds a major second higher
clarinette en ré (f)	
clarinetto in re (i)	
clarinetto piccolo in re (i)	
Klarinette in D (g)	Stravinsky, *The Rite of Spring*
petite clarinette en ré (f)	
piccolo clarinet in D	
CLARINET in E♭	(𝄞) Sounds a minor third higher
clarinetto piccolo (i)	
Klarinette in Es (g)	
petite clarinette (f)	Stravinsky, *The Rite of Spring*
clarinette en mi♭ (f)	
piccolo clarinet (i)	
clarinette en si♭ (f)	Sounds a major second lower
See clarinet in B♭	
clarinette en la (f)	Sounds a minor third lower
See clarinet in A	
clarinette en mi♭ (f)	Sounds a minor third higher
See clarinet in E♭	
clarinette alto (f)	Sounds a major sixth lower
See alto clarinet	
clarinette alto en fa (f)	(𝄞) Sounds a perfect fifth lower
See alto clarinet in F	(𝄢) Sounds a perfect fourth higher
clarinette basse en la (f)	(𝄞) Sounds a minor tenth lower
See bass clarinet in A	(𝄢) Sounds a minor third lower
clarinette basse en si♭ (f)	(𝄞) Sounds a major ninth lower
See bass clarinet	(𝄢) Sounds a major second lower

clarinette contrebasse en la (f) (𝄞) Sounds an octave + a minor tenth lower
    See contrabass clarinet in A (𝄢) Sounds a minor tenth lower

clarinette contrebasse en si♭ (f) (𝄞) Sounds an octave + a major ninth lower
    See contrabass clarinet (𝄢) Sounds a major ninth lower

clarinette contrebasse en mi♭ (f) (𝄞) Sounds 2 octaves + a major sixth lower
    See contrabass clarinet in E♭ (𝄢) Sounds an octave + a major sixth lower

clarinette en ut (f)
    See clarinet in C

clarinette en ré (f) Sounds a major second higher
    See clarinet in D

clarinetto in si♭ (i) Sounds a major second lower
    See clarinet

clarinetto in la (i) Sounds a minor third lower
    See clarinet in A

clarinetto alto in mi♭ (i) Sounds a major sixth lower
    See alto clarinet

clarinetto basso in la (i) (𝄞) Sounds a minor tenth lower
    See bass clarinet in A (𝄢) Sounds a minor third lower

clarinetto basso in si♭ (i) (𝄞) Sounds a major ninth lower
    See bass clarinet in B♭ (𝄢) Sounds a major second lower

clarinetto contralto in fa (i) Sounds a perfect fifth lower
    See alto clarinet in F

clarinetto in do (i)
    See clarinet in C

clarinetto in re (i) Sounds a major second higher
    See clarinet in D

clarinetto piccolo (i) Sounds a minor third higher
    See clarinet in E♭

clarinetto piccolo in re (i) Sounds a major second higher
   See clarinet in D

clarino (i)
   See piccolo trumpet

clarone contrabasso in la (i) (𝄞) Sounds an octave + a minor tenth lower
   See contrabass clarinet in A (𝄢) Sounds a minor tenth lower

clarone contrabasso in si♭ (i) (𝄞) Sounds an octave + a major ninth lower
   See contrabass clarinet (𝄢) Sounds a major ninth lower

clarone contrabasso in mi♭ (i) (𝄞) Sounds 2 octaves + a major sixth lower
   See contrabass clarinet in E♭ (𝄢) Sounds an octave + a major sixth lower

clarone in la (i) (𝄞) Sounds a minor tenth lower
   See bass clarinet in A (𝄢) Sounds a minor third lower

clarone (in si♭) (i) (𝄞) Sounds a major ninth lower
   See bass clarinet (𝄢) Sounds a major second lower

clavecin (f)
   See harpsichord

claves
   Holzstab (g) Prokofiev, Symphony no. 6

clavicembalo (i)
   See harpsichord

clavier (f)
   See piano

cloches (f)
   See chimes

cloches de vaches (f)
   See cowbell

cloches plaques (f)
   See bell plates

cloches tubes (f)
    See chimes

concertina (i)
    See accordion

conga drums
    tumbao
    tumbas   Stockhausen, *Gruppen*

contrabass   Sounds an octave lower
    See bass

contrabass clarinet in A   (𝄞) Sounds an octave + a minor tenth lower
    clarinette contrebasse en la (f)   (𝄢) Sounds a minor tenth lower
    clarone contrabasso in la (i)
    Kontrabaßklarinette in A (g)   Schoenberg, Five Pieces for Orchestra
    pedal clarinet in A

contrabass clarinet (in B♭)   (𝄞) Sounds an octave + a major ninth lower
    clarinette contrebasse (f)   (𝄢) Sounds a major ninth lower
    clarone contrabasso (i)
    Kontrabaßklarinette (g)   Henze, Symphony no. 7
    pedal clarinet

contrabass clarinet in E♭   (𝄞) Sounds 2 octaves + a major sixth lower
    clarinette contrebasse en mi♭ (f)   (𝄢) Sounds an octave + a major sixth lower
    octocontrebasse clarinette
        en mi♭ (f)
    clarone contrabasso in mi♭ (i)
    Kontrabaßklarinette in Es (g)
    pedal clarinet in E♭

contrabass sarrusophone   Sounds an octave lower
    See sarrusophone

contrabass saxhorn in B♭   (𝄞) Sounds an octave + a major ninth lower
    saxhorn contrebasse en si♭ (f)   (𝄢) Sounds a major ninth lower
    (bass saxophone, contrabass clarinet)   Stravinsky, *Threni*

contrabass saxophone in E♭   (𝄞) Sounds 2 octaves + a major sixth lower
    saxophone contrebasse en mi♭ (f)   (𝄢) Sounds an octave + a major sixth lower
    Kontrabaß Saxophon in Es (g)
    sassofono contrabasso in mi♭ (i)

contrabass trombone   (𝄢)
    trombone contrebasse (f)
    double-bass trombone
    Kontrabaß Posaune (g)   Henze, Symphony no. 7
    trombone contrabasso (i)

contrabasso (i)   Sounds an octave lower
    See bass

CONTRABASSOON   (𝄢) Sounds an octave lower
    controfagotto (i)
    contrebasson (f)
    double bassoon   Ravel, Piano Concerto in G
    Kontrafagott (g)

controfagotto (i)   Sounds an octave lower
    See contrabassoon

contralto bugle (i)   Sounds a major second lower
    See flügelhorn

contralto clarinet (in E♭)   Sounds a major sixth lower
    See alto clarinet

contralto clarinet in F   Sounds a perfect fifth lower
    See alto clarinet in F

contrebasse (f)   Sounds an octave lower
    See bass

contrebasse d'harmonie (f)
    See ophicleide

contrebasson (f)   Sounds an octave lower
    See contrabassoon

cor (f)
See horn

cor à piston (f)
See horn

cor anglais (f)   Sounds a perfect fifth lower
See English horn

cor anglé (f)   Sounds a perfect fifth lower
See English horn

cor chromatique (f)
See horn

cor de basset (f)   (𝄞) Sounds a perfect fifth lower
See basset horn   (𝄢) Sounds a perfect fourth higher

cor de chasse (f)
See natural horn

cor en fa (f)   Sounds a perfect fifth lower
See horn in F

cor en fa♯ (f)   Sounds a diminished fifth lower
See horn in F♯

cor en la (f)   Sounds a minor third lower
See horn in A

cor en la basse (f)   Sounds a minor tenth lower
See horn in low A

cor en la♭ (f)   Sounds a major third lower
See horn in A♭

cor en la♭ basse (f)   Sounds a major tenth lower
See horn in low A♭

cor en mi (f)   Sounds a minor sixth lower
See horn in E

cor en mi♭ (f) Sounds a major sixth lower
   See horn in E♭

cor en ré (f) Sounds a minor seventh lower
   See horn in D

cor en ré♭ (f) Sounds a major seventh lower
   See horn in D♭

cor en si (f) Sounds a minor ninth lower
   See horn in B

cor en si alto (f) Sounds a minor second lower
   See horn in high B

cor en si♭ (f) Sounds a major ninth lower
   See horn in B♭

cor en si♭ alto (f) Sounds a major second lower
   See horn in high B♭

cor en sol (f) Sounds a perfect fourth lower
   See horn in G

cor en ut (f) Sounds an octave lower
   See horn in C

cor en ut alto (f)
   See horn in high C

cor simple (f)
   See natural horn

cornemusa (i)
   See bagpipes

cornemuse (f)
   See bagpipes

cornet
   cornet à bouquin (f)
   cornet à pistons (f)

Cornett (g)
cornetta (i)
cornette (f)
cornetto (i)
Kornett (g)
pistone (i)
Zinke (g)
(trumpet)

cornet in A (𝄞) Sounds a minor third lower
  cornet à pistons en la (f)
  cornetta in la (i)
  Kornett in A (g) Berlioz, *Symphony fantastique*
  (trumpet)

cornet (in B♭) (𝄞) Sounds a major second lower
  cornet à pistons en si♭ (f)
  cornetta in si♭ (i)
  Kornett in B (g) Stravinsky, *Petrouchka*
  (trumpet)

cornet in G (𝄞) Sounds a perfect fifth higher
  cornet à pistons en sol (f)
  cornetta in sol (i)
  Kornett in G (g) Berlioz, *Symphonie fantastique*
  (trumpet)

cornet à bouquin (f)
  See cornet

cornet à pistons (f)
  See cornet

cornet à pistons en la (f) Sounds a minor third lower
  See cornet in A

cornet à pistons en si♭ (f) Sounds a major second lower
  See cornet in B♭

cornet à pistons en sol (f) Sounds a perfect fifth higher
  See cornet in G

Cornett (g)
See cornet

cornetta (i)
See cornet

cornetta in la (i)   Sounds a minor third lower
See cornet in A

cornetta in si♭ (i)   Sounds a major second lower
See cornet in B♭

cornetta in sol (i)   Sounds a perfect fifth higher
See cornet in G

cornette
See cornet

cornetto (i)
See cornet

corno (i)
See horn

corno da caccia (i)
See natural horn

corno di bassetto (i)   (𝄞) Sounds a perfect fifth lower
See basset horn   (𝄢) Sounds a perfect fourth higher

corno di posta (i)
See trumpet

corno in do (i)   Sounds an octave lower
See horn in C

corno in do alto (i)
See horn in high C

corno in fa (i)   Sounds a perfect fifth lower
See horn (in F)

corno in fa♯ (i) — Sounds a diminished fifth lower
   See horn in F♯

corno in la (i) — Sounds a minor third lower
   See horn in A

corno in la basso (i) — Sounds a minor tenth lower
   See horn in low A

corno in la♭ (i) — Sounds a major third lower
   See horn in A♭

corno in la♭ basso (i) — Sounds a major tenth lower
   See horn in low A♭

corno in mi (i) — Sounds a minor sixth lower
   See horn in E

corno in mi♭ (i) — Sounds a major sixth lower
   See horn in E♭

corno in re (i) — Sounds a minor seventh lower
   See horn in D

corno in re♭ (i) — Sounds a major seventh lower
   See horn in D♭

corno in si (i) — Sounds a minor ninth lower
   See horn in B

corno in si alto (i) — Sounds a minor second lower
   See horn in high B

corno in si♭ (i) — Sounds a major ninth lower
   See horn in B♭

corno in si♭ alto (i) — Sounds a major second lower
   See horn in high B♭

corno in sol (i) — Sounds a perfect fourth lower
   See horn in G

corno inglese (i)   Sounds a perfect fifth lower
    See English horn

corno naturale (i)
    See natural horn

corno ventile (i)
    See horn

coup de pistolet (f)
    See pistol [shot]

cowbell
    Almglocken (g)
    Alpenglocken (g)
    Alpine herd bells
    campanaccio (i)
    campane da gregge (i)
    campane da pastore (i)
    campanelli di vacca (mucca) (i)   R. Strauss, *Alpine Symphony*
    cloches de vaches (f)
    Glockengeläute (g)
    Herdengeläute (g)
    Herdenglocken (g)
    Kuhglocken (g)
    sonnailles de troupeau (f)

crécelle (f)
    See rattle

crécelle à manivelle (f)
    See rattle

crotales   (𝄞) Sound two octaves higher
    Antike Zimbeln (g)
    antique cymbals
    cimbali antichi (i)
    crotali (i)
    crotali a dita (i)   Debussy, *Prelude to the Afternoon of a Faun*
    crotali antichi (i)
    cymbales antiques (f)
    Greek cymbals

crotali (i)   Sound two octaves higher
    See crotales

crotali a dita (i)   Sound two octaves higher
    See crotales

crotali antichi (i)   Sound two octaves higher
    See crotales

cuica (i)
    See lion roar

cymbale sur tiges (f)
    See sizzle cymbal

cymbales (f)
    See cymbals

cymbales antiques (f)   Sound two octaves higher
    See crotales

cymbales digitales (f)
    See finger cymbals

cymbale suspendue (f)
    See suspended cymbal

cymbalom
    See cimbalom

CYMBALS
    Becken (g)
    cinelli (i)
    cymbales (i)
    piatti (i)   Tchaikovsky, *1812 Overture*
    Tellern (crashed) (g)
    cymbales (f)

cytharra
    See zither

Donnerblech (g)
   See thunder sheet

Donnermaschine (g)
   See thunder machine

double bass   Sounds an octave lower
   See bass

double bassoon   Sounds an octave lower
   See contrabassoon

double-bass trombone
   See contrabass trombone

Drehleier (g)
   See hurdy-gurdy

drum set
   trap set

Dudelsack (g)
   See bagpipes

dulcimer
   See cimbalom

effetto colpo di pistola (i)
   See pistol [shot]

enclume (f)
   See anvil

Englisch Horn (g)   Sounds a perfect fifth lower
   See English horn

ENGLISH HORN   (𝄞) Sounds a perfect fifth lower
   Althoboe (g)
   cor anglais (f)
   cor anglé (f)

corno inglese (i)
Englisch Horn (g)
hautbois de chasse (f)
hautecontre de hautbois (f) Berlioz, *Roman Carnival Overture*
hunting oboe
oboe contralto (i)
oboe da caccia (i)
taille (f)
tenor oboe
See Prokofiev Symphony No. 5 for rarely used alto clef

eufonio (i)
   See euphonium

euphonium
   eufonio (i)
   flicorno basso in si♭ (i) Holst, *The Planets*
   tenor tuba

éoliphone (f)
   See wind machine

Fagott (g)
   See bassoon

fagotto (i)
   See bassoon

fiddle
   See violin

field drum
   See tenor drum

finger cymbals
   cimbalini (i)
   cymbales digitales (f) Berio, *Circles*
   Fingerzimbeln (g)

Fingerzimbeln (g)
   See finger cymbals

fipple flute
>	See recorder

fisarmonica (i)
>	See accordion

flageolet (i)
>	See recorder

flautino (i)   Sounds an octave higher
>	See piccolo

flauto (i)
>	See flute

flauto a culisse (i)
>	See slide whistle

flauto basso (in do) (i)   Sounds an octave lower
>	See bass flute

flauto contralto (in sol) (i)   Sounds a perfect fourth lower
>	See alto flute

flauto contralto in fa (i)   Sounds a perfect fifth lower
>	See alto flute in F

flauto diritto (i)
>	See recorder

flauto dolce (i)
>	See recorder

flauto grande (i)
>	See flute

flauto in Do (i)
>	See flute

flauto piccolo (i)   Sounds an octave higher
>	See piccolo

flauto traverso (i)
  See flute

flautone (i)   Sounds a perfect fourth lower
  See alto flute

flessatono (i)
  See flexatone

Flexaton (g)
  See flexatone

flexatone
  flessatono (i)
  Flexaton (g)   Schoenberg, *Variations for Orchestra*
  See also musical saw

flicorno basso (i)   (𝄢) Sounds a major second lower
  buccina (i)
  flicorno basso in si♭ (i)   Respighi, *The Pines of Rome*
  (euphonium, horn, trombone)

flicorno basso in si♭ (i)   (𝄢) Sounds a major second lower
  See flicorno basso

flicorno contralto in Mi♭ (i)   Sounds a major sixth lower
  See buccina (i)
  See Flügelhorn

flicorno soprano (i)   (𝄞) Sounds a major second lower
  buccina (i)
  (Flügelhorn, cornet, trumpet)   Respighi, *The Pines of Rome*

flicorno tenore (i)   (𝄞) Sounds a major second lower
  baritono (i)
  buccina (i)   Respighi, *The Pines of Rome*
  (Flügelhorn, baritone, horn)

flicorno tenore in Si♭ (i)   (𝄞) Sounds a major second lower
  See flicorno tenore

Flöte (g)
   See flute

Flügelhorn   (𝄞) Sounds a major second lower
   bugle
   bugle à clefs (f)
   bugle à pistons (f)
   Clairon (g)   Mahler, Symphony no. 3
   contralto bugle (i)
   flicorno contralto in Mi♭ (i)
   Flügelhorn (g)
   (trumpet)

FLUTE   (𝄞)
   flauto (i)
   flauto grande (i)
   flauto in Do (i)
   flauto traverso (i)
   Flöte (g)
   flûte (f)   Beethoven, Symphony no. 3
   flûte traversière (f)
   grande flûte (f)
   grosse Flöte (g)
   Querflöte (g)
   transverse flute

flute in G   Sounds a perfect fourth lower
   See alto flute

flûte (f)
   See flute

flûte alto (f)   Sounds a perfect fourth lower
   See alto flute

flûte basse (f)   Sounds an octave lower
   See bass flute (in C)

flûte douce (f)
   See recorder

flûte traversière (f)
See flute

flûte-à-bec (f)
See recorder

Flügel (grand piano) (g)
See piano

flûte alto en fa (f)   Sounds a perfect fifth lower
See alto flute in F

fortepiano (i)
See piano

fouet (f)
See whip

French horn   Sounds a perfect fifth lower
See horn

friction drum
See lion roar

frusta (i)
See whip

frusta di verghe (i)
See whip

Geige (g)
See violin

Gerassel (g)
See rattle

Glasharmonika (g)   Sounds an octave higher
See glass harmonica

glass harmonica   (𝄞𝄢) Sounds an octave higher
  Glasharmonika (g)

Harmonika (g) Saint-Saens, *The Carnival of the Animals*
(flute, synthesizer)

Glocken (g)
See chimes

Glockengeläute (g)
See cowbell

Glockenspiel (g) Sounds two octaves higher
See orchestra bells

glockenspiel à clavier (f) Sounds two octaves higher
See keyboard Glockenspiel

Glöckchen (g) Sound two octaves higher
See orchestra bells

gong
   gong (f)
   Gong (g) Puccini, *Turandot*
   gong (i)

gourd
See maracas

gran cassa (i)
See bass drum

grande flûte (f)
See flute

Greek cymbals Sound two octaves higher
See crotales

grelots (f)
See sleigh bells

grosse Flöte (g)
See flute

grosse Trommel (g)
See bass drum

grosse-caisse (f)
See bass drum

guiro
    reco-reco
    (washboard with thimbles)

guitar   (𝄞 ⁸) Sounds an octave lower
    chitarra (i)
    guitare (f)   Webern, Five Pieces for Orchestra, Op. 10
    Guitarre (g)
    (harp, synthesizer)

Guitarre (g)   Sounds an octave lower
    See guitar

Hackbrett (g)
    See cimbalom

Hammer (g)
    See hammer[blow]

hammer[blow]
    Hammer (g)
    Hammerschlag (g)
    marteau (f)   Mahler, Symphony no. 6
    martello (i)

Hammerklavier (g)
    See piano

Hammerschlag (g)
    See hammer[blow]

hand horn
    See horn

Harfe (g)
    See harp

Harmoniebaβ (g)
  See ophicleide

Harmonika (g)
  See accordion

Harmonika (g)   Sounds an octave higher
  See glass harmonica

Harmonium (g)
  See harmonium

harmonium   (𝄞 𝄢)
  armonium (i)
  Harmonium (g)
  organetto (i)   Webern, Five Pieces for Orchestra, Op. 10
  orgue de salon (f)

harness bells
  See sleigh bells

HARP   (𝄞 𝄢)
  arpa (i)
  Harfe (g)   Tchaikovsky, *Romeo and Juliet* Fantasy-Overture
  harpe (f)

harpe (f)
  See harp

harpsichord   (𝄞 𝄢)
  Cembalo (g)
  cimbalo (i)
  clavecin (f)   Strauss, *Capriccio*
  clavicembalo (i)
  Keilflügel (g)

hautbois (f)
  See oboe

hautbois baryton (f)   Sounds an octave lower
  See heckelphone

hautbois d'amour (f)   Sounds a minor third lower
    See oboe d'amore

hautbois de chasse (f)   Sounds a perfect fifth lower
    See English horn

hautboy
    See oboe

hautecontre de hautbois (f)   Sounds a perfect fifth lower
    See English horn

hängendes Becken (g)
    See suspended cymbal

Heckelphon (g)   Sounds an octave lower
    See heckelphone

heckelphone   (𝄞 𝄢) Sounds an octave lower
    baritone oboe
    Baßoboe (g)
    bass oboe
    basset oboe   R. Strauss, *Salome*
    hautbois baryton (f)
    Heckelphon (g)
    oboe baritono (i)

Herdengeläute (g)
    See cowbell

Herdenglocken (g)
    See cowbell

Hoboe (g)
    See oboe

Holz- und Strohinstrument (g)   Sounds an octave higher
    See xylophone

Holzblock (g)
    See wood block

Holzklapper (g)
See whip

Holzstab (g)
See claves

Holztrompete (g)   Sounds a major second lower
See tarogato

Horn (g)
See horn

Horn in A (g)   Sounds a minor third lower
See horn in A

Horn in tief A (g)   Sounds a minor tenth lower
See horn in low A

Horn in As (g)   Sounds a major third lower
See horn in A♭

Horn in tief As (g)   Sounds a major tenth lower
See horn in low A♭

Horn in B (g)   Sounds a major ninth lower
See horn in B♭

Horn in hoch B (g)   Sounds a major second lower
See horn in high B♭

Horn in C (g)   Sounds an octave lower
See horn in C

Horn in hoch C (g)
See horn in high C

Horn in D (g)   Sounds a minor seventh lower
See horn in D

Horn in Des (g)   Sounds a major seventh lower
See horn in D♭

Horn in E (g)   Sounds a minor sixth lower
    See horn in E

Horn in Es (g)   Sounds a major sixth lower
    See horn in E♭

Horn (in F) (g)   Sounds a perfect fifth lower
    See horn (in F)

Horn in Fis (g)   Sounds a diminished fifth lower
    See horn in F♯

Horn in G (g)   Sounds a perfect fourth lower
    See horn in G

Horn in H (g)   Sounds a minor ninth lower
    See horn in B

Horn in hoch H (g)   Sounds a minor second lower
    See horn in high B

HORN   (𝄞 𝄢 𝄡(A))
    cor (f)
    cor chromatique (f)
    cor à piston (f)
    corno (i)
    corno ventile (i)
    French horn   Tchaikovsky, Symphony no. 5
    handhorn
    Horn (g)
    valve horn
    Ventilhorn (g)
    See also horn (in F)

horn in A   (𝄞 𝄢) Sounds a minor third lower
    cor en la (f)
    corno in la (i)   Beethoven, Symphony no. 7
    Horn in A (g)

horn in low A   (𝄞 𝄢) Sounds a minor tenth lower
    cor en la basse (f)

corno in la basso (i) Horn in tief A (g)		Verdi, *Don Carlo*
horn in A♭ cor en la♭ (f) corno in la♭ (i) Horn in As (g)	(𝄞 𝄢) Sounds a major third lower	Verdi, Requiem
horn in low A♭ cor en la♭ basse (f) corno in la♭ basso (i) Horn in tief As (g)	(𝄞 𝄢) Sounds a major tenth lower	Verdi, *Falstaff*
horn in B cor en si (f) corno in si (i) Horn in H (g)	(𝄞 𝄢) Sounds a minor ninth lower	Brahms, Symphony no. 1
horn in high B cor en si alto (f) corno in si alto (i) Horn in hoch H (g)	(𝄞 𝄢) Sounds a minor second lower	
horn in B♭ cor en si♭ (f) corno in si♭ (i) Horn in B (g)	(𝄞 𝄢) Sounds a major ninth lower	Beethoven, Symphony no. 9
horn in high B♭ cor en si♭ alto (f) corno in si♭ alto (i) Horn in hoch B (g)	(𝄞 𝄢) Sounds a major second lower	Schumann, Symphony no. 1
horn in C cor en ut (f) corno in do (i) Horn in C (g)	(𝄞 𝄢) Sounds an octave lower	Brahms, Symphony no. 1
horn in high C cor en ut alto (f) corno in do alto (i) Horn in hoch C (g)	(𝄞 𝄢)	Haydn, Symphony no. 48

horn in D (𝄞𝄢) Sounds a minor seventh lower
   cor en ré (f)
   corno in re (i)   Brahms, Symphony no. 2
   Horn in D (g)

horn in D♭   (𝄞𝄢) Sounds a major seventh lower
   cor en ré♭ (f)
   corno in re♭ (i)   Bizet, *Carmen*
   Horn in Des (g)

horn in E   (𝄞𝄢) Sounds a minor sixth lower
   cor en mi (f)
   corno in mi (i)   R. Strauss, *Don Juan*
   Horn in E (g)

horn in E♭   (𝄞𝄢) Sounds a major sixth lower
   Althorn (g)
   alto horn
   cor en mi♭ (f)
   corno in mi♭ (i)   Beethoven, Symphony no. 3
   Horn in Es (g)
   mellophone

horn in F   (𝄞𝄢 𝄡(A)) Sounds a perfect fifth lower
   cor en fa (f)
   corno in fa (i)   Beethoven, Symphony no. 6
   Horn in F (g)

horn in F♯   (𝄞𝄢) Sounds a diminished fifth lower
   cor en fa♯ (f)
   corno in fa♯ (i)   Massenet, *Manon*
   Horn in Fis (g)

horn in G   (𝄞𝄢) Sounds a perfect fourth lower
   cor en sol (f)
   corno in sol (i)   Mozart, Symphony no. 40
   Horn in G (g)

Hungarian wooden clarinet
   See tarogato

hunting horn
   See natural horn

hunting oboe   Sounds a perfect fifth lower
   See English horn

hurdy-gurdy
   Drehleier (g)
   organistrum   Haydn, Concerto in F, Hob.VIIh:4
   lira organizzata (i)
   vielle a roue (f)

incudine (i)
   See anvil

Jagdhorn (g)
   See natural horn

jeu de timbres (f)   Sound two octaves higher
   See orchestra bells, keyboard Glockenspiel

jeu de timbres à clavier (f)   Sounds two octaves higher
   See keyboard Glockenspiel

jingles
   See sleigh bells

Kastagnetten (g)
   See castanets

Ketten (g)
   See chains

kettle-drums
   See timpani

keyboard Glockenspiel   Sounds two octaves higher
   campanelli a tastiera (i)
   glockenspiel à clavier (f)
   jeu de timbres à clavier (f)   Mozart, *The Magic Flute*
   Klaviaturglockenspiel (g)

Stabglockenspiel (g)
　See also orchestra bells

Keilflügel (g)
　See harpsichord

Klappenbaß (g)
　See ophicleide

Klarinette in B (g)   Sounds a major second lower
　See clarinet in B♭

Klarinette in A (g)   Sounds a minor third lower
　See clarinet in A

Klarinette in C (g)
　See clarinet in C

Klarinette in D (g)   Sounds a major second higher
　See clarinet in D

Klarinette in Es (g)   Sounds a minor third higher
　See clarinet in E♭

Klaviaturglockenspiel (g)   Sounds two octaves higher
　See keyboard Glockenspiel

Klavier (g)
　See piano

kleine Discant-Geige (g)
　See violin

kleine Flöte (g)   Sounds an octave higher
　See piccolo

kleine Trommel (g)
　See snare drum

kleine Trompete in B (g)   Sounds a minor seventh higher
　See piccolo trumpet

Appendix B: Notation of Instruments   405

kleine Trompete in A (g)   Sounds a major sixth higher
   See piccolo trumpet in A

Knarre (g)
   See rattle

Kontrabaβ (g)   Sounds an octave lower
   See bass

Kontrabaβklarinette in A (g)   (𝄞) Sounds an octave + a minor tenth lower
   See contrabass clarinet in A   (𝄢) Sounds a minor tenth lower

Kontrabaβklarinette (in B) (g)   (𝄞) Sounds an octave + a minor ninth lower
   See contrabass clarinet in B♭   (𝄢) Sounds a major ninth lower.

Kontrabaβklarinette in Es (g)   (𝄞) Sounds 2 octaves + a major sixth lower
   See contrabass clarinet in E♭   (𝄢) Sounds an octave + a major sixth lower

Kontrabaβtuba (g)
   See tuba

Kontrabaβ Posaune (g)
   See contrabass trombone

Kontrafagott (g)   Sounds an octave lower
   See contrabassoon

Konzertina (g)
   See accordion

Kornett (g)
   See cornet

Kornett in A (g)   Sounds a minor third lower
   See cornet in A

Kornett in B (g)   Sounds a major second lower
   See cornet in B♭

Kornett in G (g)   Sounds a perfect fifth higher
   See cornet in G

Kuhglocken (g)
   See cowbell

lastra del tuono (i)
   See thunder sheet

Laute (g)
   See lute

lauto (i)
   See lute

Leier (g)
   See hurdy-gurdy

Liebesgeige (g)
   See viola d'amore

Liebesoboe (g)   Sounds a minor third lower
   See oboe d'amore

lion roar
   Brummtopf (g)
   cuica (i)
   friction drum
   ruggio di leone (i)
   ruggito del leone (i)   Varèse, *Ionisation*
   string drum
   tambour à cordes (f)
   tambour-lion (f)

lira organizzata (i)
   See hurdy-gurdy

liuto (i)
   See lute

long drum
   Provençal long drum
   tabor
   Tambourin (g)   Bizet, "*L'Arlésienne*

tambourin (f)
tambourin de Provençe (f)

long-necked lute
   See tamboritsa

Lotosflöte (g)
   See slide whistle

lute
   Laute (g)
   lauto (i)   Hindemith, *Suite of French Dances*
   liuto (i)
   luth (f)

luth (f)
   See lute

macchine del tuono (i)
   See thunder machine

macchine del vento (i)
   See wind machine

machine à tonnerre (f)
   See thunder machine

machine à vent (f)
   See wind machine

mandoline
   Mandoline (g)
   mandoline (f)   Mozart, *Don Giovanni*
   mandolino (i)

Mandoline (g)
   See mandoline

mandoline (f)
   See mandoline

mandolino (i)
   See mandoline

maracas (gourds)
   maracas (f)
   Maracas (g)   Copland, *El salón México*
   maracas (i)

marimba
   marimbafono (i)
   Marimbaphon (g)   Sessions, *Rhapsody for Orchestra*
   marimbaphone (f)

marimbafono (i)
   See marimba

Marimbaphon (g)
   See marimba

marimbaphone (f)
   See marimba

marteau (f)
   See hammer[blow]

martello (i)
   See hammer[blow]

Martenot waves
   onde Martenot (i)
   ondes Martenot (f)   Honegger, *Jeanne d'Arc au bûcher*
   tone generator

mellophone   Sounds a major sixth lower
   See horn in E♭

melodica   Michael Daugherty, *Ghost Ranch*
   (synthesizer)

metal block
   bloc de metal (f)

blocco di metallo (i)
   Metallblock (g)

metal plates
   See bell plates

Metallblock (g)
   See metal block

Metallröhren (g)
   See chimes

metallofono (i)
   See metallophone

metallophone
   metallofono (i)   Orff, *Catulli Carmina*
   (vibraphone)

mezzaluna (i)
   See bell tree

military drum
   See tenor drum

Militärtrommel (g)
   See tenor drum

musical saw
   scie musicale (f)
   sega cantante (i)
   sega musicale (i)   Henze, *Elegy for Young Lovers*
   Spielsäge (g)
   See also flexatone

nacchere (i)
   See castanets

Naturhorn (g)
   See natural horn

natural horn   (𝄞𝄢)
   cor de chasse (f)
   cor simples (f)
   corno da caccia (i)
   hand horn
   hunting horn   Brahms, Horn Trio
   Jagdhorn (g)
   Naturhorn (g)
   Waldhorn (g)

Nietenbecken (g)
   See sizzle cymbal

Oboe (g)
   See oboe

OBOE   (𝄞)
   hautbois (f)
   hautboy
   oboe (i)   Bizet, Symphony in C
   Hoboe (g)
   Oboe (g)

oboe baritono (i)   Sounds an octave lower
   See heckelphone

oboe contralto (i)   Sounds a perfect fifth lower
   See English horn

oboe da caccia (i)   Sounds a perfect fifth lower
   See English horn

oboe d'amore   (𝄞) Sounds a minor third lower
   hautbois d'amour (f)
   Liebesoboe (g)
   oboe d'amore (i)   R. Strauss, *Symphonia Domestica*
   oboe luongo (i)

oboe luongo (i)   Sounds a minor third lower
   See oboe d'amore

octocontrebasse clarinette en mi♭ (f)   (𝄞) Sounds 2 octaves + a major sixth lower
   See contrabass clarinet in E♭   (𝄢) Sounds an octave + a major sixth lower

oficleide (i)
   See ophicleide

onde Martenot (i)
   See Martenot waves

ondes Martenot (f)
   See Martenot waves

ophicleide   (𝄢)
   bass ophicleide
   contrebasse d'harmonie (f)
   Harmoniebaβ (g)
   Klappenbaβ (g)
   oficleide (i)   Mendelssohn, *A Midsummer Night's Dream*
   Ophikleide (g)
   ophicléide (f)
   tuba mirabilis

ophicléide (f)
   See ophicleide

Ophikleide (g)
   See ophicleide

orchestra bells   (𝄞 𝄢) Sound two octaves higher
   bell lyre
   campanelli (i)
   campanelli a tastiera (i)
   campanetta (i)
   cariglione (i)
   carillon (f)   Dukás, *The Sorcerer's Apprentice*
   Glockenspiel (g)
   Glöckchen (g)
   jeu de timbres (f)
   See also keyboard Glockenspiel

organ (𝄞 𝄢)
   organo (i)
   Orgel (g)   R. Strauss, *Also sprach Zarathustra*
   orgue (f)
   pipe organ

organetto (i)
   See harmonium

organistrum
   See hurdy-gurdy

organo (i)
   See organ

Orgel (g)
   See organ

orgue (f)
   See organ

orgue de salon (f)
   See harmonium

ottavino (i)   Sounds an octave higher
   See piccolo

papier de verre (f)
   See sandblocks

Pauken (g)
   See timpani

pavillon chinois (f)
   See bell tree

pedal clarinet in A   (𝄞) Sounds an octave + a minor tenth lower
   See contrabass clarinet in A   (𝄢) Sounds a minor tenth lower

pedal clarinet (in B♭)   (𝄞) Sounds an octave + a major ninth lower
   See contrabass clarinet in B♭   (𝄢) Sounds a major ninth lower

pedal clarinet in E♭   (𝄞) Sounds 2 octaves + a major sixth lower
   See contrabass clarinet in E♭   (𝄢) Sounds an octave + a major sixth lower

Peitsche (g)
   See whip

petit bugle en mi♭ (f)   Sounds a minor third higher
   See sopranino saxhorn in E♭

petit saxhorn en si♭ alto (f)   (𝄞) Sounds a minor seventh higher
   (sopranino saxophone)   Berlioz, *Te Deum*

petite trompette (en si♭) (f)   Sounds a minor seventh higher
   See piccolo trumpet

petite trompette en la (f)   Sounds a major sixth higher
   See piccolo trumpet in A

petite clarinette (in E♭) (f)   Sounds a minor third higher
   See clarinet in E♭

petite clarinette en ré (f)   Sounds a major second higher
   See clarinet in D

petite flûte (f)   Sounds an octave higher
   See piccolo

PIANO   (𝄞 𝄢)
   clavier (f)
   Flügel (grand piano) (g)
   fortepiano   Stravinsky, *Petrouchka*
   Hammerklavier (g)
   Klavier (g)
   pianoforte (i)

pianoforte (i)
   See piano

piatti (i)
   See cymbals

piatti chiodati (i)
   See sizzle cymbal

piatto chiodato (i)
   See sizzle cymbal

piatti sfrigolanti (i)
   See sizzle cymbal

piatto sospeso (i)
   See suspended cymbal

piccoli timpani orientali (i)
   See Roto-tom

Piccolo in Des (g)   Sounds a minor ninth higher
   See piccolo in D♭

Piccolo in Es (g)   Sounds a minor tenth higher
   See piccolo in E♭

Piccolo in G (g)   Sounds an octave + a perfect fifth higher
   See piccolo in G

PICCOLO (in C)   (𝄞) Sounds an octave higher
   flautino (i)
   flauto piccolo (i)
   kleine Flöte (g)
   ottavino (i)   Rossini, *The Barber of Seville*
   petite flûte (f)
   piccolo (i)

piccolo clarinet   Sounds a minor third higher
   See clarinet in E♭

piccolo clarinet in D   Sounds a major second higher
   See clarinet in D

piccolo en mi♭ (f)   Sounds a minor tenth higher
   See piccolo in E♭

Appendix B: Notation of Instruments 415

piccolo en ré♭ (f)   Sounds a minor ninth higher
   See piccolo in D♭

piccolo en sol (f)   Sounds an octave + a perfect fifth higher
   See piccolo in G

piccolo in D♭   (𝄞) Sounds a minor ninth higher
   Piccolo in Des (g)
   piccolo en ré♭ (f)   Spohr, *Jessonda*
   piccolo in re♭ (i)

piccolo in E♭   (𝄞) Sounds a minor tenth higher
   Piccolo in Es (g)
   piccolo en mi♭ (f)
   piccolo in mi♭ (i)

piccolo in G   (𝄞) Sounds an octave + a perfect fifth higher
   Piccolo in G (g)
   piccolo en sol (f)
   piccolo in sol (i)

piccolo in mi♭ (i)   Sounds a minor tenth higher
   See piccolo in E♭

piccolo in re♭ (i)   Sounds a minor ninth higher
   See piccolo in D♭

piccolo in sol (i)   Sounds an octave + a perfect fifth higher
   See piccolo in G

piccolo trumpet in B♭   (𝄞) Sounds a minor seventh higher
   Baroque trumpet
   clarino (i)
   kleine Trompete (g)
   petit trompette (f)
   sopranino trumpet
   tromba piccola (i)

piccolo trumpet in A   (𝄞) Sounds a major sixth higher
   kleine Trompete in A (g)

petit trompette en la (f)
tromba piccola in la (i)

pipe organ
   See organ

Pistol [shot]
   coup de pistolet (f)
   effetto colpo di pistola (i)
   Pistolenschuss (g)
   pistolettata (i)
   revolver
   rivoltella (i)

Pistolenschuss (g)
   See pistol [shot]

pistolettata (i)
   See pistol [shot]

pistone (i)
   See cornet

Plattenglocken (g)
   See bell plates

Posaune (g)
   See trombone

posthorn
   See trumpet

Provençal long drum
   See long drum

Querflöte (g)
   See flute

raganella (i)
   See rattle

ratchet
>   *See* rattle

Ratsche (g)
>   *See* rattle

rattle
>   crécelle (f)
>   crécelle à manivelle (f)
>   Gerassel (g)
>   Knarre (g)
>   raganella (i)   R. Strauss, *Till Eulenspiegels lustige Streiche*
>   ratchet
>   Ratsche (g)
>   Schnarre (g)
>   wasamba
>   Wasamba-Rassel (g)

reco-reco
>   *See* guiro

recorder
>   Blockflöte (g)
>   fipple flute
>   flageolet (i)
>   flauto (i)
>   flauto diritto (i)
>   flauto dolce (i)   Bach, Brandenburg Concerto no. 2
>   flûte douce (f)
>   flûte-à-bec (f)
>   Schnabelflöte (g)
>   whistle flute

revolver
>   *See* pistol [shot]

rivoltella (i)
>   *See* pistol [shot]

Rollschellen (g)
>   *See* sleigh bells

Roto-tom (tunable)   (𝄞 𝄢)
    Rototom (f)
    Roto-tom-tom (i)
    piccoli timpani orientali (i)   Davies, *Eight Songs for a Mad King*
    Tom-Tom-Spiel (g)

Roto-tom-tom (i)
    See Roto-tom

Rototom (f)
    See Roto-tom

Röhrenglocken (g)
    See chimes

ruggio di leone (i)
    See lion roar

ruggito del leone (i)
    See lion roar

Rute (g)
    See switch

Ruthe (g)
    See switch

Rührtrommel (g)
    See tenor drum

Sackpfeife (g)
    See bagpipes

salterio tedesco (i)
    See cimbalom

sandblocks
    blocchi di carta ventrata (i)
    carta vetrata (i)
    ceppi di carta di vetro (i)   Berio, *Circles*
    papier de verre (f)
    Sandblöcke (g)

Sandblöcke (g)
   See sandblocks

sarrusofono (i)   Sounds an octave lower
   See sarrusophone

Sarrusophon (g)   Sounds an octave lower
   See sarrusophone

sarrusophone   Sounds an octave lower
   contrabass sarrusophone
   sarrusophone (f)
   sarrusofono (i)   Ravel, *Rapsodie Espagnole*
   Sarrusophon (g)
   (contrabassoon, tuba)

sarrussophone (f)   Sounds an octave lower
   See sarrusophone

sassofono baritono in mi♭ (i)   Sounds an octave + a major sixth lower
   See baritone saxophone in E♭

sassofono basso in si♭ (i)   Sounds an octave + a major ninth lower
   See bass saxophone in B♭

sassofono contralto in mi♭ (i)   Sounds a major sixth lower
   See alto saxophone in E♭

sassofono contrabasso in mi♭ (i)   (𝄞) Sounds 2 octaves + a major sixth lower
   See contrabass saxophone in E♭ (𝄢) Sounds an octave + a major sixth lower

sassofono sopranino in fa (i)   Sounds a perfect fourth higher
   See sopranino saxophone in F

sassofono sopranino in mi♭ (i)   Sounds a minor third higher
   See sopranino saxophone in E♭

sassofono soprano in si♭ (i)   Sounds a major second lower
   See soprano saxophone in B♭

sassofono tenore in si♭ (i)   (𝄞) Sounds a major ninth lower
   See tenor saxophone in B♭   (𝄢) Sounds a major second lower

saxhorn
    See petit saxhorn en si♭ alto
    See sopranino saxhorn in E♭
    See soprano saxhorn in B♭
    See alto saxhorn in E♭
    See tenor saxhorn in B♭
    See bass saxhorn in B♭
    See bass saxhorn in E♭
    See contrabass saxhorn in B♭

saxhorn alto (i)   Sounds a major sixth lower
    See alto saxhorn in E♭

saxhorn baryton en si♭ (f)   (𝄞) Sounds a major ninth lower
    See bass saxhorn in B♭   (𝄢) Sounds a major second lower

saxhorn contralto en si♭ (f)   Sounds a major second lower
    See soprano saxhorn in B♭

saxhorn contrebasse en mi♭ (f)   Sounds an octave + a major sixth lower
    See bass saxhorn in E♭

saxhorn contrebasse en si♭ (f)   (𝄞) Sounds two octaves + a major ninth lower
    See contrabass saxhorn in B♭   (𝄢) Sounds a major ninth lower

saxhorn tenore in si♭ (i)   Sounds a major ninth lower
    See tenor saxhorn in B♭

saxhorn ténor en mi♭ (f)   Sounds a major sixth lower
    See alto saxhorn in E♭

saxophone
    See sopranino saxophone in F
    See sopranino saxophone in E♭
    See soprano saxophone in B♭
    See alto saxophone in E♭
    See tenor saxophone in B♭
    See baritone saxophone in E♭
    See bass saxophone in B♭
    See contrabass saxophone in E♭

saxophone alto en mi♭ (f)   Sounds a major sixth lower
  See alto saxophone in E♭

saxophone baryton en mi♭ (f)   Sounds an octave + a major sixth lower
  See baritone saxophone in E♭

saxophone basse en si♭ (f)   Sounds an octave + a major ninth lower
  See bass saxophone in B♭

saxophone contrebasse en mi♭ (f)   (𝄞) Sounds 2 octaves + a major sixth lower
  See contrabass saxophone in E♭   (𝄢) Sounds an octave + a major sixth lower

saxophone sopranino en fa (f)   Sounds a perfect fourth higher
  See sopranino saxophone in F

saxophone sopranino en mi♭ (f)   Sounds a minor third higher
  See sopranino saxophone in E♭

saxophone soprano en si♭ (f)   Sounds a major second lower
  See soprano saxophone in B♭

saxophone ténor en si♭ (f)   (𝄞) Sounds a major ninth lower
  See tenor saxophone in B♭   (𝄢) Sounds a major second lower

Schellen (g)
  See sleigh bells

Schellenbaum (g)
  See bell tree

Schellentrommel (g)
  See tambourine

Schnabelflöte (g)
  See recorder

Schnarre (g)
  See rattle

scie musicale (f)
  See musical saw

sega cantante (i)
    See musical saw

sega musicale (i)
    See musical saw

Serpent (g)
    See serpent   Sounds a major second lower

serpent in B♭
    Serpent (g)
    serpente (i)
    serpent d'église (f)   Mendelssohn, *Calm Sea and Prosperous Voyage*
    serpentone (i)
    (tuba, contrabassoon)

serpente (i)
    See serpent

serpent d'église (f)
    See serpent

serpentone (i)
    See serpent

side drum
    See snare drum

sifflet à coulisse (f)
    See slide whistle

silofono (i)
    See xylophone

siren
    sirena (i)
    Sirene (g)   Hindemith, *Kammermusik no. 1*
    sirène (f)

sirena (i)
    See siren

Sirene (g)
>   See siren

sirène (f)
>   See siren

sistro (i)
>   See spurs

sistrum
>   See spurs

sizzle cymbal
>   cymbale sur tiges (f)
>   Nietenbecken (g)
>   piatti chiodati (i)
>   piatti sfrigolanti (i)
>   piatto chiodato (i)

slapstick
>   See whip

sleigh bells
>   grelots (f)
>   harness bells
>   jingles
>   Rollschellen (g)   Mahler, Symphony no. 4
>   Schellen (g)
>   sonagli (i)
>   sonagliera (i)
>   tintinnie (i)

slide trombone
>   See trombone

slide trumpet
>   soprano trombone
>   tromba da tirarsi (i)
>   trompette à coulisse (f)   Gluck, *Orfeo ed Euridice*
>   Zugtrompette (g)
>   (cornet, flügelhorn, trumpet)

slide whistle
   flauto a culisse (i)
   Lotosflöte (g)
   sifflet à coulisse (f)
   swanee whistle

                                        Ravel, *L'enfant et les sortilèges*

SNARE DRUM
   caisse claire (f)
   kleine Trommel (g)
   side drum   Rossini, Overture to *La Gazza Ladra*
   tamburo piccolo (i)
   tamburo rollo (i)

sonagli (i)
   See sleigh bells

sonagliera (i)
   See sleigh bells

sonnailles de troupeau (f)
   See cowbell

sopranino saxhorn in E♭   Sounds a minor third higher
   petit bugle en mi♭ (f)
   soprano saxhorn in E♭   Gounod, *Faust*
   (sopranino saxophone in E♭)

sopranino saxophone en fa   Sounds a perfect fourth higher
   See sopranino saxophone in F

sopranino saxophone en mi♭   Sounds a minor third higher
   See sopranino saxophone in E♭

sopranino saxophone in E♭   Sounds a minor third higher
   sassofono sopranino in mi♭ (i)
   saxophone sopranino en mi♭ (f)
   Sopranino-Saxophon in Es (g)

sopranino saxophone in F   Sounds a perfect fourth higher
   sassofono sopranino in fa (i)
   saxophone sopranino en fa (f)   Ravel, *Bolero*
   Sopranino-Saxophon in F (g)

sopranino trumpet
   See piccolo trumpet

Sopranino-Saxophon in Es (g)   Sounds a minor third higher
   See sopranino saxophone in E♭

Sopranino-Saxophon in F(g)   Sounds a perfect fourth higher
   See sopranino saxophone in F

soprano saxhorn in B♭   Sounds a major second lower
   bugle en si♭ (f)
   saxhorn contralto en si♭ (f)
   (soprano saxophone in B♭)

soprano saxhorn in E♭   Sounds a minor third higher
   See sopranino saxhorn in E♭

soprano saxophone en si♭   Sounds a major second lower
   See soprano saxophone in B♭

soprano saxophone in B♭   Sounds a major second lower
   sassofono soprano in si♭ (i)
   saxophone soprano en si♭ (f)   Ravel, *Bolero*
   Soprano-Saxophon in B (g)

soprano trombone
   See slide trumpet

Soprano-Saxophon in B (g)   Sounds a major second lower
   See soprano saxophone in B♭

spazzola (i)
   See switch

spazzolino (i)
   See switch

Spielsäge (g)
   See musical saw

spurs
   sistro (i)
   sistrum

Stabglockenspiel (g)　　　　　　　　　　　　　Sounds two octaves higher
   See keyboard Glockenspiel

Stahlstäbe (g)
   See metal plates

string bass　　　　　　　　　　　　　　　　　　Sounds an octave lower
   See bass

string drum
   See lion roar

suspended cymbal
   cymbale suspendue (f)
   hängendes Becken (g)　　　　　　　　Rimsky-Korsakov, *Capriccio español*
   piatto sospeso (i)

swanee whistle
   See slide whistle

switch
   Rute (g)
   Ruthe (g)
   spazzola (i)
   spazzolino (i)　　　　　　　　　　　　Mahler, Symphony no. 2
   verga (i)
   verge (f)

tabor
   See long drum

taille (f)
   See English horn

TAM-TAM
   tam-tam (f)
   Tamtam (g)　　　　　　　　　　　　Mussorgsky-Ravel, *Pictures at an Exhibition*
   tamtam (i)

tamborino (i)
   See tambourine

tamboritsa
   long-necked lute
   tambourizza (f)
   tambura
   tanbura

                                          Lehar, *The Merry Widow*

tambour à cordes (f)
   See lion roar

tambour de basque (f)
   See tambourine

tambour-lion (f)
   See lion roar

tambour militaire (f)
   See tenor drum

Tambourin (g)
   See long drum

Tambourin (g)
   See tambourine

tambourin (f)
   See long drum

tambourin de Provence (f)
   See long drum

tambourine
   Schellentrommel (g)
   tamborino (i)
   tambour de basque (f)
   Tambourin (g)
   tamburello (i)
   Tamburin (g)
                                      Rimsky-Korsakov, *Capriccio español*
   tamburino (i)
   tamburo basco (i)
   timbrel
   tymbyr

tambourizza (f)
See tamboritsa

tambours de frein (f)
See brake drums

tambura (i)
See tamboritsa

tamburello (i)
See tambourine

Tamburin (g)
See tambourine

tamburino (i)
See tambourine

tamburo basco (i)
See tambourine

tamburo dei freno (i)
See brake drums

tamburo di legno (i)
See wood block

tamburo grande (i)
See bass drum

tamburo militare (i)
See tenor drum

tamburo piccolo (i)
See snare drum

tamburo rollo (i)
See snare drum

tamburo rullante (i)
See tenor drum

Appendix B: Notation of Instruments   429

Tamtam (g)
    See tam-tam

tamtam (i)
    See tam-tam

tarogato   (𝄞)
    Holztrompete (g)
    Hungarian wooden clarinet   Thern, *Svatopluk*
    tarogato (i)
    See English horn

tavoletta (i)
    See wood block

Tellern (Becken-Paar) (g)
    See cymbals

Tempelblock (g)
    See temple block

temple block
    bloc chinois (f)
    blocco di legno cinese (i)
    blocco di legno coreano (i)   Grofé, *Grand Canyon Suite*
    Tempelblock (g)
    temple-bloc (f)

temple-bloc (f)
    See temple block

tenor "Wagner" tuba (in B♭)   (𝄞𝄢) Sounds a major ninth lower
    tube ténor en si♭ (f)
    tenor tuba in B♭   Bruckner, Symphony no. 7

tenor "Wagner" tuba in E♭   (𝄞𝄢) Sounds a major sixth lower
    tube ténor en mi♭ (f)
    tenor tuba in E♭   Wagner, *Götterdammerung*

tenor drum
    caisse roulante (f)
    cassa rullante (i)

field drum
military drum
Militärtrommel (g)
Rührtrommel (g)   Strauss, *Till Eulenspiegels lustige Streiche*
tambour militaire (f)
tamburo militare (i)
tamburo rullante (i)
Tenortrommel (g)
Wirbeltrommel (g)

tenor oboe (g)   Sounds a perfect fifth lower
    See English horn

tenor saxhorn in B♭   (𝄞) Sounds a major ninth lower
    saxhorn ténor en mi♭ (f)
    saxhorn tenore in mi♭ (i)
    tenorhorn   Mahler, Symphony no. 7
    Tenorhorn in B (g)
    (baritone, tuba)

tenor saxophone in B♭   (𝄞) Sounds a major ninth lower
    sassofono tenore in si♭ (i)   (𝄢) Sounds a major second lower
    Tenor-Saxophon in B (g)
    saxophone ténor en si♭ (f)   (𝄞) Gershwin, *Rhapsody in Blue*
          (𝄢) Prokofiev, *Lieutenant Kijé*

tenor trombone
    See trombone

tenor tuba
    See euphonium

tenor tuba (in B♭)   Sounds a major ninth lower
    See tenor "Wagner" tuba

tenor tuba in E♭   Sounds a major sixth lower
    See tenor "Wagner" tuba in E♭

Tenor-Posaune (g)
    See trombone

Tenor-Saxophon in B (g)   (𝄞) Sounds a major ninth lower
    See tenor saxophone in B♭   (𝄢) Sounds a major second lower

Tenorhorn in B (g)   Sounds a major ninth lower
    See tenor saxhorn in B♭

tenorhorn   Sounds a major ninth lower
    See tenor saxhorn in B♭

Tenortrommel (g)
    See tenor drum

thunder machine
    Donnermaschine (g)
    macchine del tuono (i)   R. Strauss, *Alpine Symphony*
    machine à tonnerre (f)

thunder sheet
    Donnerblech (g)
    lastra del tuono (i)   Henze, Symphony no. 6
    tôle pour imiter le tonnerre (f)

tiefe Glocken (g)
    See chimes

timbales (f)
    See timpani

timbrel
    See tambourine

TIMPANI   (𝄢)
    kettle-drums
    Pauken (g)
    timbales (f)   Prokofiev, *Peter and the Wolf*
    timpani (i)

tintinnie (i)
    See sleigh bells

Tom-Tom (g)
: *See* tom-tom

tom-tom
: Tom-Tom (g)
: tom-tom (f)   Stravinsky, *Agon*
: tom-tom (i)

Tom-Tom-Spiel (g)
: *See* Roto-tom

tone generator
: *See* Martenot waves

tôle pour imiter le tonnere (f)
: *See* thunder sheet

transverse flute
: *See* flute

trap set
: *See* drum set

Triangel (g)
: *See* triangle

TRIANGLE
: Triangel (g)
: triangle (f)   Copland, *Appalachian Spring* Suite
: triangolo (i)

triangolo (i)
: *See* triangle

tromba (i)
: *See* trumpet

tromba alto in fa (i)   Sounds a perfect fifth lower
: *See* alto trumpet in F

tromba basso in do (i)   Sounds an octave lower
   See bass trumpet in C

tromba basso in mi (i)   Sounds a minor sixth lower
   See bass trumpet in E

tromba basso in mi♭ (i)   Sounds a major sixth lower
   See bass trumpet in E♭

tromba basso in re (i)   Sounds a minor seventh lower
   See bass trumpet in D

tromba basso in re♭ (i)   Sounds a major seventh lower
   See bass trumpet in D♭

tromba bassa in si (i)   Sounds a minor ninth lower
   See bass trumpet in B

tromba basso in si♭ (i)   Sounds a major ninth lower
   See bass trumpet in B♭

tromba contralta in fa (i)   Sounds a perfect fifth lower
   See alto trumpet in F

tromba da tirarsi (i)
   See slide trumpet

tromba in do (i)
   See trumpet in C

tromba in fa (i)   Sounds a perfect fourth higher
   See trumpet in F

tromba in fa♯ (i)   Sounds an augmented fourth higher
   See trumpet in F♯

tromba in la (i)   Sounds a minor third lower
   See trumpet in A

tromba in la♭ (i)   Sounds a major third lower
   See trumpet in A♭

tromba in mi (i) — Sounds a major third higher
    See trumpet in E

tromba in mi♭ (i) — Sounds a minor third higher
    See trumpet in E♭

tromba in re (i) — Sounds a major second higher
    See trumpet in D

tromba in re♭ (i) — Sounds a minor second higher
    See trumpet in D♭

tromba in si (i) — Sounds a minor second lower
    See trumpet in B

tromba in si♭ (i) — Sounds a major second lower
    See trumpet in B♭

tromba in sol (i) — Sounds a perfect fifth higher
    See trumpet in G

tromba piccola (i) — Sounds a minor seventh higher
    See piccolo trumpet

tromba piccola in la (i) — Sounds a major sixth higher
    See piccolo trumpet in A

TROMBONE (𝄞 𝄢 𝄡(A) 𝄡(T))
    Posaune (g)
    tenor trombone
    Tenor-Posaune (g) — Ravel, *Bolero*
    trombone à coulisse (f)
    trombone a tiro (i)
    trombone (i)
    Zugposaune (g)

trombone a tiro (i)
    See trombone

trombone à coulisse (f)
    See trombone

trombone à pistons (f)
    See valve trombone

trombone basse (f)
    See bass trombone

trombone basso (i)
    See bass trombone

trombone contrabasso (i)
    See contrabass trombone

trombone contrebasse (f)
    See contrabass trombone

trombone ventile (i)
    See valve trombone

Trompete (g)
    See trumpet

Trompete in A (g)   Sounds a minor third lower
    See trumpet in A

Trompete in As (g)   Sounds a major third lower
    See trumpet in A♭

Trompete in B (g)   Sounds a major second lower
    See trumpet in B♭

Trompete in C (g)
    See trumpet in C

Trompete in D (g)   Sounds a major second higher
    See trumpet in D

Trompete in Des (g)   Sounds a minor second higher
    See trumpet in D♭

Trompete in E (g)   Sounds a major third higher
    See trumpet in E

Trompete in Es (g)   Sounds a minor third higher
See trumpet in E♭

Trompete in F (g)   Sounds a perfect fourth higher
See trumpet in F

Trompete in Fis (g)   Sounds an augmented fourth higher
See trumpet in F♯

Trompete in G (g)   Sounds a perfect fifth higher
See trumpet in G

Trompete in H (g)   Sounds a minor second lower
See trumpet in B

trompette (f)
See trumpet

trompette alto en fa (f)   Sounds a perfect fifth lower
See alto trumpet in F

trompette à coulisse (f)
See slide trumpet

trompette basse en mi (f)   Sounds a minor sixth lower
See bass trumpet in E

trompette basse en mi♭ (f)   Sounds a major sixth lower
See bass trumpet in E♭

trompette basse en ré (f)   Sounds a minor seventh lower
See bass trumpet in D

trompette basse en ré♭ (f)   Sounds a major seventh lower
See bass trumpet in D♭

trompette basse en si (f)   Sounds a minor ninth lower
See bass trumpet in B

trompette basse en si♭ (f)   Sounds a major ninth lower
See bass trumpet in B♭

trompette basse en ut (f) Sounds an octave lower
　See bass trumpet in C

trompette en fa (f) Sounds a perfect fourth higher
　See trumpet in F

trompette en fa♯ (f) Sounds an augmented fourth higher
　See trumpet in F♯

trompette en la (f) Sounds a minor third lower
　See trumpet in A

trompette en la♭ (f) Sounds a major third lower
　See trumpet in A♭

trompette en mi (f) Sounds a major third higher
　See trumpet in E

trompette en mi♭ (f) Sounds a minor third higher
　See trumpet in E♭

trompette en ré (f) Sounds a major second higher
　See trumpet in D

trompette en ré♭ (f) Sounds a minor second higher
　See trumpet in D♭

trompette en si (f) Sounds a minor second lower
　See trumpet in B

trompette en si♭ (f) Sounds a major second lower
　See trumpet in B♭

trompette en sol (f) Sounds a perfect fifth higher
　See trumpet in G

trompette en ut (f)
　See trumpet in C

TRUMPET
　corno di posta (i)

posthorn (g)
tromba (i)
Trompete (g)
trompette (f)
See also trumpet (in B♭)

trumpet in A (𝄞) Sounds a minor third lower
    tromba in la (i)
    Trompete in A (g) Beethoven, Symphony no. 7
    trompette en la (f)

trumpet in A♭ (𝄞) Sounds a major third lower
    tromba in la♭ (i)
    Trompete in As (g) Verdi, *Aida*
    trompette en la♭ (f)

trumpet in B (𝄞) Sounds a minor second lower
    tromba in si (i)
    Trompete in H (g) Brahms, Symphony no. 2
    trompette en si (f)

trumpet in B♭ (𝄞) Sounds a major second lower
    tromba in si♭ (i)
    Trompete in B (g) Beethoven, Symphony no. 4
    trompette en si♭ (f)

trumpet in C
    tromba in do (i)
    Trompete in C (g) Beethoven, Symphony no. 1
    trompette en ut (f)

trumpet in D (𝄞) Sounds a major second higher
    tromba in re (i)
    Trompete in D (g) Beethoven, Symphony no. 2
    trompette en ré (f)

trumpet in D♭ (𝄞) Sounds a minor second higher
    tromba in re♭ (i)
    Trompete in Des (g) Wagner, *Götterdammerung*
    trompette en ré♭ (f)

trumpet in E   (𝄞) Sounds a major third higher
   tromba in mi (i)
   Trompete in E (g)   Dvořák, Symphony no. 9
   trompette en mi (f)

trumpet in E♭   (𝄞) Sounds a minor third higher
   tromba in mi♭ (i)
   Trompete in Es (g)   Beethoven, Symphony no. 3
   trompette en mi♭ (f)

trumpet in F   (𝄞) Sounds a perfect fourth higher
   tromba in fa (i)
   Trompete in F (g)   Brahms, Symphony no. 3
   trompette en fa (f)

trumpet in F♯   (𝄞) Sounds an augmented fourth higher
   tromba in fa♯ (i)
   Trompete in Fis (g)
   trompette en fa♯ (f)

trumpet in F, alto   Sounds a perfect fifth lower
   See alto trumpet in F

trumpet in G   (𝄞) Sounds a perfect fifth higher
   tromba in sol (g)
   Trompete in G (g)   Halévy, *La Juive*
   trompette en sol (g)

TUBA   (𝄢)
   Baβtuba (g)
   bass tuba
   bombardone (i)
   cimbasso (i)   Berlioz, *Symphonie fantastique*
   Cimbasso (g)
   Kontrabaβtuba (g)
   tuba (f)
   tuba basse (f)

tuba (f)
   See tuba

tuba basse (f)
    See tuba

tuba mirabilis
    See ophicleide

tubafono (i)   Sounds an octave higher
    See tubaphone

tubaphone   Sounds an octave higher
    tubafono (i)

tuba basse en fa (f)   Sounds an octave + a perfect fifth lower
    See bass "Wagner" tuba

tuba ténor en si♭ (f)   Sounds a major ninth lower
    See tenor "Wagner" tuba

tubes des cloches (f)
    See chimes

tubular bells
    See chimes

tubular chimes
    See chimes

tumbao
    See conga drums

tumbas
    See conga drums

tymbyr
    See tambourine

tympanon
    See cimbalom

typophone (f)
    See cimbalom

ukelele (𝄞)
   (banjo, synthesizer)

valve horn
   See horn

valve trombone (𝄞 𝄢 𝄡$^{(A)}$ 𝄡$^{(T)}$)
   trombone à pistons (f)
   trombone ventile (i)
   Ventil-Posaune (g)

Ventil-Posaune (g)
   See valve trombone

Ventilhorn (g)
   See horn

verga (i)
   See switch

verge (f)
   See switch

vibrafono (i)
   See vibraphone

vibraharp
   See vibraphone

Vibraphon (g)
   See vibraphone

VIBRAPHONE (𝄞)
   vibrafono (i)
   vibraphone (f) Berg, *Lulu*
   vibraharp
   Vibraphon (g)

vielle a roue (f)
   See hurdy-gurdy

VIOLA (𝄡(A)𝄞)
    alto (f)
    viola (i)   Berlioz, *Harold in Italy*
    Bratsche (g)

viola d'amore (𝄡(A))
    Liebesgeige (g)
    viole d'amour (f)   Puccini, *Madama Butterfly*
    viola d'amore (i)

viole d'amour (f)
    See viola d'amore

VIOLIN (𝄞)
    fiddle
    Geige (g)
    kleine Discant-Geige (g)
    Violine (g)   Strauss, *Ein Heldenleben*
    violino (i)
    violino piccolo (i)
    violon (f)

Violine (g)
    See violin

violino (i)
    See violin

violino piccolo (i)
    See violin

violon (f)
    See violin

Violoncelle (g)
    See cello

violoncell (f)
    See cello

violoncello (i)
    See cello

violone (i)
   See bass

                                      Sounds an octave lower

Wagner tuba
   See tenor "Wagner" tuba
   See bass "Wagner" tuba

Waldhorn (g)
   See natural horn

wasamba
   See rattle

Wasamba-Rassel (g)
   See rattle

whip
   fouet (f)
   frusta (i)
   frusta di verghe (i)
   Holzklapper (g)   Mahler, Symphony no. 5
   Peitsche (g)
   slapstick

whistle flute
   See recorder

wind chimes
   Windglocken (g)   Crumb, *A Hunted Landscape*

wind machine
   Aeolophon (g)
   éoliphone (f)
   macchine del vento (i)   R. Strauss, *Alpine Symphony*
   machine à vent (f)
   Windmaschine (g)

Windglocken (g)
   See wind chimes

Windmaschine (g)
   See wind machine

Wirbeltrommel (g)
    See tenor drum

wood block
    bloc de bois (f)
    blocco di legno (i)
    cassa di legno (i)
    cassettina (i)
    Holzblock (g)
    tamburo di legno (i)
    tavoletta (i)

    Copland, *Appalachian Spring* Suite

Xylophon (g)   Sounds an octave higher
    See xylophone

xilofono (i)   Sounds an octave higher
    See xylophone

XYLOPHONE   (𝄞) Sounds an octave higher
    Holz- und Strohinstrument (g)
    silofono (i)
    xilofono (i)
    Xylophon (g)   R. Strauss, *Salome*
    xylophone (f)
    zilafone (i)

Ziehharmonika (g)
    See accordion

zilafone (i)   Sounds an octave higher
    See xylophone

Zinke (g)
    See cornet

Zither (g)
    See zither

zither   (𝄞𝄢)
    cetra (i)
    cythare (f)

cithara (i) 　　　　　　　　　　J. Strauss, *Tales from the Vienna Woods*
cytharra (i)
Zither (g)

Zugposaune (g)
   See trombone

Zugtrompete (g)
   See slide trumpet

APPENDIX C

Harmonics

A *harmonic* is a pitch produced when an open string or portion thereof is divided into two or more equal portions. This procedure is achieved by touching the string lightly at any of the dividing points called *nodes* (◇), causing all partials to vibrate on their own and producing an identical pitch with an eerie, flutelike timbre. If the placement of the finger on the node is imprecise, the harmonic will not speak. The conductor must be aware that string players' entrances may be delayed while they attempt to find the exact spot of the chosen node.

If a harmonic is produced on an open string, it is called a *natural harmonic*. Neither pitch alteration nor vibrato is possible with a natural harmonic.

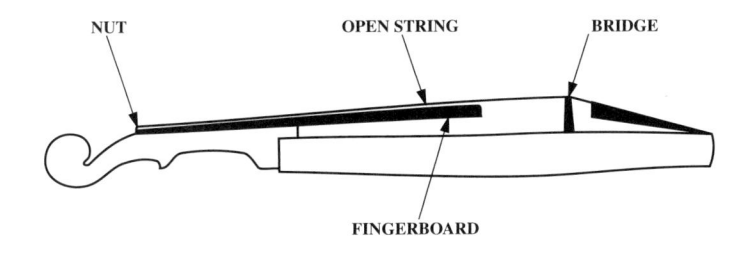

NATURAL HARMONIC (OPEN STRING)
Example: 3 Partials

String divides into three equal vibrating partials.
Each partial sounds the same pitch.

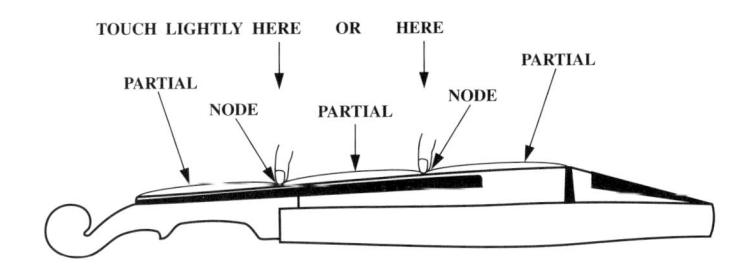

448 APPENDIX C: HARMONICS

Example: NATURAL HARMONIC (4 partials)

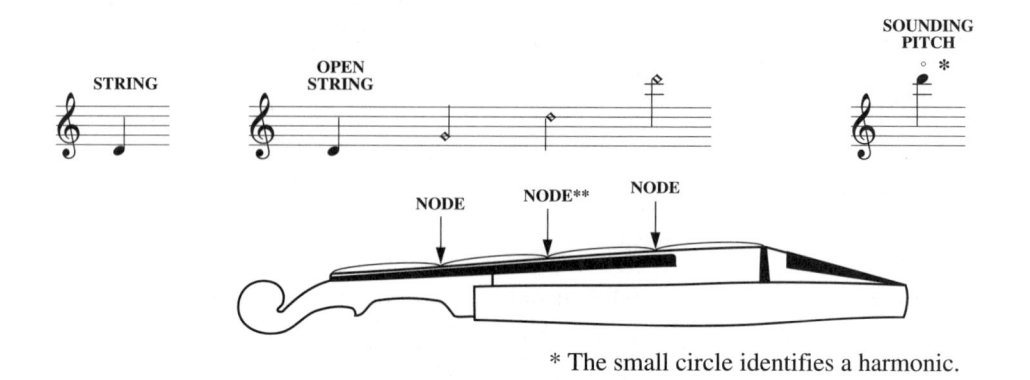

STRING   OPEN STRING   SOUNDING PITCH

NODE   NODE**   NODE

* The small circle identifies a harmonic.

Notations identifying sounding pitch only or sounding pitch and string:

SUL RE   III   D STR.

Notations identifying string and node, sounding pitch and node or all three:

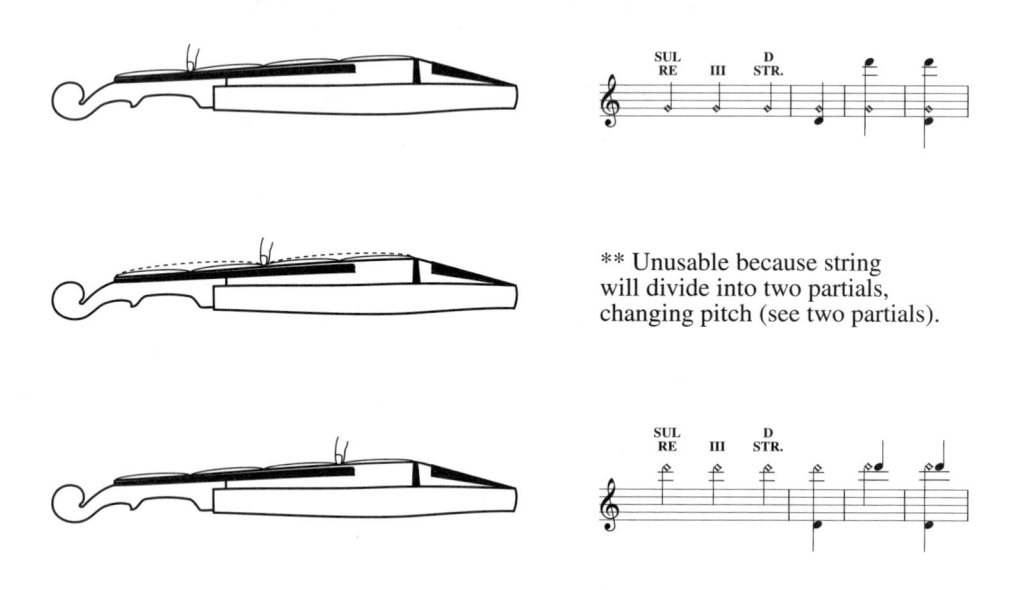

SUL RE   III   D STR.

** Unusable because string will divide into two partials, changing pitch (see two partials).

SUL RE   III   D STR.

ARTIFICIAL HARMONICS

An *artificial harmonic* utilizes the identical production process as the natural harmonic, except that the open string in use is shortened first, with the remainder of the string being divided into equal partials. At a chosen pitch, the first finger presses the string down firmly onto the fingerboard, setting up a new fundamental, while the third or forth finger touches the now shortened string lightly at any of the dividing points (nodes), separating the remainder of the string into the desired equal number of partials. With the artificial harmonic, pitch flexibility is possible, as is a limited use of vibrato.

ARTIFICIAL HARMONIC (STOPPED STRING)
Example: 4 Partials

With one finger, press string to fingerboard to establish the desired pitch. Then, with another finger, divide the remainder of the string into the desired number of partials.

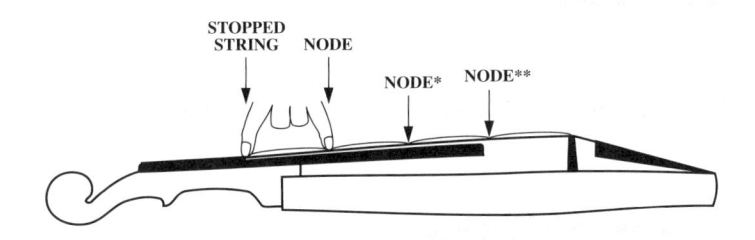

* Unusable because string will divide into two partials.

** Unusable because stretch between stopped note and node is too wide to be executed.

450   APPENDIX C: HARMONICS

Example: ARTIFICIAL HARMONIC (4 partials)

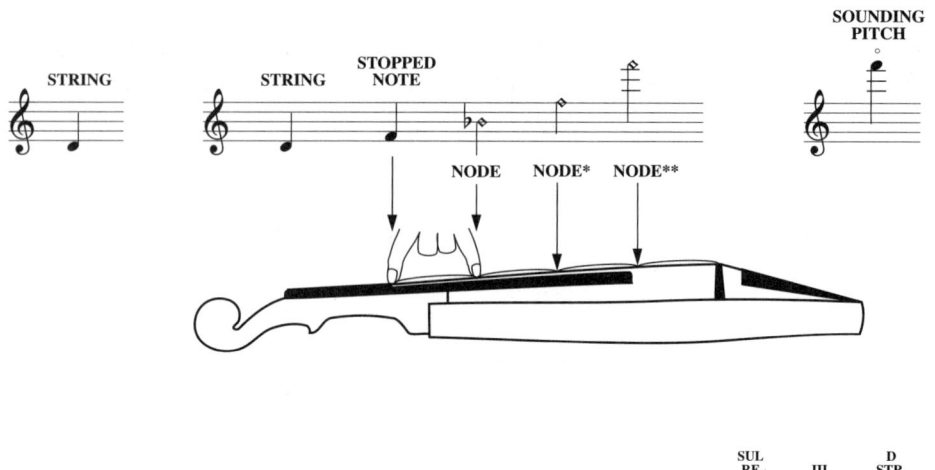

Notations identifying sounding pitch only or sounding pitch and string:

Notations identifying stopped pitch and node or stopped pitch, node & sounding pitch:

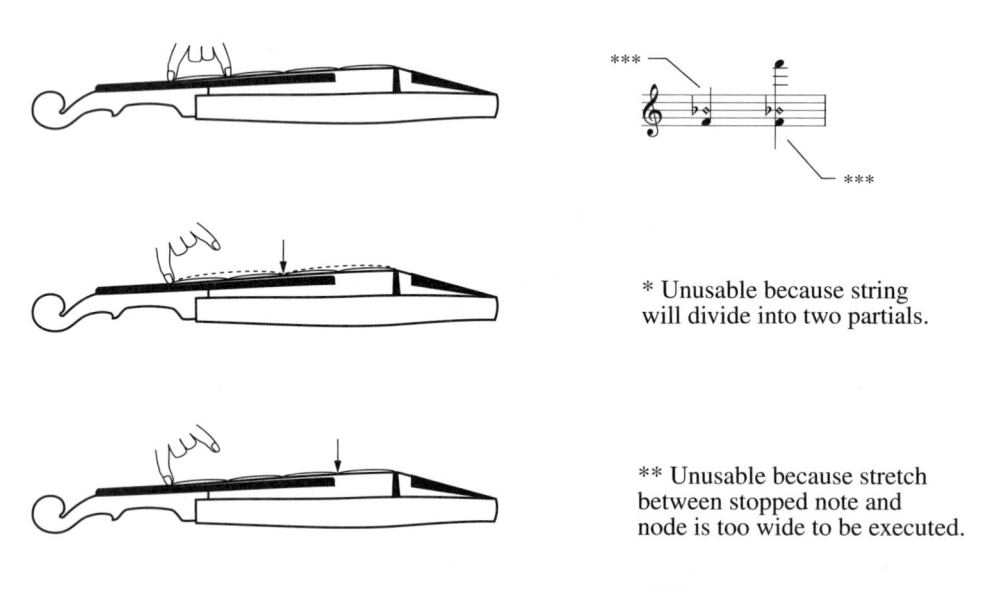

* Unusable because string will divide into two partials.

** Unusable because stretch between stopped note and node is too wide to be executed.

(*** Most common notations)

Appendix C: Harmonics

The theory behind the artificial harmonic is based on the shortening or *stopping* of a string to create a new "open" string of different length (different from the actual open string), to which the principle of natural harmonics now applies. The intervallic relationships between the shortened string (fundamental pitch), the node(s), and the resulting harmonic are, therefore, identical to those of the full-length open-string harmonic (the natural harmonic).

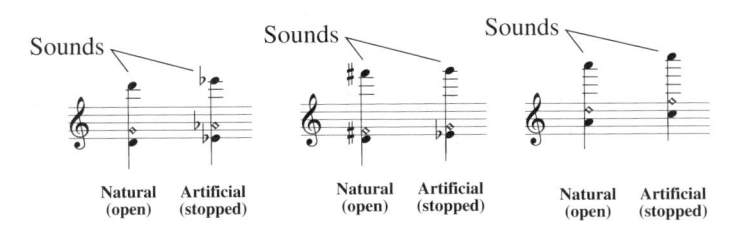

Composers may notate only the pitch of the node, which generally indicates a natural harmonic. In a few cases, depending on which open string is utilized, a given node can yield two different pitches. In general, the player will choose the upper string on which to produce the harmonic.

As the distance between the stopped note and the node becomes smaller, the practical execution of a harmonic becomes more difficult, and the margin for error increases proportionately. For this reason, string players, when given several options, will generally choose the harmonic with the fewest number of partials. The decision may be influenced by the connecting notes on either side of the harmonic. Conductors need to be aware that the sound of the harmonic cannot reach a dynamic level louder then *mf*.

A thorough knowledge of the notation of harmonics for the various string instruments is essential. Conductors must be aware that some composers notate only the pitch of the dividing point or node (◇), leaving it to the individual performer to identify the resulting pitch. Other composers notate harmonics by writing the desired pitch with a circle above the note (o). The choice of string and node, and the choice of natural versus artificial harmonic, are left to the individual player.

APPENDIX C: HARMONICS

Ravel, *Daphnis and Chloé*, Suite no. 2, bar 2

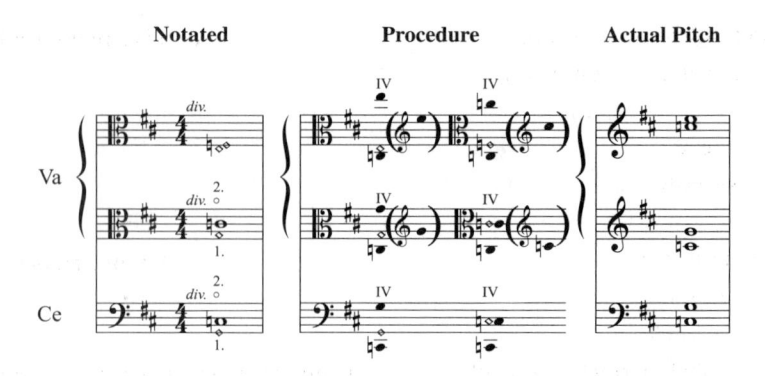

Henze, *Elegy for Young Lovers* (first edition), act 1, bar 737*

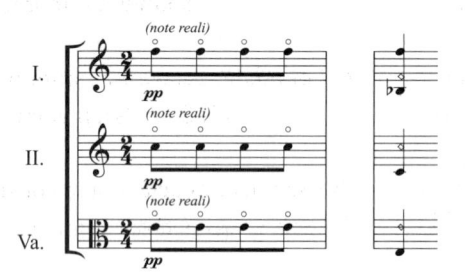

The second violin and viola approach the fingerboard from above the instrument with the fourth finger on the stopped note and the thumb on node.

Some notated harmonics cannot be executed (see Ravel's *Mother Goose Suite* or Prokofiev's *Sinfonia Concertante*). In addition the harmonic sign (o) does not always indicate a harmonic; sometimes a composer uses it merely to request that the note be played on an open string.

---

*© 1961. Revised version © 1989 Schott Music. All Rights Reserved. Used by permission of European American Music Distributors LLC, sole U.S. and Canadian agent for Schott Music.

APPENDIX D

Harmonics Charts

LIST OF EXAMPLES

1. List of Open Strings
2. Natural Harmonic: 2 Partials
3. Natural Harmonic: 3 Partials
4. Natural Harmonic: 4 Partials
5. Natural Harmonic: 5 Partials
6. Natural Harmonic: 6 Partials
7. Artificial Harmonic: 3 Partials
8. Artificial Harmonic: 4 Partials

List of Open Strings

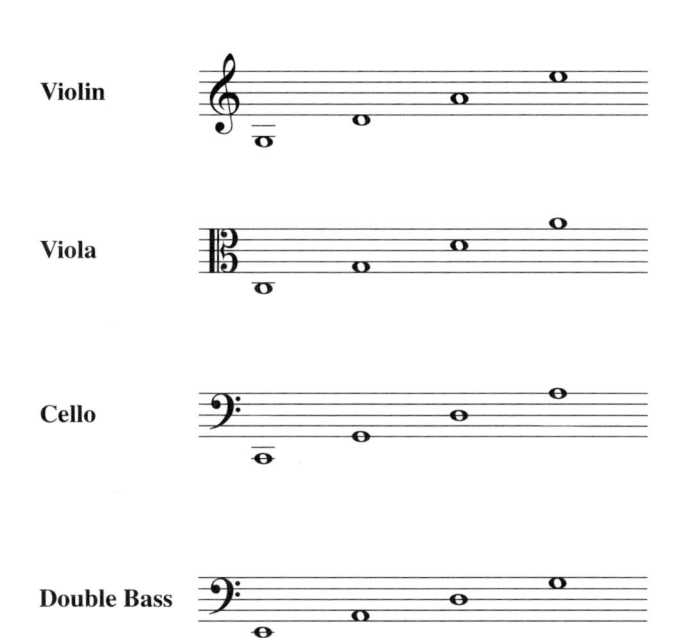

APPENDIX D: HARMONICS CHARTS

Some basses have an extension for their E string, which creates four new lower pitches (E♭, D, D♭, and C). Because each new pitch is locked in by a mechanical device, once activated, each pitch represents an open string on which the normal array of natural harmonics can be produced.

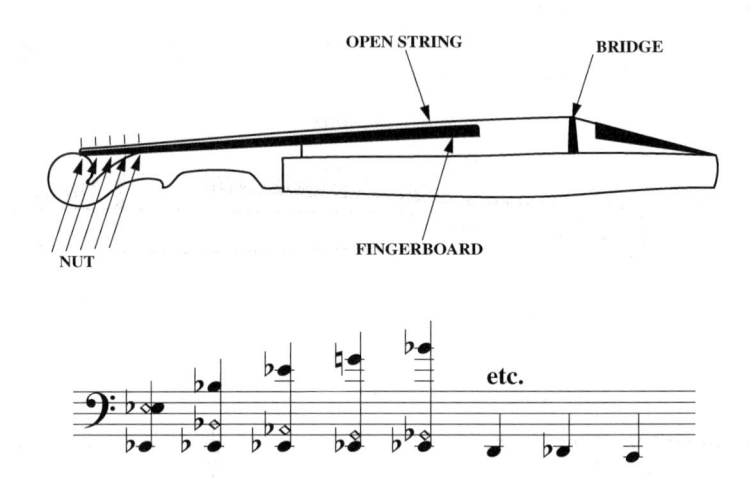

Appendix D: Harmonics Charts 455

Example: NATURAL HARMONIC (2 partials)

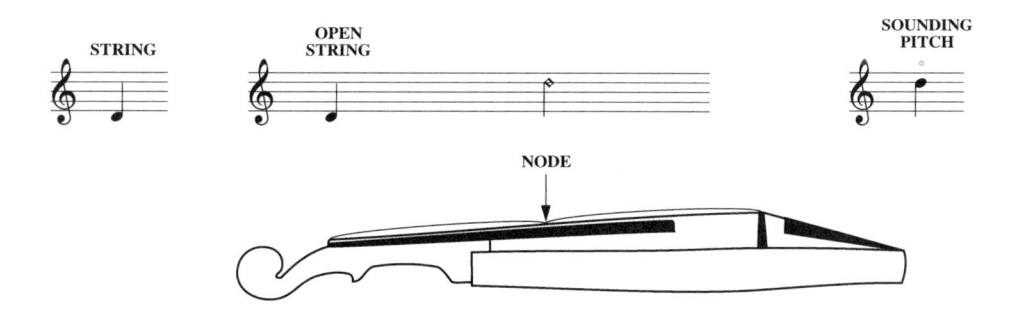

Notations identifying sounding pitch only or sounding pitch and string:

Notations identifying string and node, sounding pitch and node or all three:

456   APPENDIX D: HARMONICS CHARTS

Example: NATURAL HARMONIC (3 partials)

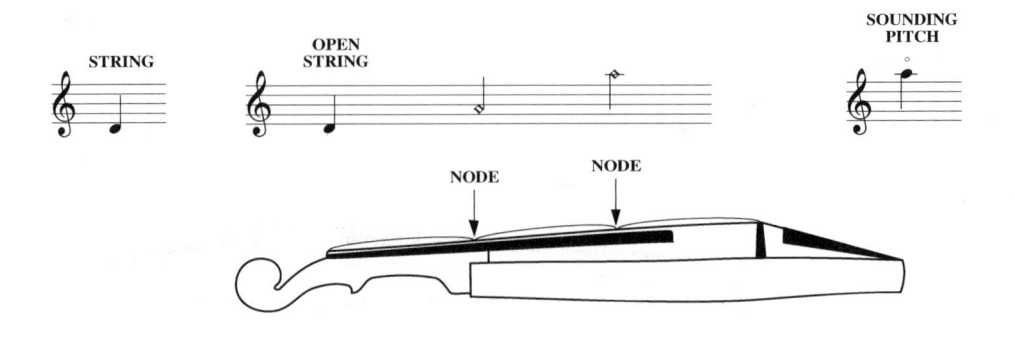

STRING   OPEN STRING   SOUNDING PITCH

                    NODE   NODE

**Notations identifying sounding pitch only
or sounding pitch and string:**

SUL RE   III   D STR.

Notations identifying string and node, sounding pitch and node or all three:

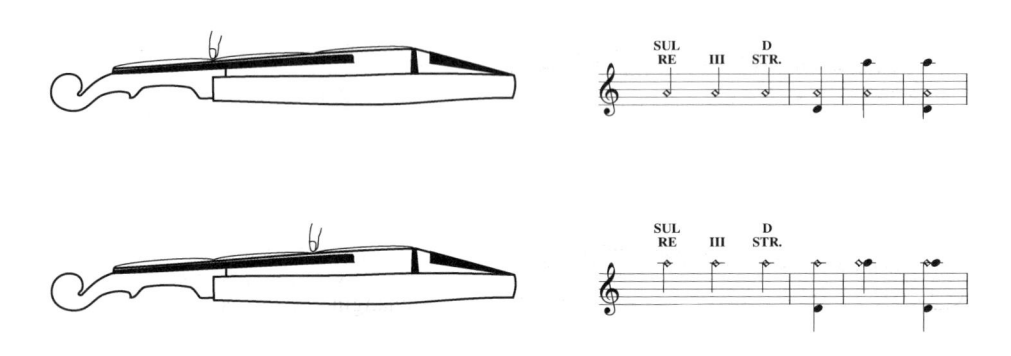

SUL RE   III   D STR.

SUL RE   III   D STR.

Appendix D: Harmonics Charts 457

Example: NATURAL HARMONIC (4 partials)

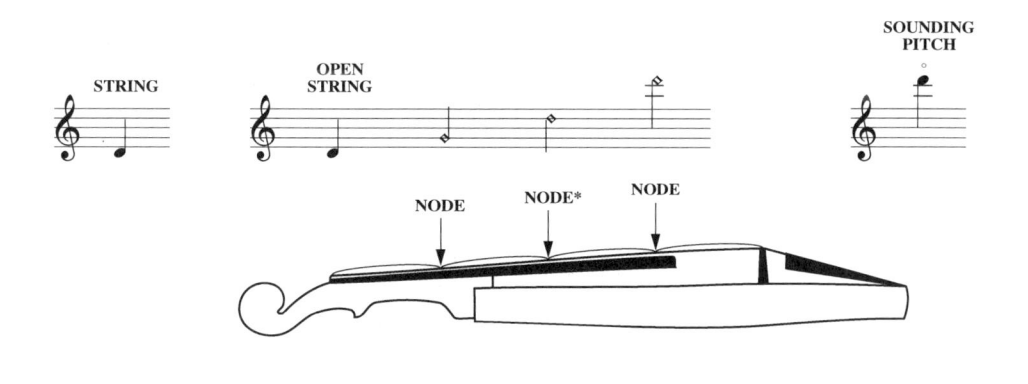

STRING

OPEN STRING

SOUNDING PITCH

NODE   NODE*   NODE

Notations identifying sounding pitch only or sounding pitch and string:

SUL RE   III   D STR.

Notations identifying string and node, sounding pitch and node or all three:

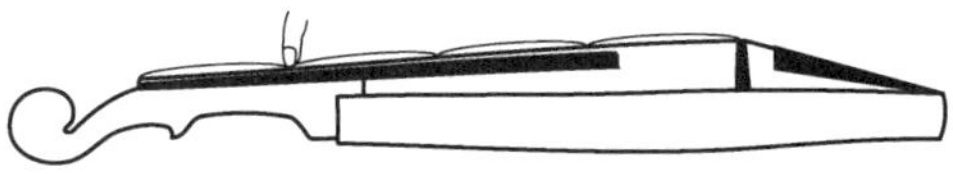

SUL RE   III   D STR.

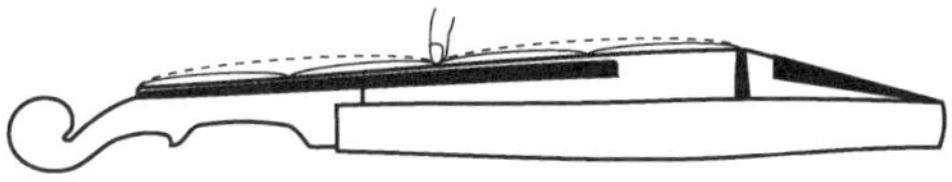

* Unusable because string will divide into two partials, changing pitch (see two partials).

SUL RE   III   D STR.

458 APPENDIX D: HARMONICS CHARTS

Example: NATURAL HARMONIC (5 partials)

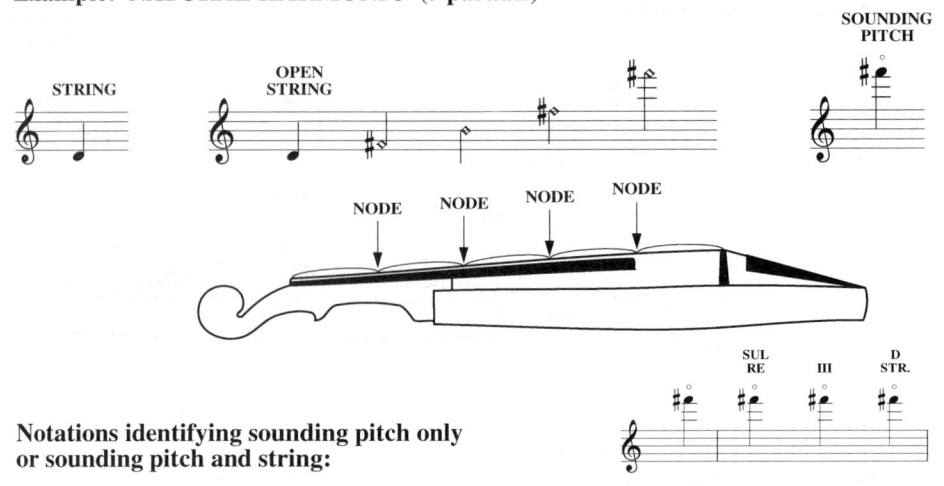

Notations identifying sounding pitch only
or sounding pitch and string:

Notations identifying string and node, sounding pitch and node or all three:

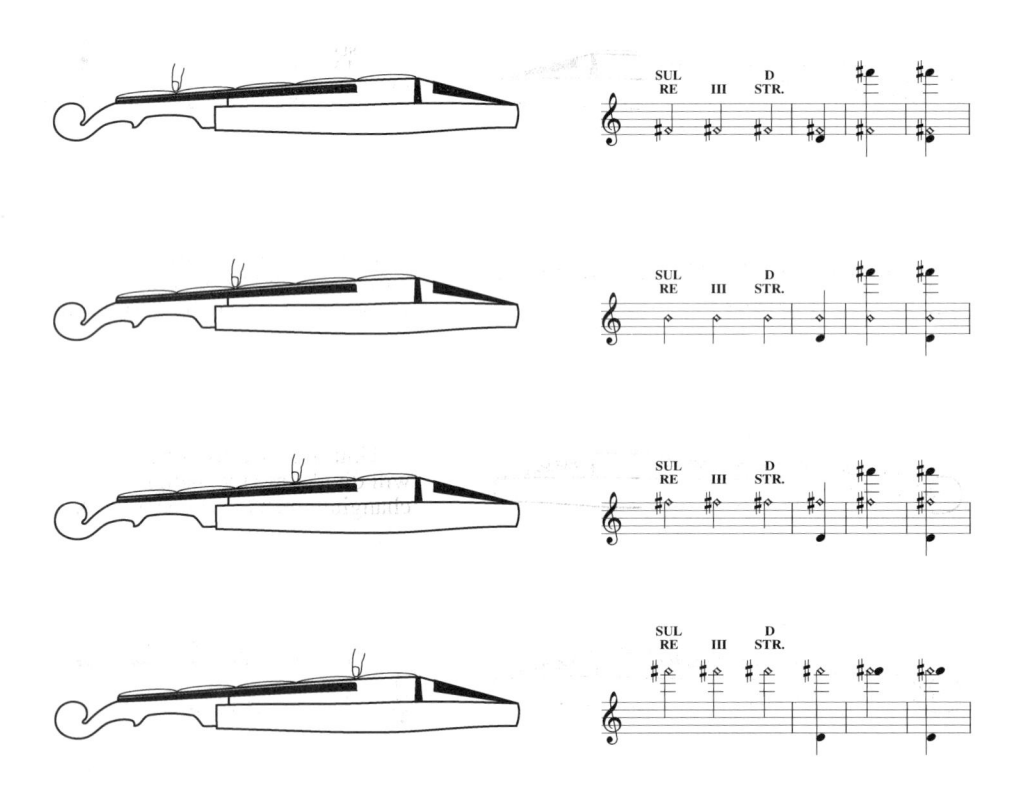

Appendix D: Harmonics Charts 459

**Example: NATURAL HARMONIC (6 partials)
only used for Double Bass**

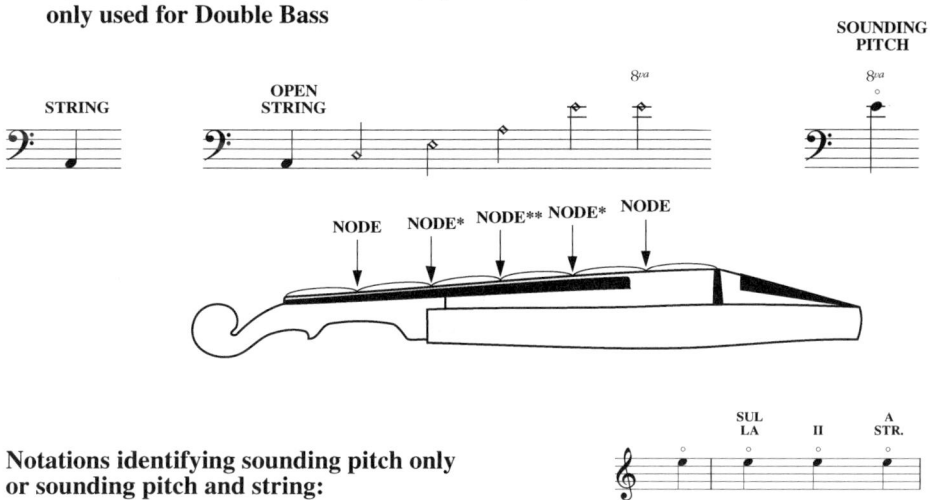

**Notations identifying sounding pitch only
or sounding pitch and string:**

Notations identifying string and node, sounding pitch and node or all three:

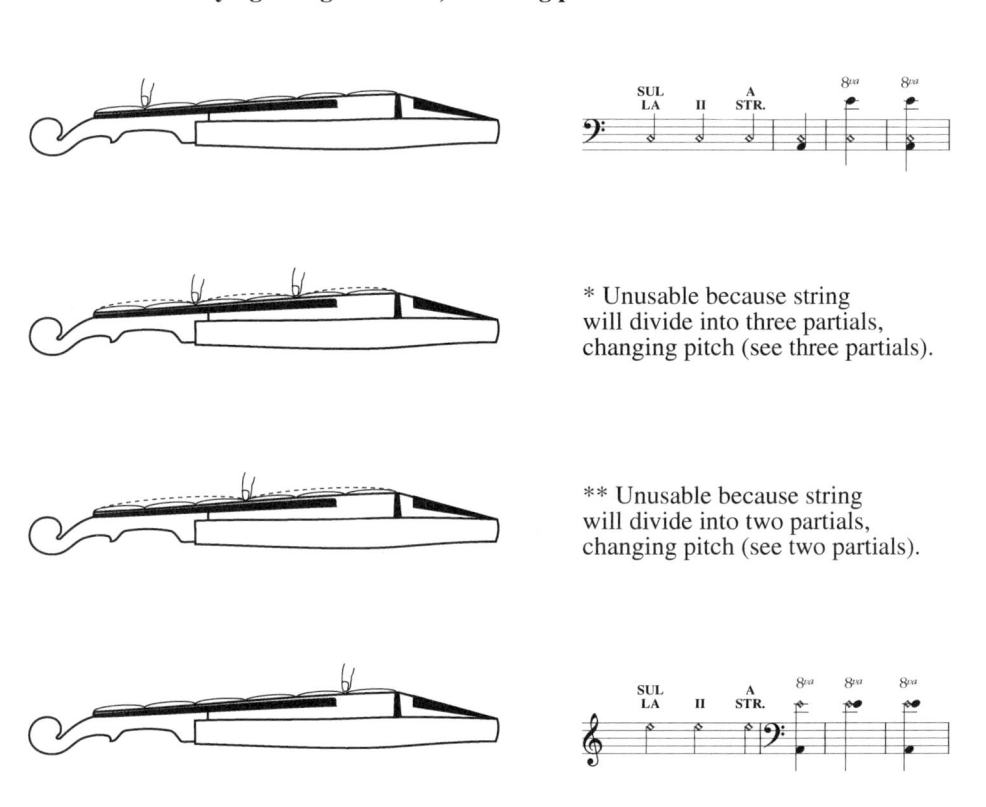

* Unusable because string
will divide into three partials,
changing pitch (see three partials).

** Unusable because string
will divide into two partials,
changing pitch (see two partials).

APPENDIX D: HARMONICS CHARTS

Example: ARTIFICIAL HARMONIC (3 partials)

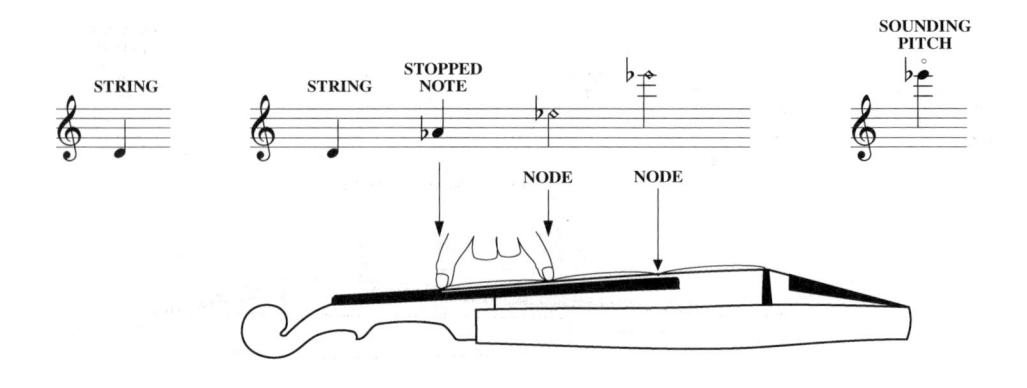

Notations identifying string, stopped note, node and sounding pitch:

Notations identifying stopped note, node and sounding pitch:

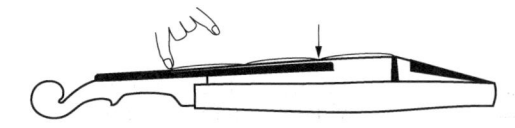

* Unusable because stretch between stopped note and node is too wide to be executed.

Appendix D: Harmonics Charts   461

Example: ARTIFICIAL HARMONIC (4 partials)

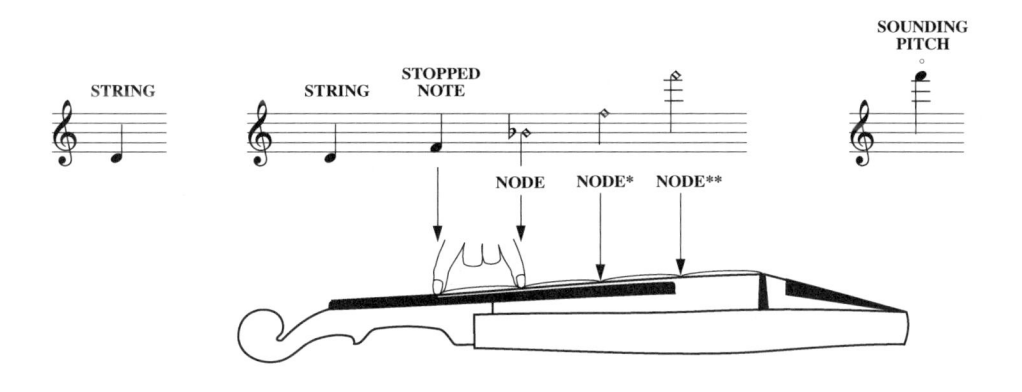

Notations identifying sounding pitch only or sounding pitch and string:

Notations identifying stopped pitch and node or stopped pitch, node & sounding pitch:

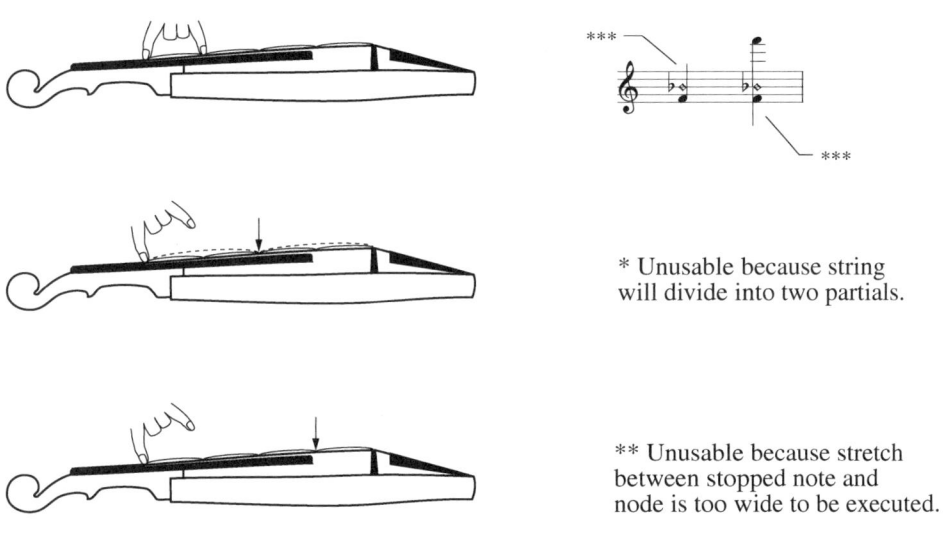

* Unusable because string will divide into two partials.

** Unusable because stretch between stopped note and node is too wide to be executed.

(**** Most common notations*)

APPENDIX E

Cross-Rhythm Charts

INDEX OF EXAMPLES

1	3:2	8	8:3
2	5:2	9	3:4
3	7:2	10	5:4
4	2:3	11	7:4
5	4:3	12	3:5
6	5:3	13	4:5
7	7:3	14	5:7

The examples on the following pages demonstrate how to execute two different rhythmic patterns simultaneously. After the time signature, the upper line shows the basic pulse of the measure. The lower line indicates the number of notes to be played against that pulse. The first bar is followed by a subdivision relating to both the basic pulse and the new independent grouping and concludes with an alternate notation of the new compounded grouping. It is suggested that the conductor practice each example slowly at first and gradually increase the speed, always counting the counterrhythm aloud. If tapping, one may use a pencil in one hand to create two different sounds. The second note *must* be correct to set up the counterrhythm properly. The succeeding notes of the counterrhythm will fall into place accurately after that.

464 APPENDIX E: CROSS-RHYTHM CHARTS

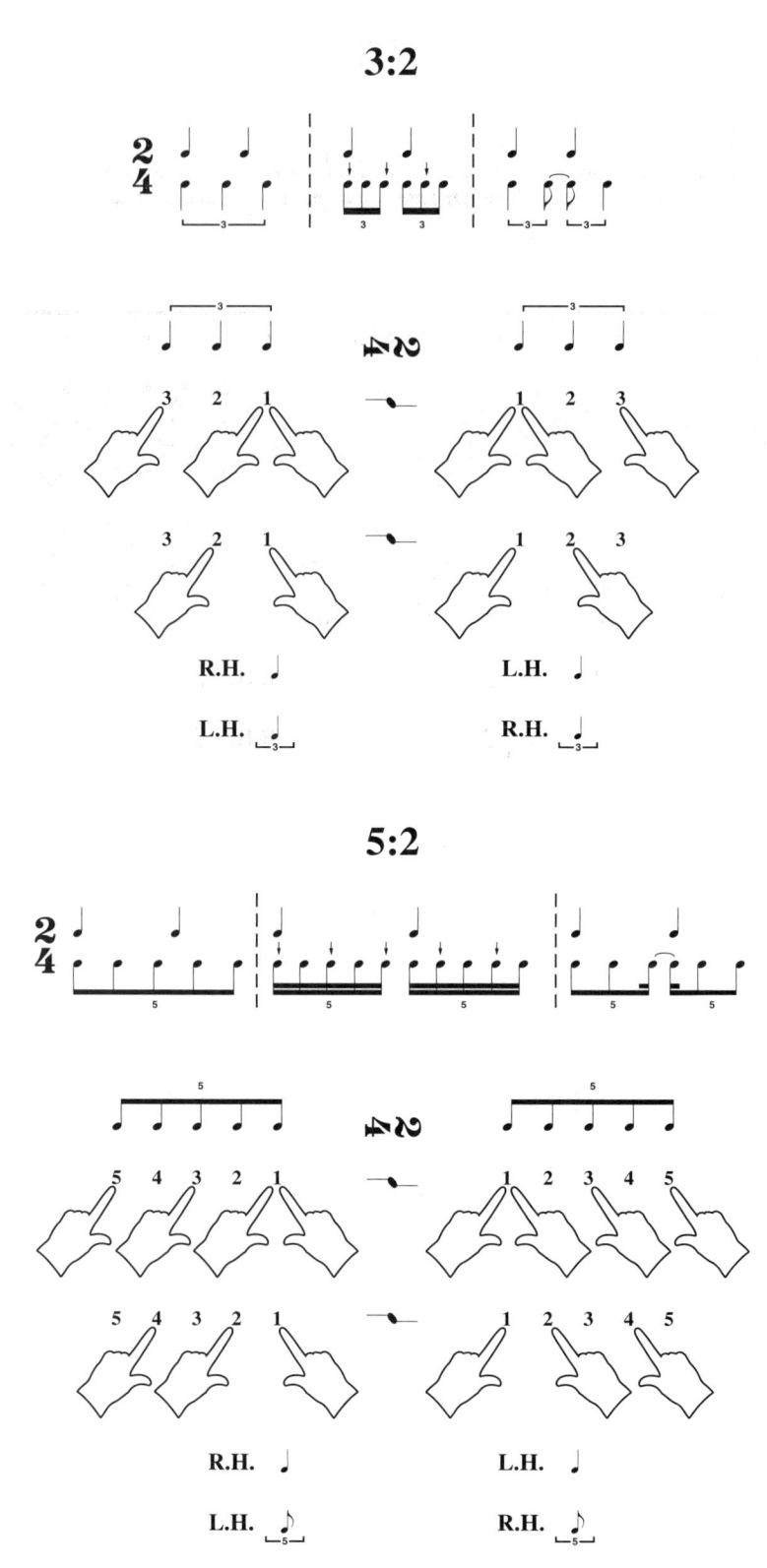

Appendix E: Cross-Rhythm Charts 465

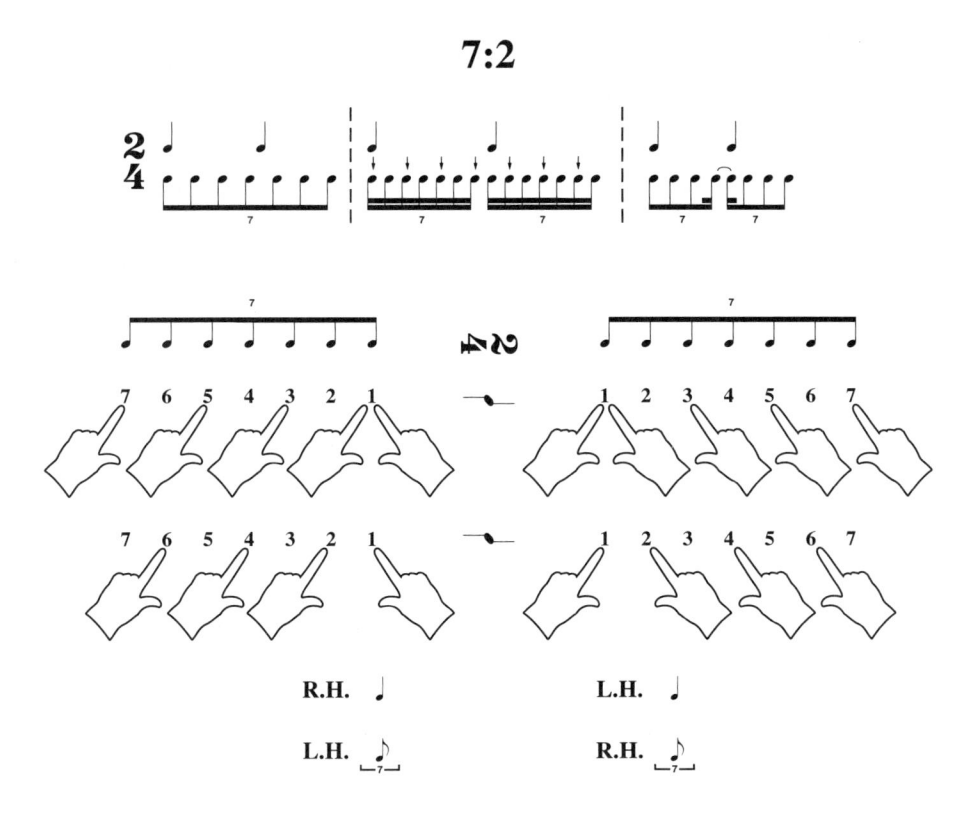

7:2

R.H. ♩

L.H. ♪

L.H. ♩

R.H. ♪

APPENDIX E: CROSS-RHYTHM CHARTS

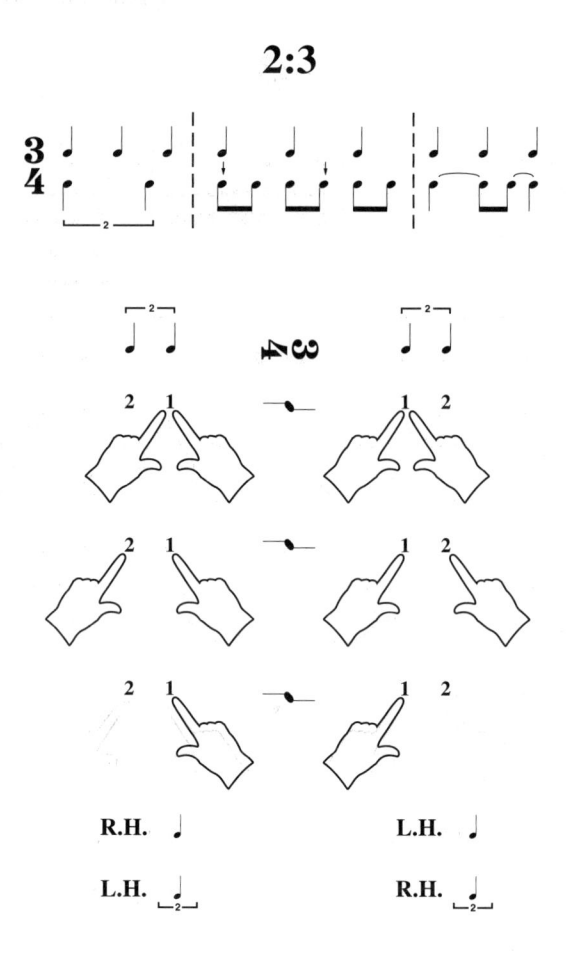

2:3

R.H. ♩

L.H. ♩

L.H. ♩

R.H. ♩

Appendix E: Cross-Rhythm Charts 467

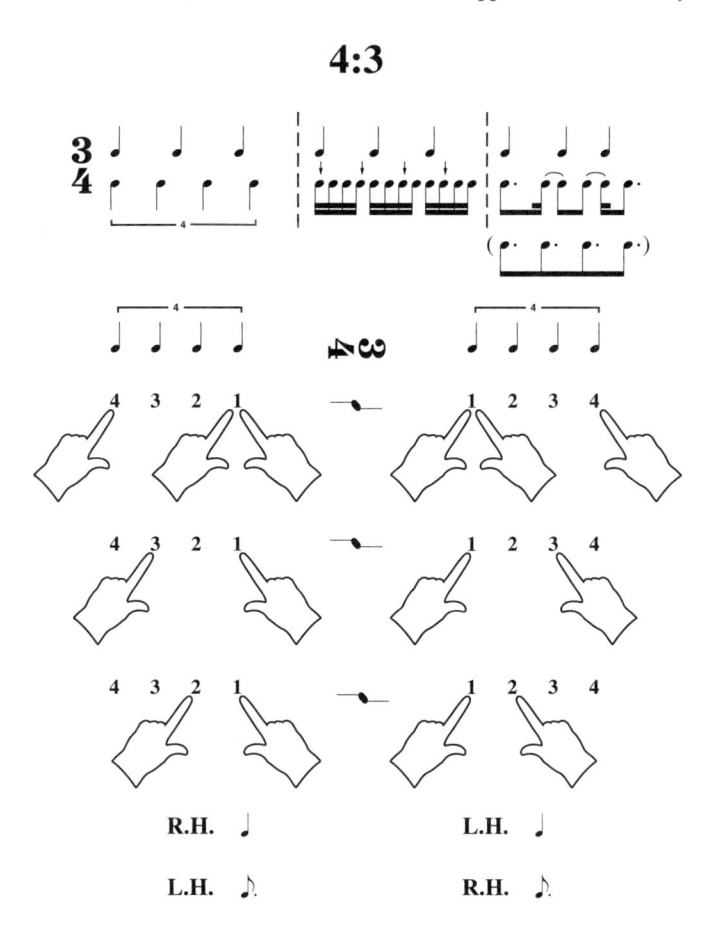

4:3

468 APPENDIX E: CROSS-RHYTHM CHARTS

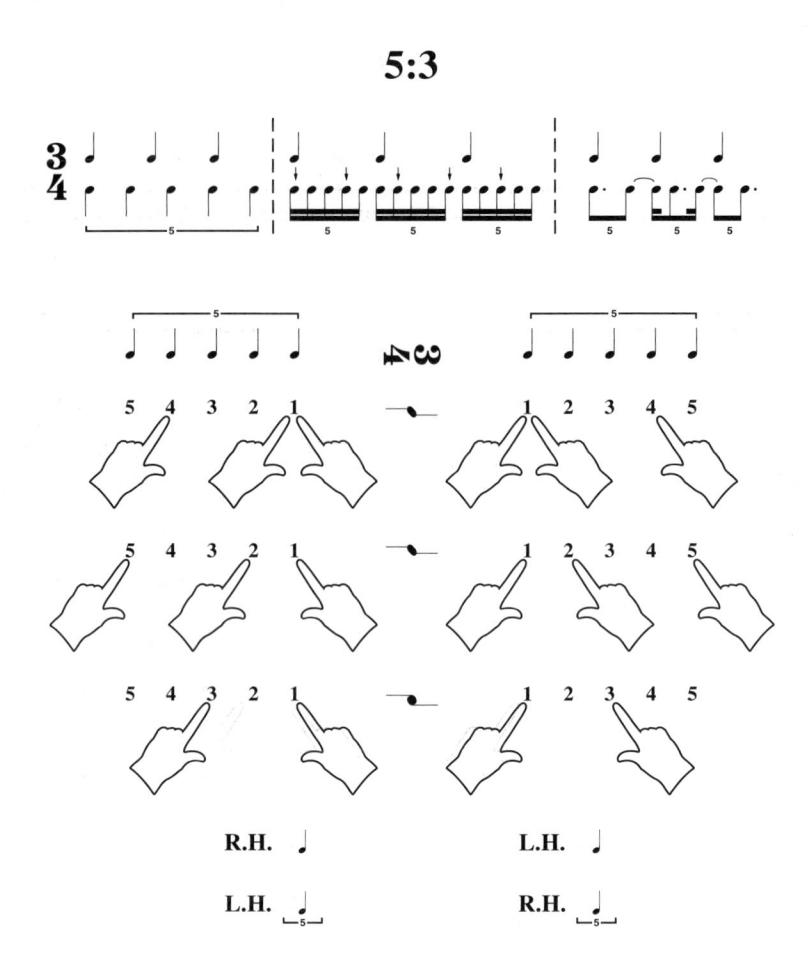

5:3

Appendix E: Cross-Rhythm Charts 469

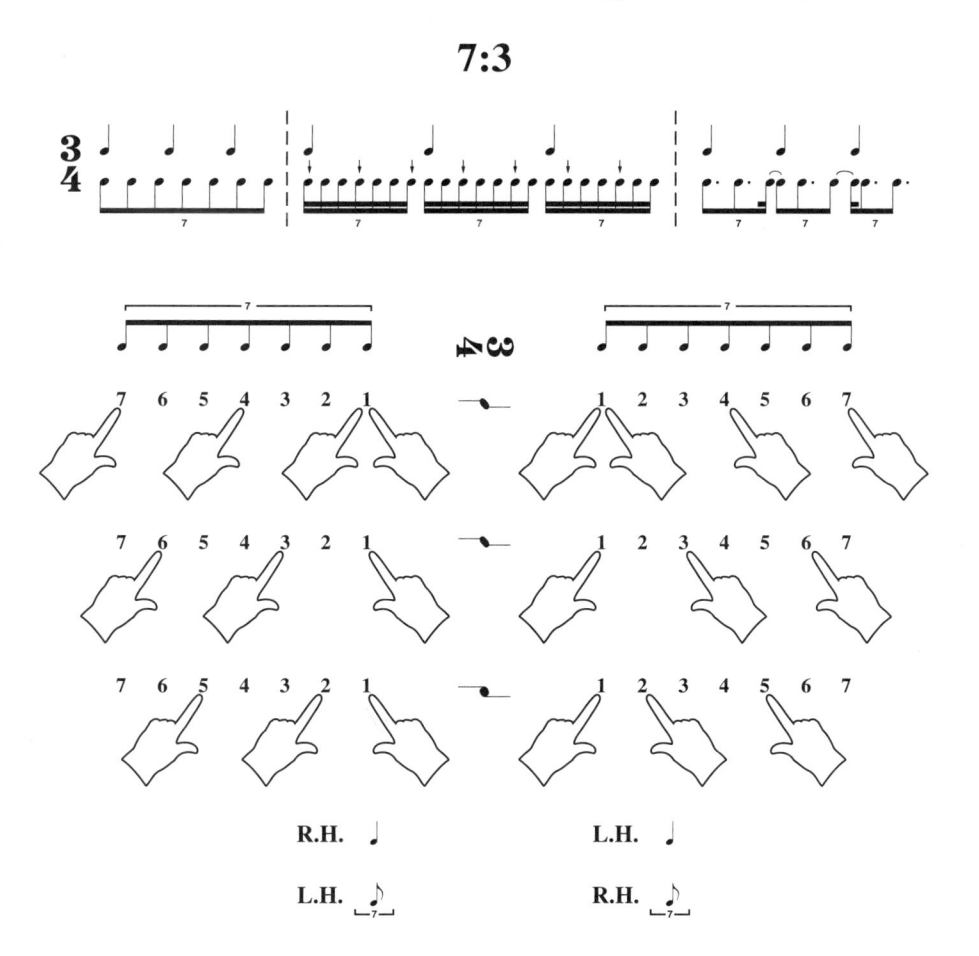

7:3

R.H. ♩

L.H. ♪

L.H. ♩

R.H. ♪

470 APPENDIX E: CROSS-RHYTHM CHARTS

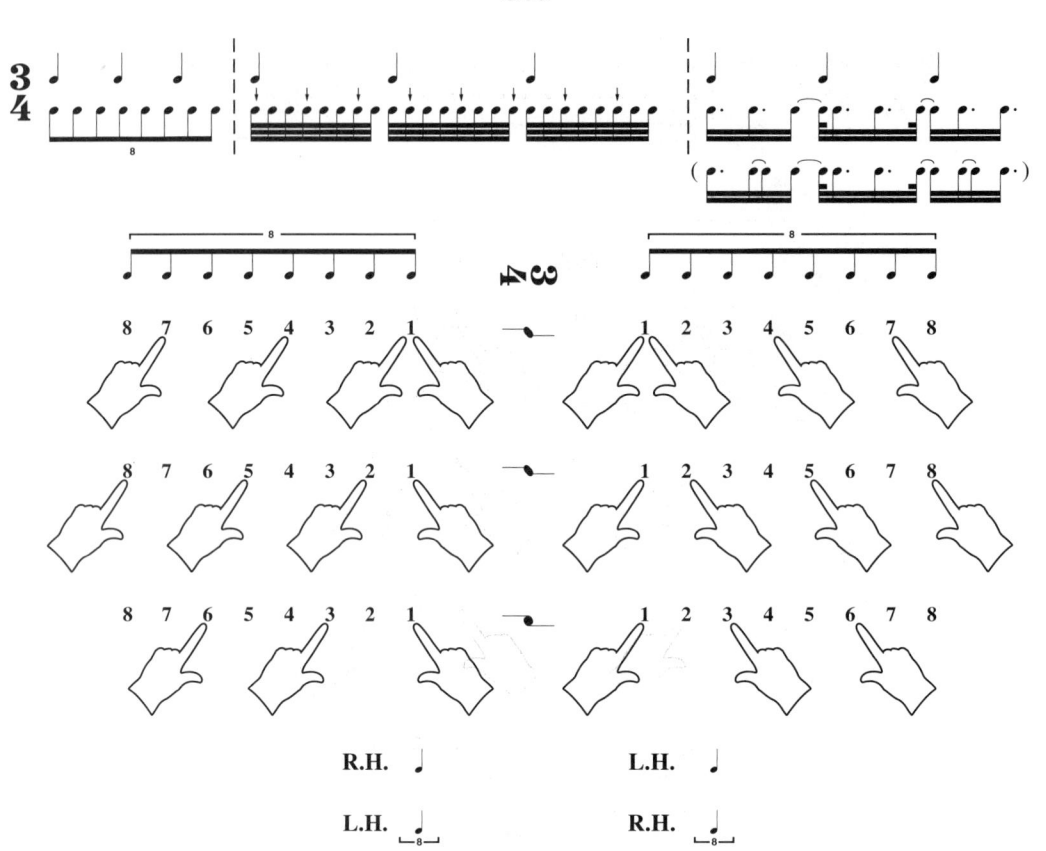

8:3

Appendix E: Cross-Rhythm Charts 471

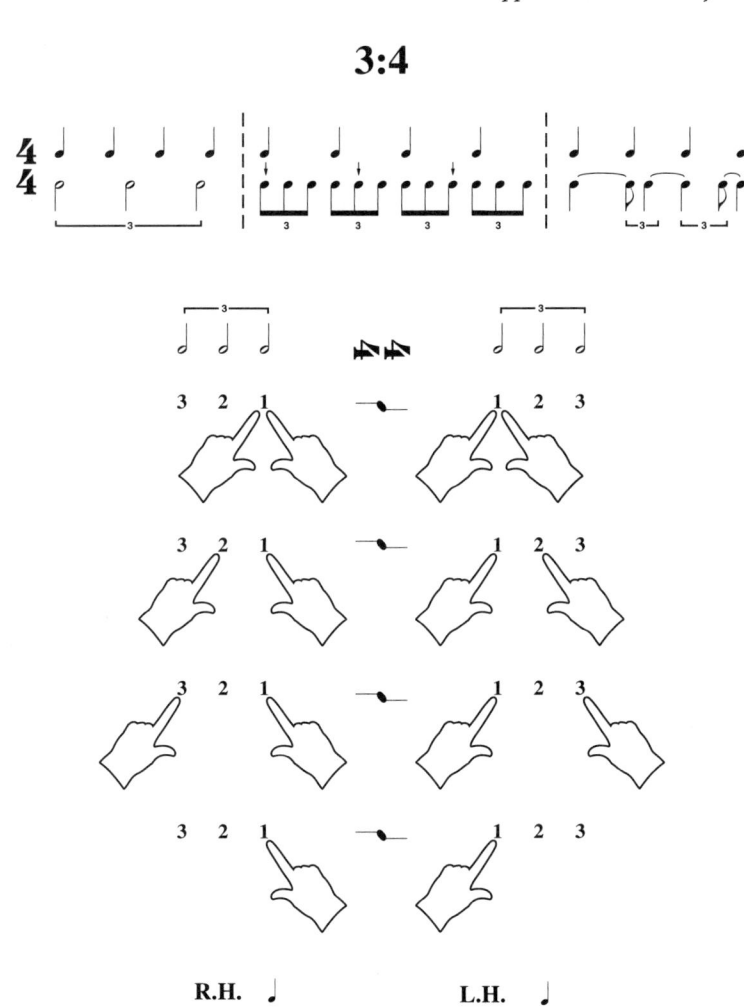

3:4

R.H. ♩   L.H. ♩

L.H. ♩   R.H. ♩
    3   3

472 APPENDIX E: CROSS-RHYTHM CHARTS

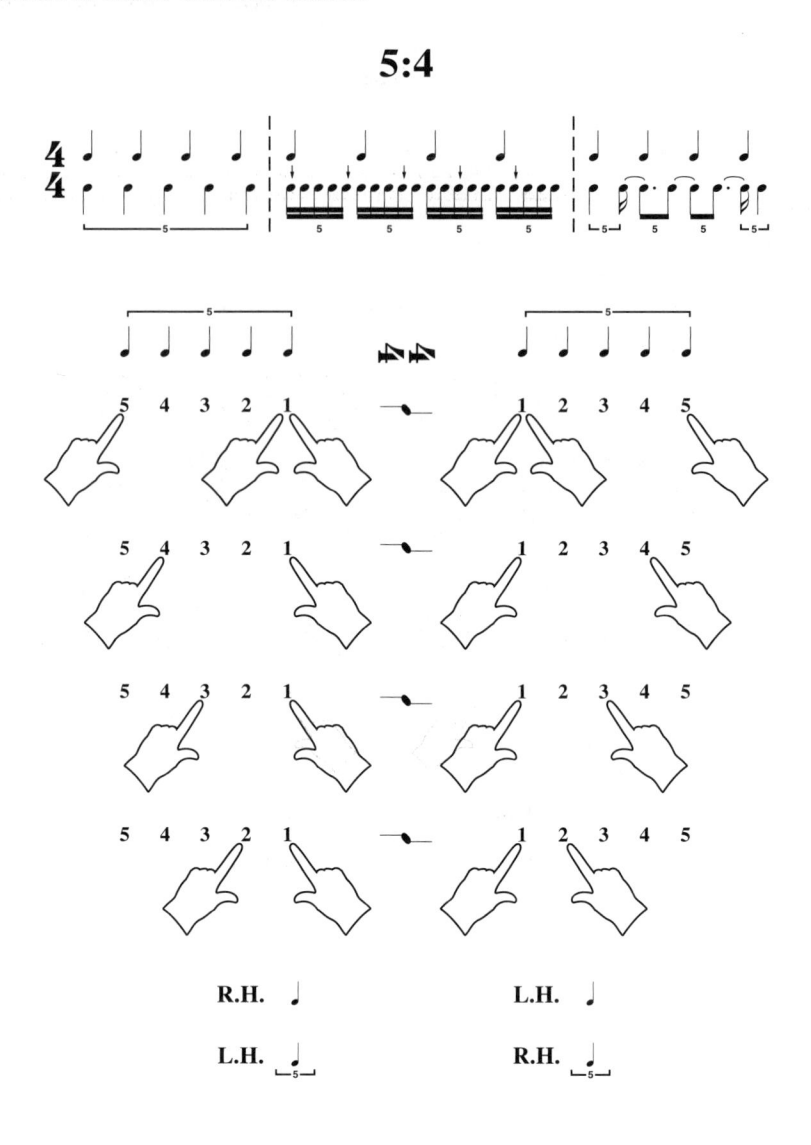

5:4

R.H. ♩

L.H. ♩ (5-tuplet)

L.H. ♩

R.H. ♩ (5-tuplet)

Appendix E: Cross-Rhythm Charts 473

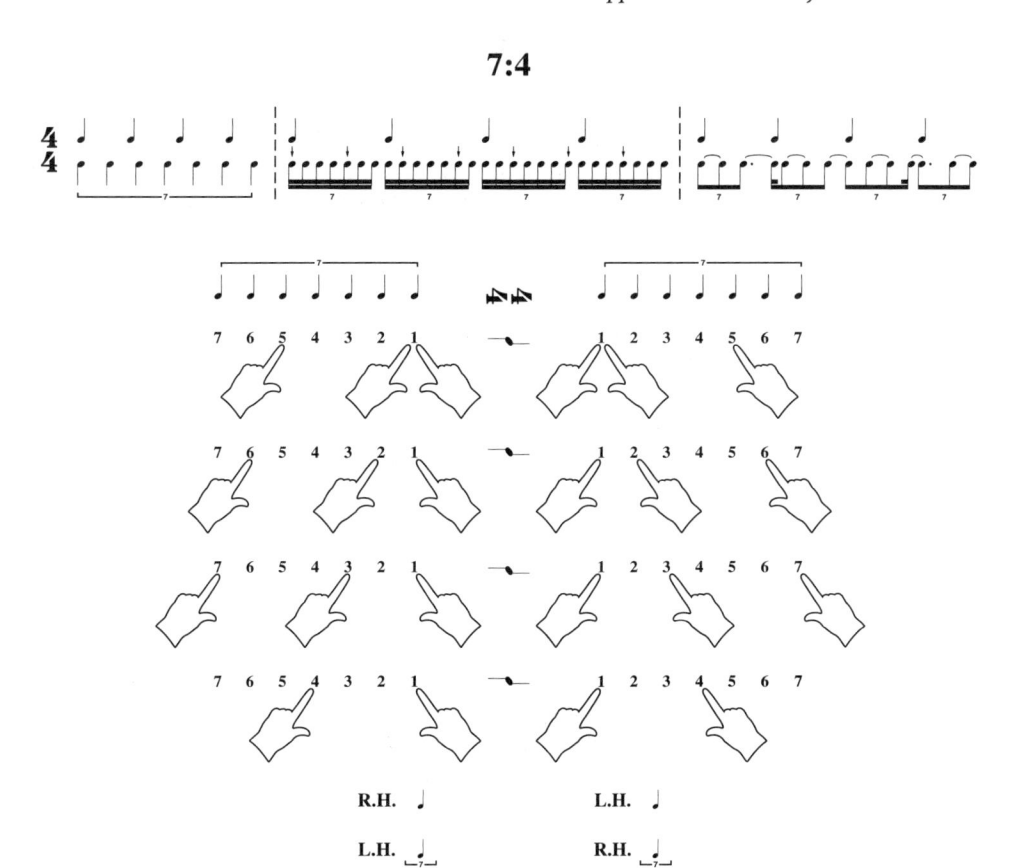

7:4

R.H. ♩

L.H. ♩ (7)

L.H. ♩

R.H. ♩ (7)

474 APPENDIX E: CROSS-RHYTHM CHARTS

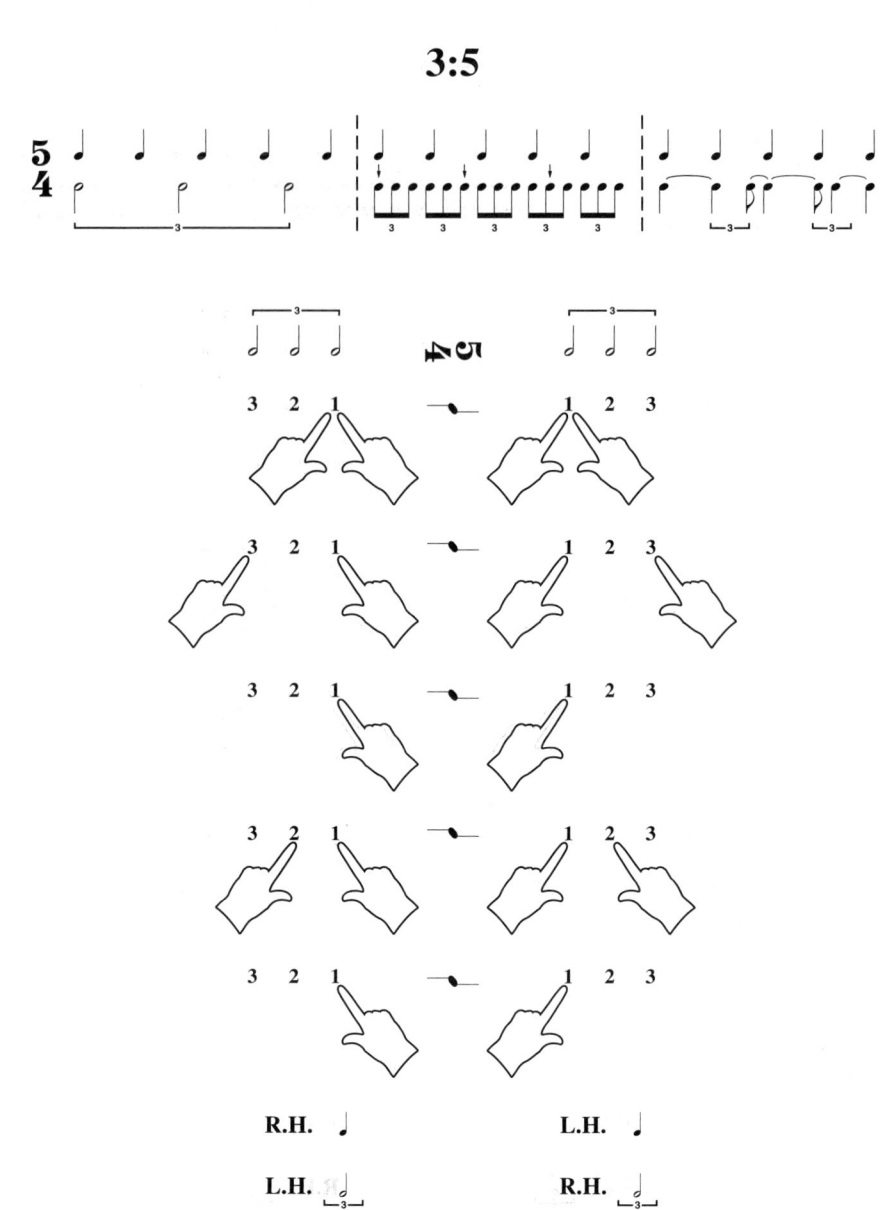

3:5

R.H. ♩

L.H. ♩

L.H. ♩

R.H. ♩

Appendix E: Cross-Rhythm Charts 475

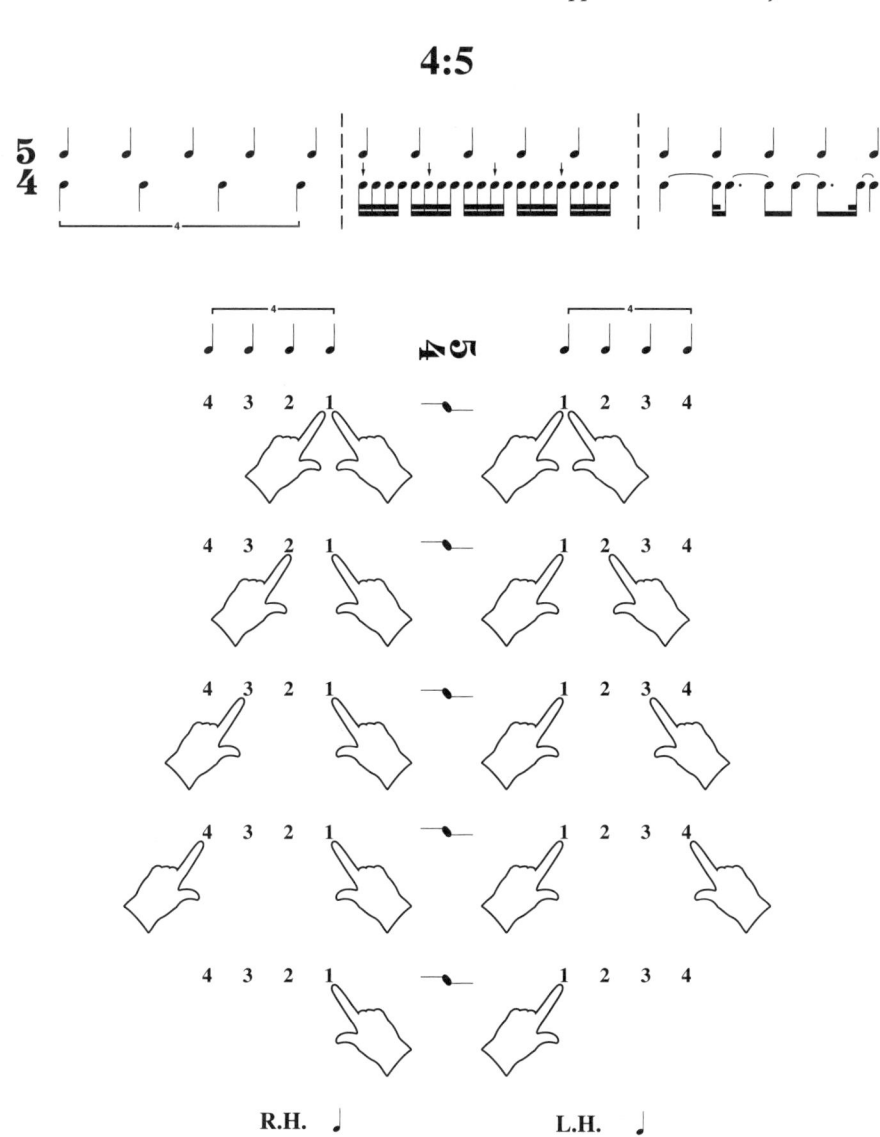

4:5

R.H. ♩

L.H. ♩ (4)

L.H. ♩

R.H. ♩ (4)

476 APPENDIX E: CROSS-RHYTHM CHARTS

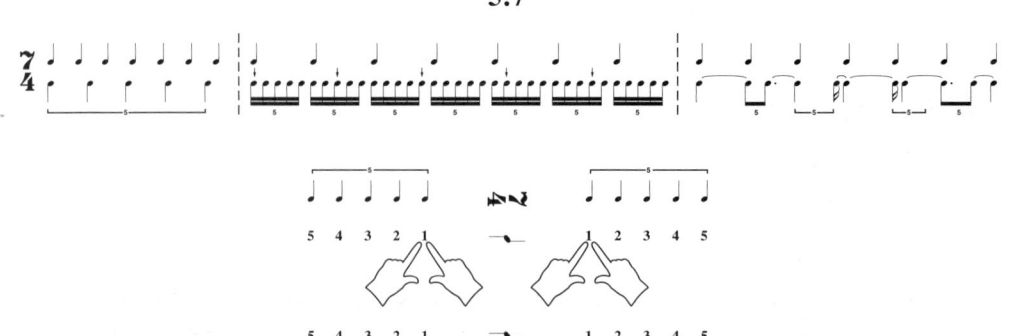

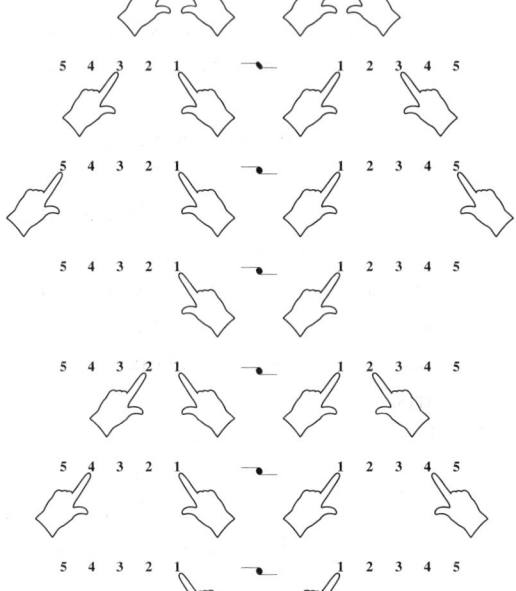

5:7

R.H. ♩   L.H. ♩

L.H. ♪   R.H. ♪

ACKNOWLEDGMENTS

Special thanks to Emy, whose editing was indispensable. She stood by me with unending support, at times going line by line with me while I figured out what I really wanted to say.

Without Bill Grossman's dedication, painstaking proofreading, countless hours of work, and collaboration with Oxford University Press, the book could not have been finished. Bill added new material and charts and put the final touches on the book.

I am indebted to Karen Nixon, who gave many hours to the project, made excellent suggestions, researched the four language charts, and assisted in creating symbols; Robert Snarrenberg, Daniel Panner, and Rebecca Schwartz-Bishir for assisting with editing; and Julien Benichou and Simeone Tartaglione for reviewing the French and Italian in the language charts.

I am grateful to Paul Boylan, Dean of the School of Music at the University of Michigan, and Phillip Nelson, Dean of the School of Music at Yale University, for granting me sabbaticals during which major portions of this book were written. Both Gunther Schuller and Leon Fleisher were highly supportive during my many summers in Tanglewood.

Others, friends, former students, and colleagues were helpful in many important ways: Marin Alsop, Mark Gibson, Ben Loeb, Donald Schleicher, and Beverly Taylor read the final draft and provided useful comments. Advice and encouragement also came from Sam Adler, Steven Baxter, Phyllis Boros, Emily Brown, Marti Burlingham, Richard and Penny Crawford, Wolfgang Justen, Fred Lerdahl, Joan Lowenstein, Antonio Pappano, Morris Risenhoover, Bill Robertson, Hannah Rosen, Rico Saccani, Carl St. Clair, Johannes Schlaefli, Jeffrey Sharkey, Robert Sirota, Eileen Soskin, Mark Springer, Brian Stone, Jonathan Trobe, Richard Turits, and Glen Watkins. Special recognition to Judith Liegner and Bob and Jean Tellalian for their unflagging personal support and interest in the book.

Finally, my thanks to Steve Jarvi who introduced me to Joanne Brownstein, my very capable and enthusiastic agent, along with special appreciation to my patient, creative, and supportive associates at Oxford: Suzanne Ryan, Senior Music Editor, Liz Smith, Production Editor, and Norman Hirschy, Associate Music Editor. My gratitude also goes to those of you whom I may have neglected to name but wish to thank whole heartedly.

ADDITIONAL MUSIC CREDITS

OF MICE AND MEN
By Carlisle Floyd
© 1971 by Carlisle Floyd
Boosey & Hawks, Inc., Sole Agent
Reprinted by permission.

RHAPSODY IN BLUE
By George Gershwin
© 1924 (renewed) WB Music Corp
All Rights Reserved. Used by permission of Alfred Publishing Co., Inc.

RHAPSODY ON A THEME BY PAGANINI, OP. 43
By Sergei Rachmaninoff
© 1934 (renewed) Charles Foley, Inc.
All Rights Reserved and Administered by Boosey & Hawkes Music Publishers, Ltd. (Publishing)
And Alfred Publishing Co, Inc., (Print)
All Rights Reserved. Used by permission of Alfred Publishing Co., Inc.

SYMPHONIC DANCES, OP 45
By Sergei Rachmaninoff
© 1942 (renewed) Charles Foley, Inc.
All Rights Reserved and Administered by Boosey & Hawkes Music Publishers, Ltd. (Publishing)
And Alfred Publishing Co, Inc., (Print)
All Rights Reserved. Used by permission of Alfred Publishing Co., Inc.

CONCERTO FOR ORCHESTRA
By Bela Bartok
© 1946 by Hawkes & Son (London) Ltd.
Reprinted by permission.

DIVERTIMENTO FOR ORCHESTRA
By Leonard Bernstein
© 1980 Amberson Holdings, LLC
Leonard Bernstein Music Publishing LLC, Publishers
Boosey & Hawkes, Inc. sole agent
All Rights Reserved. Reprinted by permission.

SYMPHONIC DANCES FROM WEST SIDE STORY
By Leonard Bernstein
© Copyright 1967 by Amberson Holdings LLC and Stephen Sondheim
Copyright renewed. Leonard Bernstein Music Publishing LLC, Publishers

Boosey & Hawkes, Inc. sole agent
All Rights Reserved. Reprinted by permission.

APPALACHIAN SPRING
By Aaron Copland
© 1945 The Aaron Copland Fund for Music, Inc.
Copyright renewed
Boosey & Hawkes, Inc. sole licensee
Reprinted by permission.

CLASSICAL SYMPHONY IN D
By Serge Prokofieff
© Copyright 1928 by Hawkes & Son (London) Ltd.
Reprinted by permission.

PIANO CONCERTO NO. 2
By Serge Rachmaninoff
© Copyright 1901 by Hawkes & Son (London) Ltd.
Reprinted by permission.

MOVEMENT FOR PIANO AND ORCHESTRA
By Igor Stravinsky
© Copyright 1960 by Hawkes & Son (London) Ltd.
Reprinted by permission.

PETROUCHKA
By Igor Stravinsky
© Copyright 1912 by Hawkes & Son (London) Ltd.
Revised version © copyright 1948 by Hawkes & Son (London) Ltd.
Reprinted by permission.

PULCINELLA SUITE
By Igor Stravinsky
© Copyright 1924 by Hawkes & Son (London) Ltd.
Revised version © copyright 1949 by Hawkes & Son (London) Ltd.
Reprinted by permission.

THE RITE OF SPRING
By Igor Stravinsky
© Copyright 1912, 1921 by Hawkes & Son (London) Ltd.
Reprinted by permission.

BALLAD OF BABY DOE
Words and Music by John Latouche and Douglas Moore
© 1958 (Renewed) Chappell & Co, Inc.
All Rights Reserved. Used by permission of Alfred Publishing Co., Inc.

SYMPHONY #5
Gustav Mahler
Copyright © 1964 by C. F. Peters Corporation.
All Rights Reserved. Used by permission.

SUITE FOR STRINGS
Ullysses Kay
Copyright © 1961 by C. F. Peters Corporation.
All Rights Reserved. Used by permission.

THREE MOVEMENTS FOR ORCHESTRA
George Perle
Movement II, bar 61, from TIME CYCLE—Foss (Carl Fisher)
Movement II, bar 39, from THREE MOVEMENTS FOR ORCHESTRA (Theodor Presser)
Reprinted by permission.

CONCERTO FOR PIANO NO. 1
By Leon Kirchner
Copyright © 1957 (Renewed) by Associated Music Publishers, Inc.
International Copyright Secured. All Rights Reserved.
Reprinted by permission.

DOUBLE CONCERTO FOR HARPSICHORD AND PIANO
By Elliott Carter
Copyright © 1962 (Renewed) by Associated Music Publishers, Inc.
International Copyright Secured. All Rights Reserved.
Reprinted by permission.

THE SOLDIER'S TALE
Music by Igor Stravinsky
Libretto by Charles Ferdinand Ramuz
Copyright © 1924 Chester Music Limited.
New Edition © 1987, 1992 Chester Music Limited
All Rights Reserved. International Copyright Secured.
Reprinted by permission.

EL SOMBRERO DE TRES PICOS
(Three Cornered Hat)
Music by Manuel de Falla
Scenario by Gregorio Martinez Sierra
Copyright © 1921. New Edition © Copyright 1999 for all countries
Chester Music Limited, 14–15 Berners Street, London W1t 3LJ, United Kingdom
Co-published for Spain and Spanish speaking territories (and including Portugal but excluding Brazil) with Manuel de Falla Ediciones
All Rights Reserved. Reprinted by permission.

INDEX OF MUSICAL EXAMPLES

Bach, J. C., Symphony, op. 18, no. 4, 225
Bartók, *Concerto for Orchestra*, 32, 52–54, 57, 66, 72, 87, 164, 175, 225, 228, 252, 280–84, 290–97
Beethoven
   Coriolan Overture, 31, 60, 86
   Egmont Overture, 16, 203, 208–10, 235, 269–72
   Leonore Overture, 53, 79, 148
   Piano Concerto no. 3, 45
   Piano Concerto no. 4, 300, 303–4
   Piano Concerto no. 5, 303, 307–8
   Symphony no. 1, 25, 45, 79, 127, 136
   Symphony no. 2, 22, 30, 51, 55–56, 60, 64, 67, 73–74, 79, 87, 89, 124, 132, 137–41, 163, 195, 197–98, 213, 226, 248, 258–65, 268–69
   Symphony no. 3, 29, 32, 34, 36, 74, 80, 132, 143–47, 160, 162, 166, 171, 177–79, 182, 184–85, 192–93, 196, 199, 201, 205–7, 211–12, 214–16, 221, 240–41
   Symphony no. 4, 44, 59, 74, 125–26, 171, 232
   Symphony no. 5, 25, 32, 49, 60, 73, 81, 84, 123–24, 137, 163, 181, 185, 192–93, 200–202, 223–24, 244
   Symphony no. 6, 46, 143, 173, 180, 188–89, 200, 224, 227, 242
   Symphony no. 7, 27, 32, 35–36, 56, 58, 78, 81, 85, 122, 160, 174, 188, 253
   Symphony no. 8, 34, 37, 142
   Symphony no. 9, 32, 51, 54, 57, 85, 90, 116, 134
   Triple Concerto, 307
Berlioz
   Overture to *Beatrice and Benedict*, 34
   Roman Carnival Overture, 116
   Symphonie fantastique, 57, 63, 88, 127–28, 133, 159, 165, 171, 181–83, 298
Bernstein
   Divertimento for Orchestra, 42, 110
   Symphonic Dances from "West Side Story" (revised edition), 109
Bizet
   Carmen, 202
   Symphony no. 1, 12, 218–20, 355
Brahms
   Academic Festival Overture, 54
   Piano Concerto no. 2, 54, 118, 307
   Serenade, Op. 11, 49

Symphony no. 1, 14, 29, 45, 87, 100, 111, 114, 132, 162–63, 194, 196–97, 224–25, 237, 250, 256
Symphony no. 2, 21, 30, 62, 64, 87, 160, 162, 168, 172, 180, 207, 227, 234
Symphony no. 3, 36, 67, 74, 87, 235, 238
Symphony no. 4, 27, 36, 86, 161, 196–99, 223, 225, 245, 247, 249, 254–56
Tragic Overture, 106

Carter, Double Concerto for Harpsichord and Piano, 66, 99, 120–21
Chopin, Piano Concerto no. 1, 306
Copland, *Appalachian Spring* Suite, 87, 119, 284–85

Debussy
   La mer, 110, 123, 165
   Nocturnes, 29
   Prelude to the Afternoon of a Faun, 65, 84, 86, 88, 91, 94, 111, 159, 224, 275–80
Dukas, *The Sorcerer's Apprentice*, 15, 52, 85
Dvořák
   Symphony no. 7, 25
   Symphony no. 8, 11, 49
   Symphony no. 9 (*From the New World*), 45, 55, 96, 164, 174, 187, 225, 228–29

Falla, *The Three-Cornered Hat*, Suite no. 2, 23, 33, 68, 106
Floyd, *Of Mice and Men*, 40–41
Foss, *Time Cycle*, 40
Franck, Symphony in D minor, 158, 167–68, 170, 186–87

Gershwin, *Rhapsody in Blue*, 81
Gluck, Overture to *Alceste*, 27

Handel
   Messiah, 62
   Water Music, 27
Haydn
   The Creation, 327
   Sinfonia concertante, 327–29
   Symphony no. 88, 136
   Symphony no. 93, 16

Haydn (*continued*)
  Symphony no. 94, 57
  Symphony no. 99, 57
  Symphony no. 100, 133
  Symphony no. 101, 12
  Symphony no. 103, 230–31
  Symphony no. 104, 86
Hindemith
  Kammermusik, 20
  Symphonie Mathis der Maler, 17, 157–58

Kay, *Suite for Strings*, 42
Kirchner, Concerto for Violin, Cello, Ten Winds, and Percussion, 39

Liszt
  Les Préludes, 31
  Totentanz, 302

Mahler
  Symphony no. 2, 80, 207
  Symphony no. 5, 169, 172
Mendelssohn
  Fingal's Cave Overture, 195
  A Midsummer Night's Dream, 78, 353
  Symphony no. 1, 23
  Symphony no. 4, 23, 33
Moore, *The Ballad of Baby Doe*, 42
Mozart
  The Abduction from the Seraglio, 19
  Contradances K. 609, 133
  Eine kleine Nachtmusik, 21, 26
  The Magic Flute, 62, 325–27
  The Marriage of Figaro, 322, 324
  Overture to *Così fan tutte*, 113
  Overture to *Don Giovanni*, 113
  Overture to *The Abduction from the Seraglio*, 53, 79
  Overture to *The Magic Flute*, 53, 161, 203, 233, 239
  Requiem, Dies Irae, 70
  Symphony no. 35, 194, 238
  Symphony no. 38, 62
  Symphony no. 39, 73, 84, 86, 95, 113, 135
  Symphony no. 40, 86
  Symphony no. 41, 58, 73
Mussorgsky
  Night on Bald Mountain, 64
  Pictures at an Exhibition (arr. Ravel), no. 5, 28

Perle, *Three Movements for Orchestra*, 165
Prokofiev, *Classical Symphony*, 174
Puccini, *La Bohème*, 50, 80

Rachmaninoff
  Piano Concerto no. 2, 107
  Rhapsody on a Theme of Paganini, 301
  Symphonic Dances, 355

Ravel, *Daphnis and Chloé*, 34
Reger, *Four Tone Poems after Arnold Böcklin*, 175
Rimsky-Korsakov, *Scheherazade*, 24, 48, 80, 115, 119
Rossini
  Overture to *La scala di Seta*, 28, 36
  Overture to *L'Italiana in Algeri*, 24

Salieri, Sinfonia, 30
Schubert, Symphony no. 9, 48–49
Schumann
  Symphony no. 1, 23, 78, 80
  Symphony no. 2, 25
  Symphony no. 3, 22–23, 35, 79
  Symphony no. 4, 20, 26, 28, 81
Shostakovich
  Symphony no. 5, 20
  Symphony no. 12, 106
Sibelius
  Symphony no. 1, 91
  Symphony no. 2, 106
  Violin Concerto, 273–75
Smetana, Overture to *The Bartered Bride*, 22
Strauss, J.
  On the Beautiful Blue Danube, 46
  Tales from the Vienna Woods, 49, 52
Strauss, R.
  Also sprach Zarathustra, 63
  Death and Transfiguration, 84, 112, 183–84, 186, 193
  Don Juan, 25, 72–73
  Ein Heldenleben, 171, 192
  Till Eulenspiegels lustige Streiche, 79, 106, 165, 185, 305
Stravinsky
  Firebird Suite (1919 version), Berceuse, 27
  Firebird Suite (1919 version), Danse infernale du roi Kastcheï, 28, 167–68
  Firebird Suite (1919 version), finale, 191
  Firebird Suite (1919 version), Introduction, 217
  Firebird Suite (1919 version), Ronde des princesses, 168, 204
  L'histoire du soldat, Royal March, 41
  L'histoire du soldat, The Devil's Dance, 66
  L'histoire du soldat, The Soldier's March, 23
  Movements for Piano and Orchestra, 338–39
  Petrouchka (1947 version), 67, 105, 109, 117–19, 168
  Pulcinella Suite, 26
  The Rite of Spring, 149, 169

Tchaikovsky
  1812 Overture, 148–49
  Piano Concerto no. 1, 23, 33
  Romeo and Juliet Fantasy-Overture, 69, 132, 285–89
  Serenade, 26, 50

Symphony no. 1, 15
Symphony no. 2, 250
Symphony no. 4, 30–31, 37, 54, 59, 63, 100, 114–15, 143, 251
Symphony no. 5, 57–58, 63, 68, 83, 90, 107–8, 110, 116, 246
Symphony no. 6, 29–32, 40, 42, 59, 64, 67–68, 78, 162

Verdi
Falstaff, 117
La Traviata, 310
Overture to *Nabucco*, 48
Requiem, Sanctus, 332–34

Wagner
A Faust-Overture, 176
Overture to *Rienzi*, 11
Overture to *The Flying Dutchman*, 25

Weber
Oberon Overture, 88
Overture to *Der Freischütz*, 13, 25, 55, 80, 82–83, 88

Webern, Symphony, op. 21, 92–93

GENERAL INDEX

accelerandos
   Appalachian Spring Suite, 284–85
   circular beat, 32
   common denominator, 111–12, 124–27
   definition, 99
   Luftpause, 72
   opera rehearsals, 309
   organic ritardando, 47
   recitatives, 321
   subdivision, 47–48
accompanying
   articulations, 299
   ballet, 335–36
   breathing, 299
   cuing, 300–301
   duets, 308
   entrances, 302
   negotiations, 299
   ornamental figures, 301
   piano concertos, 306
   preparatory beats, 302, 308
   recitatives, 308
   rehearsals, 299, 308–9, 311
   rhythms, 302
   ritardandos, 299
   soloists, 299, 307–8
   strings, 305
   tempos, 299
acoustics, 128, 151, 155–56, 335
Adagio, 141
agility, 313, 315, 331
alla breve, 34
Allegro, 98, 105–6, 108, 111, 125
Allegro con brio, 272
alto saxophones, 153
altos, 330
amateurs, 335
Andante, 98, 105–6, 108
Andante maestoso, 110
apex, 7, 26–27, 88
Appalachian Spring Suite, 284–85, 346
applause, 343
appoggiatura, 135, 270
arco, 257
arias, 299, 312–13, 318
arpeggios, 238, 240–41, 306, 341

articulations
   accompanying, 299
   ballet, 335
   band conducting, 334–35
   beat patterns, 18
   cuing, 142
   forte-pianos (*fp*), 129
   groups of bars, 50
   inhalation, 354
   modified subdivision, 46
   notation, 133–34, 149
   preparatory beats, 10
   rehearsals, 350
   score study, 98, 129, 132, 141, 298
   sforzatos, 129
artificial common denominators, 115, 124–28
artificial harmonics, 453, 460–61
assistant conductor, 351–52
attacca, 350
attitude, 344
auditions, 312–13, 312n4, 345, 347–49
aural skills, 3

Bach, 346
backstage conducting, 336
backstage speakers, 309
ballet, 318–20, 335–36
band conducting, 334–35
baritones, 332
baroque period, 152, 358
bars of silence, 84–85
Bartók, 228, 280–84, 290–98, 353
basic meters, 38
bass clarinet, 153, 164
bass clef, 331
bass line, 256–57, 309
basses, 330, 454
bassoons, 153–54
batons, 6, 18, 324, 342–43
beamed, 65
beat patterns
   articulations, 18
   basic meters, 38
   batons, 18
   conductor's craft, 342
   cutoffs, 18

beat patterns (*continued*)
   dictating, 69
   full subdivision, 44–45
   groups of bars, 50–53
   hemiola, 62–65
   irregular meters, 37–44
   modified subdivision, 45–46
   notation, 149
   preparatory beats, 17–19
   rebarring, 63–65
   rebeaming, 65–66
   recitatives, 321
   rhythmic unit, 48–50
   ritardandos, 46–47
   Romeo and Juliet Fantasy-Overture, 285
   stopping the beat, 88
   zigzag way, 257
beat unit
   accelerandos, 47
   body language, 7
   choosing, 61
   composers and, 61n4
   facial expressions, 7
   notation for, 7, 61
   placement of, 6
   polyrhythmic sections, 66–67
   size of, 6–7
   time signature, 61
Beethoven
   Egmont Overture, 269–72
   Emperor Concerto, 346
   Eroica, 166, 204–5, 210–12, 216, 221, 240–41
   one-composer concerts, 346
   Symphony no. 1, 136
   Symphony no. 2, 141, 258–69
   Symphony no. 3, 354
   Symphony no. 5, 289
   Symphony no. 6, 227
   Symphony no. 9, 50, 166, 329, 346
behavior, 344
Berlioz, 298
Bernstein, Leonard, 119, 127, 346
Bizet, 11–12, 336, 354–55
blocking, 310, 310n1
body language, 5–7, 309, 344, 350–51
boomerang motion, 9, 17
bowings
   Concerto for Orchestra, 283
   conductor directions, 354
   groups of bars, 50
   harmonic progression, 354
   Luftpause, 77
   notation, 141, 149
   score study, 133, 257
   tempos, 98
Brahms, 14, 237, 346

brasses
   cuing, 166, 206–7
   doublings, 142
   Eroica, 166
   Firebird Suite, 217
   intonation problems, 352
   preparatory beat, 9–10
   seating arrangement, 154–55, 154n2
   symbols, seating, 164–69
   Symphony no. 9 (Beethoven), 166
breathing. *See also* exhalation; inhalation
   accompanying, 308
   breath control, 331–32
   breath mark, 74
   choral conducting, 355
   conductor's craft, 354
   Luftpause, 77
   musical line, 354
   opera rehearsals, 309
   Prelude to the Afternoon of a Faun, 275, 354
   preparatory beats, 9
   soloists, 354
   stopping the beat, 88
   Symphonie Mathis der Maler, 16
   upbeats, 22
Brinkmann, Reinhold, 131
buffo, 316n5

cadential chords V-I, 321–22
cadenza, 302
caesura, 74
callbacks, 349
capella chorus, 329
Carmen, 336
Carter, 120–21
Carvalho, Eleazar de, 243
celesta, 152, 155–56, 156n3
cellos, 152, 256
chamber music, 129, 310, 342
choral concert, 68–69, 152
choral conducting, 329–34, 355
chords, 232–36, 341
choreography, 335–36
choruses
   clefs, 330–31
   cuing, 332–34
   entrances, 332
   opera chart, 318–20
   programming for, 346
   rehearsals, 330, 334
   vocal ranges, 331
circular beat, 28–29, 32
Clarinet Concerto, 346
clarinets, 153
classical period, 229–30, 229n1
Classical Symphony, 346
clefs, 98, 330–31, 361–445

coaches, 309
col legno, 132, 257
colla parte, 141, 308
colla voce, 308
common denominator
   accelerandos, 111–12, 124–27
   Allegro, 105–6, 108, 111, 125
   Andante, 105–6, 108, 110
   Appalachian Spring Suite, 284–85
   artificial common denominators, 115, 124–28
   Bernstein and, 119, 127
   composers, 105–7
   conductor's craft, 105–7, 115, 128
   definition, 102, 105
   Double Concerto for Harpsichord and Piano, 120–21
   heartbeat motif, 112
   Largo tempo, 112
   Leitmotiv, 115
   metronome markings, 102–5, 107, 109n4, 110n6, 113
   Moderato assai e molto maestoso, 110
   Moderato con anima, 114
   notation, 109
   Prelude to the Afternoon of a Faun, 111, 279–80
   Presto, 110–11
   rhythmic unit, 103
   ritardandos, 111–12, 124–27
   score study, 115–19
   subito tempo changes, 55, 127
   Symphony no. 2 (Beethoven), 263
   Symphony no. 4 (Tchaikovsky), 115
   tempos, 55, 105
   Un poco agitato, 112
   Un poco sostenuto, 111
   upbeats, 111, 122–25
   Violin Concerto (Sibelius), 273
communications
   ballet, 335–36
   body language, 344
   choral conducting, 329–30, 334
   conductor's craft, 5–6
   cosmetics, 343
   rehearsals, 5, 344
   rhythmic markings, 98–99
   score study, 3
composers
   beat unit, 61n4
   choruses, 331
   common denominator, 105–7
   concert rituals, 343
   and the conductor, 131
   cross-rhythms, 336
   cutoffs, 71
   divisions, 189
   fermata, 74
   full subdivision, 44
   metronomic tempos, 98–99
   operas, 311
   orchestration, 223
   rehearsals, 346
   rubato, 100
compoundings, 47, 306
con sordino, 283
concert hall, 128–29
concert pitch, 97, 237
concertmaster, 305, 344, 354
concerto, 299
Concerto for Orchestra, 228, 280–84, 290–98, 353
conducted beats, 18–19
conductor's craft
   accompanying, 299–308
   attitude, 344
   auditions, 345
   backstage conducting, 336
   ballet, 335–36
   band conducting, 334–35
   batons, 6
   beat patterns, 342
   body language, 5–6, 344
   breathing, 354
   choral conducting, 329–34
   common denominator, 105–7, 115, 128
   communications, 5–6
   and the composer, 131
   cosmetics, 342–43
   cross-rhythms, 336–38
   ear training, 341
   function of, 5
   Luftpause, 76–77, 77n8
   metronomic tempos, 99
   operatic conductors, 308–29
   oratorios, 327
   pitch, 97, 237
   recitatives, 321–25
   rehearsals, 350–52
   score study, 3
   seating arrangement, 151
   socializing, 344
   specialization, 342
   stopping the beat, 88
   syncopations, 82
   zigzag way, 257
Cone, Edward T., 131
continuo player, 321
contrabassoon, 153, 164
contralto, 330
Cook, Nicholas, 131
Copland, 284–85, 346
cosmetics, 342–43
counterrhythm, 337–38, 463–76
countertenors, 330
Creation, 313

crescendos, 136, 141, 224
crooks, 229
crossover, 8
cross-rhythms, 278, 336–38, 463–76
cuing
    accompanying, 300–301
    Appalachian Spring Suite, 284
    articulations, 142
    brasses, 166, 206–7
    choruses, 332–34
    definition, 142
    dynamics, 142
    Egmont Overture, 270
    ensemble playing, 5
    entrances, 206
    Eroica, 204–5, 211–12
    fugatos, 218–20
    fugues, 218–20
    inhalation, 354
    instrumentation, 186–89, 192
    memorization, 192, 218
    opera rehearsals, 310
    pivots, 143–47
    recitatives, 323
    Romeo and Juliet Fantasy-Overture, 287
    score study, 221, 298
    seating arrangement, 151–52
    soloists, 142, 152
    standard beats, 18
    strings, 191–92
    symbols, 156–69, 186–89
    Symphony no. 2 (Beethoven), 262
    traffic patterns, 151
    winds, 192
    zigzag way, 243, 257
cutoffs
    beat patterns, 18
    ensemble playing, 5
    fermata, 74–75
    preparatory beats, 71
    sudden silences, 88
    traffic patterns, 151
    zigzag way, 257
cymbals, 155

dancers, 335–36
Debussy, 111, 275–80, 354
Der Freischütz (Overture), 13
diagonal division, 176–86, 192, 211
dictating
    band conducting, 335
    choral concert, 68–69
    Concerto for Orchestra, 281
    definition, 68
    neutral beat, 69
    preparatory beats, 69
    rebound, 70–71
    rehearsals, 70
    staccato beat, 70
diminuendos, 136, 141, 224
distinto marking, 283
divisions
    Concerto for Orchestra, 281
    preparatory beats, 10
    strings, 189–90
    Symphony no. 103 (Haydn), 231
    winds, 194–203
doppio movimento, 282
double basses, 10, 152
Double Concerto for Harpsichord and Piano, 120–21
double fugue, 332
double reeds, 10, 194–95, 352
double stop, 10
double tonguing, 339
doublings
    brasses, 142
    notation, 142
    orchestration, 223, 225
    score study, 132
    seating arrangement, 151
    symbols, seating, 159
    syncopations, 223
    tremolos, 223
    winds, 142
downbeat
    basic symbols, 8
    circular beat, 32
    pivots, 145–46
    polyrhythmic sections, 66–67
    recitatives, 322n7
    splitting a single preparatory beat, 59–60
drums, 155
duets, 308
Dukas, 15
duple meter, 45
Dvořák, 11, 228–29
dynamics
    acoustics, 128
    ballet, 335
    band conducting, 334–35
    beat patterns, 18
    choruses, 331
    crescendos, 136
    cuing, 142
    cutoffs, 71
    feedback, 128–29
    groups of bars, 50
    interpretive decisions, 128–29, 128n10
    intonation problems, 352
    melodic line, 224
    notation, 133–34, 149
    opera rehearsals, 309
    preparatory beats, 10

rehearsals, 350–51
score study, 98, 129, 132, 257, 298
subito tempo changes, 53–58

ear training, 341
earphones, 336
E♭ clarinet, 164
Egmont Overture, 269–72
embellishments, 223, 308
Emperor Concerto, 346
English horn, 153, 164
ensemble playing, 5, 351
entrances
    accompanying, 302
    choruses, 332
    cuing, 206
    diagonally, 176–86
    Eroica, 204–5, 221
    Firebird Suite, 204
    horizontally, 183
    mirroring, 203
    notation, 169, 221
    preparatory beats, 10–11
    recitatives, 322
    soloists, 302
    strings, 170–92, 170n4
    traffic patterns, 208–21
    vertically, 183
    winds, 192–206
Epstein, David, 131
Eroica
    brasses, 166
    cuing, 204–5, 211–12
    entrances, 221
    fanfare, 240–41
    strings, 210–12, 216
    traffic patterns, 210–12, 216, 221
exhalation, 9, 354. *See also* breathing
exposition, 137

F rhythms, 244–48, 252–56
Fach system, 312–18
facial expressions, 7, 244, 343, 350–51
fanfare, 240–41
feedback, 3, 128–29, 342
fermata
    ballet, 335
    definition, 74
    ensemble playing, 5
    excerpts, 78–81
    measured rest, 76
    preparatory beats, 55, 74–77
    soloists, 36
    subito tempo changes, 55
    tacet sections, 76
    upbeats, 75–76
fingerboard, 454

fingering, 5
Firebird Suite, 204, 217
first violins, 5
flexibilities, 312
flutes, 153
flutist, 5
flutter-tonguing, 10
forte (f), 77
Forte, Allen, 131
forte-pianos (fp), 10, 129
fortissimo (ff), 55–58, 60
fugatos, 218–20
fugues, 218–20
full subdivision, 44

gestures, 342
grand pause (G.P.), 31, 84–85
grievances, 345
groups of bars, 41, 50–53

harmonic progression
    bass line, 256–57
    bowings, 354
    charts, 453–61
    groups of bars, 50
    inhalation, 354
    preparatory beats, 10
    rhythmic texture, 89
    rubato, 100
    score study, 147–49, 257
harmony
    Eroica, 241
    New World Symphony, 229
    orchestration, 223
    pedal point, 226
    Symphony no. 103 (Haydn), 231
harp, 152, 155–56
harpsichord, 151, 321
Haydn, 12, 135–36, 230–31, 313
heartbeat motif, 112
hemiola, 61–65, 277, 281, 283
Hindemith, 16
horizontal division, 183, 192, 194

ictus or impulse
    alterations to basic symbols, 8
    definition, 8–9
    exhalation, 9
    inhalation, 9
    legato beat, 29–30
    multiple preparatory beats, 33
    neutral beat, 31
    nondurational preparatory upbeat, 35
    notation, 7
    pickups, 24
    pivots, 143
    preparatory beats, 11, 15–17

ictus or impulse (*continued*)
    splitting a single preparatory beat, 59–60
    staccato beat, 27–28
    standard beats, 26–27
    Symphonie Mathis der Maler, 16
    upbeats, 21–22
Il Trovatore, 336
improvisation, 306, 341
impulse. *See* ictus or impulse
individual bars, 48–53
inhalation. *See also* breathing
    articulations, 354
    cuing, 354
    ictus or impulse, 9
    nondurational preparatory upbeat, 35
    pickups, 24
    pitch, 354
    and posture, 343
    preparatory beats, 354
    rhythms, 244, 354
inner woodwinds, 195
inner-beat, 34
instrumental charts, 357–59
instrumentalists, 342
instrumentation, 186–89, 192, 334–35, 346
instruments, 131–33, 327–29, 347–49, 361–445
intermission, 345
intonation problems, 236–37, 350–53
irregular meters, 37–44, 149
Ives, 346

jazz ensembles, 33
Jeremiah Symphony, 346

keyboard, 129, 321, 352

La Bohème, 324
La Forza del Destino, 269
Largo tempo, 112, 141
left-hand cutoff, 12, 24, 74–75, 322
legato beat
    alterations to basic symbols, 8
    beat patterns, 18
    Concerto for Orchestra, 281
    full subdivision, 45
    Prelude to the Afternoon of a Faun, 276
    preparatory beats, 29–30
Leitmotiv, 115
Lento, 98
librarian, 344, 351–52
libretto, 311
litigation, 345
loudspeakers, 336
Luftpause
    accelerandos, 72
    bowings, 77
    breathing, 77

    conductor's craft, 76–77, 77n8
    definition, 72
    preparatory beats, 72
    pull-back motion, 73n7
    push-away motion, 73n7
    rebound, 67–68
    tempos, 72–73
    winds, 77

M (majority), 249–56
The Magic Flute, 233, 325–26
Mahler, 336, 346
mallets, 155
Marriage of Figaro, 312n4
measured rest, 76
measured silence, 84
measured to unmeasured beat, 8, 72, 141
melodic line, 223–24, 231, 237–39
melody, 223
memorization, 192, 218, 341–42
meters, 19, 47
metronome markings
    common denominator, 102–5, 107, 109n4, 110n6, 113
    definition, 100
    subdivision, 101–2
    tremolos, 141
metronomic tempos, 98
metronomic unit, 44–45, 48, 61–65
Meyer, Leonard B., 131
mezzo-sopranos, 330, 332
mini-cutoff, 325–26
mirroring, 203, 282
Moderato assai e molto maestoso, 110
Moderato con anima, 114
modified subdivision, 45–46
monitors, 347, 349
Morse code punctuations, 282
Mozart
    brasses, 166
    The Magic Flute, 233, 325–26
    Marriage of Figaro, 312n4
    one-composer concerts, 346
    Symphony no. 39, 134–35
    Symphony no. 40, 166
multiple preparatory beats, 33–34, 42. *See also* preparatory beats
multiple rhythms, 339
music director, 349
musical line, 351, 354
musicians
    articulations, 129
    auditions, 347–49
    aural skills, 3
    beat unit, size of, 7
    cutoffs, 71
    dictating, 70

feedback, 3
M (majority), 249–56
metronomic tempos, 98
orchestra committee meetings, 344–45
preparatory beats, 10
probation, 345
rehearsals, 350–52
mutes, 10, 132, 257

narrators, 343
natural harmonic, 453–59
negotiations, 299
neutral beat
  alterations to basic symbols, 8
  dictating, 69
  ictus or impulse, 31
  preparatory beats, 31
  recitatives, 321, 325
  subito tempo changes, 55
New World Symphony, 228–29
nodes, 10, 455–61
nondurational preparatory upbeat, 35–36
nonrebound beat, 30, 82
notation
  alterations to basic symbols, 8
  articulations, 133–34, 149
  basic symbols, 8
  beat patterns, 149
  beat unit, 7, 61
  bowings, 141, 149
  common denominator, 109
  concert pitch, 97
  crescendos, 136
  doublings, 142
  dynamics, 133–34, 149
  entrances, 169, 221
  exposition, 137
  feedback, 133–34
  harmonics charts, 455–61
  ictus or impulse, 7
  instruments, 361–445
  irregular meters, 149
  numbers, 169
  oratorios, 327
  orchestration, 136, 149
  phrasings, 141, 149
  pitch, 149
  Prelude to the Afternoon of a Faun, 280
  preparatory beats, 7
  quattro battute, 149
  recapitulation, 134, 137
  rehearsals, 350
  score study, 97, 129, 133–42, 147–49
  security, 147–49
  symbols, seating, 164
  Symphony no. 1 (Beethoven), 136
  Symphony no. 2 (Beethoven), 141, 267

Symphony no. 39 (Mozart), 134–35
Symphony no. 88 (Haydn), 135–36
time signature, 149
traffic patterns, 151, 208–21
tre battute, 149
voice leading, 142
numbers
  brasses, 206–7
  notation, 169
  rehearsals, 350–51
  strings, 170–92
  traffic patterns, 208–21
  winds, 192–206

oboes, 153, 352
octave doubling, 353
offbeat, 83
one-composer concerts, 346
open strings, 453–61
operas, 310–12, 342
operatic conductors
  casting decisions, 311–12
  opera chart, 318–20
  piano dress rehearsals, 310
  rehearsals, 308–11
  seating arrangement, 152
  Sitzprobe, 310, 310n2
  star system, 311, 311n3
  voice categorization, 312–13
  voice charts, 313–18
oratorios, 312–13, 318n6, 327, 342
orchestras
  backstage conducting, 336
  choral conducting, 330
  clefs used, 98
  committee, 344–45
  instrumental charts, 357–59
  opera chart, 318–20
  recitatives, 327–29
  rituals for, 343
orchestration
  arpeggios, 238
  ballet, 335–36
  chords, 232–36
  Concerto for Orchestra (Bartok), 228
  crescendos, 224
  cutoffs, 71
  doublings, 223, 225
  Eroica, 240–41
  groups of bars, 50
  harmony, 223
  intonation problems, 236–37, 353
  The Magic Flute, 233
  melodic line, 223–24, 237–39
  New World Symphony, 228–29
  notation, 136, 149
  pedal point, 226–27, 237

orchestration (*continued*)
   pitch, 232, 236–37
   preparatory beats, 10–17
   rehearsals, 351
   score study, 223
   seating arrangement, 151
   sorting, 223–42, 256–57
   Symphony no. 1 (Brahms), 237
   Symphony no. 6 (Beethoven), 227
   Symphony no. 103 (Haydn), 230–31
   syncopations, 239
   traffic patterns, 208
   zigzag way, 243, 256–57
organic ritardando, 47
ornamental figures, 301
ornamentations, 223, 308
Oster, Ernst, 131
outer woodwinds, 195
Overture to *Der Freischütz*, 13

page turning, 152
Parsifal, 353
partials, 455–61
pedal point, 226–27, 231, 237
percussion section
   band conducting, 335
   cutoffs, 71
   rehearsals, 351
   seating arrangement, 151, 151n1, 155–56
   tremolos, 141
personnel manager, 344, 347
phrasings
   accompanying, 299
   groups of bars, 50
   notation, 141, 149
   score study, 129
   tempos, 98
pianissimo (*pp*), 71
piano (*p*), 55–58, 60, 77
Piano Concerto in G, 353
pianos
   ballet, 335
   concertos, 306
   ear training, 341
   piano concertos, 346
   piano dress rehearsals, 310
   seating arrangement, 152, 155–56, 156n3
piccolos, 153, 164
pickups, 22–26
Piston, Walter, 131
pitch
   accompanying, 302
   band conducting, 335
   brasses, 166
   capella chorus, 330
   conductor's craft, 97, 237
   ear training, 341

   fermata, 75
   inhalation, 354
   intonation problems, 352
   notation, 149
   oboes, 352
   oratorios, 327
   orchestration, 232, 236–37
   score study, 257
   sounding pitch, 455–61
pivots, 143–47
pizzicatos
   bowings, 354
   Prelude to the Afternoon of a Faun, 276
   preparatory beats, 10, 15
   score study, 132, 257
   splitting a single preparatory beat, 59–60
poco a poco più, 282
poco rit., 112
polyphony, 208
polyrhythmic sections, 66–67, 99
posture, 342–43
Prelude to the Afternoon of a Faun
   breathing, 275, 354
   common denominator, 111, 279–80
   soloists, 275, 354
   subdivision, 278–80
   zigzag way, 275–80
preparatory beats
   accompanying, 302, 308
   articulations, 10
   band conducting, 335
   beat patterns, 17–19
   boomerang motion, 9, 17
   brasses, 10
   breathing, 9
   circular beat, 32
   to count 1, 15–17, 39–42
   counts other than 1, 19–21
   cutoffs, 71
   definition, 8
   dictating, 69
   divisions, 10
   double stop, 10
   dynamics, 10
   fermata, 55, 74–77
   groups of bars, 41
   harmonic progression, 10
   ictus or impulse, 11, 15–17
   inhalation, 354
   irregular meters, 43
   left-hand cutoff, 12, 24
   Luftpause, 72
   multiple preparatory beats, 33–34, 42
   musicians, 10
   mutes, 10
   neutral beat, 31
   nonrebound beat, 30

notation, 7
orchestration and, 10–17
Overture to *Der Freischütz*, 13
pickups, 22–26
pizzicatos, 10, 15
rebound, 17, 67–68
recitatives, 321–24
response to, 10
rhythmic unit, 42, 244
rhythms, 40–42
Rienzi, 10–11
secondary preparatory beats, 33–34, 49
soloists, 36–37, 88
Sorcerer's Apprentice, 15
splitting a single preparatory beat, 59–60
staccato beat, 27–29
stopped pitches, 10
stopping the beat, 88
strings, 10
subito tempo changes, 53–58
Symphonie Mathis der Maler, 16–17
Symphony no. 1 (Bizet), 11–12
Symphony no. 1 (Brahms), 14
Symphony no. 1 (Tchaikovsky), 15
Symphony no. 8 (Dvořák), 11
Symphony no. 101 (Haydn), 12
tacet bars, 84
tempos, 17, 40–42
time signature, 48–50
types of beats, 26–32
upbeats, 21–26, 21n1, 43–44, 48–49
Presto, 110–11, 285
probation, 345
programming, 345–46
Prokofiev, 346
Puccini, 324, 336
pull-back motion, 73n7
punta d'arco, 283
push-away motion, 73n7

quattro battute, 86, 149

Rachmaninoff, 346, 355
rallentando, 119
range, 313, 315, 316n5, 317–18
Ravel, 353
rebarring, 63–65
rebeaming, 65–66
rebound
    cutoffs, 71
    dictating, 70–71
    fermata, 74
    irregular meters, 37–39
    legato beat, 29–30
    Luftpause, 67–68
    nonrebound beat, 30

preparatory beats, 17, 67–68
ritardandos, 46–47
sforzatos, 58–59
staccato beat, 27–28
standard beats, 27
subito tempo changes, 53–54
syncopations, 83
tempos, 46–47
tied-over, 68
recapitulation, 134, 137
recitals, 310
recitatives
    accelerandos, 321
    accompanying, 308
    auditions, 312
    batons, 324
    beat patterns, 321
    downbeat, 322n7
    entrances, 322
    neutral beat, 321, 325
    orchestra, 327–29
    preparatory beats, 321–24
    recitativo accompagnato, 321
    recitativo secco, 321
    rhythms, 321
    ritardandos, 321
    specialization, 342
    staccato beat, 322
    tacet bars, 321–24
    tempos, 322–23
    types of, 321
    upbeats, 322n7
    winds, 324
    zigzag way, 325–26
recordings, 336, 341–42
regular to neutral beat, 8
regular to strong ictus, 8
rehearsals
    accompanying, 299, 308–9, 311
    articulations, 350
    assistant conductor, 351–52
    ballet, 335–36
    band conducting, 335
    body language, 309, 350–51
    chamber music, 310
    choruses, 330, 334
    communications, 5, 344
    composers, 346
    conductor's craft, 350–52
    dictating, 70
    dynamics, 128–29, 350–51
    ensemble playing, 351
    facial expressions, 350–51
    intonation problems, 350–51
    musicians, 350–52
    opera chart, 318–20
    operatic conductors, 308–11

rehearsals (*continued*)
  programming, 346
  score study, 350
  star system, 311, 311n3
  strings, 351
  tempos, 351
  time limits, 3
  winds, 351
  zigzag way, 243
repertoire, 334–35
Requiem (Verdi), 332–34
rest, 75
retenu, 278
rhythmic texture, 89–96
rhythmic unit
  artificial common denominators, 115
  beat patterns, 48–50
  common denominator, 103
  hemiola, 61–62
  preparatory beats, 42
rhythms
  accompanying, 302
  bass line, 256–57
  beat unit, 6
  cross-rhythms, 278, 336–38, 463–76
  ear training, 341
  F rhythms, 244–48, 252–56
  facial expressions, 244
  inhalation, 354
  multiple rhythms, 339
  preparatory beats, 40–42
  recitatives, 321
  score study, 243–44
  upbeats, 21
  zigzag way, 243–44
Rienzi, 10–11
right-hand cutoff, 75
ritardandos
  accompanying, 299
  beat patterns, 46–47
  common denominator, 111–12, 124–27
  Concerto for Orchestra, 283
  definition, 46, 99
  opera rehearsals, 309
  Prelude to the Afternoon of a Faun, 276, 278
  rebound, 46–47
  recitatives, 321
  subdivision, 47
Rite of Spring, 353
ritmo di quattro battute, 50–51
ritmo di tre battute, 50
rituals, 343
Romeo and Juliet Fantasy-Overture, 285–89
Rorschach mirroring, 282
Rosen, Charles, 131
Rothstein, William, 131
rubato, 99, 100, 141

Salzer, Felix, 131
saxophones, 153
Schachter, Carl, 131
Schenker, Heinrich, 131
Schubert, 346
score study
  analysis, 131
  arco, 257
  articulations, 98, 129, 132, 141, 298
  artificial common denominators, 128
  band conducting, 334–35
  beat unit, 61
  bowings, 133, 257
  chamber music, 129
  choral conducting, 329–34
  col legno, 132, 257
  common denominator, 115–19
  conductor's craft, 3
  cuing, 221, 298
  doublings, 132
  dynamics, 98, 129, 132, 257, 298
  ear training, 341
  F rhythms, 244–48, 252–56
  harmonic progression, 147–49, 257
  instrumental charts, 357–59
  instruments, 131–33
  M (majority), 249–56
  memorization, 341–42
  metronomic tempos, 98
  mirroring, 203
  mutes, 132, 257
  notation, 97, 129, 133–42, 147–49
  opera chart, 318–20
  orchestration, 223
  phrasings, 129
  pitch, 257
  pizzicatos, 132, 257
  rehearsals, 350
  rhythms, 243–44
  seating arrangement, 152
  security, 147–49
  slur, 129
  symbols, seating, 157
  tacet bars, 131
  tempos, 98–100, 257, 298
  transitions, 257
  zigzag way, 243–44, 298
seating arrangement
  brasses, 154–55, 154n2
  cuing, 151–52
  percussion section, 151, 151n1, 155–56
  strings, 151–52
  symbols, 156–69
  winds, 151–54
secondary preparatory beats, 33–34, 49
sectionals, 351–52

security
  memorization, 341–42
  opera rehearsals, 310
  Prelude to the Afternoon of a Faun, 277
  score study, 147–49
  Symphony no. 2 (Beethoven), 266
Sessions, Roger, 131
sforzato (*sfz*), 10, 58, 129
Shostakovich, 353
Sibelius, Violin Concerto, 273–75
signaling, 5
singers, 309, 321, 331–32, 342. *See also* soloists
single reeds, 10, 194–95
Sitzprobe, 310, 310n2
slur, 129
socializing, 344
solfeggio, 341
soloists
  accompanying, 299, 307–8
  auditions, 312–13
  breathing, 354
  concert rituals, 343
  cuing, 142, 152
  entrances, 302
  fermata, 36
  intonation problems, 353
  opera chart, 318n6
  orchestral recitatives, 327–29
  ornamental figures, 301
  Prelude to the Afternoon of a Faun, 275, 354
  preparatory beats, 36–37, 88
  programming, 345–46
  upbeats, 36
  Violin Concerto (Sibelius), 274–75
sopranos, 330
Sorcerer's Apprentice, 15
sorting, 334–35
Sostenuto, ma non troppo, 269
sounding pitch, 455–61
soutenu, 276
specialization, 342
specified duration, 8
staccato beat
  circular beat, 32
  dictating, 70
  ictus or impulse, 27–28
  modified subdivision, 46
  phrasings, 129
  Prelude to the Afternoon of a Faun, 276
  preparatory beats, 27–29
  rebound, 27–28
  recitatives, 322
  tempos, 28
stage director, 309, 311–12
staging rehearsals, 310
standard beats, 18, 26–27, 37
star system, 311, 311n3

sternum, 26
stopped pitches, 10
Strauss, R., 305, 353
Stravinsky, 204, 217, 353
stringendo, 288
strings
  accompanying, 305
  circular beat, 28–29, 32
  cuing, 191–92
  cutoffs, 71
  divisions, 189–90
  entrances, 170–92, 170n4, 190–92
  Eroica, 210–12, 216
  harmonics charts, 453–61
  intonation problems, 352
  Luftpause, 77
  numbers, 170–92
  preparatory beats, 10
  rehearsals, 351
  seating arrangement, 151–52
  slur, 129
  splitting a single preparatory beat, 59–60
  string divisi chart, 189–90
  symbols, 156–59
  traffic patterns, 170n4
  tremolos, 141
subdivision
  accelerandos, 47–48
  beat unit, 61
  Concerto for Orchestra, 281
  cross-rhythms, 336–38, 463–76
  full subdivision, 44–45
  metronome markings, 101
  modified subdivision, 45–46
  Prelude to the Afternoon of a Faun, 278–80
  ritardandos, 47
  Romeo and Juliet Fantasy-Overture, 286
  Symphony no. 2 (Beethoven), 265
subito tempo changes, 53–58, 127, 136, 263
sudden silences, 86
sul ponticello, 132, 142
supertitles, 311
symbols, 156–69, 186–89
Symphonic Dances, 355
Symphonie fantastique, 298
Symphonie Mathis der Maler, 16–17
Symphonies. *See individual composers*
syncopations
  conductor's craft, 82
  doublings, 223
  offbeat, 83
  orchestration, 239
  Prelude to the Afternoon of a Faun, 276–77
  rebound, 83
  Symphony no. 2 (Beethoven), 266
  tempos, 82–84
  Violin Concerto (Sibelius), 274

tacet bars
    preparatory beats, 84
    recitatives, 321, 324
    score study, 131
    symbols, seating, 164, 166
    upbeats, 84
tacet sections, 69, 76
Tanglewood, 243
Tchaikovsky
    concertos, 345–46
    one-composer concerts, 346
    Romeo and Juliet Fantasy-Overture, 285–89
    Symphony no. 1, 15
    Symphony no. 4, 115
    Symphony no. 6, 141, 346
tempos
    accelerandos, 48
    accompanying, 299
    Allegro, 98
    artificial common denominators, 115
    ballet, 335
    beat unit, 61
    bowings, 98
    circular beat, 32
    common denominator, 55, 105
    counts other than 1, 19–21
    jazz ensembles, 33
    Luftpause, 72–73
    modified subdivision, 46
    multiple preparatory beats, 33
    nondurational preparatory upbeat, 35–36
    opera rehearsals, 309
    preparatory beats, 17, 40–42
    rebound, 46–47
    recitatives, 322–23
    rehearsals, 351
    ritardando, 46–48
    rubato, 99
    score study, 98–100, 257, 298
    staccato beat, 28
    subito tempo changes, 55
    syncopations, 82–84
tenors, 330
tenutos
    Appalachian Spring Suite, 284
    modified subdivision, 46
    phrasings, 129
    preparatory beats, 10
    recitatives, 322
tessitura, 316n5
tied-over, 68
Till Eulenspiegels lustige Streiche, 305
time signature
    beat unit, 61
    cross-rhythms, 336–38, 463–76
    full subdivision, 44–45
    groups of bars, 50, 51n3

metronomic unit, 48
notation, 149
polyrhythmic sections, 66–67
preparatory beats, 48–50
rebarring, 64–65
timpani, 155, 229–30, 229n1
timpanists, 142
traffic patterns
    cuing, 151
    Egmont Overture, 270–71
    entrances, 208–21
    Eroica, 210–12, 216, 221
    Firebird Suite, 217
    fugatos, 218–20
    fugues, 218–20
    notation, 151, 208–21
    numbers, 208–21
    strings, 170n4
transitions, 115, 128, 257
translations, 327, 331, 361–445
transposition, 97, 361–445
tre battute, 86, 149
treble clef, 331
tremolos, 223, 228–29, 240–41
très retenu, 279
triangle, 155
trills, 223
trios, 308
triple tonguing, 339
trombones, 154, 168
trumpets, 5, 154, 168
tubas, 154, 168
tuning procedures, 229, 352
Turandot, 336
tutti passages, 299, 351

Un poco agitato, 112
Un poco sostenuto, 111
union representative, 344–45, 347, 349
unusual instruments, 358–59
upbeats
    breathing, 22
    common denominator, 111, 122–25
    fermata, 75–76
    ictus or impulse, 21–22
    nondurational preparatory upbeat, 35–36
    preparatory beats, 21–26, 21n1, 43–44, 48–49
    recitatives, 322n7
    rhythms, 21
    secondary preparatory beats, 33–34, 49
    soloists, 36
    tacet bars, 84

valves, 166
Verdi, 269, 332–34, 336
vertical division, 183, 192, 194–95

vibratos, 354
videos, 342
violas, 152
violins, 152
vocal line, 309, 311, 321, 327
vocal ranges, 331
voice categorization, 312–13, 316n5
voice charts, 313–18
voice leading, 142

Wagner, 10–11, 353
warm-up room, 349
Weber, 13
wedge, 129
winds
   band conducting, 335
   bass line, 256
   cuing, 192
   cutoffs, 71
   divisions, 194–203
   doublings, 142
   entrances, 192–206
   Eroica, 204–5, 210–12
   inner woodwinds, 195
   intonation problems, 352
   Luftpause, 77
   multiple preparatory beats, 33
   outer woodwinds, 195
   preparatory beats, response to, 10
   recitatives, 324
   rehearsals, 351
   seating arrangement, 151–54

slur, 129
splitting a single preparatory beat, 59–60
symbols, seating, 159–65
Symphony no. 101 (Haydn), 12
wrist action, 30

Yale University, 243

zigzag way
   Appalachian Spring Suite, 284–85
   band conducting, 334–35
   beat patterns, 257
   choral conducting, 330–34
   Concerto for Orchestra (Bartók), 280–84, 290–98
   conductor's craft, 257
   cuing, 243, 257
   cutoffs, 257
   definition, 243
   Egmont Overture, 269–72
   La Forza del Destino, 269
   orchestration, 243, 256–57
   Prelude to the Afternoon of a Faun, 275–80
   recitatives, 325–26
   rehearsals, 243
   rhythms, 243–44
   Romeo and Juliet Fantasy-Overture, 285–89
   score study, 243–44, 298
   Symphonie fantastique, 298
   Symphony no. 2 (Beethoven), 258–69
   Symphony no. 5 (Beethoven), 289
   Violin Concerto (Sibelius), 273–75